# GENDER AND COMMUNICATION AT WORK

# Gender and Organizational Theory Series

Series Editor: Dr. Emma Jeanes,
*School of Business and Economics,*
*University of Exeter, UK*

The aim of this series is to provide research monographs and edited volumes on all topics within the area of gender and management, broadly defined. The series is intended to encompass different perspectives within feminism (for example liberal, post-structuralist and Marxist) as well as the interplay of feminist perspectives with other forms of identity and discourse. The series also aims to provide books that explore notions of masculinities in an organizational context.

*Forthcoming titles in the series:*

The Making of Women Trade Unionists
*Gill Kirton*
ISBN 0 7546 4569 X

Masculinities and Management in Agricultural Organisations Worldwide
*Barbara Pini*
ISBN 0 7546 4734 X

# Gender and Communication at Work

*Edited by*

MARY BARRETT
*University of Wollongong, Australia*

and

MARILYN J. DAVIDSON
*The University of Manchester, UK*

## ASHGATE

Published by
Ashgate Publishing Limited
Gower House
Croft Road
Aldershot
Hampshire GU11 3HR
England

Ashgate Publishing Company
Suite 420
101 Cherry Street
Burlington, VT 05401-4405
USA

Ashgate website: http://www.ashgate.com

**British Library Cataloguing in Publication Data**
Gender and communication at work. - (Gender and organizational theory)
  1.Communication in organizations 2.Sex role in the work
  environment 3.Sex discrimination in employment
  4.Communication - Sex differences
  I.Barrett, Mary II.Davidson, Marilyn
  302.3'5

**Library of Congress Cataloging-in-Publication Data**
Gender and communication at work / edited by Mary Barrett and Marilyn
  J. Davidson.
     p. cm. -- (Gender and organizational theory)
  Includes bibliographical references and index.
  ISBN 0-7546-3840-5
  1. Communication in organizations--Sex differences. 2. Communication
  in management--Sex differences. 3. Sex role in the work environment.
  4. Organizational behavior--Sex differences. 5. Career development
  --Sex differences. 6. Sex discrimination against women. I. Barrett,
  Mary. II. Davidson, Marilyn. III. Series.

  HD30.3.G455 2006
  650.01'4--dc22

                                                                    2005034779

Printed and bound in Great Britain by MPG Books Ltd. Bodmin, Cornwall.

# Contents

**Part IV: Communicating to Get Things Done**

# List of Figures

# List of Tables

# List of Contributors

JUDITH BAXTER
Department of Applied Linguistics, The University of Reading, UK.

MARK J. BROSNAN
Department of Psychology, University of Bath, UK.

PATRICE M. BUZZANELL
Department of Communication, Purdue University, West Lafayette, IN, USA.

LAURA BYRA
Department of Management and Marketing, The Hong Kong Polytechnic University, Hong Kong.

LINDA L. CARLI
Department of Psychology, Wellesley College, Wellesley, MA, USA.

THERESA A. DOMAGALSKI
College of Business, Florida Institute of Technology, Melbourne, FL, USA.

DAVID A. FOSTER
Psychology Division, Western Oregon University, Monmouth, OR, USA.

MARGARET FRANKEN
School of Education, University of Waikato, Hamilton, New Zealand.

CAROL D. HANSEN
Andrew Young School of Policy Studies, Georgia State University, Atlanta, GA, USA.

JEFF HEARN
Department of Management and Organisation, Swedish School of Economics, Helsinki, Finland, Tema Genus, Linköping University, Sweden and Department of Behavioural Science, University of Huddersfield, UK.

MERLE KELLEY
Psychology Division, Western Oregon University, Monmouth, OR, USA.

GARY L. MAY
School of Business, Clayton State University, Morrow, GA, USA.

REBECCA J. MEISENBACH
Department of Communication, University of Missouri-Columbia, Columbia, USA.

BEVERLY D. METCALFE
The Business School, University of Hull, UK.

JOAN MULHOLLAND
School of English, Media Studies and Art History, The University of Queensland, Brisbane Qld, Australia.

CATHERINE W. NG
Department of Management and Marketing, The Hong Kong Polytechnic University, Hong Kong.

SU OLSSON
Department of Communication and Journalism, College of Business, Massey University, Palmerston North, New Zealand.

KATHRYN S. O'NEILL
Rock-Tenn Company, Norcross, GA, USA.

NIKI PANTELI
School of Management, University of Bath, UK.

ISABELLA PAOLETTI
Communication Science Department, University of Bologna, Italy.

WENDY PARKIN
Formerly of the Department of Health, Social Work and Community Studies, University of Huddersfield, UK.

JENNIFER J. PECK
Department of Linguistics, Division of Linguistics and Psychology, Macquarie University, Sydney, Australia.

VICTOR SAVICKI
Psychology Division, Western Oregon University, Monmouth, OR, USA.

MONICA SEELEY
Mesmo Consultancy, London, UK.

LEONIE V. STILL
Graduate School of Management, University of Western Australia, Perth, Australia.

ALICE F. STUHLMACHER
Department of Psychology, DePaul University, Chicago, IL, USA.

ROB THOMSON
Department of Psychology, University of East London, UK.

CATHERINE WALLACE
Department of Communication and Journalism, Massey University, Palmerston North, New Zealand.

REBECCA B. WINKLER
Department of Psychology, DePaul University, Chicago IL, USA.

# Acknowledgements

The editors are greatly indebted to Dr Tom Mylne for the many hours of typing, proofreading and incidental research that he contributed to this project.

The editors also wish to acknowledge the loss of one of the chapter contributors, Su Olsson, who died a few months before the book was published. Her work on women's leadership archetypes is well known. She will be much missed by her family, friends, students and the wider academic community.

# List of Acronyms

| | |
|---|---|
| ACD | Automatic Call Distribution |
| ANOVA | Analysis of Variance |
| BSRI | Bem Sex Role Inventory |
| CDA | Critical Discourse Analysis |
| CEE | Central and Eastern Europe |
| CEO | Chief Executive Officer |
| CIS | Communication and Information Systems |
| CMC | Computer-mediated Communication |
| CO | Concern for Other |
| CofP | Communities of Practice |
| CS | Concern for Self |
| CSCW | Computer Supported Cooperative Work |
| CSO | Customer Support officer |
| CSR | Customer Service Representative |
| EO | Equal Opportunity |
| EOC | Equal Opportunities Commission |
| GNP | Gross National Product |
| GSS | Group Support System |
| HRD | Human Resource Development |
| ICT | Information and Communication Technology |
| ILO | International Labour Organization |
| IS | Information Systems |
| IT | Information Technology |
| KSA | Knowledge, Skills and Abilities |
| LTSI | Learning Transfer System Inventory |
| MENA | Middle East and North Africa |
| MNC | Multinational Corporation |
| MUD | Multi-User-Dimension |
| PDA | Personal Digital Assistant |
| RIP | Rest in Peace |
| SIDE | Social Identity and Deindividuation (model) |
| SMS | Short Message Service |
| WAP | Wireless Application Protocol |
| WWW | World Wide Web |
| Y2K | Year 2000 |

# About the Editors

**Mary Barrett** is Professor of Management at the University of Wollongong, Australia. She studied French and literary theory and taught in those fields at the University of Queensland, Australia for some years. She worked in HRM in university administration and government in Australia and the US before becoming a management academic in 1992 and gaining an MBA in 1993. Mary researches women in management, especially as business owners and in family business, and workplace communication.

**Marilyn J. Davidson** is Professor of Work Psychology in the Manchester Business School at the University of Manchester, UK. She is currently Head of the Occupational Psychology Group and Co-Director of the Centre for Diversity and Work Psychology. Her research interests are in the fields of the management of diversity, occupational stress, equal opportunities, women in management and female entrepreneurs. She has published over 150 academic articles and twenty books and is a Fellow of the British Psychological Society and Royal Society of Arts.

Chapter 1

# Gender and Communication at Work: An Introduction

Mary Barrett and Marilyn J. Davidson

## Introduction

The last three to four decades have seen a rapid increase in numbers of women in the workplace worldwide, with more women also entering managerial ranks. However, despite legislation in many countries aimed at furthering women's capacities to move to the top of their organizations, the phenomenon of the 'glass ceiling' persists (Davidson and Burke, 2004; Ryan and Haslam, 2005). Public policy documents, academic research and popular books advocating government, industry and organization-level policy initiatives to facilitate women's advancement continue to be published. So-called 'business case' arguments, that is, arguments to the effect that organizations that fail to acknowledge and use the skills of all members of their workforce will find themselves at a competitive disadvantage, seem to have had much less effect than similar arguments for other kinds of business and organizational change. Nevertheless, over the past decade or so, there has been a shift from equal opportunities (EO) initiatives aimed at reducing discrimination in organizations to the phenomenon of managing diversity in the workplace (Cassell, 1997; Liff and Wajcman, 1996). Failure of 1980s policies and practices was often linked to degrees of 'backlash' and resistance from majority groups (often white males) who felt excluded and the unrealistic expectations placed on employees of different gender and backgrounds (Davidson and Burke, 2000). Conversely, the concept of managing diversity both values and harnesses the talents of individual differences. These differences, in turn, transform the varying sets of skills that every employee possesses into a business advantage. According to Davidson and Fielden (2003: xxii):

> Through the fostering of difference, team creativity, innovation and problem-solving can often be enhanced. The focus is, therefore, much more on the individual rather than the group. Having a diverse workforce not only enables organizations to understand and meet customer demand better, but also helps attract investors and clients, as well as reduce the costs associated with discrimination.

Evidence from a variety of fields suggests that communication issues contribute to the creation of barriers to women's advancement in organizations or, at least, to a variety of misunderstandings between women and men at work. Differences between men's and women's communication have been part of the academic literature in linguistics for more than two decades. Some of the findings have also entered the popular 'battle of the sexes' management literature, especially through books such as Deborah Tannen's (1990) *You Just Don't Understand: Men and Women in Conversation* and (1994) *Talking from 9 to 5*, Marian Woodall's (1990) *How to Talk so Men Will Listen*, and John Gray's (1992) *Women are from Venus, Men are from Mars*.

The popularity of these books and many others like them suggests their findings are intuitively attractive to many women worldwide. Many are based on excellent research. Deborah Tannen, for example, is a linguistics scholar and researcher of international repute, as well as an author of a number of bestsellers in the popular 'gender wars at work' arena. However, much of the original research on which the 'communication advice' literature is based was done in the United States. Accordingly, such work typically recommends directness, forcefulness and simplicity to produce effective communication, and this has been criticized as being based on implicit models of communication that are male and American (for example Woodall, 1990). Moreover, since the research data was gathered more than a decade ago, it is important to consider how much resonance these ideas have with women and workplaces now. Certainly, they were very much based on the EO model of assimilation rather than the diversity model, whereby communication differences were to be valued and incorporated as part of a diverse organizational culture. As well, findings and advice based on – and addressed to – the experience and interests of white, 'corporate' women in conventional office settings, will not necessarily address the gender-related aspects of 'new' workplaces, such as teleworking, various forms of e-business and computer-mediated communication, non-managerial work, or special work environments such as emergency call centres.

Globalization and the rise of the service sector, with its emphasis on people skills, have both been touted as factors creating the work environments of the future. Both phenomena have been argued to create work situations requiring a high level of communication skills and, indeed, the empathetic styles of communication that have been popularly thought to be more 'natural' for women. As a result, it is often held (for example, Wajcman, 1999) that women's ways of working and women's leadership styles, especially as these relate to communication, ought to further women's advancement at work and even persuade men to adopt more 'female' approaches to communication, management and leadership. This would follow as part of a more general reliance on participative management that, in turn, has been seen as characteristic of 'female' approaches to leadership, as described by authors such as Rosener (1990). On the other side, however, more critical views point to the emotional labour demands of some 'remote' and service sector work, and the risks of renewed stereotyping and undervaluing of women at work through the focus on 'naturally female' skills (for example, Brody and Hall, 2000; Hess et al., 2000).

The complexity and range of gender issues in workplace communication is also reflected in the paucity of serious and comprehensive 'handbook' material directed at people such as human resource managers who have a professional interest in communication and gender issues at work. Many major 'gender and work' texts deal only minimally with communication issues and, conversely, texts on organizational communication usually deal only minimally with gender. For example, Powell's (1999) *Handbook of Gender and Work* is comprehensive in its treatment of a range of work problems for women and men, but includes little discussion of communication issues. Jablin and Putnam's (2001) *The New Handbook of Organizational Communication: Advances in Theory, Research, and Methods* deals with gender issues on only about 30 pages out of a hefty 911 pages in the volume as a whole.

This book brings together current debates and findings around these issues, and is divided into five parts:

- gender and communication situations in the employment lifespan;
- gender, communication and organizational boundaries: linkages and violations;
- gender and communication channels in special workplace environments;
- communicating to get things done; and
- the future: gender and computer-mediated communication at work.

## Gender and Communication Situations in the Employment Lifespan

The chapters in the first part of the book review current research concerning the communication experience of men and women in relation to three different situations or events during the employment lifespan: the employment interview; employment training, especially training in communication and leadership skills; and promotion. These three situations, it would be agreed, are critical phases or events in employment and crucial both to securing basic job security and achieving advancement at work. Gender issues as they relate to the employment relationship are, of course, not new research concerns. The academic and professional literature surrounding equal employment opportunity and affirmative action, and the more recent diversity movement have long focused on the potential for systemic and non-systemic bias in recruitment and selection processes, development opportunities including training for organizational leadership, and promotion processes (for example, Smith, 2003). Ways in which these situations and opportunities are presented and framed at individual, organizational and societal levels can all mitigate against women's opportunities for getting ahead at work. The focus in terms of remedial action has typically been on organizational policies and strategies that aim to ensure that selection processes and later work opportunities are based on merit. In more complex discussions, the nature of merit has been problematized, leading to its redefinition to take account of organizational and societal constraints on women and individuals from diverse groups. In Part II, we broaden the discussion to include the minutiae of gender differences in communication strategies and how they are differentially valued.

Patricia Buzzanell and Rebecca Meisenbach begin the process in Chapter 2 by reviewing existing and potential research approaches to the employment interview. They view employment interview research through four different lenses, as explored by Ashcraft (2004) in her work on the interlinkages of gender, organization and discourse. Ashcraft's four lenses, briefly put, are firstly, the *outcome* or *effect* lens, in which discourse is seen as an outcome of gender. Research from this viewpoint (which is also the viewpoint adopted by most existing research into the employment interview) focuses on how gender shapes individual linguistic choices, interactional strategies and style. The second lens, *performance*, presents the reciprocal viewpoint to the first, focusing on how individual talk shapes the performance of gendered identity. The two remaining frames move beyond perceptions by and of the individual to encompass *organizational* and *social* levels of discourse, which both enable and constrain gender in ways likely not to be perceived by participants in the employment interview, just as they remain largely hidden in other areas of organizational and social life. The four lenses taken together provide tools for uncovering different assumptions underlying existing and potential research into the employment interview and other similar workplace situations. The authors also discuss how the four lenses suggest ways of achieving more equitable outcomes for women and diverse individuals in employment interviews.

Kathryn O'Neill, Carol Hansen and Gary May pursue a similar agenda in Chapter 3 in their review of research into problems associated with the transfer of organizational training, especially training aimed at producing better interpersonal communication and leadership at work. They first consider how societal culture shapes gender schemas and prescribed social roles, and then how gender-related theories are linked to organizational culture. Organizational culture, in turn, is linked to the issue of training transfer in the workplace, since the cultural environment of the organization affects individuals' capacity and motivation to transfer to the workplace the skills of communication and leadership they have learned in training situations. Problems often arise because the behaviours taught in typical interpersonal skills workshops are frequently seen as feminine and therefore tend to be resisted by learners. Often, the learned behaviours are extinguished by a masculine-oriented organizational culture before they can be put into effect in the workplace. The authors conclude that training interventions aimed at changing approaches to interpersonal communication need to be considered as interventions at the level of organizational culture, rather than as simple workplace training. Like other culture changes, and as emphasized in the organizational culture literature, such interventions will fail in the absence of strong modelling and support by senior management.

In Chapter 4, Jennifer Peck undertakes a more micro-level analysis of communication factors affecting formal promotion and other processes underlying women's advancement at work. In her discussion of workplace promotion and linguistic interactions, she discusses the problems created by different sex-role expectations of men and women at work. According to traditional sex-role norms as they translate to the workplace, women are expected to be dependable, cooperative, intuitively perceptive and to exhibit the 'soft' skills of management. Men, on the other hand, are required to be intelligent, analytical, 'dynamic' and to excel at 'hard' skills in the management arena. However, following traditional female sex-role patterns frequently does not result in women reaching executive positions, since the skills required for executive positions seem to be associated with the managerial views of men that both genders hold. A double bind for women is created both by the fact that skills of organizational success are associated with men, and also because for women to exhibit skills regarded simply as 'natural' for them means that they are less likely to receive acknowledgement of these skills in formal evaluation or promotional processes. This is despite the fact that the 'new' management skills for the twenty-first century are often seen as 'soft' or 'women's' skills.

## Gender, Communication and Organizational Boundaries: Linkages and Violations

In Part II of the book, the emphasis shifts from communication within specific and crucial employment events to more routine instances of workplace communication and the gender issues associated with them. In addition, rather than focusing on people's attempts to move vertically through the organizational hierarchy via the processes of entry, training and promotion, the chapters in this part focus on lateral relationships. These include general workplace groups, as well as lateral relationships external to the organization, such as advising customers or clients in a professional setting and managing organizational relationships in the international arena. Part II focuses on gender issues in how organizational boundaries are both maintained and crossed, including (as in the last chapter in the part) when the crossing of boundaries represents violation.

Linda Carli, in Chapter 5, provides a detailed summary of empirical academic research on gender differences in communication, particularly in work groups. She pays particular attention to research that either reinforces or questions stereotypical views of women as communal, collaborative communicators and of men as agentic, forceful communicators. She argues that most research does indeed reveal women to be warmer and more communal in their communication styles, but that various situational factors in workplaces have been found to moderate this. For example, both men and women communicate more warmly towards women, and features associated with typical 'male' and 'female' differences in communication styles are more marked in same-sex than in mixed-sex groups. In addition, factors related to people's expectations of their own and other people's behaviour, their relative power in the situation, and their perceptions about what type of behaviour will increase their influence in a situation all play a role in determining communication styles. While this is consistent with the general finding that men tend to communicate in a more mitigated and less dominant manner to men and to exhibit more dominance towards women, there are factors that can alter the situation for women. These include women being seen in a leadership role, or the topic of the communication being one on which the particular woman – or women in general – are perceived to know a good deal about. As Peck and other authors in the book point out, however, this still leaves a double bind for women. Appearing competent can actually reduce a woman's influence because it makes her less likeable, since behaviour seen as competent often asserts status and uses fewer qualities of communality. Women need to combine competence with communality to overcome resistance to their influence, while still acting in accordance with traditional expectations of their role. The way through the double bind seems to be for women to exercise transformational leadership and to do this more than men do. Transformational leadership combines communal qualities and leadership effectiveness, in ways that allow women to excel as leaders and still maintain their traditional communal styles of communication. This is discussed in more depth in Chapters 13 and 14.

Joan Mulholland, in Chapter 6, expands on the reservations presented by Carli about when and whether gender determines communication style, and suggests how other factors in a workplace situation may reduce or even nullify its influence. Mulholland's discussion of professional communications with clients highlights that while gender problems in communication have been thought to occur because of profound differences in men's and women's preferred ways of knowing and understanding and in their preferences for different social relations between the participants, different problems occur in communications between advisor and client simply because of the nature of 'advice' itself, as well as the nature of 'advisorhood' and 'clienthood'. The nature of advice giving may make at least as much difference as gender to what participants consider an appropriate response in a particular situation. Clients signal, by the language they adopt, what role they feel themselves to be in. These roles can range from one of complete ignorance and helplessness, to one where clients believe themselves to have a great deal of knowledge, or one where they are generally knowledgeable but lack one element of required information, and so on. In addition, general trends towards the casualization of language signal affiliation in ways that are beginning to even out gender differences. In summary, rather than asking what gender the participants are in a advisor–client exchange, researchers of advisor–client communications are discerning a continuum of affiliative-instrumental communicative styles that, increasingly, transcend gender issues.

Beverly Metcalfe, in Chapter 7, continues and develops Mulholland's more complex view of gender differences in language with her insights drawn from the realm of international business. Like many authors in the book, Metcalfe takes issue with both the 'difference' paradigm ('men and women speak differently because of early socialization') and the 'dominance' paradigm ('gender-based language differences reveal the economic dominance that men still typically exercise over women'). Both, she argues, present an overly simple view of a phenomenon that is better understood as multi-layered and fluid. She uses three different approaches to elucidate this view. First, in a way similar to Mulholland, she takes Butler's (1990, 1993) notions of gender as a performative social construct to examine how individuals employ a wide range of linguistic repertoires. Second, she draws on the idea of 'communities of practice' (CofP), or the ways individuals' attachments to a wide range of different communities with different norms and practices allow them to adopt different identity positions within specific groups. Finally, she uses critical discourse analysis, which focuses on the ways language creates and sustains gendered power relations. All of them are used in her discussion of gender and communication issues as seen in the light of insights from international business. She draws on two rapidly changing environments: the Middle East and Eastern Europe, which present different communication approaches as 'typically' male or female, to argue along with Holmes et al. (2003) that masculinity and femininity are not opposites, but mutually overlapping constructs giving rise to multiple masculinities and femininities.

While the developments put forward in Part II present some potential ways to understand and manage the practical difficulties of workplace communication for women, Jeff Hearn and Wendy Parkinson in Chapter 8, writing in the critical theory tradition, end this part on a warning note. They examine the connections between communication and violation at work, including gender relations. In their view, communication can never be gender neutral. The ways male power is structured into the very fabric of organizational processes means the potential for communication violations range from the silence and noise ('din') of exclusions and unresolved tensions, through to harassment, bullying and even physical violence. They review the processes and practices of a broad range of organizational violations and finally consider contemporary social changes in communication, gender and violation, with special attention to globalization, multinational corporations (MNCs) and information and communication technologies (ICTs). They urge the development of policies on communication and practices of communication that reduce and abolish forms of violation.

## Gender and Communication Channels in Special Workplace Environments

Part III of the book, which includes two case study chapters, examines the special constraints and possibilities of communication carried out in some particular workplace situations and environments, such as virtual environments, management board meetings, call centres and emergency rooms. It shows how these constraints may heighten, but also potentially reduce, the gender issues around workplace communication.

Catherine Ng and Laura Byra in Chapter 9 discuss a range of gender issues in face-to-face situations and compare them with non-face-to-face communication. They briefly examine the literature on traditional views of gender differences in communication, arguing, in a similar way to Mulholland's work in Chapter 6 on the advisor–client relationship, that the relationship between communication and gender is mediated by situational specifics rather than by gender alone. This is also true for choice of communication channel, whether face-to-face or virtual. For example, task characteristics and equivocality of the message have been shown to have the greatest impact on the choice of communication medium, with individual preferences only coming into play when equivocality is low, such as when a manager simply wants to inform their staff of the time and venue for a meeting. Thus, gender differences may be only one of the factors that influence communication channel choice. Nevertheless, traditional debates and concerns about women's experience of the workplace still come into play. For instance, women may be perceived as less adept with the technologies needed for virtual workplaces, or training in their use may be less available to women. Alternatively, women may be seen as 'naturally' advantaged through their (by now) traditional advantage in keyboarding skills. All this suggests the need for more research, for example, into effects of choice of communication channel in more traditionally gender-based societies, the effects of other diversity factors such as race, and how changes to communication channels may affect – or be affected by – existing social and power structures in organizations.

Communication constraints derived from the environment itself are also the concern of Margaret Franken and Catherine Wallace, in Chapter 10, who consider gender and language use in call centres. While both men and women can work in call centres, this work environment is overwhelmingly the preserve of women. Issues around communication as a commodity arise from conflicting demands on front-line staff to be customer oriented, but also to 'do the business', that is, get through making or receiving a large number of calls. The chapter discusses the ways in which women are seen as particularly suited to call centre practices that require them to act as 'aesthetic labour'. The authors explore situation-specific issues of the call centre environment, including the difficulties they create for research, and then analyse various aspects of call centre language, including language prescriptions, typical talk patterns and the nature of communication as a commodity. The chapter concludes with some implications for researchers and call centre managers, including the issues of aesthetic labour and women's work (for which previous research on women and emotional labour ought to be illuminating) and how call centre training could draw on the experiences of call centre operators themselves both to alleviate some of the less satisfying aspects of call centre work and to reduce turnover problems.

Judith Baxter, in Chapter 11, presents a case study of part of a management board meeting. This setting constitutes a special environment in that management boards in most business organizations worldwide still typically have fewer female than male members. This chapter uses a post-structuralist research perspective to challenge essentialist views of gender differences, including essentialist views of women's speech patterns, for example, the notion that women prefer a more cooperative, supportive speech style. She thus argues against the presumption that 'discourses of gender will necessarily override the impact of other discourses in constructing mixed-sex spoken interactions'. Rather, speakers' identities, including that of the sole female participant in the board meeting, 'Sarah', are shown to be negotiated within meetings and to be governed by a mix of competing and interwoven discourses. The author's analysis shows that while Sarah, the only woman member of the board, has a degree of dominance constructed through the power discourses particular to that organization's management, there are still gendered undercurrents associated with her colleagues' reactions to her. Sarah, and by extrapolation, women at work in general, need to be considered as multi-faceted individuals constituted by different sets of power relationships. Nevertheless, women who occupy minority positions as women within a 'boysy' culture may have a more limited range of identities to which they have access in management meetings.

Isabella Paoletti, in Chapter 12, also uses a case study, this time of a phone call to the emergency number in an Italian city, to study what is involved in 'doing gender' at work. The work environment of the ambulance control centre is supported by complex information technology systems, an issue that is taken up again in the final part of the book. Here, however, the technology is less the issue than the analysis of gender stereotypes and their effects during control room interactions. The issues of emotional labour considered by Franken and Wallace in Chapter 10 reappear here, as control and regulation of emotional expression is a regular feature of emergency control room interactions. But more important for this context is the issue of 'framing'. As Paoletti says, problems often arise in emergency centre control rooms because callers tend to treat requesting an ambulance as similar to ordering a pizza or a taxi, and this conflicts with the requirement on the person taking the call to elicit specific information in order to know what kind of help to send. All this is complicated further by the ways gender is embedded into the status hierarchy of the control room. By examining an emergency phone call that went wrong as a result of framing problems, Paoletti illustrates how the analysis of the interactions between a male doctor and a female control room operator turn out to be source of empowerment for the operator. This is not because of the operator's recognition of sexism in the conversation (although this was clearly apparent to the analyst) but through the operator having the opportunity to revisit, investigate and learn from her own constructions of what had happened in the conversation. The case presents possibilities for empowering control room personnel and also for countering sexism.

## Communicating to Get Things Done

Part IV groups together discussions of gender issues surrounding leadership, negotiation and the expression of emotion at work. Leadership is sometimes defined as getting people to do things they would not otherwise do and negotiation refers to particular bargaining behaviours to achieve specific goals. Expressing emotion at work has links both to the capacity to express power overtly and the need at times to conceal power sources. Both of these issues have been linked to gender. In addition, the concept of emotional labour has extended the discussion of the expression or suppression of emotions at work to the use of emotion for achieving organizational goals.

Leonie Still, in Chapter 13, presents an overview of the very slow progress in organizational leadership attainments of women at work in Australia and elsewhere. She reviews the explanations for this in terms of sex-role stereotypes, women's supposed lack of ambition, their preference for support rather than line roles, difficulties in accommodating work and family responsibilities, and so on. Using a managerial rather than a social or psycho-social perspective, Still surveys the research into traditional, male, 'heroic' models of leadership in management and research into gender differences in management styles, and links the two issues to gender-related communication styles. It appears that women fall short not only in terms of the old, 'heroic' leadership models (despite women being rated as having the skills, women are not seen culturally as leaders), but also, ironically, in terms of the traits associated with the 'new' leadership models of empathy: capacity for listening, relationship ability, and so on. The problem is that these 'feminine' characteristics have already been incorporated into mainstream discourse according to the rules of the old leadership paradigm. The same has happened with women's leadership styles and female speech patterns: both are assessed in terms of contrast with male norms, which means they are linked with subordinate roles rather than leadership. Still points to the need to recognize the different languages of men and women created through varying gender cultures, and the need for women to learn 'leadership speak' and the language of 'salesmanship' as well as the languages of their other roles.

A potential remedy for the problems identified in Still's chapter is suggested by Su Olsson in Chapter 14. Olsson discusses the content of organizational stories about the (male) senior manager as a heroic and transformational leader, stories that are fed by myths such as Theseus killing the Minotaur and Mercury the winged messenger. Like Still in the previous chapter, Olsson identifies the marginalization of women that stems from these internal and public images of the male executive as hero. Olsson proposes a way to break through the masculinist appropriation of leadership models: the propagation of organizational stories about a female archetype of workplace leadership, 'Xena'. Xena, both through the connotations of her name, the 'stranger', and by virtue of the fact that she is a modern invention rather than an 'original' mythical figure, invokes the dynamic and evolving nature of women's leadership. Xena stories, which are the stories that women executives tell to each other, embody women's competence as a 'given', and use humour to parody and thereby subvert traditional views of women, and assert women's rightful place as organizational leaders.

Alice Stuhlmacher and Rebecca Winkler, in Chapter 15, review research findings about the differences in outcomes, behaviours and perceptions that occur when women and men negotiate, as well as the theoretical explanations for these differences and their implications. In experimental tests of negotiation outcomes, men appear to earn higher profits or other forms of better outcomes than do women and to make more use of formal dispute resolution procedures compared to women. It appears that women are more likely to try to resolve the situation themselves, or simply to leave the situation. While the reasons for this may lie in differences in negotiating behaviours, the fact that outcome differences appear even when male and female negotiation behaviours are identical suggests that differences in perceptions are important. For example, men may be perceived as tough negotiators and to possess negotiation skills, whereas for women to be seen as tough negotiators is not congruent with perceptions of sex-typical roles. This is complicated further by the phenomenon of stereotype threat (where the fear of confirming a stereotype actually leads to lower outcomes), and other non-gendered factors in the situation, including differential power of the participants to the negotiation, the role of organizational norms and culture, levels of rank and experience, information differences, and even the mode of exchange. The authors' suggestions for further research include widening the definitions of negotiation success and paying more attention to the design of negotiation experiments to include, for example, the need to consider long-term relationships, which are a regular feature of real negotiations. Women should be trained in negotiation techniques to strengthen their self-efficacy, and to increase the attention they pay to achieving specific negotiation goals. Organization members need to recognize sources of power differences, provide ways of resolving conflicts and pay attention to equity issues.

Theresa Domagalski, in Chapter 16, considers issues of emotional expression at work. She first reviews prevailing gender stereotypes around emotions, then explores how gender relates to organizational norms about expressing emotions and, finally, discusses links between emotions, gender and status relationships at work. Domagalski points out how gender stereotypes along the lines of 'women are more emotional than men' can obscure how individual and situational differences affect the expression of emotion. She also reminds us that men and women have been found, at least in physiologically based experiments, to experience emotions to a very similar degree. The work context makes the task of understanding emotional expression more difficult, since the 'rules' about expressing emotion at work are not necessarily congruent with the expectations of society at large. As a result, it is not clear whether organizational demands that employees express or suppress particular emotions in the interests of achieving organizational goals (both are forms of emotional labour) are damaging, and, if so, whether this is also gender related. However, since expressing emotions such as anger can be a way of affirming and maintaining one's place in the organizational hierarchy, but anger is stereotypically a male emotion, dilemmas arise for women in the extent to which they are 'permitted' to exercise this indicator of status. As Domagalski concludes, there is much that remains unknown about emotional expression in work organizations along gendered lines, but it is likely that women's situation concerning the expression of emotion is more precarious than that of men.

## The Future: Gender and Computer-mediated Communication at Work

Part V, the final part of the book, explores the gender issues of 'new' work environments, particularly virtual environments, or those relying heavily on email and other electronic forms of communication. Information technology-supported work has been touched on in some other chapters, such as that by Franken and

Wallace, but here the gender issues around electronic communication come in for specific attention.

Rob Thomson, in Chapter 17, explores whether men and women speak, use and interpret language differently in the arena of electronic discourse. He first addresses the features of electronic discourse that link it to, or distinguish it from, ordinary written or face-to-face discourse. For example, computer-mediated communication (CMC) often has features of informal, interpersonal speech, such as informal greetings and sign-offs and, as in electronic discussion groups, conversations may be carried out synchronously. However email use is typically asynchronous. It is also possible in CMC discussions, especially in non-work environments, to conceal one's gender. The question then arises as to what extent gender-predictive features of spoken language are likely to be found in CMC environments. On the one hand, and as predicted by communication accommodation theory, gender-linked language differences have been observed to be more salient in same-gender electronic discussions than in mixed-gender discussions. Similarly, in mixed-gender discussions, or in discussions on typically male or female topics, researchers have found that both males and females tend to adopt the speech styles they perceive as appropriate to the gender of the other speaker or the topic, reducing gender-predictive language differences. On the other hand, in some CMC environments, especially anonymous ones, or ones where other social cues are reduced, males still appear to dominate discussions. Thomson concludes that although there is much flexibility in how men and women use language, there are gender effects in how we produce, interpret and communicate with electronic language as with other media. Nevertheless, in the absence of cues about personal identity, including gender, other aspects of social identity, such as workplace status or job, can influence language use more than gender.

Niki Panteli and Monica Seeley, in Chapter 18, focus on email, particularly its text-based attributes, as an issue in CMC. Following a review of the literature on information richness theory as it relates to email communication, they analyse a series of emails sent within a university department over several months. They point out how gender cues emerge in the text-based features of these messages, especially gender differences, which are also encoded in other organizational features such as hierarchical levels. As a result, they argue that the place of email as a 'lean' medium in terms of information richness theory should be questioned. They conclude with some suggestions for how organizations can cultivate email's capacity to indicate social context in order both to further organizational goals and to relax traditional patterns of interaction across organizational hierarchies and between male and female users.

Mark Brosnan, in Chapter 19, takes a less optimistic view of email's capacity to equalize communication differences between men and women at work. On the one hand, email, which women use as much as men, presents a salient instance of equalizing technology uptake between the genders. As such, it is an exception to the 'digital divide' that has been posited to exist between women and men as a result of findings of higher computer anxiety among women compared to men, and other ways women's access to computer technology has been restricted compared to men. On the other hand, processes surrounding email use in organizations may reassert gender differences. Specifically, the very limitations of the medium, its 'affect-limited' nature, may serve traditionally male approaches to communication better than female approaches. Women, by inserting politeness markers and making other attempts to re-insert a more social dimension into their email messages, take longer to send each email message. This may mean that female users are regarded as more inefficient at using email at work. They may also suffer less 'message agreement' as a result of misunderstandings arising, for example, from misinterpretations of the tone in email messages. Brosnan speculates about how these issues will play out as videophoning and texting become more prominent communication tools at work.

Finally, Victor Savicki, David Foster and Merle Kelley, in Chapter 20, examine gender issues in CMC in terms of how they affect the performance of virtual teams. Effective team communication is linked to the dual task of all teams, that is, to undertake both 'task' and 'maintenance' activities. Difficulties arise because maintenance activities have been under-recognized as part of what the team needs to do. This issue is amplified in the CMC environment, which is generally taken as less 'information-rich' than face-to-face environments. At an individual level, this is important for women members of virtual teams, since research has consistently shown women to be more sensitive than men to non-verbal communication and therefore more affected both by its presence in face-to-face communication and its loss in CMC. Nevertheless, even in anonymous virtual communications, it is often possible to tell by the presence of features of women's language, such as attenuated assertions, apologies, questions, a personal orientation, and so on, that a communication has come from a woman. In short, CMC mimics face-to-face communication, regardless of the lack of more obvious cues. The question then arises as to how group performance is affected by these gender-related features of virtual group communication. It is important to note that in group CMC situations, group culture is affected by the proportions of women or men in the group. In particular, the communication patterns generated by all-women virtual groups seem able to overcome the bareness of text-based communication. This is important for group or team performance since, with tasks that require high levels of group 'preference' as well as simply 'task' or 'intellective' activity, it is important to achieve a balanced concern for working on the task itself and maintaining positive socio-emotional dynamics within the virtual group.

What is evident from the material presented throughout this book, is that while there are clearly many similarities in men's and women's approaches to communication in the work environment, there are also many differences. These differences are not only dependent on the sex of the communicators, but also on a variety of situational factors ranging from individuals' expectations of their own and other people's behaviour to the perceived status of the communicators. What is also clear is that until relatively recently, EO practices and policies have tended to imply that so-called 'female' communication differences, based on the 'male' approach as 'the norm', are in some way often inferior. The emphasis has traditionally been on women needing to change and adapt to male ways of communicating in workplace environments in order to assimilate and succeed in predominantly male cultures. The management of diversity, on the other hand, seeks to fully develop the potential communication skills of each employee (regardless of gender, ethnicity, disability, age, and so on) and turn the different sets of skills that each employee brings into a business advantage. According to Davidson and Fielden (2003), it is through the fostering of these types of differences (including communications) that innovation, team creativity and problem-solving can be enhanced.

## Research Directions

What the authors in this book advocate about the directions for future research suggests that more complex, nuanced and inter-disciplinary research approaches will have most to offer in increasing our understanding of gender and communication issues at work. Several of the authors in this book have looked at new or 'virtual' communication technologies and speculated about the extent to which communication using these technologies will tend to retain or change previous research findings about male and female communication patterns, suggest new, variant patterns, or require new research frameworks entirely to understand the gender implications of the interchanges that take place. From their conclusions, it is clear that it still too early to make judgements about this. Other contributors, however, have looked more closely at already established communication situations and workplace phenomena and sought to apply more complex research approaches to them to better understand the nature and role of gender at work. Many of their research recommendations indicate the potential for new ways of understanding gender issues in relation to familiar workplace concepts or events, such as the employment interview, the transfer of formal workplace training, promotion processes, or the international assignment, or ideas about work and organizations, such as leadership, hierarchy, the nature of 'advice' or 'clienthood', workplace story-telling, or even the meaning of silence in organizations. Still others have drawn insights from special workplace environments, such as emergency rooms, call centres or top-level management meetings to achieve new understandings of the role of gender. Typically, these authors have stressed how organizational discourse both constrains gender and is constrained by it, but also how renewed close inspection of these familiar situations reveals a more complex view of communication. The situations are seen as offering a range of strategic positions or discourses that both women and men can draw upon to achieve their goals at work. In various ways, they emphasize the nature of gender as 'performance'. This, in turn, suggests that gender issues in communication are best understood less in simple, 'essentialist', 'female vs. male' terms, and more in terms of a range of strategies, positions, identities, workplace roles and discourse genres that influence and are influenced by various gender schema. The interplay of all of these factors needs to be taken into account if we are to understand both how women may still be being disempowered at work and also how they may be accessing new ways of being and acting so as to reduce various types of workplace barriers. Diversities of ways of understanding will be at least as important as diversity policies in knowing and managing gender at work in future.

## References

Ashcraft, K. L. (2004), 'Gender, discourse, and organization: Framing a shifting relationship', in D. Grant, C. Hardy, C. Oswick and L. L. Putnam (eds), *Handbook of Organizational Discourse*. London: Sage. pp. 275–98.

Brody, L. and Hall, J. (2000), 'Gender, emotion, and expression', in M. Lewis and J. Haviland-Jones (eds), *Handbook of Emotions*, 2nd edn. New York: The Guilford Press. pp. 338–49.

Butler, J. (1990), *Gender Trouble*. New York: Routledge.

Butler, J. (1993), *Bodies that Matter*. New York: Routledge.

Cassell, C. (1997), 'The business case for equal opportunities: Implications for women in management', *Women in Management Review*, **12**(1): 11–16.

Davidson, M. J. and Burke, R. (eds) (2000), *Women in Management: Current Research Issues, Vol. 2*. London: Sage.

Davidson M. J. and Burke R. (eds) (2004), *Women in Management Worldwide – Facts, Figures and Analysis*. London: Ashgate.

Davidson, M. J. and Fielden, S. L. (eds) (2003), *Individual Diversity and Psychology in Organizations*. Chichester: Wiley.

Gray, J. (1992), *Women are from Venus, Men are from Mars*. London: Thorsons.

Hess, U., Senecal, S., Kirouac, G., Herrera, P., Philppot, P. and Kleck, R. (2000), 'Emotional expressivity in men and women: Stereotypes and self-perceptions', *Cognition and Emotion*, **14**(5): 609–42.

Holmes, J., Burns, L., Marra, M., Stubbe, M. and Vine, B. (2003), 'Women managing discourse in the workplace', *Women in Management Review*, **18**(8): 414–24.

Jablin, F. M. and Putnam, L. L. (eds) (2001), *The New Handbook Of Organizational Communication: Advances in Theory, Research, and Methods*. Thousand Oaks, CA: Sage.

Liff, S. and Wajcman, J. (1996), '"Sameness" and "difference" revisited: Which way forward for equal opportunity initiatives?', *Journal of Management Studies*, **33**(1): 79–94.

Powell, G. (ed.) (1999), *Handbook of Gender and Work*. Thousand Oaks, CA: Sage.

Rosener, J. B. (1990), 'Ways women lead', *Harvard Business Review*, **68** (November–December): 119–25.

Ryan, M. K. and Haslam, S. A. (2005), 'The glass cliff: Evidence that women are over-represented in precarious leadership positions', *British Journal of Management*, **16**: 81–90.

Smith, M. (2003), 'Bias in job selection and assessment techniques', in M. J. Davidson and S. L. Fielden (eds), *Individual Diversity and Psychology in Organizations*. Chichester: Wiley. pp. 331–52.

Tannen, D. (1990), *You Just Don't Understand: Women and Men in Conversation*. New York: William Morrow.

Tannen, D. (1994), *Talking from 9 to 5*. New York: William Morrow.

Wajcman, J. (1999), *Managing Like a Man: Women and Men in Corporate Management*. St Leonards: Allen and Unwin.

Woodall, Marian K. (1990), *How to Talk so Men will Listen*. Lake Oswego, OR: Professional Business Communications.

# PART I
# Gender and
# Communication Situations in
# the Employment Lifespan

Chapter 2

# Gendered Performance and Communication in the Employment Interview

Patrice M. Buzzanell and Rebecca J. Meisenbach

## Introduction

Gender is noticeably absent from many popular and academic materials about employment interviewing. With the exceptions of empirical investigations analysing the roles and outcomes of same- and cross-sex applicant–recruiter dyads (for example, Graves and Powell, 1995, 1996), research is lacking into how gender underlies the assumptions, structures and outcomes of employment interviewing processes. (For exceptions, see Buzzanell, 1999, 2002; Ralston and Kinser, 2001; Kinser, 2002) In this chapter, we make a start on rectifying this situation by adapting Ashcraft's (2004) four modes of framing the relationships among gender, discourse and organization to review the findings, nuances and assumptions of theory and research on employment interviewing.

## Overview of Current Research

Despite challenges to the employment interview's reliability, validity and usefulness in employers' selection and recruitment, as well as in applicants' decision making about job offers, the interview is still the most popularly used device in these processes (Eder and Ferris, 1989; Posthuma et al., 2002). Over the years, numerous reviews, textbooks, popular books and articles, and websites have described and discussed roles and sequences in interview scripts, how to construct good-quality questions, interview schedules and question–answer interactions, proper interview attire and demeanour, how to construct documents (for example, resumés, curricula vitae and cover letters), and how to manage impressions so as to gain favourable responses from the other party in the interview exchange (for example, QuintCareers.com, 2003; Schultz, 2003; Stewart and Cash, 2003; Taylor and Small, 2002). In these materials, employment interviewing often is divided into first (screening) interviews and second ('fit') assessments. During screening procedures, applicants and potential employers are scrutinized for desirability (for example, applicants' knowledge, skills and abilities; organizational policies and culture), 'fit' (for example, person–job, – organization, and/or –industry) and other functions (for example, public relations, marketing and environmental monitoring) (see Avery and Campion, 1982; Diboye, 1989; Kristof-Brown, 2000; Rynes, 1989; Rynes and Gerhart, 1990; Stewart and Cash, 2003). Second interviews entail more elaborate assessments of person–organization fit, images, potential mutual treatment and information quality, as well as rudimentary socialization processes for potential newcomers (for example, Fink et al., 1994; Jablin, 1987, 2001; Miller and Buzzanell, 1996; Ralston and Kirkwood, 1999; Rynes and Boudreau, 1986; Rynes et al., 1991; Taylor and Bergmann, 1987).

As mentioned earlier, we shall use Ashcraft's (2004) four modes of framing the relationships among gender, discourse, and organization to classify theory and research on the gendered nature of employment interviewing processes.

Within the first frame, we outline findings from studies on biological sex in employment interviewing that view discourse as an outcome of sex and gender. We then explore studies that describe gender as a constitutive feature of employment interviewing in three other frames, that is, at the interactional, institutional and societal levels of discourse. After discussing each frame, we provide examples of research that enhances the frame's potential to provide insight into gendered employment interviewing processes. We conclude our chapter with recommendations for researchers and practitioners to create more equitable conditions for women and men in interviewing processes and outcomes.

Employment interviews are pivotal points in most individuals' lives because they provide entry into paid work conditions and employer–employee contracts that set the stage for employability security, advancement opportunities, dignity as productive members of society and certain standards of living. Whether individuals earn their livelihoods in corporate, government, or not-for-profit venues, employment interviewing is a gateway to paid work. The exceptions are people who cannot or have no need to earn their livelihood and those who are entrepreneurs or perhaps members of family-run or small businesses. Moreover, job searches involve multiple employment interviews with the same and different organizational representatives over a longer period of time than these searches did a decade earlier (Dunham, 2003). Globally, interest in acquiring a labour force with the 'right' mix of technical skills, drive, personality types and work ethics means that companies may stage elaborate three-stage processes in which candidates are interviewed intensively and on-site for person–job, –organization, and –industry fit over a year after a resumé check indicates KSA (knowledge, skills, and abilities) acceptability (Jeremy Appleton, Director for Media Relations for AlpineStars; personal correspondence, October, 14 2003, at corporate headquarters in Asolo (TV), Italy).

For most people, then, trends in the new or post-Fordist economy mean that employment interviewing is poised to become more frequent and lengthier for diverse occupations, for bricks-and-mortar as well as virtual organizations, and for global enterprises (Arthur et al., 1999; Cheney et al., 2004; Kirkman et al., 2002). To be more specific, research on careers in the new economy indicates that individuals are experiencing multiple employment arrangements in different organizations and industries, as both individual motivations for financially secure growth and industry requirements for labour force flexibility escalate (Arthur et al., 1999). However, these new careers and social contracts about work expectations establish fairly rigid notions of success for both parties and disadvantage people without financial safety nets, high educational levels, superior networking abilities, and ideal worker profiles (Buzzanell, 2000). Trends towards increased restructuring, team-based work, telework, inter-organizational connections (for example, joint ventures or strategic alliances) and outsourcing mean that individuals bid for jobs and project contracts at a higher rate than previously (Cheney et al., 2004) and need particular personality and technical profiles as well as excellent interpersonal and political skills for virtual team work and telework (Cascio, 2000; Kirkman et al., 2002). Underlying these and other changes are tensions between Fordism and neo- or post-Fordism (simply put, the differences between standardized mass production and flexible specialization as well as their associated discourses, work arrangements and relationships) that are being discussed from structural, technological, economic, production, political, sociological, gendered, geographic and other viewpoints (for an overview, see Townsley, 2002). As a result, it is even more important to understand employment interviewing processes and make them more equitable.

## Frames for Re-examining Employment Interviewing

Ashcraft (2004; see also Ashcraft and Mumby, 2004) organizes literature on gender, discourse and organization by posing four frames or ways of seeing the character and function of discourse, to illuminate how discourse is constituted by and constitutes these areas and their intersections (see Table 2.1). Although Ashcraft's aim is to overview how these four processes are presented differently in research studies cutting across organizational communication, organization theory, gender and feminist studies, and management, her frames are useful for organizing theory and research on gender and employment interviewing because they offer lenses for extracting and focusing on gendered aspects of the interviewing process differently from the typical literature and narrative reviews.

Her four frames are not mutually exclusive but are established as different ways of viewing the relationships between gender, discourse and organizations for discussion purposes. The frames are:

- *outcome* or *effect*, meaning that this lens positions discourse as an outcome of gender, focusing on how gender shapes linguistic choices, interactional strategies, and style;
- *performance*, meaning that this frame shifts attention to the ways individual talk shapes the performance of gendered identity;
- *organizational text–conversation dialectic*, meaning that organizations cyclically offer narratives of gender and power relations that coalesce into organizational discourses and structures that further enable and constrain

gender; and

- *social texts*, meaning that broad societal discourses produce gendered selves, relations, and organizing.

**Table 2.1   Gendered frames for viewing and revisiting employment interviewing**

| Frame | Definition | Implications for research and practice |
|---|---|---|
| Outcome | Gender shapes interactional tendencies in employment interviewing | • Researchers need to continue looking for sex differences so that corrections can be made in employment interviewing processes and outcomes.<br>• Practitioners can takes steps to lessen control processes and managerial biases by approximating ideal speech situations and fair treatment standards. |
| Performance | Discourse shapes gendered identity performance in employment interviewing | • Researchers need to investigate how discourses of employment interviewing in specific contexts construct particular gendered performances.<br>• Practitioners can be trained to examine how organizational representatives and applicants follow ritualized gendered scripts and how these scripts can be disrupted productively. |
| Text–conversation dialectic | Employment interviewing structure enables and constrains gender | • Researchers need to examine the ways that structures and ideal applicant profiles produce gendered differences in employment interviewing.<br>• Practitioners can design, implement and participate in training that shows how structural discourses constrain applicants and interviewers in certain gendered ways. |
| Social texts | Societal narratives (en)gender employment interviewing | • Researchers need to analyse the socio-historical and gendered bases of employment interviewing as well as popular depictions of employment interviewing.<br>• Practitioners can make changes in popular renderings of employment interviewing. |

Ashcraft suggests that each frame offers a different way of defining and understanding the relationships between gender, discourse and organization. These four lenses, therefore, can be used to map out assumptions of existing research on gender issues and employment interviewing and to chart new areas for research and exploration.

*Outcome: How Gender Shapes Interactional Tendencies in Employment Interviewing*

In this first frame, gender guides and determines employment interviewing discourse. Outcome-focused employment interviewing researchers see gender as being fixed in identity and organized fairly consistently around biological sex and expectations associated with sex stereotypes and feminine/masculine cultures. Most existing research on sex and gender issues in employment interviewing employs this frame.

The impetus for many empirical studies on applicant–recruiter sex in employment interviews rests on sameness–difference arguments. According to a sameness stance, if employment policies, procedures and practices produce no noticeable differences in processes and outcomes for women or men, then fairness has been achieved. Fairness typically corresponds with procedural (procedures), interactional (treatment) and distributive (outcome) justices (see Bies and Moag, 1986; Sheppard et al., 1992) and provides the basis for US laws such as the Civil Rights Act of 1964, Title VII, in which anything calling attention to special categories, such as age, race, and sex/gender, is classified as unlawful (Stewart and Cash, 2003). On the other hand, if there are differences, then researchers would anticipate being able to pinpoint where, when and how in the process these sex differences occur, with the hope either that corrections can be made or that feminine qualities will be considered superior.

However, researchers have found contradictory results for employment interviewing that have necessitated more complex examinations of gender as a predictor than sameness–difference arguments would imply. For instance, in cross-sex applicant–interviewer dyads, Graves and Powell (1995, 1996) found that female recruiters regarded applicants as more similar to themselves (recruiters) resulting in offering more favourable impressions of interactions and more desirable outcomes to the 'similar' applicants (except when similarity held negative connotations, such as when femaleness was associated with lower status for the female applicants). In another example, influence tactics in employment interviewing were differentially effective depending on the sex of the applicant and the type of job for which the applicant was interviewing (Buttner and McEnally, 1996). Males were more likely to receive job offers if they used assertive tactics, whereas females were more likely to be hired if they used rational, unemotional approaches. Male and female applicants were rated as more capable for cost accounting and sales representative jobs, respectively (for additional evidence of sex-role and job stereotyping, see Avery et al., 1987). In both the research on similarity and on influence tactics, the results did not portray across-the-board disadvantages for female applicants. Rather, interactions between recruiter and applicant sources of similarity or applicant sex and job type produced more complex findings.

Sameness research also extends to notions of fit, or the match between applicant and job or organizational characteristics (Kristof, 1996). In rational-legal bureaucracies, fit should mean needed or complementary skills and abilities (possible heterogeneity), whereas in value-rational organizations, such as cooperatives, fit may mean similarity in key values and attitudes (possible homogenization) (see Rothschild-Whitt, 1979). It is unclear, according to conceptual and empirical studies surveyed by Posthuma et al. (2002), whether fit is close to similarity, contributes substantively to effect size or acts as biasing factor. In Judge et al.'s (2000; see also Jelf, 1999) overview of fit's relevance to employment interviewing, they note that there are few empirical studies of the role of person–organization fit conducted within the context of the interview, but that such research could align with such areas as culture and image analyses to design interviewer training interventions. It also could align with applicant–interviewer gender characteristics, particularly the ways interactants 'do gender' in different employment interviewing phases (see West and Zimmerman, 1987), as well as with ways the organizational culture for which fit is being assessed is gendered.

The outcome perspective has also been employed in research on videoconference interview scenarios with conflicting results. Chapman and Rowe (2001) found that both female and male interviewers rated applicants more highly in videoconference situations than in face-to-face exchanges. One possible explanation was that the interviewers felt that applicants deserved the benefit of the doubt and inflated their evaluations to correct for applicant inexperience with videoconferencing. However, with regard to sex, female interviewers rated applicants higher when using unstructured interview techniques than when using structured techniques, but 'higher levels of interview structure eliminated the disparity between male and female interviewers' ratings' (p. 292), as would be expected based on Campion et al.'s (1997) review of, and recommendations regarding, structure. Although not dealing with new technology use in employment interviewing, Posthuma et al.'s (2002) conclusions in their review of same-sex and cross-sex interviewing dyads still apply to the studies mentioned in this section of our chapter. Namely, inconsistent findings with regard to demographic and attitudinal similarity may be adjudicated by examining other forms of group identity, such as life events and social similarity.

In short, reviews have found contradictory results in applicant–recruiter same- and cross-sex interactional patterns, attributions and consequences. These contradictions are problematic, since the outcome approach is static and has difficulty accounting for people and situations that do not fit the common patterns. In general, outcome studies focusing on engrained personal styles anticipate few variations within and across groups in discursive proclivities, practices and styles. The fixed nature of this frame highlights how public beliefs in the outcome frame can affect interviewing outcomes. That is, if individuals believe and act according to the prognoses of these studies, then their own behaviours during interviews may be guided by and end up fulfilling these expectations. However, when the outcome lens situates employment interviewing as a site in which women and men may present themselves and be treated differentially, and where masculine culture becomes privileged, then additional research needs to be generated. As Ashcraft and Mumby (2004) point out, the first frame 'suffers from a general lack of context – cultural, political, institutional, historical, and structural' such that power and difference arguments (difference-but-equal and difference-but-superior claims) are ineffective (pp. 7–8).

As an example of the outcome frame's possible extensions in employment interviewing, Ralston and Kirkwood (1995) suggest how the parties in employment interviewing processes can overcome managerialist biases. Although theirs is not a study explicitly focused on gender, they elaborate on gendered and contextualized cultural approaches beyond simple sameness–difference and personal (including influence) styles approaches. Underlying much of their analysis and recommendations is a focus on feminine and feminist values (that is, values of caring, connecting and relating combined advocacy for change on behalf of vulnerable groups) and on emancipatory effects of interviewing to offer a counterpoint to masculinity and to restrictions on informational exchanges.

Specifically, Ralston and Kirkwood (1995) note that recommendations for, and use of, standardized interviewing techniques increasingly demand control over interviewing content, relationships, effects and sequencing. These techniques and characteristics are inherently masculine and disadvantage applicants who want to gather information, ask questions (especially questions that are not the 'right' ones to ask) and frame the interview as more of a power-sharing collaboration. Because most employment interviewing does not meet applicants' information needs, Ralston and Kirkwood (1995) insist that more equitable and satisfying interactions can be achieved through use of Habermas's ideal speech situation in which both parties question claims, ask what is of concern to them, participate with candour and in good faith, and share rights to control and direct interviewing processes. Thus, by recognizing that there are different outcomes and different applicant–interviewer interests than those typically investigated in employment interviewing research, scholars and practitioners may be better able to develop and implement interviewing practices that accommodate both men and women.

By socially constructing employment interviewing along the lines of feminine-feminist values and approaches, researchers and practitioners may find creative ways of adjusting to minority applicants. These ways would be more complex, nuanced and contextualized than the sameness–difference arguments and traditional outcomes of same- and cross-sex applicant–recruiter research. There is no research known to us that describes what actually happens in interviewing dyads if informational approaches and fair treatment standards are different from current norms.

However, Ralston (2000) does provide a training exercise in which Rawls's (1971) ethical approach to understanding and empathizing with the needs and interests of different parties come into play. Buzzanell (2002, p. 261) describes a particular circumstance in which 'normal' employment interviewing procedures and power dynamics were disrupted, thus allowing for different types of information exchange (that is, the aftermath of terrorist strikes in the United States, or post September 11,

2001). These two examples suggest that special applicants or circumstances require unusual approaches. However, if researchers and practitioners assume that all individuals are differentiated and, thus, have unique needs (as Ralston and Kirkwood, 1995, maintain), then employment interviewing would begin with a negotiated and mutually empowering stance towards each interview for all applicants and all interviewers. (For additional ways in which individuals can be differentiated without succumbing to sameness–difference double binds, see Vogel's (1990) analysis of equality and special treatment positions and Taub and Williams's (1985) case for gender-neutral approaches.) Research that starts with alternative premises, infuses context and investigates conditions under which equitable and satisfying employment interviewing takes place would productively extend thinking and practice associated with outcome-focused employment interviewing.

*Performance: How Discourse Shapes Gendered Identity Performance in Employment Interviewing*

In the second or performance frame, discourse temporarily fixes but simultaneously offers opportunities for change in gender enactment that is located in mundane interactions. That is, interpersonal discourse produces gender. In a sense, this frame is the response to the first frame; it suggests that not only does gender organize discourse, but discourse also organizes conceptions of gender. In this lens, people accomplish or 'do gender' with 'particular contexts afford[ing] a range of acceptable behaviour and resources to assist the performance' (Ashcraft, 2004, p. 279; see also West and Zimmerman, 1987). As Ashcraft and Mumby (2004, p. 12) point out, the ways discourse constitutes gender may be manifest in the construction and implementation of institutional norms, such as those associated with occupational cultures that present identity dilemmas and opportunities for resolving them. Furthermore, this lens focuses on individual discourses, rather than organizational or societal discourses as the source of gendered identities. Thus, the performance frame can highlight an individual, micro-level perspective on the constitutive nature of discourse in employment interviewing.

The ongoing activity of organizing and disorganizing gender is revealed by studies that are not focused directly on employment interviewing but that, nonetheless, inform interviewing and attendant gendered performances within specific contexts. For instance, the ways in which professional women (and increasingly men) discipline their bodies to conform to appropriate gendered and externally successful images is described by Trethewey (2000) and Nadesan and Trethewey (2000). These authors focus on the paradoxical and ironic renderings of women's discourses and actions in which they strive for, and are constantly denied, entrepreneurial (masculine) ideals. As Nadesan and Trethewey note, career – and, we would argue, employment interviewing – success is 'contingent upon individual women's ability to perform an entrepreneurial subjectivity that draws upon extant articulations of hegemonic masculinity, tempered by social adroitness and image awareness' (p. 231). How these ideals manifest themselves in employment interviewing and how women *and* men enact performative resistance remains under-explored.

As another example of how discourses surrounding interviewing can construct gender, in an empirical study of white middle-class family men who have lost their managerial or professional jobs, Buzzanell and Turner (2003) found interlocking interactional processes by which the men and their family members discursively constructed positive feelings, normalcy, and gender. Although not focused specifically on employment interviewing, job search processes were underlying tensions that surfaced throughout members' talk. Members engaged in emotion work or a complex, situated production of discourse and gendered identities. Partners and children discussed their spouses' and fathers' up-and-down cycles of hope and despair, enthusiastic preparation for interviews and sadness or feelings of hopelessness during post-interview phases, and engagement with family members prior to interviews and withdrawal when there was silence from company representatives. For instance, the teenaged daughter of 'Brad' spoke about her father's up-and-down emotional pattern: 'When he had job interviews, he was really happy. [When] they gave it to someone who had experience, after that he was sad for a day or two but after that he was happy again.' Brad attempted to construct a particular form of masculinity that placed him in the public world of work, in the breadwinner's role, despite lack of earned income, and so on. In these job loss situations, femininity required that partners support the men and sequester their own concerns and questions about employment termination. All parties engaged in elaborate gendered performances that enabled adaptation to changing circumstances and hopefulness that the traditional breadwinner role would be reinstated for the men.

Overall, the performance frame is gaining popularity as scholars begin to focus on the negotiation of gendered identity. But it has rarely been used in studies of employment interviewing processes. Such studies could explore how individual interactions enact gender within employment interviews, particularly the ways gender identities (re)surface differently and politically. Gherardi (1994) shows how routine interaction follows ritualized gendered scripts and how these scripts can be disrupted productively. Examination of how interactants repair and fail to repair gendered scripts following interviewers' introduction of unlawful questions (described in detail by Stewart and Cash, 2003, especially pp. 176–80), could provide insight into gendered performance. Furthermore, studies that focus on screening and second employment interviewing discourses, practices and processes during multiple career and life phases would be beneficial for understanding gendered employment interviewing processes over individuals' lifetimes.

*Text–conversation Dialectic: How Employment Interviewing Structure Enables and Constrains Gender*

In the third frame, organization 'supplies a text that guides discursive activity' or conversation (Ashcraft, 2004, p. 281). The text side of the text–conversation dialectic is typically favoured within existing research, although the dialectic implies the opportunity to focus on how 'organization is both the subject and object of gendered discourse' (Ashcraft, 2004, p. 284). In other words, this frame focuses on collective narratives about organizing that engender and are engendered by interviewing conversations and discourses. Here, organizationally managed employment interviewing processes and structures produce, and are a product of, gendered discourse. Ashcraft says that researchers have emphasized:

> discourse as a collective narrative of gender and power relations that crystallizes into organizational form or design. Accordingly, authors in this perspective stress the discursive construction of gender at the 'meso' (that is, intermediate, institutional) level, where it carries abstract, symbolic, structural, and normative force. (2004, p. 282)

In this sense, employment interviewing is gendered in its design and execution. It has become scripted interaction that admits little variation (Tullar, 1989) not only for reliability and validity purposes (Campion et al., 1997), but also for equality reasons. Structure produces gendered differences such that women and diverse applicants may be dissuaded by bureaucratic language, impersonal norms, written documentation, standard questions, hierarchical relationships and objective rules from introducing the personal (see Ashcraft and Mumby, 2004, p. 15; Buzzanell, 1999).

The ways these tensions are examined and managed in employment interviewing have not been studied empirically. However, recent work on alternative organizing and on gendered employment interviewing structures provides insight into how innovative interviewing research can be accomplished. For instance, Ashcraft (2001), Buzzanell et al. (1997), and Gottfried and Weiss (1994) offer contrastive sites for explorations of organizing that could be extended to employment interviewing processes. These authors studied both hybrid forms of organizing that melded (albeit paradoxically) feminist-bureaucratic structures and alternative organizational forms that coincided with empowering interactions through invitational and dramaturgical leadership. These alternative sites may provide insight into how different gendered discourses and practices can become possible if organizational structures deviate from the usual systems.

More to the point of employment interviewing, recent critiques and empirical studies both confirm and counter assumptions that applicants can emulate the ideal applicant profile and that employment interviewing structures are neutral sites for interactions. The ideal applicant profile focuses on the applicant as the primary factor in interview and employment decisions. Some research has indicated that there are fairly narrow ranges of acceptability between ideal and real applicants (Van Vianen and Willemsen, 1992). Selected candidates must have masculine personality types and be attractive, verbally fluent and adept at turn-taking, interviewer–interviewee role switching and engaged non-verbal communication displays (Babbitt and Jablin, 1985; Engler-Parish and Millar, 1989; Ragan, 1983; Stewart and Cash, 2003; Tengler and Jablin, 1983; Van Vianen and Van Schie, 1995).[1] This profile, coupled with 'normal' and preferred ways of structuring employment interviewing, poses dilemmas for applicants who deviate from the standard applicant (Buzzanell, 1999, 2002; Ralston and Kinser, 2001; Van Vienen and Willemsen, 1992).

In a critique of the ideal applicant as a key player in employment interviewing dramas, Kinser (2002) focused on gendered interviewing structures by using a theatrical metaphor. In this way, employment interviewing becomes an organizational drama in which applicants have to manage dramaturgical challenges. Kinser's focus was not on individual performance, but on interviewing as inherently structured to (re)produce members' behaviours, expectations, feelings and desires in gendered ways for particular outcomes (such as plant trips and job offers). She describes verbal and non-verbal behaviours that are so carefully regulated or scripted, but so taken-for-granted that the reader is momentarily surprised but quickly sees how structural discourses constrain applicants and interviewers in certain gendered ways. While Kinser provides details from numerous employment interviewing and inter-disciplinary materials to support her claims, at this point we do not have empirical investigations and critiques of the dramaturgical processes she describes.

The dialectic frame shows the organization as an active agent in constructing interview discourses, adding a middle-level perspective to the ways that discourse is viewed as a constitutive process. Furthermore, this perspective rejects the idea of isolated, sexist individuals discriminating in a neutral interviewing context. Instead, the interview format and the organizations determining it are viewed as contributing to the gendered nature of the interview process and its interactions. Future research can address the text side of the dialectic, assessing how interviewing processes and structures are fundamentally gendered. This frame proposes that transformation is needed for greater gender equity.

In addition, just as Ashcraft (2004) encourages increased focus on the conversation/discourse side of the dialectic, employment interviewing research can address how these interviews are gendered through discourses about the processes. Such research differs from the performance frame by moving beyond the mundane, individual conversations to the collective narratives associated with organizing.

*Social texts: How Societal Narratives (En)gender Employment Interviewing*

In the final frame, employment interviewing as a societal narrative emphasizes public and popular discourses about gender institutions and members' participation in these institutions, such as work. Aligning partly with a critical perspective, this frame focuses on and critiques the power of societal discourses in employment interviewing. Questions that would be posed in this frame could be:

- What is it about contemporary society that makes employment interviewing such an important process in organizational entry?
- Why do organizational and societal members cling to interviewing despite questionable aspects and refuse to locate other means of recruiting and selecting newcomers?
- What are the depictions of interviewing in media representations and what do they present about the gendered nature and the participation of individuals in these processes?

- How and when do individuals use and resist dominant images in interviewing? How do the presumed fairness and equity in employment interviewing processes and images (re)create the American Dream, hope for under-classes, rights of passage into adult status, differential treatment for applicants of different occupations, ages, or backgrounds, and so on (for example, Ehrenreich, 2001; Newman, 1999)?

As Ashcraft and Mumby (2004) note, this frame has 'potential to hone our understandings of linkages among discourse, history and material conditions' (p. 23). By requiring that researchers analyse the socio-historical and gendered bases of employment history as well as its popular depictions over time, we better grasp why this selection device has such a hold on the business imagination. These studies are yet to be done.

## Conclusion

In this chapter, we have used Ashcraft's (2004) framework for viewing the relationships among gender, discourse and organization and for (re)considering research and issues on gender and employment interviewing. We did not re-cover in detail already reviewed discussions of sex differences in individual recruiter and applicant behaviours, expectations, and outcomes, same- and cross-sex dyads, or similarity and appearance studies in employment interviewing, as these reviews have already been published (for example, Avery and Campion, 1982; Harris, 1989; Posthuma et al., 2002). Instead, we addressed two basic questions:

- How might several frames that foreground different aspects of gender, discourse and employment interviewing help generate new ways of thinking about employment interviewing policies, structures, practices and interactions?
- What is missing in studies of gender in employment interviewing?

In response to these questions, we have uncovered some characteristics of Ashcraft's categorization pattern that could be extended for employment interviewing. Specifically, Ashcraft's first two frames are in a structurational relationship with one another. The first frame (outcome) allows readers to see how gender organizes discourse, while the second frame (performance) focuses on how discourse organizes gender, creating a cycle of structuration. Gender both organizes and is organized by discourse. In contrast, the third frame encompasses how meso- or middle-level organization engenders discourse and, to a lesser extent, how discourses engender organizations. Discourse both engenders and is engendered by organizations and organizing. Thus, Ashcraft has included in one category what she broke into two categories with the first two frames (that is, the whole cycle is covered within the one frame). In the fourth frame, Ashcraft moves to the macro-level of societal discourses, considering how these broad discourses engender organizing processes. While the cyclical nature of this fourth frame is not explicitly addressed (that is, how societal discourses both engender and are engendered by organizing processes), the potential certainly exists.

Drawing from these frames in our overview of gendered employment interviewing, we found that while most existing studies that address gender/interviewing intersections employ an outcome perspective, there are ways to expand outcome research in pursuit of equitable interviewing processes. In particular, the findings of outcome studies themselves can be used to formulate and structure interviews so as to equalize opportunities for male and female applicants. Such a structure might have women interviewing women using the styles research describes as feminine. However, in consideration of the contradictory and inconclusive findings of outcome studies, such moves are highly problematic for a couple of reasons. They can further constrain and limit acceptable patterns of interaction for both men and women, and individuals who fail to use the predicted and prescribed communication styles may continue to be disadvantaged by the interviewing process.

In addition, a feminized interviewing process could well be positioned as lesser and easier, creating significant problems for individuals who are offered jobs through this alternative process. However, researchers can further address the possibilities of interviewing processes that integrate both masculine and feminine styles as discovered through outcome research. In a move that pushes past sameness–difference critiques, researchers also could study interviewing processes that assume diverse informational and contextual needs for all parties rather than emphasizing only sex and gender styles.

Ashcraft's other three frames reveal many avenues for future research on gender issues in employment interviewing. Still missing from research programmes are: analyses of employment interviewing as gendered performances embedded within specific contexts; investigations of how employment interviewing structures enable and constrain interactions; and critiques of the cultural products, such as popular films and corporate training materials, that (re)produce (and are produced by) certain aspects and discourses of contemporary society. We hope that, by paying greater attention to the assumptions and logical extensions of current research on gendered employment interviewing, we can encourage more complex and nuanced analyses of gendered interviewing processes within and across micro-meso-macro levels of analysis.

## Note

1. Based on changes in the new economy indicating greater need for participatory practices, relational skills and team work, one might assume that findings from previous studies indicating masculine biases within the ideal applicant profile would become outdated (that is, studies indicating that more feminine female applicants are not selected for employment would no longer be the case; for example, see Van Vianen and Van Schie, 1995; Van Vianen and Willemsen, 1992). Yet, some recent findings indicate continued disadvantage for many female applicants. Specifically testing the assumption in employment interviewing that a more

feminized workplace might enable women (and men) to act in a more communal fashion, Rudman and Glick (1999) found that female job applicants had to carefully negotiate tensions among feminine approaches, competence and assertiveness within very narrow ranges despite job descriptions as masculine or feminine.

Moreover, there may be increased biases against women as professional and managerial women ascend corporate hierarchies. The reasons for these biases are that managers' roles are associated more with masculine than feminine values and characteristics, and that managers are supposed to be more rational and ambitious, whether female or male (Calás and Smircich, 1993; Collinson and Hearn, 1996; Fondas, 1997; Marshall, 1993; Powell, 1993). Despite meta-analyses indicating that male and female leaders are equally effective, men are viewed as more effective in roles that are defined as more masculine and when positions are in numerically male-dominated contexts (Eagly et al., 1995). So strong is the association of masculine with professional and managerial, that managerial roles override gender roles (Eagly and Johnson, 1990).

Managers (as opposed to non-managers) have a stronger preference for masculine cultures that emphasize male values (Van Vianen and Fischer, 2002). Managers, whether female or male, adhere to and prefer masculine cultural norms (for example, for competition, achievement and work pressure) (Van Vianen and Fischer, 2002). Female managers either incorporate more masculine behaviours into their own personal styles over time or they may be more attracted to these careers because of pre-existing preferences for masculine norms and cultures. To test assumptions of adaptation and self-selection, Van Vianen and Fischer used career starters and seasoned managers to find that the second explanation, self-selection, seemed to account for female managers' behaviours.

## References

Arthur, M. B., Inkson, K. and Pringle, J. K. (1999), *The New Careers: Individual Action And Economic Change*. London: Sage.

Ashcraft, K. L. (2001), 'Organized dissonance: Feminist bureaucracy as hybrid organizational form', *Academy of Management Journal*, **44**: 1301–22.

Ashcraft, K. L. (2004), 'Gender, discourse, and organization: Framing a shifting relationship', in D. Grant, C. Hardy, C. Oswick and L. L. Putnam (eds), *Handbook of Organizational Discourse*. London: Sage. pp. 275–98.

Ashcraft, K. L. and Mumby, D. K. (2004), *Reworking Gender: A Feminist Communicology Of Organization*. Thousand Oaks, CA: Sage.

Avery, R. D. and Campion, J. E. (1982), 'The employment interview: A summary and review of recent research', *Personnel Psychology*, **35**: 281–322.

Avery, R. D., Miller, M., Gould, E. and Burch, P. (1987), 'Interview validity for selecting sales clerks', *Personnel Psychology*, **40**: 1–12.

Babbitt, L. V. and Jablin, F. M. (1985), 'Characteristics of applicants' questions and employment screening interview outcomes', *Human Communication Research*, **11**: 507–35.

Bies, R. J. and Moag, J. S. (1986), 'Interactional justice: Communication criteria of fairness', in R. J. Lewicki, B. H. Sheppard and M. H. Bazerman (eds), *Research On Negotiation in Organizations* (Vol. 1). Greenwich, CT: JAI Press. pp. 43–56.

Buttner, E. H. and McEnally, M. (1996), 'The interactive effect of influence tactic, applicant gender, and type of job on hiring recommendations', *Sex Roles*, **34**: 581-91.

Buzzanell, P. M. (1999), 'Tensions and burdens in employment interviewing processes: Perspectives of non-dominant group applicants', *The Journal of Business Communication*, **36**: 134–62.

Buzzanell, P. M. (2000), 'The promise and practice of the new career and social contract: Illusions exposed and suggestions for reform', in P.M. Buzzanell (ed.), *Rethinking Organizational And Managerial Communication From Feminist Perspectives*. Thousand Oaks, CA: Sage. pp. 209–35.

Buzzanell, P. M. (2002), 'Employment interviewing research: Ways we can study underrepresented group members' experiences as applicants', *The Journal of Business Communication*, **39**, 257–75.

Buzzanell, P. M. and Turner, L. H. (2003), 'Emotion work revealed by job loss discourse: Backgrounding–foregrounding of feelings, construction of normalcy, and (re)instituting of traditional masculinities', *Journal of Applied Communication Research*, **31**: 27–57.

Buzzanell, P. M., Ellingson, L., Silvio, C., Pasch, V., Dale, B., Mauro, G., Smith, E., Weir, N. and Martin, C. (1997), 'Leadership processes in alternative organizations: Invitational and dramaturgical leadership', *Communication Studies*, **48**: 285–310.

Calás, M. B. and Smircich, L. (1993), 'Dangerous liaisons: The "feminine-in-management" meets "globalization"', *Business Horizons*, **36**(2): 71–81.

Campion, M. A., Palmer, D. K. and Campion, J. E. (1997), 'A review of structure in the selection interview', *Personnel Psychology*, **50**: 655–702.

Cascio, W. F. (2000), 'Managing a virtual workplace', *Academy of Management Executive*, **14**, 81–90.

Chapman, D. S. and Rowe, P. M. (2001), 'The impact of videoconference technology, interview structure, and interviewer gender on interviewer evaluations in the employment interview: A field experiment', *Journal of Occupational and Organizational Psychology*, **74**: 279–98.

Cheney, G., Christensen, L., Zorn, T. and Ganesh, S. (2004), *Organizational Communication in an Age of Globalization: Issues, Reflections, Practices*. Prospect Heights, IL: Waveland.

Collinson, D. L. and Hearn, J. (eds). (1996), *Men As Managers, Managers As Men: Critical Perspectives On Men, Masculinities And Managements*. Thousand Oaks, CA: Sage.

Diboye, R. L. (1989), 'Threats to the incremental validity of interviewer judgments', in R. W. Eder and G. R. Ferris (eds), *The Employment Interview: Theory, Research and Practice*, Newbury Park, CA: Sage. pp. 45–60.

Dunham, K. J. (2003, July, 15), 'Career journal: The jungle', *Wall Street Journal*: B6.

Eagly, A. H. and Johnson, B. T. (1990), 'Gender and leadership style: A meta-analysis', *Psychological Bulletin*, **18**: 233–56.

Eagly, A. H., Karau, S. J. and Makhijani, M. G. (1995), 'Gender and the effectiveness of leaders: A meta-analysis', *Psychological Bulletin*, **117**: 125–45.

Eder, R. W. and Ferris, G. R. (eds), (1989), *The Employment Interview: Theory, Research, and Practice*. Newbury Park, CA: Sage.

Ehrenreich, B. (2001), *Nickel And Dimed: On (Not) Getting By in America*. New York: Henry Holt.

Engler-Parish, P. G. and Millar, F. E. (1989), 'An exploratory relational control analysis of the employment screening interview', *Western Journal of Speech Communication*, **53**: 30–51.

Fink, L. S., Bauer, T. N. and Campion, M. A. (1994), 'Job candidates' views of site interviews', *Journal of Career Planning and Employment*, Spring: 32–8.

Fondas, N. (1997), 'Feminism unveiled: Management qualities in contemporary writings', *Academy of Management Review*, **22**: 257–82.

Gallois, C., Callan, V. J. and Palmer, J.-A. M. (1992), 'The influence of applicant communication style and interviewer characteristics on hiring decisions', *Journal of Applied Social Psychology*, **22**: 1041–60.

Gherardi, S. (1994), 'The gender we think, the gender we do in our everyday organizational lives', *Human Relations*, **47**: 591–610.

Gottfried, H. and Weiss, P. (1994), 'A compound feminist organization: Purdue University's Council on the Status of Women', *Women and Politics*, **14**: 23–44.

Graves, L. M. and Powell, G. N. (1995), 'The effect of sex similarity on recruiters' evaluations of actual applicants: A test of the similarity-attraction paradigm', *Personnel Psychology*, **48**: 85–98.

Graves, L. M. and Powell, G. N. (1996), 'Sex similarity, quality of the employment interview and recruiters' evaluation of actual applicants', *Journal of Occupational and Organizational Psychology*, **69**: 243–61.

Harris, M. M. (1989), 'Reconsidering the employment interview: A review of recent literature and suggestions for future research', *Personnel Psychology*, **42**: 691–726.

Jablin, F. M. (1987), 'Organizational entry, assimilation, and exit', in F. M. Jablin, L. L. Putnam, K. H. Roberts and L. W. Porter (eds), *Handbook Of Organizational Communication: An Interdisciplinary Perspective*. Newbury Park, CA: Sage. pp. 679–740.

Jablin, F. M. (2001), 'Organizational entry, assimilation, and disengagement/exit', in F .M. Jablin and L. L. Putnam (eds), *The New Handbook Of Organizational Communication: Advances in Theory, Research and Methods*. Thousand Oaks, CA: Sage. pp. 732-810.

Jelf, G. S. (1999), 'A narrative review of post-1989 employment interview research', *Journal of Business and Psychology*, **14**: 25–58.

Judge, T. A., Higgins, C. A. and Cable, D. M. (2000), 'The employment interview: A review of recent research and recommendations for future research', *Human Resource Management Review*, **10**: 383–406.

Kinser, A. (2002), Gendered performances in employment interviewing: Interpreting and designing communication research', *Journal of Business Communication*, **39**: 245–56.

Kirkman, B. L., Rosen, B., Gibson, C. B., Tesluk, P. E. and McPherson, S. O. (2002), 'Five challenges to virtual team success. Lessons from Sabre, Inc.', *Academy of Management Executive*, **16**: 67–79.

Kristoff, A. L. (1996), 'Person–organization fit: An integrative review of its conceptualizations, measurement, and implications', *Personnel Psychology*, **49**: 1–49.

Kristof-Brown, A. L. (2000), 'Perceived applicant fit: Distinguishing between recruiters' perceptions of person–job and person–organization fit', *Personnel Psychology*, **53**, 643-71.

Marshall, J. (1993), 'Viewing organizational communication from a feminist perspective: A critique and some offerings', in S. Deetz (ed.), *Communication Yearbook 16*. Newbury Park, CA: Sage. pp. 122–43.

Miller, V. D. and Buzzanell, P. M. (1996), 'Toward a research agenda for the second employment interview', *Journal of Applied Communication Research*, **24**, 165–80.

Nadesan, M. H. and Trethewey, A. (2000), 'Performing the enterprising subject: Gendered strategies for success (?)', *Text and Performance Quarterly*, **20**: 223–50.

Newman, K. S. (1999), *No Shame in My Game: The Working Poor in the Inner City*. New York: Vintage Books/Russell Sage Foundation.

Posthuma, R. A., Morgenson, F. P. and Campion, M. A. (2002), 'Beyond employment interview validity: A comprehensive narrative review of recent research and trends over time', *Personnel Psychology*, **55**: 1–81.

Powell, G. (1993), *Women and Men in Management*. Newbury Park, CA: Sage.

QuintCareers.com. (2003), 'Traditional employment interview questions'. Retrieved November 1, 2003 from www.quintcareers.com/interview_questions.html.

Ragan, S. L. (1983), 'A conversational analysis of alignment talk in job interviews', in R. N. Bostrom (ed.), *Communication Yearbook 7*. Beverly Hills, CA: Sage. pp. 502–17.

Ralston, S. M. (2000), 'The "veil of ignorance": Exploring ethical issues in the employment interview', *Business Communication Quarterly*, **63**: 50–52.

Ralston, S. M. and Kinser, A. (2001), 'Intersections of gender and employment interviewing', in L. P. Arliss and D. J. Borisoff (eds), *Women And Men Communicating: Challenges and Changes*. Prospect Heights, IL: Waveland. pp. 185–211.

Ralston, S. M. and Kirkwood, W. G. (1995), 'Overcoming managerial bias in employment interviewing', *Journal of Applied Communication Research*, **23**: 75–92.

Ralston, S. M. and Kirkwood, W. G. (1999), 'The trouble with applicant impression management', *Journal of Business and Technical Communication*, **13**: 190–207.

Rawls, J. (1971), *The Theory Of Justice*. Cambridge, MA: Harvard University Press.

Rothschild-Whitt, J. (1979), 'The collectivist organization: An alternative to rational-bureaucratic models', *American Sociological Review*, **44**: 509–27.

Rudman, L. A. and Glick, P. (1999), 'Feminized management and backlash toward agentic women: The hidden costs to women of a kinder, gentler image of middle managers', *Journal of Personality and Social Psychology*, **77**: 1004–10.

Rynes, S. L. (1989), 'The employment interview as a recruitment device', in R. W. Eder and G. R. Ferris (eds), *The Employment Interview: Theory, Research, and Practice*. Newbury Park, CA: Sage. pp. 127–41.

Rynes, S. L. and Boudreau, J. W. (1986), 'College recruiting in large organizations: Practice, evaluation, and research implications', *Personnel Psychology*, **39**, 729–57.

Rynes, S. L., Bretz, R. D., Jr and Gerhart, B. (1991), 'The importance of recruitment in job choice: A different way of looking', *Personnel Psychology*, **44**: 487–521.

Rynes, S. L. and Gerhart, B. (1990), 'Interviewer assessments of applicant "fit": An exploratory investigation', *Personnel Psychology*, **43**: 13–35.

Schultz, B. (2003), 'Interviewing acumen: Establishing job competencies and using behavioral event interviewing can lead you to the perfect hire', *Networking World*, **20**(33): 53.

Sheppard, B. H., Lewicki, R. J. and Minton, J. W. (1992), *Organizational Justice: The Search For Fairness In The Workplace*. New York: Lexington Books.

Steinpreis, R. E., Anders, K. A. and Ritzke, D. (1999), 'The impact of gender on the review of the curricula vitae of job applicants and tenure candidates: A national empirical study', *Sex Roles*, **41**: 509–28.

Stewart, C. J. and Cash, W. B., Jr. (2003), *Interviewing: Principles and Practices*, 10th edn. Boston, MA: McGraw-Hill.

Taub, N. and Williams, W. W. (1985), 'Will equality require more than assimilation, accommodation, or separation from existing social structure?' *Rutgers Law Review*, **37**: 825–44.

Taylor, M. S. and Bergmann, T. J. (1987), 'Organizational recruitment practices and applicants' reactions at different stages of the recruitment process', *Personnel Psychology*, **40**: 261–85.

Taylor, P. J. and Small, B. (2002), 'Asking applicants what they *would do* versus what they *did do*: A meta-analytic comparison of situational and past behaviour employment interview questions', *Journal of Occupational and Organizational Psychology*, **75**: 277–94.

Tengler, C. D. and Jablin, F. M. (1983), 'Effects of question type, orientation, and sequencing in the employment screening interview', *Communication Monographs*, **50**: 243–63.

Townsley, N. (2002), 'A Discursive Approach to Embedded Gender Relations in a (Swedish) Global Restructuring', unpublished dissertation, Purdue University, West Lafayette, IN.

Trethewey, A. (2000), 'Revisioning control: A feminist critique of disciplined bodies', in P. M. Buzzanell (ed.), *Rethinking Organizational and Managerial Communication from Feminist Perspectives*. Thousand Oaks, CA: Sage. pp. 107–27.

Tullar, W. L. (1989), 'The employment interview as a cognitive performing script', in R. W. Eder and G. R. Ferris (eds), *The Employment Interview: Theory, Research and Practice*. Newbury Park, CA: Sage. pp. 233-45.

Van Vianen, A. E. M. and Fischer, A. H. (2002), 'Illuminating the glass ceiling: The role of organizational culture preferences', *Journal of Occupational and Organizational Psychology*, **75**: 315–37.

Van Vianen, A. E. M. and Van Schie, E. C. M. (1995), 'Assessment of male and female behaviour in the employment interview', *Journal of Community and Applied Social Psychology*, **5**: 24–357.

Van Vianen, A. E. M. and Willemsen, T. M. (1992), 'The employment interview: The role of sex stereotypes in the evaluation of male and female job applicants in the Netherlands', *Journal of Applied Social Psychology*, **22**: 471–91.

Vogel, L. (1990), 'Debating difference: Feminism, pregnancy, and the workforce', *Feminist Studies*, **16**, 9–32.

West, C. and Zimmerman, D. H. (1987), 'Doing gender', *Gender and Society*, **1**: 125–51.

Chapter 3

# The Effect of Gender on the Transfer of Interpersonal Communication Skills Training to the Workplace

Kathryn S. O'Neill, Carol D. Hansen and Gary L. May

## Introduction

Skilful interpersonal communication is essential to managerial and leadership success. The move to team-focused organizational structures (Barry and Watson, 1996; Carmichael, 1995) has put extra importance on communication, which already takes up three-quarters of a manager's time (Barry and Watson, 1996). Participative management approaches are well documented as important for organizational effectiveness (Campbell et al., 1993; Kabakoff, 1998; Penley et al., 1991; Rosener, 1990) and oral communication skills are predictive of vertical mobility (Shockley-Zabalak et al., 1988). Kabakoff (1998) recommends training for managers focused on empathy, listening skills, sensitivity to interpersonal differences and the ability to give effective and constructive feedback. Since these skills are all sex-linked to the feminine in many national cultures (Hofstede, 1980), gendered thinking could impede the use and effectiveness of these skills in a workplace culture dominated by male communication paradigms and thus interfere with career mobility. This concern is supported by a recent report from the International Labour Organization (Wirth, 2001) indicating that the gap in male and female authority has worsened in many male-oriented industrialized countries as well as in some societal cultures that have traditionally been seen as more feminine. In the clash of masculine and feminine cultural behaviours, communication skills training crystallizes the struggle.

In the case of North American organizations, interpersonal communication, as a skill area, is vulnerable to training transfer barriers, that is, to the use of newly learned skills on the job, as identified by findings published in *The 2000 ASTD Learning Outcomes Report* (Bassi and Ahlstrand, 2000). In the report, transfer rates for supervisors in training are only 34 per cent for management/supervisory skills and 27 per cent for interpersonal skills. Not only is the low rate of transfer costly in terms of organizational performance, it is costly in terms of budgeted training expenditures. US employers spent $54 billion on formal training in 2000, and 81 per cent of companies provided leadership training, including communication skills (*Training Magazine*, 2000). Leadership development as a percentage of total training expenditures is growing rapidly, with 42 per cent of firms devoting 10 to 25 per cent of total training expenditures on leadership training. In addition, 57 per cent of respondents to a 1998 ASTD survey of human resource development (HRD) executives put communication as the number one skill of good leaders (ASTD, 1998).

In this chapter, we will first introduce the three theories of societal culture, gender schemas and social roles, and their potential to influence one's communication orientation to the workplace. Our premise is that societal culture shapes gender schemas and prescribes social roles. Second, we will link the gender-related theories to organizational culture and the issue of training transfer in the workplace. We believe that gender schemas and social roles interact to produce sex-typed thinking that, in turn, influences capacity and motivation to transfer skills. This explains why the feminine sex-linked behaviours taught in typical interpersonal skills workshops are often resisted by learners and ultimately extinguished by a masculine-oriented organizational culture, accounting for the low rates of transfer reported in the literature (see Figure 3.1). We then discuss the implications of this phenomenon for theory and practice, including the notion that training interventions designed to change interpersonal communication behaviour are, in reality, cultural interventions that require strong modelling from the senior management level to be successful. Finally, we conclude the discussion with suggestions for further research.

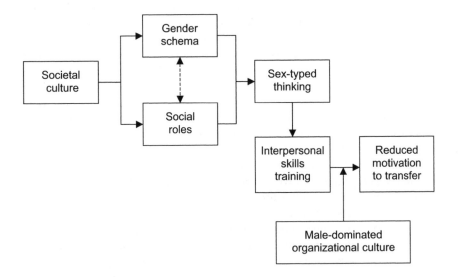

**Figure 3.1    Origin of sex-typed thinking and its effects in motivation to transfer**

## Overview of Current Research

*Gender Models and Societal Cultures*

Gender models vary and are shaped by the cultural norms of the societies in which they reside (Hofstede, 1980). As a construct, Hofstede's (1991) definition of culture is one of the best known. He defines culture as 'the collective programming of the mind' (p. 5), that is, as a manifestation of the value systems of various groups which is able to sustain itself over long periods of time. In the work environment, when beliefs are shared by members of the same culture or subculture, they become a kind of code for 'meaning-making', which can influence, for example, ways to resolve conflict, the information needed for sound decision making, the criteria for promotion and the appropriate level of assertiveness.

The issue of culture, its societal origins and its impact on the workplace has grown in importance in recent years. Globalization has brought this issue to the forefront. As more and more companies cross national boundaries, scholars have begun to question the relative importance of socio-cultural (national and regional) and organizational frames (for example, Laurent 1986; Trompenaars, 1993). In a landmark study in 1979 (Hofstede, 1980) that was later replicated (Hofstede, 2001), Hofstede found that work behaviour was more a factor of the local national culture than the parent organization. In fact, societal culture may be where the largest difference in values and beliefs of cross-cultural organizations reside. As culture is learned and not inherited, gender role patterns are typically demonstrated by one's parents or other family members and internalized at a very young age. Thus, work beliefs are shaped during childhood and the depth of this early orientation remains relatively constant and more powerful than the temporary effect of organizational affiliation.

Anthropologists suggest that gender issues are common world wide (Inkeles and Levinson, 1969). Hofstede (1980, 2001) confirmed this premise by identifying femininity and masculinity as a dimension of societal culture on which national value systems vary. This construct has widespread appeal to the international business community (Adler, 1997).

From his study of IBM employees in 53 countries and three regions, Hofstede (1980) developed an index on which nations that score high on masculinity exhibit a greater tendency to be competitive and assertive and are greatly affected by job earnings, recognition and advancement. Conversely, feminine cultures are characterized as being more modest, nurturing and concerned with the quality of life. Masculine cultures are interested more in equity, while those countries whose characteristics are associated with femininity are concerned with equality. Moreover, it is in masculine cultures that there is the greatest distinction between social gender roles. The Scandinavian countries tend to score high on femininity, while Japan and the United States score high on masculinity. It is not surprising that Japanese men and women do not find comparable career opportunities (Behrman and Zheng, 1995) and that Laurent (1986) found that Swedish managers saw their role as facilitative rather than directive or controlling. Meanwhile, the *International Herald Tribune* (1995) reported that a Norwegian shelter for abused women opened its doors to men who had been battered and tyrannized by their wives and girlfriends.

It follows that how a national culture defines its gender orientation will influence the role of men and women in the workplace as well as their occupational orientation. In highly masculine cultures, gender characteristics are attributed to occupations. Hofstede (1980, 2001) found that salesmen who were paid on commission and worked in a highly competitive environment were considered to be highly masculine, while nurses and teachers who were expected to be nurturing and charitable were associated with femininity.

## Gender Schema Theory

Gender schema theory (Bem, 1981; Hudak, 1993) complements social role theory, to be discussed next, and offers a way to understand how expectations surrounding the behaviour of men and women could obstruct the use of learned interpersonal skills. A schema is a network of interrelated elements that defines a concept for individuals (Crockett, 1988). Thus, individuals form schemas to define expectations about the behaviour of men and women. According to Bem (1977), being masculine or feminine is a fairly central aspect of self-concept for many people. In American society, she states, masculinity and femininity are seen as opposites, and a person is therefore taking a risk of sorts when they venture into the other sex's behavioural territory.

Gender schema theory proposes that the phenomenon of sex-typing derives, in part, from gender-based schematic processing, that is, from a generalized readiness to process information on the basis of the sex-linked associations that constitute the gender schema. Individuals are relatively schematic or aschematic with respect to gender. Gender is theorized to be particularly salient for gende- schematic individuals, serving as a primary schema for sorting and conceptualizing information, since the self-concept itself gets assimilated to the gender schema. Masculine (schematic) men are thus most prone to see women as stereotypically high in femininity and low on masculinity. Bem (1981) describes several studies that demonstrate that sex-typed individuals do, in fact, have a greater readiness to process information, including information about the self, in terms of the gender schema. She speculates that gender-based schematic processing derives, in part, from the society's insistence on the functional importance of the gender dichotomy. Using this theory as a lens, it is easy to see how the use of feminine sex-linked skills in a workplace structured to a masculine paradigm, could be problematic for individuals of either gender.

## Social Role Theory

Eagly (1987) sees differences in the behaviour of men and women through the lens of her social role theory of sex differences. In the realm of psychology, 'sex' is defined as the grouping of humans into two biological categories, male and female, and 'sex difference' refers to findings when females and males have been shown to differ on a particular measure or set of measures. 'Gender' refers to meanings that societies and individuals ascribe to female and male categories and 'gender roles' are those social roles a society defines for women and men. 'Social role' refers to specific social roles assigned to men and women in a society – especially occupational and family roles.

With these definitions in place, then, Eagly theorizes that people are expected to behave consistently in accord with societal gender roles. These expectations arise from men's and women's occupancy of different social roles. Karau and Eagly (1999, p. 322) cite three roles as particularly important to male-dominated societies:

- men's concentration in roles with greater power and status;
- differential concentrations of men and women in certain paid occupations;
- men's concentration in the family role of primary resource provider and women's concentration in the family role of primary homemaker.

They also note that research has demonstrated that men are expected to have high levels of agentic attributes (independent, masterful, assertive, competent) and that women are expected to have high levels of communal attributes (friendly, unselfish, concerned with others, emotionally expressive).

When these expectations are held up to expected leadership behaviours required of supervisors and managers, disconnects emerge. Leadership is significantly correlated with masculinity (Bem, 1974; Kolb, 1999), requiring women who wish to fill that social role to adopt a masculine behaviour pattern to be chosen as leaders and to be successful in the job. Since feminine communication routines are devalued in the workplace, both men and women in the roles of supervisor and manager may resist applying interpersonal communication skills learned in training.

**Implications**

*Gender Role and Interpersonal Skills in the Organization*

Organizations, like national societies, have cultures and abide by a set of mostly unconscious beliefs about appropriate and inappropriate work behaviour. Likewise, organizational cultures are highly influenced by the gender orientation of the societies in which they operate.

Movement towards flatter, team-based organizations and increases in workplace diversity have given rise to predictions that leadership styles in organizational cultures will shift from a directive to a more participative focus, requiring excellent interpersonal skills. Much of the training in management/supervisory skills and interpersonal communication skills seeks to assist supervisors to meet increasing demands for participation from the workforce and to enable interactive leadership styles that will keep the organization viable in an economic climate of rapid change (Billard, 1992; Rosener, 1990).

A possible problem in this specific training context is that the skills involved are traditionally sex-linked to women (Lee, 1994). In more masculine-oriented societies, supervision in most organizational cultures is still a male-dominated activity and power relationships in organizations are shaped to traditional male paradigms (Carmichael, 1995; Davidson and Ferrario, 1992; Morrison et al., 1992). Assumptions about characteristics that are typically associated with men and women carry over into the area of interpersonal skills, so that feminine sex-linked behaviours are not regarded in a favourable light (Bem, 1994; Kinser, 2002; Larwood and Wood, 1995; Reavley, 1989; Tannen, 1995). Male behaviour patterns are more valued than feminine characteristics in the workplace (Helgesen, 1995; Hudak, 1993; Kanter, 1977; Powell et al., 1984), creating potential barriers to the transfer of newly learned interpersonal communication skills and behaviour to the workplace.

Traditionally, workplace behaviours and communication styles in countries rated high in masculine values favour the male paradigm, requiring such qualities as risk taking, aggressiveness and task orientation (Borisoff and Hahn, 1995; Fagenson, 1990). As previously noted, however, developments in total quality management and team-based organizational frameworks have begun to require of managers and supervisors a new style that includes such qualities as empathy, listening and providing support that are associated with females in the social context (Carr-Ruffino, 1993; Claes, 1999; Korabik and Ayman, 1989; Lee, 1994; Penley et al., 1991; Rosener, 1990). In addition, in assessments and research into competencies most needed for success as a manager, communication and interpersonal abilities typically turn up high on the list (Davids, 1995; Shockley-Zabalak et al., 1988).

*Transfer Rates*

As important as they seem to be, however, when carrying out interpersonal skills training, transfer rates are low where the predominating gender orientation favours the male (Broad and Newstrom, 1992; Facteau et al., 1995). As previously cited, *The 2000 ASTD Learning Outcomes Report* (Bassi and Ahlstrand, 2000) shows transfer rates in the United States, expressed as 'change of performance on course objectives' by the supervisors of trained employees, are low for management/supervisory skills and interpersonal skills. Indeed, for one essential skill, listening, one of the few empirical field studies of transfer found no transfer at all (May and Kahnweiler, 2000).

One possible reason for low rates of transfer may be the resistance of learners, as members of a culture dominated by male behaviours, to using feminine sex-linked behaviours in the workplace. Skills addressed in training often include asking questions, listening, sharing information, enhancing the self-worth of others and promoting participation, all stereotypical feminine behaviours (Helgesen, 1995; Moskal, 1997; Rosener, 1990). Female leaders in the workplace have been socialized into their leadership roles in the male-centred organizational paradigm so that research often shows little difference in style between men and women, and styles are characterized by a masculine orientation (Eagly, 1987; Eagly and Johnson, 1990; Kanter, 1977; Karau and Eagly, 1999; Kolb, 1999).

*Theory and Practice*

From a theoretical perspective, we are still in the early stages of model building in regard to learning transfer and research has only been conducted in male-dominated societies. This chapter has contributed to the theoretical dialogue by identifying a component of transfer that has been neglected in the transfer literature: the effect of gender-based role perceptions. Deep-seated beliefs about appropriate role behaviours, interacting with organizational norms, may block an individual's willingness to act on what is learned in some context-specific areas of training, such as interpersonal skills. A similar disconnect may be expected in international business where communication barriers await the expatriate whose style and role expectations differ greatly from the gender schemas of the societal culture of foreign colleagues.

One role of theory development is to determine research priorities (Torraco, 1997). Three theoretical perspectives, gender schema, social role and cultural orientation, demonstrate that trainee characteristics related to gender role perceptions can play an important role in the transfer process and should be made a priority in terms of future research.

This discussion also raises interesting questions for HRD practice. Current approaches to soft skills training are probably a waste of time and money in terms of real transfer. One reason may be the gender effect. The theory suggests that a trainee with masculine schematic thinking may have difficulty transferring feminine-linked skills training. Transfer is further complicated if the business culture and communities of discourse are programmed for masculinity in terms of leadership styles. If gender-based role perceptions and cultural norms do indeed play a significant role in the transfer equation, what can a practitioner do?

There are several possible strategies, all needing validation through field research. Validated instruments exist to test the effect of gender upon transfer of interpersonal skills, including the Bem Sex Role Inventory (BSRI) (Bem, 1974) and the Learning Transfer System Inventory (LTSI) (Bates and Holton, 1999; Naquin and Holton, 2001; Ruona et al., 1999). These can be used in conjunction with workplace populations of trainees undergoing training in interpersonal communication skills to gather data on possible effects. One project that attempted to correlate high masculine scores on the BSRI with low scores for transfer on the LTSI, however, showed no effects (O'Neill, 2003).

One approach would be a pre-training intervention, designed to facilitate self-discovery through the use of instruments such as the BSRI and the LTSI. Another might be to introduce, during the training, a cognitive-behavioural model for relapse prevention (Marx, 1982), which offers a systematic approach to the maintenance of behaviour in the face of an environment hostile to the trained skills. A third approach is to employ post-training coaching or mentoring support (Joyner, 2001). Whatever the intervention, it is clear that the problem of gender effect offers a number of opportunities to engage in the theory–research–development–practice cycle for the purpose of enhancing training transfer.

On the other hand, a case can be made that traditional training is the wrong paradigm for changing interpersonal communication skills behaviour in an organization. What may be needed is a culture change intervention, not a training intervention. Changing a company's culture and aligning it with strategy are among the most challenging responsibilities of management (Sims, 2000). Schein (1985) argues that employees learn what behaviours are valued most in an organization by watching their leaders. Leader-founders also control cultural models, as Schein noted, through the reward systems and succession plans that they create. If this is the case, HRD practitioners must devise a strategy to develop and engage senior management as role models for effective interpersonal communication skills. This strategy means a personalized leadership development process involving assessment and personal coaching (McCauley et al., 1998).

## Recommendations for Research

There has been, to date, little, if any, research into the relationship of gender schema to transfer of training. Because gender is so pervasive a part of everyone's thinking and of the society, broad awareness of its effects is generally low. As Tannen (1995, 1996) notes, conversational routines for men and women are formed in childhood, so that differences, if we were ever aware of them, are long forgotten by adulthood. This finding complements the premise of Hofstede et al. (1990) that societal norms shape gender models by the age of puberty.

Because men and women at work are, in general, speaking what we all see as the same language, all of us make assumptions that what we are saying and how we are saying it come across clearly with our meaning intact. Tannen's linguistic research demonstrates that this assumption is often incorrect and that faulty assumptions about what men and women mean when they speak can negatively affect assessments of job performance and, subsequently, opportunities. Thus, while the phenomenon is important and worthy of study, its effects are generally below the conscious awareness of potential researchers as members of the same society.

Opportunities for research also exist in the cross-cultural context, especially using ethnographic and qualitative methods. Because beliefs about appropriate male and female behaviour exist in the societal/cultural fabric of a society, effects of these beliefs upon transfer of interpersonal communication skills training may vary across cultures. The existing instruments, which may be useful in the United States, would require validation cross-nationally to be usable in other cultures. Ethnographic methods, such as those described by Spradley (1979), permit a study of perceived appropriate behaviours for men and women through a cultural lens, especially communication behaviours.

## Conclusion

In these days of economic downturn, companies feel more pressure than ever before to keep employees motivated and productive, since many of them are doing more work than before with fewer resources at their disposal. The burden for productivity and employee motivation falls onto the shoulders of managers and supervisors and presses them to employ and improve every management skill they have. These circumstances require excellent HRD practice. Practitioners are obligated to do their best in identifying skills and knowledge critical to the business strategy, and to craft and deliver learning experiences that address gaps in skill and knowledge. As we have discovered, however, an excellent learning experience does not necessarily translate into improved performance unless there is cultural support for the transfer of skill and knowledge from the training room to the job.

As they develop, more complete models of training transfer are enabling more thorough examination of variables affecting this very important issue. To the extent that scholars can map the specifics of the variables involved, practitioners and organizations can take action to design transfer systems before and after training that more effectively move new skills into the workplace. In so doing, HRD can fulfil its role as a partner in the creation of organizational effectiveness and success in the marketplace.

## References

Adler, N. (1997), *The International Dimensions of Organizational Behavior*, 3rd edn. Cincinnati, OH: Southwestern Publishing.

ASTD (1998), *National HRD Executive Survey*. Retrieved February 2, 2005 from www.astd.org/virtual_community/research/nhrd_executive_survey_98ld.html.

Barry, B. and Watson, M. R. (1996), 'Communication aspects of dyadic social influence in organizations: A review and integrations of conceptual and empirical developments', in B. R. Burleson and A. W. Kunkel (eds), *Communication Yearbook 19*. Thousand Oaks, CA: Sage. pp. 269–317.

Bassi, L. and Ahlstrand, A. (2000), *The 2000 ASTD Learning Outcomes Report*. Alexandria, VA: ASTD.

Bates, R. A. and Holton, E. F. (1999), 'Learning transfer in a social service agency: Test of an expectancy model of motivation', paper presented at the Academy of Human Resource Development, Arlington, VA.

Behrman, J. and Zheng, Z. (1995), 'Gender issues and employment in Asia', *Asian Development Review*, **13**(2): 1–49.

Bem, S. L. (1974), 'The measurement of psychological androgyny', *Journal of Consulting and Clinical Psychology*, **42**(2): 155–62.

Bem, S. L. (1977), 'Bem Sex Role Inventory (BSRI)', in J. E. Jones and J. W. Pfeiffer (eds), *The 1977 Annual Handbook for Group Facilitators*. San Diego, CA: Pffeiffer. pp. 83–7.

Bem, S. L. (1981), 'Gender schema theory: A cognitive account of sex typing',

*Psychological Review*, **88**(4), 354–71.

Bem, S. L. (1994), 'In a male-centered world, female differences are transformed into female disadvantages', *The Chronicle of Higher Education*, **40**(50), B1–B3.

Billard, M. (1992), 'Do women make better managers?', *Working Woman*, **17**: 68–71, 106–07.

Borisoff, D. and Hahn, D. (1995), 'From research to pedagogy: Teaching gender and communication', *Communication Quarterly*, **43**(4): 381–94.

Broad, M. and Newstrom, J. (1992), *Transfer of Training*. Reading, MA: Perseus Books.

Campbell, D. J., Bommer, W. and Yeo, E. (1993), 'Perceptions of appropriate leadership style: Participation versus consultation across two cultures', *Asia Pacific Journal of Management*, **10**(1): 1–19.

Carmichael, J. L. (1995), 'What do we believe makes a good manager?', *Management Development Review*, **8**(2): 7–10.

Carr-Ruffino, N. (1993), 'He said ... she said: Communicating effectively', in N. Carr-Ruffino *The Promotable Woman*. Belmont, CA: Wadsworth Publishing. pp. 209–52.

Claes, M. T. (1999), 'Women, men and management styles', *International Labour Review*, **138**(4): 431–46.

Crockett, W. H. (1988), 'Schemas, affect, and communication', in L. Donohew, L., H. E. Sypher and E. T. Higgins (eds), *Communication, Social Cognition and Affect*, Hillsdale, NJ: Lawrence Erlbaum Associates. pp. 33–51.

Davids, M. (1995), 'Where style meets substance', *Journal of Business Strategy*, **16**(1): 48–60.

Davidson, M. and Ferrario, M. (1992), 'A comparative study of gender and management style', *Target Management Development Review*, **5**(1): 13–17.

Eagly, A. H. (1987), *Sex Differences in Social Behaviour: A Social-Role Interpretation*. Hillsdale, NJ: Lawrence Erlbaum Associates.

Eagly, A. H. and Johnson, B. T. (1990), 'Gender and leadership style: A meta-analysis', *Psychological Bulletin*, **108**(2): 233–56.

Facteau, J. D., Dobbins, G. H., Russell, J. E. A., Ladd, R. T. and Kidisch, J. D. (1995), 'The influence of general perceptions of the training environment on pretraining motivation and perceived training transfer', *Journal of Management*, **21**(1): 1–25.

Fagenson, E. A. (1990), 'Perceived masculine and feminine attributes examined as a function of individuals' sex and level in the organizational power hierarchy', *Journal of Applied Psychology*, **75**(2): 204–11.

Helgesen, S. (1995), *The Female Advantage: Women's Ways of Leadership*. New York: Currency Doubleday.

Hofstede, G. (1980), *Culture's Consequences: International Differences in Work Related Values*, 1st edn. Newbury Park, CA: Sage.

Hofstede, G. (1991), *Cultures and Organizations: Software of the Mind*. London: McGraw-Hill.

Hofstede, G. (2001), *Culture's Consequences: Comparing Values, Behaviours,*

*Institutions, and Organizations Across Nations*, 2nd edn. Thousand Oaks, CA: Sage.

Hofstede, G., Neuijen, B., Ohayv, D. D. and Sanders, G. (1990), 'Measuring organizational cultures: A qualitative and quantitative study across twenty cases', *Administrative Science Quarterly*, **35**(2): 286–316.

Hudak, M. A. (1993), 'Gender schema theory revisited: Men's stereotypes of American women', *Sex Roles*, **28**(5/6): 279–93.

Inkeles, A. and Levinson, D. J. (1969), 'National character: The study of modal personality and sociocultural systems', in G. Lindsey and E. Aronson (eds), *The Handbook of Social Psychology* (Vol. 4), 2nd edn. Reading, MA: Addison-Wesley.

*International Herald Tribune* (1995, March 2), 'European topics: Norwegian men beating at door of shelter for abused women', *International Herald Tribune*, cited in R. Mead, (1998), *International Management*. Oxford: Blackwell. p. 41.

Joyner, T. (2001, September 4), 'Bully bosses find their gentler side', *The Atlanta Journal-Constitution*: E1, E3.

Kabakoff, R. I. (1998), 'Gender differences in organizational leadership; A large sample study', paper presented at the annual convention of the American Psychological Association, San Francisco, CA, August.

Kanter, R. M. (1977), *Men and Women of the Corporation*. New York: Basic Books.

Karau, S. J. and Eagly, A. H. (1999), 'Invited reaction: Gender, social roles and the emergence of leaders', *Human Resource Development Quarterly*, **10**(4): 321–7.

Kinser, A. E. (2002), 'Gendered performances in employment interviewing: Interpreting and designing communication research', *The Journal of Business Communication*, **39**(2), 245–56.

Kolb, J. A. (1999), 'The effect of gender role, attitude toward leadership and self-confidence on leader emergence: Implications for leadership development', *Human Resource Development Quarterly*, **10**(4): 305–20.

Korabik, K. and Ayman, R. (1989), 'Should women managers have to act like men?', *Journal of Management Development*, **8**(9): 23–32.

Larwood, L. and Wood, M. M. (1995), 'Training women for management: Changing priorities', *Journal of Management Development*, **14**(2): 54–64.

Laurent, A. (1986), 'The cross-cultural puzzle of international human resource management', *Human Resource Management*, **25**(1): 91–102.

Lee, C. (1994), 'The feminization of management', *Training Magazine*, **31**: 25–31.

Marx, R. D. (1982), 'Relapse prevention for managerial training: A model of maintenance of behaviour change', *Academy of Management Review*, 7(3): 433–41.

May, G. L. and Kahnweiler, W. M. (2000), 'The effect of a mastery practice design on learning and transfer in behaviour modeling training', *Personnel Psychology*, **53**: 353–73.

McCauley, C. D., Moxley, R. S. and Van Velsor, E. (eds) (1998), *The Center for Creative Leadership Handbook of Leadership Development*. San Francisco, CA:

Jossey-Bass.

Morrison, A. M., White, R. P., Van Velsor, E. and The Center for Creative Leadership (1992), *Breaking the Glass Ceiling*. Reading, MA: Addison-Wesley.

Moskal, G. S. (1997), 'Women make better managers', *Industry Week*, **24**: 17–19.

Naquin, S. S. and Holton, E. F. (2001), 'The effects of personality, affectivity, and work commitment on motivation to improve work through learning', paper presented at the Academy of Human Resource Development, Tulsa, OK, February–March.

O'Neill, K. S. (2003), 'The effect of masculine gender schema on the transfer of interpersonal communication skills training to the workplace', unpublished PhD thesis, Georgia State University, Atlanta, GA.

Penley, L. E., Alexander, E. R., Jernigan, I. E. and Henwood, C. I. (1991), 'Communication abilities of managers: The relationship to performance', *Journal of Management*, **17**(1): 57–76.

Powell, G. N., Posner, B. Z. and Schmidt, W. H. (1984), 'Sex effects of managerial value systems', *Human Relations*, **37**(11): 909–21.

Reavley, M. (1989), 'Who needs training: Women or organizations?', *Journal of Management Development*, **8**(6): 55–60.

Rosener, J. B. (1990), 'Ways women lead', *Harvard Business Review*, **68**(November–December): 119–25.

Ruona, W. E. A., Leimbach, M., Holton, E. F. I. and Bates, R. A. (1999), 'The relationship between learner utility reactions and predictors of learning transfer: Implications for evaluation', paper presented at the Academy of Human Resource Development, Arlington, VA.

Schein, E. H. (1985), *Organizational Culture and Leadership*. San Francisco, CA: Jossey-Bass.

Shockley-Zabalak, P., Staley, C. C. and Morley, D. D. (1988), 'The female professional: Perceived communication proficiencies as predictors of organizational advancement', *Human Relations*, **41**(7): 553–67.

Sims, R. R. (2000), 'Changing an organization's culture under new leadership', *Journal of Business Ethics*, **25**(1): 65–78.

Spradley, J. P. (1979), *The Ethnographic Interview*. New York: Harcourt Brace Jovanovich.

Tannen, D. (1995), 'The power of talk: Who gets heard and why'. *Harvard Business Review*, **73**(September–October): 138–48.

Tannen, D. (1996), *Gender and Discourse*. New York: Oxford University Press.

Torraco, R. J. (1997), 'Theory-building research methods', in R.A. Swanson and E. F. Holton (eds), *Human Resource Development Research Handbook*. San Francisco, CA: Berrett-Koehler. pp. 113–37.

*Training Magazine* (2000), 'Industry Report 2000', *Training Magazine*, **37**(10): 45–94.

Trompenaars, F. (1993), *Riding the waves of culture: Understanding cultural diversity in business.* London: Economist Books.

Wirth, L. (2001), *Breaking through the Glass Ceiling: Women in Management*. London: International Labour Office.

# Chapter 4

# Women and Promotion: The Influence of Communication Style

Jennifer J. Peck

## Introduction

Many management writers, in both the academic arena and fields that embody a more directly applied approach, describe women's struggle to succeed at high levels of business and organizations (for example Bellamy and Ramsay, 1994; Bevan and Thompson, 1992; Davidson and Burke, 1994; Davidson and Cooper, 1992; Ford, 1991; Ledwith and Colgan, 1996; Still, 1990). Some work discusses this in terms of the gender-differentiation of management style, with men's style identified as more initiating and women's as more considerate and cooperative (Davidson and Cooper, 1992). These traits are identified as the result of socialization processes, with women being socialized into roles that involve nurturing and sharing and men being socialized into roles that equate with competition and individualism (Case, 1994; Ledwith and Colgan, 1996; Still, 1990; Wajcman, 1999).

The literature shows that the qualities identified by both women and men as necessary for subordinates to be promoted are gender-differentiated: qualities that are given priority for women are that they are dependable and perceptive, while men are required to be intelligent and dynamic (Bevan and Thompson, 1992). So not only are male and female managers seen as having different qualities, they are expected to demonstrate these differences if they are to progress. This is confirmed by the finding that behaviour that equates with sex-role stereotypes is rewarded, while behaviour that fails to conform to stereotypical patterns is denigrated (Bevan and Thompson, 1992). This would suggest that, based on stylistic performance, women's management success should be unproblematic. However, this is not the case. Evidence shows that relatively few women reach senior executive positions (for example Ledwith and Colgan, 1996) and that those who do often have communication styles usually associated with traditional male management patterns (Davidson and Cooper, 1992), demonstrating what has been termed the 'Thatcher factor' (Wajcman, 1999). A major focus of this chapter is women's perception that communicative stylistic change is necessary for their advancement in the workplace.

Business management literature routinely describes communicative performances, attributes and skills in terms of generalizations. Women are said to be cooperative and have soft skills (Davidson and Cooper, 1992; Ledwith and Colgan, 1996), while men are said to be dynamic and have hard skills (Bevan and Thompson, 1992). This apparent contradiction between required attributes and success may be because generalizations do not predict success accurately. Accordingly, while it may be perceived as desirable for a woman to be cooperative, the linguistic performances associated with cooperation are not recognized or rewarded. This chapter will make connections between the generalized descriptions of gender-related skills and linguistics literature that examines how such performances are enacted. Linguistic features that equate with cooperation and collaboration or with competition will be explored, showing that in mixed-sex interactions, both collaborative and competitive features used by women are negatively sanctioned in business settings.

The contemporary relevance of this problematic may be seen in the identification of 'soft' skills as being a requirement for business success in the twenty-first century (British Institute of Management, 1994; Burton and Ryall, 1995; Ledwith and Colgan, 1996; Peters and Waterman, 1982; Wajcman, 1999). This literature describes soft skills as being 'women's skills', and it is argued that women 'will flourish as never before' (Wajcman, 1999, p. 5) in management careers because they already possess the attributes necessary for the new models of management. This chapter will argue that this outcome may be problematized by dominant concepts of organizational success as unrelated to practices associated with 'the female'. A further issue that relates directly to the generalization of skill descriptions is that performances that can be described as 'natural' are less likely to receive professional acknowledgement in formalized processes of evaluation (Wajcman, 1999).

This chapter will show that findings from linguistics can usefully explicate gendered performances and expectations about interactional behaviours. This facilitates an understanding of stylistic differences based on the specifics of linguistic performances, rather than on generalizations of gender-based attributes. It will be argued that a central problem is women's perceptions about the stylistic communication requirements needed for success, and it will be shown that these perceptions are based on women's experiences in workplace interactions. Finally, the issue of transformational management style and its relevance for women's success in business will be examined.

## Overview of Current Research

It is now well documented in the linguistics literature that women and men tend to have different communication styles in casual conversation (Coates, 1989; Fishman, 1983; Hirschman, 1973; Holmes, 1986, 1995; Maltz and Borker, 1982; Tannen, 1987; West and Zimmerman, 1983; Zimmerman and West, 1975) and that these differences result from socialization processes that encourage women and men to 'do gender' differently (Bergvall, 1999; Hodge and Kress, 1988; Lorber and Farrell, 1991a, 1991b; Peck, 2000a; West and Zimmerman, 1991). While gender and communication differences in business and the workplace have been less documented, there is now a body of evidence that shows that men and women in business tend to use different communication strategies (Coates, 1995; Edelsky, 1981; Holmes, 1992; Peck, 2000b; Tannen, 1994). This literature suggests that the gender-differential performances found in casual conversation are replicated in business settings. Some findings are that men tend to interrupt, take long, sole-speaker turns, and use direct forms, while women tend to use indirect or modalizing strategies, use inclusive communication techniques, and encourage collaborative turns and floors (for example Edelsky, 1981; Holmes, 1992). While these strong tendencies have been documented, types of turns and ways of communicating are by no means gender exclusive and women have been shown to use a range of strategies in business settings (for example Case, 1995; Stubbe et al., 2000). Some business communications literature includes reference to linguistics research (for example, Davidson and Cooper, 1992; Wajcman, 1999), but does not examine interactions in contemporary business settings at the level of micro-linguistic features.

A notable exception to this pattern is Case's (1994) examination of gendered interactional features in organizations. Pointing out that almost no attention has been paid to analysis of how people actually speak in organizational contexts, Case (1994) argues that tags (which are features, such as 'you know'; 'isn't it?') used by women outside women's speech communities are seen as indicative of uncertainty or deference, rather than enabling devices. This suggests that while women managers are expected to perform in stereotypical ways associated with women or with femininity (Bevan and Thompson, 1992), the micro-linguistic level of such performances is not valued, but denigrated. Kirner and Rayner (1999, p. 136) describe the marginalization of women, saying that they are made to feel 'invisible, ridiculous, ignorant, inadequate or exploited'. Women are put down, in a range of ways, for failing to conform to the traditional patterns of western business.

The traditional patterns are male patterns, and, as CNN Executive Vice-President Gail Evans says, 'men know the rules of business because they wrote them' (Ellis, 2002, p. 63). Holmes (1992, p. 143) states that 'most cross-gender communication problems in public contexts are women's problems, because the interactional rules in such situations are men's rules'. Not only are the problems women's, but women themselves can be constructed as 'the problem'.

The expectation of gender-stereotypical conformity helps to explain the denigration that some women face when they use direct and unmodalized linguistic forms that are usually associated with male talk (Davidson and Cooper, 1992). Women may be treated as 'deviant' (Peck, 1998, 2000b, 2005a) for performing according to typical female or male linguistic patterns. Citing turn-taking in meetings, Case (1994) points out that organizations typically foster interaction patterns that are more compatible with male styles. When women 'do gender' in line with female-stereotypical patterns in formal meetings, their performances may be ignored or overruled (Peck, 2000b, 2005b). Such situations have led to the recommendation that women adopt androgynous behavioural patterns (Bem, 1974; Davidson and Cooper, 1992) and perform in a range of voices in business settings ( Holmes, 1992; Peck, 2000b; Stubbe et al., 2000). This work supports the notion of wide-verbal-repertoire speech advanced by Case (1995). Women who adopt alternative voices may be seen as increasing their linguistic, and thereby their symbolic capital (Bourdieu, 1990, 1991). This may enable female managers to negotiate their way through contexts that do not accommodate for styles typically associated with women's speech communities, but the process may be highly stressful, as it may involve unnatural distortion of identity and self (Davidson and Cooper, 1992; Kanter, 1977).

## The Devaluation of Women's Linguistic Style

It is claimed that informal conversation constitutes the 'supergenre' from which other forms select (Heritage, personal communication). It is therefore useful to examine the ways in which casual conversation is controlled at a micro-linguistic level, in order to draw conclusions about the subgenre of professional discourse. Negative sanctions have been found in relation to women's perceived interruptions of male turns at talk, women completing men's utterances and women's use of direct forms (Peck 2005a; Talbot, 1992). Women are criticized for 'talking too much', in both face-to-face and online conversations, despite the evidence that they are talking significantly less than their male interactants ( Davidson and Cooper, 1992; Herring et al., 1992; Spender, 1980; Talbot, 1992). It seems that the conversational supergenre is an androcentric one, with women typically being criticized for deviating from an implicit male norm.

It has been documented that women and men have different notions of what constitutes interruption of a turn at talk. Men are found to prefer sole-speaker turns, and interpret any invasion into their turn as a violation of their sole-speaker rights (Coates, 1994; Edelsky, 1981; Peck, 1998; Talbot, 1992; West and Zimmerman, 1991; Zimmerman and West, 1975). This method of talking conforms to male socialized expectations in relation to the (western) value of individualism and hierarchical structures. Competition in talk is an important way of achieving a dominant position in a hierarchy. The socialization of girls and women involves a different orientation to hierarchical structures, with a preference for inclusiveness and egalitarianism being demonstrated by girls and women (Hodge and Kress, 1988; Maltz and Borker, 1982; Peck, 2000a). Women are found to prefer 'ensemble' (Tannen, 1989) or 'melded' floors (Coates, 1996), which encode inclusiveness and shared knowledge and experience. Women achieve these collaborative floors largely through overlapping speech and completion of another woman's utterance. Other features that encode collaboration will be discussed later in this chapter.

When women perform overlapping speech in mixed-sex conversation, it is often found to be problematic. A number of mechanisms are used by male interactants to silence female speakers, including loud or emphatic speech, repetition of words or phrases and silence. Typically the female speaker withdraws from the speaking floor, sometimes apologizing for her interruption (Peck, 1998, 2005a). More overt strategies on the part of male speakers are metalinguistic comments such as 'Let me finish'; 'I hadn't finished what I was saying'; 'I let you say what you think, now you must let me say my bit'; 'What I was trying to say before' (Peck, 1998, 2005a).

Women, by contrast, do not complain that they have been interrupted (Coates, 1996; Edelsky, 1981; Peck, 1998, 2005a; Zimmerman and West, 1975), presumably because the form has a different meaning for them: overlapping speech represents collaboration in the construction of talk, rather than competition for a turn.

Women are typically silenced by the negative sanctions that they receive from male speakers. They tend to abandon the speaking floor (Talbot, 1992; Peck, 1998, 2005a), and apparently internalize the negative evaluations that are placed on their interactional behaviour. This is evidenced not only by women's abandoning of the floor and of their own speaking style, but by the metacomments made by women about other women's performances. Women say that women who engage in overlapping speech with men are 'aggressive', 'dreadful', and 'rude', and sometimes repeat men's denigrations of female interruptions (Peck, 1998; 2005a). One woman evaluates her own overlapping speech style as 'a dreadful habit. I try to control myself' (Peck, 1998, 2005a). This effectively perpetuates a situation in which male meanings of stylistic features of discourse are treated as normative for all speakers. Women are constructed by men as aggressive on the basis of their linguistic style, and also construct themselves and other women in this way. Their metacomments and their style-shifting towards the single-speaker floor provide evidence that many women have internalized androcentric beliefs and values about the organization of conversation.

Men may regard female overlapping speech as extremely aggressive because men interpret women's constant overlap as representing fast-starts at the first available turn-transition place (Sacks et al., 1974). If this formulation of turn-taking is valid for male talk, to constantly start fast is to constantly compete. Men or women who compete in this way are therefore considered to be continually attacking and refusing to grant space to their conversational partner or 'opponent'. Women who use simultaneous or overlapping speech could thus be interpreted by men as behaving in an aggressive manner.

Everyday interaction is based on features that are 'taken for granted' by social actors and on shared but unstated beliefs about the communication process (Denzin, 1971; Schutz, 1962). Garfinkel (1967) claims that social interaction depends on reciprocal trust. One result of this is that deviations from expected behaviours have major significance. The trust that is jointly held (Garfinkel, 1967) is implicitly challenged and the 'taken for granted' nature of social action is disputed. The rules and rituals (Denzin, 1971) that support interaction and the social structures embedded in interaction are brought into question and, in order to maintain the status quo, deviations are negatively sanctioned. A point that goes unstated in much of the sociology, ethnomethodology and conversation analysis literature is that the rules and rituals on which mixed-sex interaction is based are derived from male communicative style. Female style is treated as 'other', as incorrect and in need of control. Men and women are involved in this control process, since women, through abandoning their interactive style, and through the articulation of androcentric values relating to interactive behaviours, effectively concur with androcentric interpretations of their communicative performance. Women are treated as deviating from social norms and they are complicit in enforcing these norms. This process is arguably aided by learned gendered performances: men use competitive strategies to assert the validity of their style as normative, and women's learned cooperation leads them to acquiesce to male controls and modify their style (see Hodge and Kress, 1988; Lorber and Farrell, 1991a; Peck, 1998, 2000a for discussion of socialization).

## Devaluation of Women's Business Communication

If, as suggested earlier, casual conversation is the 'supergenre' from which other forms are derived, business communication will include the features described above. Business style is based on male conversational style; the (usually unstated) rules and rituals of communication are androcentric rules, and women's style is treated as deviating from normative practices. Women are implicitly or explicitly censured for their deviations, and they either style-shift to conform to male expectations of communicative interaction, or are silenced. Men and women are engaged in the process of the maintenance of normative behavioural practices: men may be the ones who exercise control in the micro-interactions, but women are complicit in the process through their style-shifting, silence, and criticism of their own style and that of other women (Peck, 2005a).

Overlaps and attempts at shared floors are censured, especially in meetings, which are implicitly or explicitly based on sole-speaker floors and androcentric turn-taking models. When women complete the utterances of their male interactants, they are similarly negatively sanctioned. One woman reports a man saying to her in a meeting 'You can't read my mind, can you? So don't tell me what I am going to say' (Peck, 2005b).

The shared floor is thus constructed as an aberration in most business settings and the sole-speaker floor and androcentric models of turn-taking are the normative patterns (compare Edelsky, 1981). Thus a major stylistic feature that embodies collaborative and cooperative meanings is removed from many mixed-sex business settings. Significantly, women are found to enact collaborative floors in all-female meetings (Edelsky, 1981).

Directness and indirectness are encoded by linguistic features and enact competitive and cooperative meanings respectively. Men tend to use more features associated with directness, which inhibits contributions from other speakers. Indirectness strategies encode collaboration and their use encourages others' voices into the discourse. Some linguistic forms that encode inclusiveness and collaboration are inclusive pronouns ('we', 'us', 'let's', 'shall we'), modal verbs ('could', 'might', 'may'), and modalizers ('perhaps', 'maybe'). Directness involves egocentric pronouns, ('I', 'me'), and absence of modalizers. Indirectness strategies are common in all-female talk when the talk encodes meanings of collaboration and cooperation. These features, however, are routinely denigrated in many workplace and business settings. For instance, a female manager in banking who modalizes and uses inclusiveness strategies, beginning a proposal with 'I think maybe we should consider ...' is challenged by a man saying 'Do you know or don't you?'. Another woman commences her recommendation in an academic meeting with 'Perhaps it would be a good idea if we thought about doing ...' and is interrupted by a man who says 'Can you get to the point? Is it possible for you to do that?' (Peck, 2005b). These findings support Case's (1994) claim that tags are interpreted as indicative of uncertainty when used outside women's speech communities. Women who are treated in this way report being silenced and feeling diminished and humiliated (Peck, 2005b). Women appear to internalize male constructions of their performances and describe their communication strategies in business settings as 'unclear', and 'vague' and say that they 'don't get to the point' (Peck, 2005b).

These findings confirm Kirner and Rayner's (1999) observations. Women who are progressing in the hierarchy say that they are routinely ignored or silenced (Kirner and Rayner, 1999; Peck, 2005b). Woman's position as speaking subject is denied. It is not only the women who are the recipients of this treatment that are affected: the behaviours impact on observers, arguably confirming for both men and women that androcentric linguistic practices are the only acceptable ones and that behaviour that fails to conform to the traditional male model is liable to public censure. These are instances of the 'corrosive effect' that traditional western business culture has on women, the 'dysfunctional consequences' for themselves and their organizations that result from women adapting to the prevailing culture (Burton and Ryall, 1995, p. 24). Certainly women feel the pressure to adapt and they typically succumb to that pressure, but they seem to do so without externalizing their vision of the culture as a male one (Burton and Ryall, 1995; Still, 1994), possibly because of the absence of micro-linguistic analysis.

Linguistic features that encode collaboration are treated as aberrant. Women's evaluation of their own style in business settings resembles their evaluations of casual conversation. Women style-shift to adhere to male expectations and women who do perform in line with gender-role stereotypes state that their style is problematic and in need of correction. Women repeatedly say that they need to change their way of communicating in workplace and business settings if they are seeking to progress in the organizational hierarchy, since they do not see their communication style as equating with management success. Women cite examples from within their organizations of successful women who do not use the style that is traditionally associated with women's speech community (Coates, 1989; Peck, 2005b). These models tend to endorse other women's construction of themselves as having a communication style that is inappropriate for promotion and that therefore makes them unsuitable candidates for promotion to senior-, or even to middle-management positions (Peck, 2005b). It is an apparent contradiction, then, that women who see directness as necessary to success also condemn women who perform direct or competitive style on the basis that their behaviour is aggressive. It seems that women do make the explicit connection between communication style and the possibility of promotion that is often generalized in business literature under behavioural attributes. Men also denigrate women who demonstrate competitive linguistic strategies.

Women are denigrated by both men and women in business settings for failing to perform in accordance with sex-role stereotypes. As Bergvall (1999, p. 278) says, assertive women are 'doubly deviant': 'not male nor yet fully female'. However, women are also denigrated when they perform in linguistic sex-stereotypical style. It is arguably the case that while behaviour that is generalized as collaborative is expected of women, the linguistic features that encode collaboration are neither respected nor rewarded. This may be a consequence of the fact that the underlying rituals of social interaction are unnoticed and yet are taken for granted (Denzin, 1971; Garfinkel, 1967; Schutz, 1962).

*Performing Androgyny*

It is claimed that women could succeed in business through performing in a range of styles, effectively representing masculine as well as feminine identities through communication (for example Bem, 1974; Case, 1995). The previous section of this chapter has demonstrated that, while women may receive sanctions for performing either in female or male styles, they have the ability to perform a range of styles. As the subordinates in society, women are required to understand male style and accommodate to male linguistic needs (Baker Miller, 1986; Coates, 1996; Deuchar, 1989). This chapter has argued that women are regularly required to style-shift in mixed-sex conversation. Women therefore have developed communication skills that they can draw on in business settings, in meetings and where they perceive that an androcentric model will be effective in promotion situations.

This may be problematic, however, for it involves women's damage to their own faces while protecting those of the dominants, and possible distortion of identity and self (Davidson and Cooper, 1992; Kanter, 1977). Wajcman (1999) makes the point that women managers are required to sacrifice major elements of their gender identity. When women adapt to dominant stylistic practices, they arguably perpetuate the traditional (male) status quo at the expense of their face, needs and selves. Women effectively devalue their own histories and identities. By abandoning their 'own' voice and adopting linguistic practices with which they are not congruent, they acknowledge the relative lack of value that they attribute to their own social worth in that social space and they devalue their social history (compare Bourdieu, 1990, 1991). The situation is further problematized by research claims that sex-role stereotypical behaviours are expected from subordinates seeking promotion (Bevan and Thompson, 1992). While wide-verbal-repertoire speech is undoubtedly a useful resource for women in business (Case, 1995; Holmes, 1992), the complexity of the situation suggests that using 'male style' will not automatically result in women's voices being heard in meetings, or in their success in promotion processes. The 'new wave' model of management that has been proposed for the twenty-first century may bring with it alternative ways of communicating in business for women and men, and suggests unique opportunities for women's success.

## The 'New Wave' Management Model

The new leadership model that has been widely promoted as appropriate for twenty-first century western management is based on collective commitment, shared visions and values, inclusiveness and people-orientation, and it is argued that this is crucial to success in international markets and diverse workplaces (British Institute of Management, 1994; Burton and Ryall, 1995; Case, 1994; Rosener, 1990; Wajcman, 1999). The skills associated with this model are 'soft' skills which include 'the ability to communicate, the ability to motivate, the ability to lead and delegate, and the ability to negotiate ... they are deep and sophisticated abilities' (Burton and Ryall, 1995, p. 25). Burton and Ryall (1995) find that Australian managers need to enhance these skills. This is a general recommendation for 'western' management (British Institute of Management, 1994; Peters and Waterman, 1982; Wajcman, 1999).

The model is described as a feminine one. According to Burton and Ryall (1995, p. 8) it is:

> ... subject to characterization as more 'feminine' than the more 'masculinist' practices of convention ... In this new way of managing, increasing recognition is given to factors such as relational rather than competitive values, the need for firms to seek interdependence rather than dominance in the marketplace and for business opportunities to be nurtured in an 'emergent' manner through affiliation and cooperation rather than rationality, separation and manipulation.

New wave management is regularly described in terms of gender images (British Institute of Management, 1994; Peters and Waterman, 1982, and, according to Tom Peters, 'the time has come for men on the move to learn to play women's games' (Fierman, 1990, p. 71).

It is claimed that the contemporary leadership model embodies a unique opportunity for women in business: they will succeed as never before (Wajcman, 1999). Women executives are making it to the top 'by drawing on the skills and attitudes they developed from their shared experience as women ... They are succeeding because of – not in spite of – certain characteristics generally considered to be "feminine" and inappropriate in leaders', claims Rosener (1990, pp. 119–20). Acknowledging the changes that have formerly been required of women, Case (1994, p. 159) proposes that now, 'rather than try to change speech patterns, women can capitalize on the strength of some of the differences that emerge from their feminine heritage that are clearly suited for current organizational realities'.

The success of women is constructed as a natural and almost automatic result of the emergence of a new management paradigm. They will simply use the skills that they have learned through their socialization and histories as women. Men, by contrast, will have to not only learn new skills and ways of communicating that have not been emphasized in their earlier socialization, such as sensitivity, active listening and encouragement (Case, 1994), but will also have to embrace women's skills (Burton and Ryall, 1995) and demonstrate their new knowledge and acceptance of the feminine.

While the opportunities for women and the need for changes that are required of men are typically presented in positive and unproblematic terms, some authors are more cautious. Burton and Ryall (1995, p. 8) warn that 'the need ... to embrace the 'soft' skills, traditionally associated with women ... is bound to meet with strong resistance from the traditional manager'. Wajcman (1999) suggests that it is likely that men will appropriate 'female' style and add it their repertoire and, because it is not naturalized as part of the self, it will be rewarded as an occupational resource. Given the denigration that women's communication style receives in management settings, it seems overly optimistic to assume that the new wave model will be welcomed and that male managers will rush to learn women's skills and features of their communication style. Indeed, it has been demonstrated that men know the micro-linguistic features of female talk and they have been shown to use these features to demonstrate heterosexual masculinity when marking themselves against homosexual people (Cameron, 1997). Thus, although men know how to 'do' women's style, only in exceptional circumstances do they see it as in their interests to perform this style. The proposed new wave model involves a major shift in the beliefs and attitudes not only of men, but also of women, since women have constructed their own style as incongruent with management success.

*Problematizing the New Wave Model*

The acceptance and implementation of the management model that is variously referred to as new wave, transformational and twenty-first century management, involves an examination of the traditional western model of management and the recognition that it is an androcentric one. It requires a shift away from male-oriented management strategies towards female ones. This involves a fundamental move on the part of the dominants: they must observe and adopt the practices of the subordinates. Since a basic principle of social practices is that the subordinates adapt to the needs of the dominants (Baker Miller, 1986; Coates, 1996; Deuchar, 1989), it seems unlikely that the reverse process will be undertaken. Further, for men to adopt skills that are associated with women would risk damage to the organizational status quo. Wajcman (1999, p. 2) points out that 'management incorporates a male standard that positions women as out of place. Indeed, the construction of women as different from men is one of the mechanisms whereby male power in the workplace is maintained'. Adopting a transformational model would involve a major attitudinal shift in constructions of difference and orientations to male power and the mechanisms that uphold it.

It is important to this debate that generalizations have been made about collaboration and support (for example Davidson and Cooper, 1992), and that these qualities have been widely associated with women. This makes it unlikely that a new wave model that highlights these skills will be readily accepted by male managers who have established and preserved their hierarchical positions on the basis of 'male' qualities of dynamism and hardness. Foregrounding linguistic features rather than generalized qualities might be more useful: a model based on linguistic features such as indirectness and modalization strategies might be more readily incorporated into traditional organizational practices.

Further, the 'soft' skills identified as twenty-first century management skills are traditionally associated not only with women's skills and attributes, but with roles traditionally associated with women. It is unlikely that men will embrace or adopt a communication style that implicitly associates them with traditionally female roles of home-maker and carer, for these are precisely the roles that they have typically rejected for themselves in achieving executive success, and roles that are required to be performed by the 'other' to support their own progress.

The relative value assigned by dominant social practices to stereotypically male and female roles is demonstrated by the fact that less organization value is assigned to attributes that are perceived as naturally acquired rather than formally learned (Wajcman, 1999). Thus the skills associated with women's acquisition of nurturing roles are typically denigrated compared with the 'hard' skills that are perceived as formally learned. In fact, both skill sets are part of socialization processes that train men to be competitive and women to be cooperative (Hodge and Kress, 1988; Lorber and Farrell, 1991a; Peck, 1998, 2000a). The skills are differentially constructed and this can then be used to support the notion that male skills have been part of a more difficult learning process and therefore deserve more authority. On the basis of these points, it seems unlikely that men will welcome a management model that requires them to perform like women. As Wajcman (1999, p. 163) points out, 'men may well feel that, rather than women levelling up to them, they are levelling down to women'.

If women's communication styles and the qualities associated with women are used by men, the preference for promotion based on sex-role stereotypical performances is challenged (Bevan and Thompson, 1992). A challenge is also posed to the fact that 'women are seen as less likely to possess characteristics perceived internationally as requisite management characteristics' (Davidson and Burke, 1994, p. 48) and that gender role behaviours in line with gender stereotypes are evaluated more positively (Case, 1994). As Case (1994, p. 161) says, 'the risk of change coexists with the need for change'.

*Articulating the Model*

The success of the new wave model may depend on the way that it is articulated to organizations and specifically to senior male management. This transformational management model is expected to advance business success in an international market and with multicultural clients and in diverse workplaces. It is particularly salient to successful engagement with the rapidly growing Asian markets of China, Japan and India. If the model is described in terms of these expectations and linked to the need for diverse stylistic requirements, it could arguably be more acceptable than if it is presented as a model based on female soft skills.

Further, identifying the skill base required in terms of formal learning, rather than highlighting skills as being a result of the 'natural' socialization process of girls and women could authenticate both the skills and the model. Thus, articulating the new model and the new wave of business leadership as an innovative and learned model can lead to its acceptance and success. However, because women are typically more comfortable with the linguistic requirements of this model, they are more likely to progress through the management hierarchy. Failure to carefully construct the ways in which the new wave model is presented could result in either management failure to accept the model or the model having a short life, being abandoned when its association with women's skills and 'natural' socialization processes is recognized.

## Implications

These findings suggest that when women receive negative input for their linguistic performances, they will denigrate themselves and other women. As a result of experiences that suggest that the style of their socialized speech community is incompatible with organizational practices, they will attempt to reconstruct themselves and their linguistic performances to conform to dominant normative practices. The negative sanctions of women's linguistic style may lead to more general self-devaluation, since others have a powerful impact on the creation or destruction of the self. Goffman articulates this point clearly: 'There seems to be no agent more effective than another person in bringing a world for oneself alive or, by a glance, a gesture, or a remark, shriveling up the reality in which one is lodged' (Goffman, 1961, p. 41). These factors are implicated in women's low self-efficacy (Bevan and Thompson, 1992).

Women are likely to suffer stress and isolation if they change or attempt to change their communication style. Stress is one consequence of attempted identity reconstruction, and women who succeed in changing may find themselves isolated by their subsequent positioning outside both male and female organizational social networks (Davidson and Cooper, 1992; Ford, 1991; Still, 1990). This may result in women's attrition from organizations.

The situation is complicated by the fact that women are expected to conform to sex-role stereotypes, as confirmed by performance requirement surveys (Bevan and Thompson, 1992), while their actual gendered performances are denigrated. This leads to identity confusion for women, because performances that are recommended are negatively sanctioned rather than receiving the expected organizational rewards.

A major implication of these findings is that business loses the skills of women, which are especially important in an international market and in workplaces that are characterized by diversity. The new wave management and leadership model offers opportunities for women to succeed while maintaining their own speech styles. However, it is unlikely that most women in junior- and middle-management positions will take advantage of this opportunity unless the model is explicitly described and promoted within their organizations. The new wave model embodies the possibilities for an alternative organizational structure based on connection rather than isolation that will benefit both men and women. The adoption of this model would facilitate the approach described by Baker Miller and would promote 'an entirely different (and more advanced) approach to living and functioning … [in which] affiliation is valued as highly as, or more highly than, self-enhancement' (Baker Miller, 1986, p. 83). However, a model that requires men to adopt female practices is unlikely to succeed in most traditional western organizations. The absence of collaborative and cooperative management strategies is virtually guaranteed by the need of the dominants to maintain the traditional organizational status quo.

## Conclusion

The description of management skills in terms of generalizations may help to support sex-role stereotypical behaviours as requirements for success. When attributes are described in general terms such as competitive, dynamic, cooperative, or supportive, the actual performances that encode these behaviours may remain unanalysed. So while women are expected to be cooperative and supportive, their linguistic enactments of cooperation and support are negatively sanctioned. Negative evaluation occurs in both casual conversation and in business and workplace settings, and both women and men treat cooperative strategies such as overlapping speech or modalization as deviating from an assumed norm. Women expect to change their communication style to that of the dominant male pattern in order to succeed in business, and especially if they are aiming to be promoted. Input from women's male interactants in meetings as well as the models of successful female executives that surround them support this expectation. Major consequences to style-shifting on the part of women are that if they successfully produce the dominant communication style they are liable to be condemned by both men and women for being aggressive. They will not achieve the promotion that they strive for since they will no longer be performing the required sex-role stereotypical behaviour. A further implication is that adopting a style with which women are unfamiliar and abandoning the style that is representative of their socialized identity can be highly stressful, as the process may involve loss of self and identity.

The new wave, twenty-first century model of management and leadership that is based on 'soft' skills offers many women the opportunity to rapidly develop their management profiles while maintaining the communication styles of women's speech communities. The model may, however, be rejected since it embodies the requirement that men adopt and display skills that are associated with women, and that men re-evaluate in positive terms behaviours that they have previously denigrated. One approach to this problem might be to articulate the model in terms other than the gender-based generalizations that are currently employed.

## Recommendations

The evidence provided in this chapter suggests that the new wave or transformational model of management offers women a unique opportunity for promotion within organizational structures. They can use the 'soft' skills of collaboration and inclusiveness that they have acquired through socialization into their positions as women. In particular, women have the opportunity to demonstrate in public forums the linguistic skills that are displayed consistently in interactions in women's speech communities and that are encoded in the requirement that gender is routinely performed. Micro-linguistic features such as tags, overlapping speech, completion of another's utterances and modalization encode support and collaboration, which are crucial to contemporary management and leadership styles. It is therefore recommended that women use these linguistic features in a range of settings. It is also an empowering strategy for women to analyse their linguistic strategies at the micro-linguistic level, so that they can use their skills strategically and knowingly. This will enable women to claim their linguistic usages as part of their leadership style. The knowing use of linguistic features will also prepare women for any challenges that they face for deviating from an assumed and androcentric norm. With awareness of their own style, they are better equipped to counter attacks on their stylistic performances and are less likely to be silenced.

It is recommended that women translate experience-based skills into learned skills through processes such as formal training or education programs that are either internal to their organizations or offered by external institutions. This will authenticate the skill base and will enable women to gain the acknowledgement that is reserved for learned skills. Analysis of their linguistic strategies will enable women to re-evaluate them as valuable skills that they can then not only use in management interactions, but formalize for evaluation in promotion processes.

Women can continue to benefit from using the wide range of communication skills that they have, performing different skills in different settings and thereby demonstrating a wide skill base and versatility.

It would be useful for the literature to describe management attributes in terms of linguistic strategies, including micro-linguistic features, rather than in broad generalizations. This would facilitate the more accurate evaluation of the performances of both male and female managers. Finer definitions would also avoid discrepancies that appear to arise in defining behaviours required for success in terms of sex-role stereotypes.

## References

Baker Miller, J. (1986), *Toward a New Psychology of Women*, 2nd edn. Boston, MA: Beacon.

Bellamy, P. A. and Ramsay, K. (1994), *Barriers to Women Working in Corporate Management*. Canberra: Australian Government Publishing Service.

Bem, S. L. (1974), 'The measurement of psychological androgyny', *Journal of Consulting and Clinical Psychology*, **42**: 155–62.

Bergvall, V. L. (1999), 'Toward a comprehensive theory of language and gender', *Language in Society*, **28**: 273–79.

Bevan, S. and Thompson, M. (1992), *Merit Pay, Performance Appraisal and Attitudes to Women's Work*. Brighton: Institute of Manpower Studies.

Bourdieu, P. (1990), *In Other Words: Essays Towards a Reflexive Sociology*, trans. M. Adamson. Cambridge: Polity Press with Basil Blackwell.

Bourdieu, P. (1991), *Language and Symbolic Power*, trans. G. Raymond and M. Adamson. Cambridge: Polity Press with Basil Blackwell.

British Institute of Management (1994), *Management Development to the Millennium*. London: British Institute of Management.

Burton, C. and Ryall, C. (1995), *Enterprising Nation: Renewing Australia's Managers to Meet the Challenges of the Asia-Pacific Century: Managing for Diversity*, Research for the Industry Task Force on Leadership and Management Skills. Canberra: Australian Government Publishing Service.

Cameron, D. (1997), 'Performing gender identity: Young men's talk and the construction of heterosexual masculinity', in S. Johnson, S. and U. H. Meinhof (eds), *Language and Masculinity*. Oxford: Blackwell. pp. 47–64.

Case, S. S. (1994), 'Gender differences in communication and behaviour in organizations', in M. J. Davidson and R. J. Burke (eds), *Women in Management: Current Research Issues*. London: Paul Chapman. pp. 144–67.

Case, S. S. (1995), 'Gender, language and the professions: Recognition of wide-verbal-repertoire speech', *Studies in the Linguistic Sciences*, **25**(2): 149–92.

Coates, J. (1989), 'Gossip revisited: Language in all-female groups', in J. Coates and D. Cameron (eds), *Women in their Speech Communities*. London: Longman. pp. 94–122.

Coates, J. (1994), 'No gap, lots of overlap: Turn-taking patterns in the talk of women friends', in D. Graddol, J. Maybin B. and Stierer (eds), *Researching Language and Literacy in Social Context*. Clevedon: Multilingual Matters. pp. 177–92.

Coates, J. (1995), 'Discourse, gender and subjectivity: The talk of teenage girls', paper presented at the University of Queensland, Brisbane, June.

Coates, J. (1996), *Women Talk*. Oxford: Blackwell.

Davidson, M. J. and Burke, R. J. (1994), *Women in Management: Current Research Issues*. London: Paul Chapman.

Davidson, M. J. and Cooper, C. L. (1992), *Shattering the Glass Ceiling: The Woman Manager*. London: Paul Chapman.

Denzin, N. K. (1971), 'Symbolic interactionism and ethnomethodology', in J. D. Douglas (ed.), *Understanding Everyday Life*. London: Routledge and Kegan Paul. pp. 259–84.

Deuchar, M. (1989), 'A pragmatic account of women's use of standard speech', in J. Coates and D. Cameron (eds), *Women in their Speech Communities*. pp. 27–32.

Edelsky, C. (1981), 'Who's got the floor?' *Language in Society*, **10**: 383–421.

Ellis, A. (2002), *Women's Business Women's Wealth*. Sydney: Random House.

Fierman, J. (1990, December 17), 'Do women manage differently?' *Fortune*: 71–4.

Fishman, P. (1983), 'Interaction: The work women do', in B. Thorne, C. Kramarae and N. Henley (eds), *Language, Gender and Society*. Rowley, MA: Newbury House. pp. 89–101.

Ford, C. (1991), *Women mean Business*, Port Melbourne: Mandarin.

Garfinkel, H. (1967), *Studies in Ethnomethodology*. Englewood Cliffs, NJ: Prentice Hall.

Goffman, E. (1961), *Encounters: Two Studies in the Sociology of Interaction*. Indianapolis, IN: Bobbs-Merrill.

Herring, S., Johnson, D. and DiBenedetto, T. (1992), 'Participation in electronic discourse in a "feminist" field', in K. Hall, M. Bucholtz and B. Moonwomon (eds), *Locating Power: Proceedings of the Second Berkeley Women and Language Conference*. Berkeley, CA: Berkeley Women and Language Group. pp. 250-62. Reprinted in Coates, J. (ed.) (1998), *Language and Gender: A Reader*. Oxford: Blackwell.

Hirschman, L. (1973), 'Female–male differences in conversational interaction', paper presented at Linguistic Society of America. Cited in Thorne, B. and Henley, N. (eds), (1975), *Language and Sex: Difference and Dominance*. Rowley, MA: Newbury House.

Hodge, R. and Kress, G. (1988), *Social Semiotics*. Cambridge: Polity in association with Basil Blackwell.

Holmes, J. (1986), 'Functions of *you know* in women's and men's speech', *Language in Society*, **15**: 1–22.

Holmes, J. (1992), 'Women's talk in public contexts', *Discourse and Society*, **3**(2): 131–50.

Holmes, J. (1995), *Women, Men and Politeness*. London: Longman.

Kanter, R. M. (1977), *Men and Women of the Corporation*. New York: Basic Books.

Kirner, J. and Rayner, M. (1999), *The Women's Power Handbook*. Ringwood: Penguin.

Ledwith, S. and Colgan, F. (eds), (1996), *Women in Organisations: Challenging Gender Politics*. Macmillan: Basingstoke.

Lorber, J. and Farrell, S. A. (1991a), 'Principles of gender construction', in J. Lorber and S. A. Farrell (eds), *The Social Construction of Gender*. Newbury Park, CA: Sage. pp. 7–11.

Lorber, J. and Farrell, S. A. (1991b), 'Preface', in J. Lorber and S. A. Farrell (eds), *The Social Construction of Gender*. Newbury Park, CA: Sage. pp. 1–6.

Maltz, D. N. and Borker, R. A. (1982), 'A cultural approach to male-female miscommunication', in J. J. Gumperz (ed.), *Language and Social Identity*. Cambridge: Cambridge University Press. pp. 196–216.

Peck, J. J. (1998), 'The performance of gendered subjectivities in micro-interactions', unpublished PhD thesis, University of Queensland.

Peck, J. J. (2000a), 'The mutual process of semioticization: Linguistic acquisition and performance of social subjectivities', *Australian Journal of Linguistics*, **20**(2): 179–209.

Peck, J. J. (2000b), 'The cost of corporate culture: Linguistic obstacles to gender equity in Australian business', in J. Holmes (ed.), *Gendered Speech in Social Context*. Wellington: Victoria University Press. pp. 211–30.

Peck, J. J. (2005a), 'Deviant women: How women's communicative behaviour is controlled', unpublished manuscript.

Peck, J. J. (2005b), 'Heteroglossia: Voices of authority in twenty-first century management', unpublished manuscript.

Peters, T. and Waterman, R. (1982), *In Search of Excellence*. New York: Harper and Row.

Rosener, J. (1990), 'Ways women lead', *Harvard Business Review*, **68**(November–December): 119–25.

Sacks, H., Schegloff, E. A. and Jefferson, G. (1974), 'A simplest systematics for the organization of turn-taking for conversation', *Language*, **50**: 696–735.

Schutz, A. (1962), *Collected Papers. Vol. I.* The Hague: Martinus Nijhoff.

Spender, D. (1980), *Man Made Language*. London: Routledge and Kegan Paul.

Still, L. V. (1990), *Enterprising Women: Australian Women Managers and Entrepreneurs*. Sydney: Allen & Unwin.

Still, L. V. (1994), 'Women in management: The cultural dilemma', *Inkwel*, **3**(June): 2–5.

Stubbe, M., Holmes, J., Vine, B. and Marra, M. (2000), 'Forget Mars and Venus, let's get back to earth! Challenging gender stereotypes in the workplace', in J. Holmes (ed.), *Gendered Speech in Social Context*. Wellington: Victoria University Press. pp. 221–58.

Talbot, M. (1992), '"I wish you'd stop interrupting me!": Interruptions and asymmetries in speaker-rights in equal encounters', *Journal of Pragmatics*, **18**: 451–66.

Tannen, D. (1987), *That's Not What I Meant! How Conversational Style Makes or Breaks Relationships*. New York: Ballantine.

Tannen, D. (1989), *Talking Voices: Repetition, Dialogue, and Imagery in Conversational Discourse*. Cambridge: Cambridge University Press.

Tannen, D. (1994), *Talking from 9 to 5*. New York: William Morrow.

Wajcman, J. (1999), *Managing Like a Man: Women and Men in Corporate Management*. St Leonards: Allen & Unwin.

West, C. and Zimmerman, D. H. (1983), 'Small insults: A study of interruptions in cross-sex conversations between unacquainted persons', in B. Thorne, C. Kramarae and N. Henley (eds), *Language, Gender and Society*. Rowley, MA: Newbury House. pp. 103–18.

West, C. and Zimmerman, D. H. (1991), 'Doing gender', in J. Lorber and S. A Farrell (eds), *The Social Construction of Gender*. Newbury Park, CA: Sage. pp. 13–37.

Zimmerman, D. H. and West, C. (1975), 'Sex roles, interruptions and silences in conversation', in B. Thorne and N. Henley (eds), *Language and Sex: Difference and Dominance*. Rowley, MA: Newbury House. pp. 105–29.

# PART II
## Gender, Communication and Organizational Boundaries: Linkages and Violations

Chapter 5

# Gender Issues in Workplace Groups: Effects of Gender and Communication Style on Social Influence

Linda L. Carli

## Introduction

Popular writing on gender and language typically makes the claim that women and men differ in their communication styles. For example, Deborah Tannen in her books, *You Just Don't Understand* (1990) and *Talking from 9 to 5* (1994), characterized women's conversations as 'rapport-talk,' language that maintains social connection, and men's conversations as 'report-talk,' language that asserts male status and authority. In the academic literature, however, there is considerable debate as to whether there are gender differences in communication, or if there are, whether the differences are large enough to be of any practical importance. This may be due, in part, to the tremendous breadth of research in this field, which has examined gender differences in syntax, semantics, non-verbal behaviours, the use of particular words or expressions and other aspects of communication. Nevertheless, popular books about gender and language resonate with everyday beliefs about how men and women communicate, suggesting that gender differences may exist. Indeed, research reveals that cultural stereotypes concerning gender often do reflect actual differences between men and women (Hall and Carter, 1999). Additionally, the literature on gender stereotypes reveals that, in general, people consider men to be more agentic than women and women to be more communal than men (for example Williams and Best, 1990), stereotypes that are consistent with Tannen's popular view of gender differences in language.

In this chapter, attention is focused on gender differences in communication that are consistent with the commonly held stereotypes about women and men: that women show greater communality and other-directedness in their communications and men greater agency and self-assertion. Further, mediators of gender differences are examined in communication as well as the effect of gender differences in communication on social influence.

**Overview of Current Research**

*Gender and Communication*

Although research does not always reveal gender effects in communication, when such differences are reported, they typically reveal more status asserting, dominant and negative communications by men and more collaborative, warm and supportive communications by women (Carli, 2001; Carli and Bukatko, 2000). Men more than women, for example, display high levels of visual dominance, which is associated with power and status and is measured as the ratio of the amount of time that people maintain eye contact while talking to the amount of time that they maintain eye contact while listening to others (Dovidio, Brown et al., 1988; Dovidio, Ellyson et al., 1988). Compared with women, men more often ignore the communications of others (Fishman, 1978; Leet-Pellegrini, 1980) and issue directives (Mulac and Gibbons, 1993, cited in Mulac, 1998; Mulac et al., 1988). Moreover, a meta-analytic review revealed that men interrupt others more than women do, particularly for intrusive interruptions directed at gaining the floor in conversations (Anderson and Leaper, 1998). Finally, men also talk more than women in a wide variety of social and professional contexts (James and Drakich, 1993), and total group participation is associated with possessing formal leadership and authority in groups (Mullen et al., 1989).

Studies on gender differences in interaction style, which examine the relative amounts of task and social contributions to group interactions, also reveal greater agency in male communications and communality in female communications. A meta-analytic review of these studies revealed that men exhibit a higher percentage of task behaviours and direct disagreements than women do and women exhibit a higher percentage of positive social behaviours than men do (Carli and Olm-Shipman, 2004), although a meta-analytic review of gender differences among leaders revealed only a small gender difference in social behaviour and none in task behaviours (Eagly and Johnson, 1990). These results suggest that the role of leader may to some extent prescribe particular behaviours regardless of the gender of the leader, which would effectively reduce gender differences in leadership style. Nevertheless, two meta-analytic reviews related to communication have established differences between male and female leaders that correspond to the expected pattern of greater female communality and male agency. Compared with leaders of the other gender, female leaders display a more democratic style, encouraging collaboration and involving subordinates in decisions, whereas male leaders display a more autocratic style, discouraging participation by subordinates in favour of asserting the leader's control and authority (Eagly and Johnson, 1990; van Engen, 2001). Women leaders also exhibit higher levels of transformational leadership than their male counterparts, who in turn generally exhibit higher levels of transactional leadership (Eagly et al.; 2003). The emphasis of the transformational leader on mentoring, empowering and encouraging subordinates reflects greater communality compared to the transactional leader, who relies on enforcing authority through reward and punishment of subordinates.

Other evidence of women's communality has been found in their tendency to be warmer, more open, and more socially supportive of others. For example, meta-analyses have revealed a moderate gender effect on smiling (LaFrance et al., 2003) and a small effect on self-disclosure (Dindia and Allen, 1992), demonstrating that women smile more and disclose more personal information than men do. Furthermore, among married couples (DeFrancisco, 1991; Fishman, 1978), college students (Carli, 1990; Leet-Pellegrini, 1980; Marche and Peterson, 1993; Mulac and Bradac, 1995), and university employees (Hall et al., 2001) women expend greater effort to maintain conversations with others or encourage others to speak by nodding or verbally reinforcing others' speech (that is, by giving minimal verbal responses indicating agreement, such as 'yeah' and 'mm hmm').

Even though mitigated language has been construed as powerless (Grob et al., 1997), it can also exemplify communality, acting as a means to involve others in conversation (Fishman, 1980), which may thereby enhance the speaker's influence and appeal (Carli, 1990). This may be particularly true for speech that is somewhat mitigated. For example, Geddes (1992) reported that workers perceived managers who used moderate levels of mitigation to have more satisfied subordinates than managers who used a great deal or none at all. It has often been argued that women communicate in a more mitigated or tentative manner, which includes such behaviours as hedging (for example, adding 'I guess,' 'maybe', or 'kind of' to statements), disclaiming expertise (for example, qualifying one's opinions by saying 'I may be wrong, but …' or 'this may be crazy, but …'), or adding tag questions to statements (for example, 'This is important, don't you think?') (Carli, 1990; Crosby and Nyquist, 1977; Fishman, 1980; Hartman, 1976; Holmes, 1984; McMillan et al., 1977; Mulac and Lundell, 1986; Mulac et al., 1988; Mulac and Gibbons, 1993, cited in Mulac, 1998; Preisler, 1986). Although studies have sometimes not reported consistent gender differences in mitigated speech (for example, Grob et al., 1997; Mulac et al., 1986) and occasionally have found greater mitigation among men (for example, Mulac and Bradac, 1995), in general, when differences are found, they reveal greater mitigation by women. Therefore, women's more frequent use of mitigated speech further reflects their greater tendency towards communality.

## Gender Composition Effects in Agentic and Communal Communications

Although gender differences in communal and agentic speech are consistent with stereotypes about typical male and female behaviour, the gender differences have been shown to depend on situational factors, such as whether communication occurs in mixed- or same-sex groups. Interactions between gender differences in communication and gender composition essentially reflect gender of partner effects. Research revealing such interactions has indicated that both men and women exhibit greater warmth toward women than toward men. Meta-analytic findings show that the gender difference in smiling interacts with gender composition such that the gender difference is bigger in same- than mixed-gender interactions (LaFrance et al., 2003). This reveals greater smiling at women than at men. Although gender differences in interaction style have been reported for both mixed- and same-sex interactions, a number of studies have found stronger differences in same-sex interactions, with higher levels of positive social behaviour and lower levels of task behaviour directed at female partners (Aries, 1976; Carli, 1989; Johnson et al., 1996; Piliavin and Martin, 1978; Wheelan and Verdi, 1992). The pattern of showing greater communality toward women was also reported in a meta-analytic review of gender differences in self-disclosure (Dindia and Allen, 1992), in which both men and women self-disclosed more to women than to men. Similarly, Hall and Braunwald (1981) found that pleasant warm voices were most characteristic of conversations between women and least characteristic of conversations between men, with men and women behaving more similarly in mixed-sex interactions. Carli (1990) reported that verbal reinforcement, which conveys support and encouragement, occurred more often in interactions among women and least often in interactions among men, with no gender differences in mixed-gender interactions. Overall, communications to women appear to be warmer and more communal than those to men.

Whereas gender differences in warmth have been more pronounced in same-gender interactions, reflecting greater warmth toward women, gender differences in mitigation and dominance have been more pronounced in mixed-gender interactions, reflecting greater mitigation and less dominance toward men. For example, the gender differences in mitigated speech (Carli, 1990; McMillan et al., 1977) and visual dominance (Ellyson et al., 1992) are most pronounced in mixed-gender interactions; that is, people display greater mitigation and less visual dominance to men than to women. Other studies on non-student samples of men have likewise revealed that men speak in a more mitigated manner when talking to other men than when talking to women (Brouer et al., 1979; Sayers and Sherblom, 1987). These results suggest that interactions with women involve less hierarchy and more communality and warmth than interactions with men, whereas interactions with men elicit more competition for dominance than those with women.

Clearly, people modify their communication style depending on the gender of the person with whom they are interacting, perhaps based on their assessment of how the other person is likely to behave in that situation, how they themselves are expected to behave, as well their own relative power in the interaction. Furthermore, individuals' use of both communal and agentic behaviour may be pragmatic, depending on their perceptions of what type of behaviour will lead to increased influence in interactions with others. In particular, the tendency to communicate in a more mitigated and less dominant manner to men may reflect men's greater status and power relative to women.

*Effects of Power on Gender Differences in Communication*

In general, men possess more power than women do, particularly *legitimate power* derived from holding social roles that command authority (for example, high-status work roles) (Carli, 1999). Men also possess greater *expert power*, derived from the perception of greater male expertise and competence (Carli, 1999). Research does, in fact, reveal a double standard in evaluating men and women such that women must perform better to be considered equally competent (Biernat and Kobrynowicz, 1997; Foddy and Graham, 1987, cited in Foschi, 1992; Foschi, 1996). As a result, female leaders receive more critical evaluations than male leaders (Eagly et al., 1992) and women are viewed as less likely to possess leadership and management skills than men are (Schein, 2001).

Research suggests that legitimate power may mediate gender effects on communication. For example, in a study of romantic couples, regardless of gender the more powerful partner interrupted more than the less powerful partner and the less powerful partner displayed more verbal reinforcement (that is, back-channels) (Kollock et al., 1985). Comparable results have been found in an organizational setting, where individuals who were assigned to a leadership position spoke more than those assigned to a subordinate position (Johnson, 1994); in a courtroom setting, where those who possessed less formal education communicated with greater mitigation than those who possessed more formal education (O'Barr, 1982); and in a study of leaders of both genders, who communicated more directly with subordinates to the extent that they had greater formal authority (Hirokawa et al., 1991).

Studies also suggest that expert power may affect gender differences in communication. McMullen and Pasloski (1992) found that women hedge less when they have more familiarity with the topic of discussion. Dovidio and his colleagues reported that both men and women increase their visual dominance relative to the other gender when working on tasks that favoured the expertise of their gender (Dovidio, Brown et al., 1988). A second study demonstrated that the gender difference in visual dominance for masculine tasks was eliminated when women received special training to improve their expertise at the task (Brown et al., 1990). In addition, women show proportionately more task behaviour and men proportionally less task behaviour when working on traditionally feminine than masculine tasks (Yamada et al., 1983). Gender differences in task contributions can also be reduced by giving women feedback that they have superior ability at the task (Wood and Karten, 1986) or giving them extra experience at performing the task (Lockheed and Hall, 1976). These findings suggest that the typical gender differences in agentic communication derive from the male advantage in power and authority, but can, however, be reduced in contexts where women possess high power relative to men.

*Gender, Communication and Influence*

Gender differences in communication are of particular relevance to understanding gender effects on social influence. It is well known from research on adults that men exert greater influence than women in gender-neutral contexts (for example, Pugh and Wahrman, 1983; Wagner et al., 1986; Ward et al., 1985). A vivid illustration of this was reported by Propp (1995) who found that in group interactions, information that was introduced by men was six times more likely to influence the group decision than the same information introduced by women. Male influence has likewise been revealed in the more frequent emergence of male than female leaders in initially leaderless groups (Eagly and Karau, 1991).

What, however, is the relation of gender differences in communication to gender differences in social influence? A number of studies have revealed that both men and women exert greater influence when communicating in a gender-stereotypical manner (Burgoon et al., 1983; Buttner and McEnally, 1996). For example, displays of visual dominance increase men's influence but reduce women's (Mehta et al., 1989, cited in Ellyson et al., 1992). Nevertheless, other research reveals more serious consequences when women violate gender-role norms than when men do. In one study, female police officers who communicated in a demanding manner were perceived to be less feminine than those who communicated with less dominance, whereas male officers received comparable ratings of masculinity regardless of how they communicated (Sterling and Owen, 1982). A study by Copeland and her colleagues revealed greater dislike for non-verbally dominant women than non-verbally dominant men, but an actual preference for low dominant males over low dominant females (Copeland et al., 1995). Carli (1998) found that male confederates were equally influential and likeable whether they expressed agreement or disagreement, but female confederates who disagreed exerted less influence and were considered less likeable than those who agreed.

The ineffectiveness of highly dominant behaviour by women is perhaps not surprising. But even task contributions, such as simply expressing opinions or giving suggestions, provide less benefit for women than for men. Although task contributions are typically associated with leader emergence and influence in groups (Hawkins, 1995; Ridgeway, 1978; Stein and Heller, 1979; Wood and Karten, 1986), women's task contributions are more likely to be ignored or to evoke negative reactions (Butler and Geis, 1990; Ridgeway, 1982) and are less likely to influence others than men's task contributions are (Walker et al., 1996). Apparently, dominant, assertive, direct or even merely competent communications are particularly problematic for women. As a result, women have a narrower repertoire of behaviours for gaining social influence than men have.

Highly agentic behaviour by women violates prescriptive gender-role norms and can be perceived as an illegitimate attempt to attain status, but women's communal behaviour is consistent with both descriptive and prescriptive stereotypes about women (Carli and Eagly, 1999). As a result, women who are too agentically competent may be disliked. For example, people evaluate women who exhibit an exceptional level of managerial competence more negatively than their exceptionally competent male counterparts – seeing the competent female manager as having a less desirable personality (Heilman et al., 1995; Heilman et al., 2004). Indeed, scholars have argued that women must be more communal than men in order to be influential, because women lack the status and authority of men and communal behaviour serves to demonstrate a woman's other directedness and lack of interest in status attainment (Lockheed and Hall, 1976; Ridgeway and Diekema, 1992). Essentially, displays of communal behaviour can blunt the threat of female competence. As a result, displays of warmth and positive social behaviour enhance women's influence, but have relatively little effect on men's (Carli, 1998; Ridgeway, 1982; Shackelford et al., 1996).

Likewise, women must also avoid self-promotion and instead communicate modesty. Although self-promotion can benefit men, women receive more favourable reactions for modest than self-promoting communications (Giacalone and Riordan, 1990; Wosinska et al., 1996). Furthermore, Rudman (1998) found that self-promoting women were generally less influential and likeable than modest women. The prescription for communal behaviour in women extends to female leaders as well. According to meta-analytic findings, female leaders are rated less favourably than their male counterparts for leading in an autocratic rather than a democratic manner (Eagly et al., 1992). Again, women must adhere more closely than men do to their traditional gender role in order to overcome resistance to their agency and influence.

Men, in particular, respond less favourably to agentic women. In a study of reaction to leaders, men rated task-oriented female leaders to be less effective than task-oriented male leaders, whereas women rated male and female task leaders as equally effective (Rojahn and Willemsen, 1994). In a similar vein, men, in particular, resist female leadership and evaluate autocratic female leaders more harshly than autocratic male leaders (Eagly et al., 1991; Forsyth et al., 1997) and men, more than women, associate managerial ability with being male (Heilman, 2001).

In a study comparing the social influence of speakers who communicated using mitigated or direct speech, Carli (1990) reported that women who spoke in a mitigated fashion exerted greater influence over a male audience but less influence over a female audience than women who spoke more directly. Male speakers were equally influential with both males and females regardless of how they spoke. The male subjects reported that the direct woman was more competent but less likeable. Another study revealed that a female speaker who communicated in a highly competent manner exerted less influence over men than male speakers using the same pattern of behaviour, although women were equally influenced by the male and female speakers (Carli et al., 1995). In this study, the men rated the competent women to be less likeable and more threatening than their male counterparts. Likewise, Foschi et al. (1994) conducted a study in which they manipulated the competence of male and female job candidates and then gave undergraduates the choice of hiring the man, the woman, or no-one at all. Women preferred to hire the candidate with the better academic record, regardless of gender; men preferred to hire the better candidate when the candidate was male, but preferred to hire no-one at all to hiring a superior woman.

Although men, overall, seem more resistant to female leadership and influence, there are factors that moderate this resistance. In general, men are less resistant to the influence of a women when they stand to gain by her influence. Men are more influenced by a competent over a less competent woman when her ideas can help them achieve some goal, such as obtaining money or some other reward (Shackelford et al., 1996) and more influenced by a competent woman over a less competent man when the woman can help them improve their performance on a task (Pugh and Wahrman, 1983). As noted earlier, displays of communality enhance women's influence generally, and men in particular are more likely to accept female agency when it is tempered by displays of communal behaviour. For example, the study showing that men felt threatened by a competent woman and were not influenced by her also showed that women influenced a male audience more when they combined non-verbal warmth (for example, by smiling and nodding) with competence than when they were merely competent (Carli et al., 1995).

## Conclusion

Overall, research indicates that women's communications are more other-directed, warm and mitigated than men's, and men's communications are more dominant, status-asserting, and task-oriented than women's. Nevertheless, gender composition and power effects mediate gender differences in communication. Both men and women communicate in a less dominant manner with men and a warmer manner with women. These findings suggest that different social norms may be operating in interactions with men than with women. Perhaps people are more communal to women because they expect women to be warmer and more affiliative and believe that women will find such behaviour appealing and influential. They may also be more deferent and less agentic in communications to men because men possess higher status and authority. This possibility is underscored by reports that when women are in positions of power, stereotypical gender differences in agentic communication shrink or are eliminated. This suggests that female managers would be generally less likely than women in general to communicate in a highly communal manner, but instead would increase their use of more traditionally masculine forms of communication. Gender differences in communication continue, even for those in leadership or management positions, however, because women in management continue to possess less power and authority than men. Overall, then, it appears that both men and women communicate a way that is expedient and likely to be most effective and influential, given their power, social roles and relative position in their interactions with others.

Although it is not clear where gender differences in communication originate, in different socialization of males and females or in situational social pressure on women to conform to traditional gender-role expectations, it appears that women's greater communality enhances women's ability to influence and lead others. On one hand, people judge women's abilities more harshly than men's, holding women to a higher standard of competence and evaluating female managers and leaders more critically than their male counterparts. On the other hand, women who convey a high degree of agency and thus undermine doubts about their abilities, may be seen as too agentic to be influential. Competent behaviour can reduce a woman's influence by lowering her likeableness, because behaviour that appears competent often also appears status asserting and lacking in the communal qualities prescribed by stereotypes about women and because such behaviour may be seen as illegitimately seeking status, leadership or influence. Instead, women must combine competence with communality in order to overcome resistance to their influence while still adhering to traditional gender-role expectations.

The double bind of competence can be particularly problematic for female managers and leaders. Research has shown that people believe that good managers must possess agentic qualities, qualities that are considered more characteristic of men than of women (Schein, 2001). Hence, men are typically seen as having the qualities needed for effective management, whereas women are not. At the same time, agentic female managers are rejected for lacking sufficient warmth and femininity (Heilman et al., 1995; Heilman et al., 2004).

Female managers and leaders have responded to this dilemma by displaying higher levels of transformational leadership than men. Interestingly, transformational leadership has been found to be an effective style of leadership (Lowe et al., 1996), particularly so for women (Eagly et al., 2003). Its combination of communal qualities and leadership effectiveness has provided female managers with a means of overcoming the double bind and excelling as leaders.

## Implications

Implications of the discussion in this chapter may be summarized as follows.

- Compared with men, women have more constraints on their style of communication in order to be effective influence agents. As a result, female managers and leaders must adhere more closely to gender-role prescriptions to avoid penalties.
- Women leaders must display exceptional levels of competence to overcome the presumption that women lack the agency, competency and leadership abilities of men.
- Women who exhibit exceptional agentic competence may be evaluated unfavourably because such behaviour violates prescriptive gender-role norms, particularly in domains such as management and leadership, which are seen as stereotypically masculine.
- Gender stereotypes thus create a double bind for women, who can be penalized for showing too little or too much agency.
- Women may overcome the double bind by displaying communal behaviour, which can reduce resistance to female authority and influence. Female managers, in particular, have been shown to employ a transformational leadership style, which effectively combines communality with competent leadership.

## References

Anderson, K. J. and Leaper, C. (1998), 'Meta-analyses of gender effects on conversational interruption: Who, what, when, where, and how', *Sex Roles*, **39**: 225–52.

Aries, E. J. (1976), 'Interaction patterns and themes of male, female, and mixed groups', *Small Group Behavior*, **7**: 7-18.

Biernat, M. and Kobrynowicz, D. (1997), 'Gender and race-based standards of competence: Lower minimum standards but higher ability standards for devalued groups', *Journal of Personality and Social Psychology*, **72**: 544–57.

Brouer, D., Gerritsen, M. and de Haan, D. (1979), 'Speech differences between women and men: On the wrong track?', *Language in Society*, **8**: 33–50.

Brown, C. E., Dovidio, J. F. and Ellyson, S. L. (1990), 'Reducing sex differences in visual displays of dominance: Knowledge is power', *Personality and Social Psychology Bulletin*, **16**: 358–68.

Burgoon, M., Dillard, J. P. and Doran, N. E. (1983), 'Friendly or unfriendly persuasion: The effects of violations by males and females', *Human Communication Research*, **10**: 283–94.

Butler, D. and Geis, F. L. (1990), 'Non-verbal affect responses to male and female leaders: Implications for leadership evaluations', *Journal of Personality and Social Psychology*, **58**: 48–59.

Buttner, E. H. and McEnally, M. (1996), 'The interactive effect of influence tactic, applicant gender, and type of job on hiring recommendations', *Sex Roles*, **34**: 581–91.

Carli, L. L. (1989), 'Gender differences in interaction style and influence', *Journal of Personality and Social Psychology*, **56**: 565–76.

Carli, L. L. (1990), 'Gender, language, and influence', *Journal of Personality and Social Psychology*, **59**: 941–51.

Carli, L. L. (1998), 'Gender effects in social influence', paper presented at meeting of the Society for the Psychological Study of Social Issues, Ann Arbor, MI, June.

Carli, L. L. (1999), 'Gender, interpersonal power, and social influence', *Journal of Social Issues*, **55**: 81–99.

Carli, L. L. (2001), 'Assertiveness', in J. Worell (ed.), *Encyclopedia of Women and Gender: Sex Similarities and Differences and the Impact of Society on Gender*. San Diego, CA: Academic Press.

Carli, L. L. and Bukatko, D. (2000), 'Gender, communication, and social influence: A developmental perspective', in T. Eckes and H. M. Trautner (eds), *The Developmental Social Psychology of Gender*. Mahwah, NJ: Lawrence Erlbaum Associates. pp. 295–331.

Carli, L. L. and Eagly, A. H. (1999), 'Gender effects on social influence and emergent leadership', in G. Powell (ed.), *Handbook of Gender in Organizations*. Thousand Oaks, CA: Sage. pp. 203–22.

Carli, L. L. and Olm-Shipman, C. (2004), 'Gender differences in task and social behavior: A meta-analytic review', manuscript in preparation, Wellesley College, Wellesley, MA.

Carli, L. L., LaFleur, S. J. and Loeber, C. C. (1995), 'Non verbal behavior, gender, and influence', *Journal of Personality and Social Psychology*, **68**: 1030–41.

Copeland, C. L., Driskell, J. E. and Salas, E. (1995), 'Gender and reactions to dominance', *Journal of Social Behavior and Personality*, **10**: 53–68.

Crosby, F. and Nyquist, L. (1977), 'The female register: An empirical study of Lakoff's hypothesis', *Language in Society*, **6**: 313–22.

DeFrancisco, V. (1991), 'The sounds of silence: How men silence women in marital relations', *Discourse and Society*, **2**: 413–23.

Dindia, K. and Allen, M. (1992), 'Sex differences in self-disclosure: A meta-analysis', *Psychological Bulletin*, **112**: 106–24.

Dovidio, J. F., Brown, C. E., Heltman, K., Ellyson, S. L. and Keating, C. F. (1988), 'Power displays between men and women in discussions of gender-linked tasks: A multichannel study', *Journal of Personality and Social Psychology*, **55**: 580–87.

Dovidio, J. F., Ellyson, S. L., Keating, C. F., Heltman, K. and Brown, C. E. (1988), 'The relationship of social power to visual displays of dominance between men and women', *Journal of Personality and Social Psychology*, **54**: 233–42.

Eagly, A. H. and Johnson, B. T. (1990), 'Gender and leadership style: A meta-analysis', *Psychological Bulletin*, **108**: 233–56.

Eagly, A. H. and Karau, S. J. (1991), 'Gender and the emergence of leaders: A meta-analysis', *Journal of Personality and Social Psychology*, **60:** 685–710.

Eagly, A. H., Johannesen-Schmidt, M. C. and van Engen, M. L. (2003), 'Transformational, transactional, and laissez-faire leadership styles: A meta-analysis comparing women and men', *Psychological Bulletin*, **129**: 569–91.

Eagly, A. H., Makhijani, M. G. and Klonsky, B. G. (1992), 'Gender and the evaluation of leaders: A meta-analysis', *Psychological Bulletin*, **111**: 3–22.

Ellyson, S. L., Dovidio, J. F. and Brown, C. E. (1992), 'The look of power: Gender differences in visual dominance behavior', in C. L. Ridgeway (ed.), *Gender, Interaction, and Inequality*. New York: Springer-Verlag. pp. 50–80.

Fishman, P. M. (1978), 'Interaction: The work women do', *Social Problems*, **25**: 397–406.

Fishman, P. M. (1980), 'Conversational insecurity', in H. Giles, W. P. Robinson and P. M. Smith (eds), *Language: Social Psychological Perspectives*. New York: Pergamon. pp. 127–32.

Forsyth, D. R., Heiney, M. M. and Wright, S. S. (1997), 'Biases in appraisals of women leaders', *Group Dynamics: Theory, Research, and Practice*, **1**: 98–103.

Foschi, M. (1992), 'Gender and double standards for competence', in C. L. Ridgeway (ed.), *Gender, Interaction, and Inequality*. New York: Springer-Verlag. pp. 181–207.

Foschi, M. (1996), 'Double standards in the evaluation of men and women', *Social Psychology Quarterly*, **59**: 237–54.

Foschi, M., Lai, L. and Sigerson, K. (1994), 'Gender and double standards in the assessment of job applicants', *Social Psychology Quarterly*, **57**: 326–39.

Geddes, D. (1992), 'Sex roles in management: The impact of varying power of speech style on union members' perception of satisfaction and effectiveness', *Journal of Psychology*, **126**: 589–607.

Giacalone, R. A. and Riordan, C. A. (1990), 'Effect of self-presentation on perceptions and recognition in an organization', *The Journal of Psychology*, **124**: 25–38.

Grob, L. M., Meyers, R. A. and Schuh, R. (1997), 'Powerful/powerless language use in group interactions: Sex differences or similarities', *Communication Quarterly*, **45**: 282–303.

Hall, J. A. and Braunwald, K. G. (1981), 'Gender cues in conversations', *Journal of Personality and Social Psychology*, **40**: 270–80.

Hall, J. A. and Carter, J. D. (1999), 'Gender-stereotype accuracy as an individual difference', *Journal of Personality and Social Psychology*, **77**: 350–59.

Hall, J. A., LeBeau, L. S., Reinoso, J. G. and Thayer, F. (2001), 'Status, gender, and non verbal behavior in candid and posed photographs: A study of conversations between university employees', *Sex Roles*, **44**: 677–92.

Hartman, M. (1976), 'A descriptive study of the language of men and women born in Maine around 1900 as it reflects the Lakoff hypothesis in *Language and Women's Place*', in B. L. Dubois and I. Crouch (eds), *The Sociology of the Languages of American Women*. San Antonio, TX: Trinity University. pp. 81–90.

Hawkins, K. W. (1995), 'Effects of gender and communication content of leadership emergence in small task-oriented groups', *Small Group Research*, **26**: 234–49.

Heilman, M. E. (2001), 'Description and prescription: How gender stereotypes prevent women's ascent up the organizational ladder', *Journal of Social Issues*, **57**: 657–74.

Heilman, M. E., Block, C. J. and Martell, R. (1995), 'Sex stereotypes: Do they influence perceptions of managers?', *Journal of Social Behavior and Personality*, **10**: 237–52.

Heilman, M. E., Wallen, A. S., Fuchs, D. and Tamkins, M. M. (2004), 'Penalties for success: Reactions to women who succeed at male gender-typed tasks', *Journal of Applied Psychology*, **89**: 416–27.

Hirokawa, R. Y, Mickey, J. and Miura, S. (1991), 'Effects of request legitimacy on the compliance gaining tactics of male and female managers', *Communication Monographs*, **58**: 421–36.

Holmes, J. (1984), 'Women's language: A functional approach', *General Linguistics*, **24**: 149–78.

James, D. and Drakich, J. (1993), 'Understanding gender differences in amount of talk: A critical review of research', in D. Tannen (ed.), *Gender and Conversational Interaction*. New York: Oxford University Press. pp. 281–312.

Johnson, C. (1994), 'Gender, legitimate authority, and leadership–subordinate conversations', *American Sociological Review*, **59**: 122–35.

Johnson, C., Clay-Warner, J. and Funk, S. J. (1996), 'Effects of authority structures and gender on interaction in same sex groups', *Social Psychology Quarterly*, **59**: 221–36.

Kollock, P., Blumstein, P. and Schwartz, P. (1985), 'Sex and power in interaction: Conversational privileges and duties', *American Sociological Review*, **50**: 34–46.

LaFrance, M., Hecht, M. A. and Paluck, E. L. (2003), 'The contingent smile: A meta-analysis of sex differences in smiling', *Psychological Bulletin*, **129**: 305–34.

Leet-Pellegrini, H. M. (1980), 'Conversational dominance as a function of gender and expertise', in H. Giles, W. P. Robinson and P. M. Smith (eds), *Language: Social Psychological Perspectives*. Oxford: Pergamon. pp. 97–104.

Lockheed, M. E. and Hall, K. P. (1976), 'Conceptualizing sex as a status characteristic: Application to leadership training strategies', *Journal of Social Issues*, **32**: 111–24.

Lowe, K. B., Kroeck, K. G. and Sivasubramaniam, N. (1996), 'Effectiveness correlates of transformational and transactional leadership: A meta-analytic review of the MLQ literature', *Leadership Quarterly*, **7**: 385–425.

Marche, T. A. and Peterson, C. (1993), 'On the general differential use of listener responsiveness', *Sex Roles*, **29**: 795–816.

McMillan, J. R., Clifton, A. K., McGrath, D. and Gale, W. S. (1977), 'Women's language: Uncertainty or interpersonal sensitivity and emotionality', *Sex Roles*, **3**: 545–59.

McMullen, L. M. and Pasloski, D. D. (1992), 'Effects of communication apprehension, familiarity of partner, and topic on selected 'women's language' features', *Journal of Psycholinguistic Research*, **21**: 17–30.

Mulac, A. (1998), 'The gender-linked language effect: Do language differences really make a difference?', in D. J. Canary and K. Dindia (eds), *Sex Differences and Similarities in Communication: Critical Essays and Empirical Investigations of Sex and Gender in Interaction*. Mahwah NJ: Lawrence Erlbaum Associates. pp. 127–53.

Mulac, A. and Bradac, J. J. (1995), 'Women's style in problem solving interaction: Powerless, or simply feminine?', in P. Kalbfleisch and M. Cody (eds), *Gender, Power and Communication in Human Relationships*. Hillsdale NJ: Lawrence Erlbaum Associates. pp. 83–104.

Mulac, A. and Lundell, T. L. (1986), 'Linguistic contributors to the gender-linked language effect and sex role stereotypes', *Journal of Language and Social Psychology*, **8**: 249–70.

Mulac, A., Lundell, T. L. and Bradac, J. J. (1986), 'Male/female language differences and attributional consequences in a public speaking situation: Toward an explanation of the gender-linked language effect', *Communication Monographs*, **53**: 115–29.

Mulac, A., Wiemann, J. M., Widenmann, S. J. and Gibson, T. W. (1988), 'Male/female language differences and effects in same- and mixed-sex dyads: The gender-linked language effect', *Communication Monographs*, **55**: 315–35.

Mullen, B., Salas, E. and Driskell, J. E. (1989), 'Salience, motivation, and artifact, as contributions to the relation between participation rate and leadership', *Journal of Experimental Social Psychology*, **25**: 545–59.

O'Barr, W. (1982), *Linguistic Evidence: Language, Power, and Strategy in the Courtroom*. New York: Academic Press.

Piliavin, J. A. and Martin, R. R. (1978), 'The effects of sex composition of groups on style of social interaction', *Sex Roles*, **4**: 281–96.

Preisler, B. (1986), *Linguistic Sex Roles in Conversation*. Berlin: Mouton de Gruyter.

Propp, K. M. (1995), 'An experimental examination of biological sex as a status cue in decision-making groups and its influence on information use', *Small Group Research*, **26**: 451–74.

Pugh, M. D. and Wahrman, R. (1983), 'Neutralizing sexism in mixed-sex groups: Do women have to be better than men?', *American Journal of Sociology*, **88**: 746–62.

Ridgeway, C. L. (1978), 'Conformity, group-oriented motivation, and status attainment in small groups. *Social Psychology*, **41**: 175–88.

Ridgeway, C. L. (1982), 'Status in groups: The importance of motivation', *American Sociological Review*, **47**: 76–88.

Ridgeway, C. L. and Diekema, D. (1992), 'Are gender differences status differences?', in C. L. Ridgeway (ed.), *Gender, Interaction, and Inequality*. New York: Springer-Verlag. pp. 157–80.

Rojahn, K. and Willemsen, T. M. (1994), 'The evaluation of effectiveness and likeability of gender-role congruent and gender-role incongruent leaders', *Sex Roles*, **30**: 109–19.

Rudman, L. A. (1998), 'Self-promotion as a risk factor for women: The costs and benefits of counterstereotypical impression management', *Journal of Personality and Social Psychology*, **74**: 629–45.

Sayers, F. and Sherblom, J. (1987), 'Qualification in male language as influenced by age and gender of conversational partner', *Communication Research Reports*, **4**: 88–92.

Schein, V. E. (2001), 'A global look at psychological barriers to women's progress in management', *Journal of Social Issues*, **57**: 675–88.

Shackelford, S., Wood, W. and Worchel, S. (1996), 'Behavioral styles and the influence of women in mixed-sex groups', *Social Psychology Quarterly*, **59**: 284–93.

Stein, R. T. and Heller, T. (1979), 'An empirical analysis between leadership status and participation rates reported in the literature', *Journal of Personality and Social Psychology*, **37**: 1993–2002.

Sterling, B. S. and Owen, J. W. (1982), 'Perceptions of demanding versus reasoning male and female police officers', *Personality and Social Psychology Bulletin*, **8**: 336–40.

Tannen, D. (1990), *You Just Don't Understand: Women and Men in Conversation*. New York: William Morrow.

Tannen, D. (1994), *Talking from 9 to 5*. New York: William Morrow.

van Engen, M. L. (2001), 'Gender and leadership: A contextual perspective', doctoral dissertation, Tilburg University, The Netherlands.

Wagner, D. G., Ford, R. S. and Ford, T. W. (1986), 'Can gender inequalities be reduced?', *American Sociological Review*, **51**: 47–61.

Walker, H. A., Ilardi, B. C., McMahon, A. M. and Fennell, M. L. (1996), 'Gender, interaction, and leadership', *Social Psychology Quarterly*, **59**: 255–72.

Ward, D. A., Seccombe, K., Bendel, R. and Carter, L. F. (1985), 'Cross-sex context as a factor in persuasibility sex differences', *Social Psychology Quarterly*, **48**: 269–76.

Wheelan, S. A. and Verdi, A. F. (1992), 'Differences in male and female patterns of communication in groups: A methodological artifact?', *Sex Roles*, **27**: 1–15.

Williams, J. E. and Best, D. L. (1990), *Measuring Sex Stereotypes: A Multinational Study*. Newbury Park, CA: Sage.

Wosinska, W., Dabul, A. J., Whetstone-Dion, R. and Cialdini, R. B. (1996), 'Self-presentational responses to success in the organization: The costs and benefits of modesty', *Basic and Applied Social Psychology*, **18**: 229–42.

Wood, W. and Karten, S. J. (1986), 'Sex differences in interaction style as a product of perceived sex differences in competence', *Journal of Personality and Social Psychology*, **50**: 341–47.

Yamada, E. M., Tjosvold, D. and Draguns, J. G. (1983), 'Effects of sex-linked situations and sex composition on cooperation and style of interaction', *Sex Roles*, **9**: 541–53.

## Chapter 6

# Gender and Advisor–Client Communication

### Joan Mulholland

### Introduction

In general terms, gender problems are said to occur in communication because of differences in ways of knowing and understanding, and in preferences for different social relations between the participants, from a friendly rapport to a professional distance, with resultant differences in communication style (Belenky et al., 1986; Lakoff, 1973). When the communication is between advisor and client, a further set of problems can occur because of the nature of 'advice' itself, as well as of 'advisorhood' and 'clienthood'. This chapter will focus on these matters, illustrate them in action, and suggest where future research could assist in solving the problems they present.

### Overview of Current Research: Gender, Style, and Client Communication

In her useful paper on gendered communication in professional settings, Baker (1991) includes a major review of the research undertaken on gender style from the 1970s and this provides valuable background to any study of gender in workplace communications. Specifically, the research results she and others from that time noted (Borisoff and Merrill, 1985; Game and Pringle, 1983; Harper and Hirokawa, 1988; Pringle, 1988; Tannen, 1990, 1994; Tebeaux, 1990; Tymson, 2001) shared a focus on the major differences in communicative style between men and women, a view sparked by Robin Lakoff's seminal paper on language and women's place (Lakoff, 1973).

The differentiation school argued that women used a deal of 'affiliative' or interpersonal elements, while men preferred a more object-centred, 'instrumental' style and a more personal distance. However, how affiliation or instrumentality were enacted in practice, Baker noted (1991, p. 42), received less attention and less analysis than it deserved. Examples of these two styles can be seen in Table 6.1. The examples used in this chapter were collected by purposive sampling methods and form a data set of about 120 examples collected during 2003. These examples were analysed to produce a usefully nuanced critique by two focus groups, one of males and one of females, while material was also collected from two telephone advisors working with major service providers.

It is the language used by clients to represent their problem that provides an indication of which role the client has adopted, and it requires an alertness to these factors by the advisor so that the most appropriate mode of advice can be given. Advisors reading or listening to clients need to note such language and role differences as those illustrated in Table 6.1, which lists utterances with which clients may begin a telephone or face-to-face communication.

**Table 6.1    Gender style differences**

| | | | |
|---|---|---|---|
| Ignorant | (a) | (female) | Can you help? I am in a real mess |
| | (b) | (female) | I don't know what I am supposed to do about … |
| | (c) | (male) | These instructions are unclear |
| Partially knowing | (d) | (female) | I've done the pipe, but what do I do about the extra connection? |
| | (e) | (male) | How are we supposed to fill in the form? |
| Knowledgeable | (f) | (male) | I've done the form, where do I send it? |
| | (g) | (female) | I've got the concert series info but does it begin this Sunday? |

In (a) in Table 6.1, the reference to the situation as 'a real mess' and in (b) the client's self-description as 'not knowing' make clear the client's position of ignorance; but the male version (c) suggests that the ignorance is the result of another's fault. In (d) and (e) there is little gender differentiation other than the singular (female) 'I' and the plural (male) 'we', where the male sees himself as one of a group and hence not alone in his ignorance. In (f) one task has been completed, and in (g) most of the information is known though not one feature of it, showing in each case a high degree of knowledge. So gender may have an impact on the language the client uses, but it is less likely to influence the language used by the advisor because the people who train advisors nowadays usually teach a more unisex style (personal communication).

Since that early research, some new social factors have crept into client communication that partly displace some features of the distinction between affiliative and instrumental styles. The general casualization of communication (Fairclough, 1994) and hence of advisory communications has encouraged a degree of affiliation that evens out gender differences. In a data-set example, a male academic rings a major bank for information. The male advisor says, 'hang on, a colleague here was talking about this just yesterday, he'll know' – which neatly combines (in this order) casualization, 'female' affiliation, and 'male' instrumental style elements. And the newer advice websites intended for young clients have adopted a casual mode in language, fonts and graphics.

While this gender-in-communication research concentrates on the differences in gender style, other scholars have argued for a high degree of similarity in style, for example Goddard and Patterson (2000), Lay (1994), and Wodak (1997). In such a competing research environment, it seems best to assume that the practical purposes of understanding client communication can best be served by taking ideas from both types of study.

Meantime, since Garfinkel's work (1967) there has been a third field of communication research that did not assume that gender was a major guiding force for the individual's communication behaviour, but rather saw gender and style as properties of, and affected by, the event itself (Antaki, 1988; Drew and Heritage, 1997; Hatcher, 2001; Mulholland, 1991; West and Zimmerman, 1987). Such researchers noted that gender signs did not always appear to be an issue for the participants themselves (Schegloff, 1997, p. 182). For them, the question to ask is not what gender are the communicators, but rather how do people 'do gender' in events and where does it seems to matter to the communicators. A useful bibliography of the range of participants' orientation to gender is in Stokoe and Smithson (2001).

## Implications

### Variability of Gender and Style

On gender and style, then, it seems best to assume, first, that there is not a grand divide between men's and women's talk, but rather that there is a continuum between them, and this holds true for the affiliative-instrumental style distinction; and, second, that the style preference of any communicator may be much more affected by the nature of the event than by their own gender. Some communication events by their very nature invite communicators of both genders to use either the affiliative or the instrumental style, as Table 6.2 suggests.

**Table 6.2     A possible continuum of client communication event types**

| *Affiliation* | | | | *Instrumental* |
|---|---|---|---|---|
| stress counselling | legal advising | financial advising | equipment managing | institutional processing |

Also affecting any analysis of the communication is the fact that within a single event the value of gender can vary. Just as members of a gender group vary among themselves in degrees of male or femaleness in their communication styles, so too can an individual vary in style within a single event. Communication is negotiated between the parties, and gendering will play its part as a variable and may wax and wane as an issue of relevance (Firth, 1995; Mulholland, 1991). For example, at a large hardware store the author was unable to find a particular tool. On seeking advice from a male staff member, he said, 'Down this way' (neutered utterance) and went to the correct tool section. At this point he turned and said, 'Will you be using it yourself?' (which takes into account the possibility of a gender issue, for example wife shopping for husband, but does not assume it). On my replying that it was for me, he then offered a specific tool stating that it was at a good price (neutered utterance) and that it was small enough for my hand (gendered utterance).

The second reason to study gender and style only as it concerns the parties to a communication is the nature of advice itself and, with it, the roles adopted by client and advisor – 'clienthood' and 'advisorhood', which can reduce or even nullify the gender factor.

## *Advice as Communicative Act: An Exploration*

The act of advising, which may include the acts of informing, suggesting, teaching, explaining, answering, instructing, and others, is a dominant act to perform because of the high degree of influence the advisor assumes over the client's world (Wierzbicka, 1987, p. 113). Even when it is supplied at the request of the client, advice is intended to direct the client's future behaviour (Mulholland, 1991, pp. 148–51) and it requires skill to maintain the right kind of dominance (whether by affiliative, instrumental or other non-gendered means) to ensure relevance to the client's situation and compliance with the advice.

A glimpse of some of the areas of difficulty within the context of advice is presented in Table 6.3. First, there can be a range of the discrepancies between client and advisor: Table 6.3 mentions only a small number of the huge variety of this communication type.

**Table 6.3    Client and advisor difficulties**

| *Client* | *Advisor* |
|---|---|
| Ignorant client seeking information | Knowledgeable advisor deciding on degree and kind of information and risking insufficiency, too much detail, and so on |
| Uncertain client seeking informed advice | Knowledgeable advisor unwilling to display personal responsibility |
| Partially knowledgeable client seeking explanation | Professional advisor with technical vocabulary only partially known to client |
| Knowledgeable client seeking judgment on completed action | Advisor risking a display of paternalist criticism |

Another factor has caused the advisory situation to become more complex. Where once advisors were regular employees of the service provider and included among their major tasks the maintenance of the respect due to their institution, familiarizing clients with its procedures and maintaining conformity to its policies, nowadays many advisors have only a loose connection with their employers, as advice is outsourced, with call centres as a dominant player (Van Den Broek, 2004). Clients can experience confusion during a communication because some firms still use older ways while some have changed.

## Communication and Clienthood: Roles

The focus groups described clienthood as about not knowing, not coping, not being certain about what to do and having to surrender part of one's autonomy to someone else, as information, advice and explanations are sought from others. The nature of clienthood has changed in recent times because of the massive increase in the number of occasions when people have to seek advice, where their common sense, education and personal knowledge are insufficient to achieve the outcome they want. Though this can be frustrating, on the positive side, the extra practice that people get as clients enables some of them to learn to perform the role well. Also, more clients have become advisors, for example, in the many workplaces where more experienced staff now have as part of their employment conditions that they train new staff, and so they can see bad and good ways in which the client role can be played and so perhaps learn to improve their own performance.

As indicated above, the client role may not have gender implications, for example, when the client has an urgent need for advice, as in the case of a medical emergency or a computer crash. In such an instance, both the advisor and the client roles might be played in an non-gendered way. In a recent experience of this kind, the author sought advice as a busy professional computer user, angry with the machine's recalcitrance. As a researcher, I noted the details of the communication and asked three male colleagues to report on their communications to the same information technology (IT) specialist, on the same issue, and on the same day. It was found that we had all used the same questions, the same words, even the same swear words, as if our genders were of little significance. And we all seemed to attend to the value of the answers we were given irrespective of the gender of the advisor – indeed when asked 'was the IT advisor a man or a woman' the colleagues either responded angrily that they didn't care, or hesitated in a puzzled fashion before dredging up the gender from what seemed to be a memory of low-level interest and concern.

## Communication and Clienthood: Problems

Clients are not a homogeneous group. Some see themselves as detached questioners, while others are more involved, and they have very different advisory needs. For example, among small investors receiving a company brochure, the first type of client may want only to know what the dividends will be, while the second may want to know everything from future policies to why the directors have voted themselves a rise in salary. And, again, variation in role for a particular client is a possibility, since a client can change quickly and unpredictably from one to the other role within a single communication as well as from one communication to another, as their interest in a matter waxes or wanes. A detached client might want only an easily skimmed overall format, but an involved client might want the information to be in useful order and be fully detailed. Both types of client may ignore the needs and rights of the other and criticize the communication as inefficient.

While clients are becoming familiar users of the vocabulary of institutional discourses, this does not always mean that they understand it in the same way as the advisor. An advisor should not assume mutuality of meaning. For example, a patient in the author's database of medical consultations was asked by the doctor if she was taking any *medication*. She said 'no' but it emerged later that she took the contraceptive pill – 'medication' to her was curative not preventative. Such misunderstandings can lead to poor-quality advice. One solution is to train the advisor to expect the misuse of technicality and to check for accuracy, another is to have advisors teach clients to use the terms accurately. However, any suggestion to the client that their term is inappropriate can be taken as criticism and viewed negatively: tactics should be developed to avoid this implication or make it less negative (Mulholland, 1994). Unfortunately, clients cannot easily be trained to be efficient seekers of advice, but there are some advice providers, for example, medical centres and pharmacies, that have begun to supply brochures that provide written information and advice to augment a doctor's spoken communication in a consultation, and such materials may eventually teach correct medical vocabulary. In another context, the 'Help' facilities of most computer programs and the websites with 'Frequently Asked Questions' segments do excellent work in showing client-users how to recognize the vocabulary and style the computer world uses and hence perhaps to emulate this when next seeking advice.

One problem for current advice providers lies in their use of offshore call centres. Many clients still expect the advisor to be aware of local circumstances, and dislike telephone advisors who turn out to be thousands of miles away and unaware of the context in which the inquiry is being put. Occasionally this can mean that a client has to spend extra work deciding just which elements of their own context need to be expressed and which can be assumed to be shared. This extra work can turn an often simple request for advice into a major project. A colleague reported an irritating instance in which an adviser asked him for his telephone number: when he provided his local number he was then asked to provide his international call code – which he did not know and had to find in a telephone directory that was not in his office. In advice situations like these, both clients and advisors have to work harder at understanding the taken-for-granted assumptions of the other person, and making clearer their own circumstantial assumptions than when both are operating within the same context (Van Den Broek, 2004).

The frustration of phoning major institutions such as banks or branches of government for advice is well known and people share stories of the particular difficulties of dealing with the menus of choices presented. Although the institutions design the menus with the most likely choice in first position, as based on their research, there are people who either do not understand the generalized nature of the names given to the choices or find none of the choices connects with their specific problem. Even working through the menu can take a good deal of energy before the most fitting option is selected. This is truest where clients have very complex problems. For these troubled people there is frustration in having to listen to four or five choices, only the last of which shows even some faint chance of being relevant.

One response to this frustration by some of the smaller institutions seeking to increase their business can be seen in their advertising. They advertise themselves as affiliative in approach and willing to undertake face-to-face advisor–client interactions, and they emphasize how unusual this is. One such television advertisement, for the Bank of Queensland in Australia, shows a client couple who need advice about their new small business. They speak of their wish to 'shake someone's hand' at the bank because they are excited about what they are doing and they want a celebration of the event. And the bank advertises that it will meet such wishes. When this advertisement was presented to the focus groups, both the men and the women found the affiliative touch attractive, and very different from their own bank dealings. Of course, the problem for the larger advice providers is how to add a personal element to the advisor–client communication without excessive cost. The most pertinent issue in this regard is to understand what can best be done with the cost parameters to increase the affiliative element. One possibility is to train advisors to add a brief personal comment on the client's situation where this might be well received. (And permitting advisors to spend the few seconds it takes to add this comment without penalizing them for slowness.) An example the author experienced, and found attractive, included a phrase of sympathy from a company when contacted for advice about a loss of credit cards: '*Oh dear, how upsetting for you*. We can fix that straightaway …'.

*Communication and Advisorhood*

Any advisor needs an awareness of language and particularly style variation, so that they can analyse the client's words and design a good response. Also, advisors need to understand that their initial response to a client should be modified where necessary during the communication. Firth (1995) notes that each communication action during an encounter affects the next action, so every turn at talk or every sentence in writing affects the response it gets, and that response affects the next action, and so on (p. 34). An advisor's main goal is to ensure that the advice is sufficient not to require another call on the same issue from the same client.

Some of the problems arise, and are worsening, because of the efficiencies that providers have put in place to cut the running costs of their advisory services. In the data set, the two advisor trainers who were consulted reported that time constraints on supplying advice by telephone, as well as changes to the proformas used for advisory letters, in addition to constant monitoring, were seen by advisors as inhibiting their ability to concentrate on the advice event. Perhaps as a result of this, the focus groups used for this project complained that advice can be supplied too technically, too quickly and even too paternalistically: some advisors emphasize the penalties that will follow if the advice is not taken. The focus groups also saw some advisors as coercive, using too instructional a tone, downplaying alternatives where available, rather than leaving choices to the client. Other advisors place too much emphasis on the advice being for the client's good, which can assume too great an affiliation with the client, as if the advisor knows the client well enough to be certain of what is the client's 'good'. Even if these advices are correct, clients can resent this apparent closeness and prefer a more distanced approach.

On the other hand, advisors can offer too many choices and too many qualifications, and too many details of them, and so create confusion for the client. Even if the details are meant to assist a proper choice, for some clients this is not perceived as good advice.

*Cross-cultural Advisor–Client Communication*

As global communications become increasingly easy and more frequent, cross-cultural client communications will grow in number and will inevitably require care if the encounters are to be satisfactory to both parties. Gumperz (1982, pp. 175–9) has described a classic cross-cultural example. In it, it is the *role expectations* that cause problems rather than gender difference or language difficulties. A Pakistani male teacher has been referred to an enquiry centre set up to deal with inter-ethnic employment problems, because, although educated in England, he has insufficient communications skills for teaching in English high schools. Both he and his female English advisor regard the face-to-face occasion as an advisory session, but their expectations of the appropriate role to adopt differ greatly. During the hour-long session, many attempts are made to negotiate the roles with little success. The two are at odds about such things as the informalities of self-introduction, the client's supplying of a long and finally irrelevant life story, and the limits of the power of the advisor. Gumperz sees these particular misunderstandings as frequent with Indians and Pakistanis, who see such interviews as events in which they should act as a petitioner and use their personal hardship to persuade the other party to waive the condition that is impeding their employment opportunities. He shows how it is a person's general socio-cultural knowledge, which may or may not include gender issues, that sets expectations of client roles, and therefore cross-cultural training for advisors should include such matters. (See also Tracy, 1998.)

## Recommendations: Future Directions for Client Communication

In this chapter, providers have already been offered some suggestions for areas of improvement in client-communication. Other possibilities include the following:

- Career pathways and promotional opportunities for advisory staff should be put on a par with those available for staff in the other parts of the organization; it is well known that 'human resources' (where client communication is often placed) is still the 'poor relation' area of many businesses.

- In general, advice providers should learn to privilege cooperation with clients and to accentuate affiliation as well as instrumentality.
- Advantage could be taken of the growth in university courses in human resources and of communication skills, and more money and effort should be put into client advice since it can give the business a serious edge over its competitors.
- With respect to research on the gender of clients, research is needed to assess just where gender is and is not an issue, and for which institutions or which advisory events the gendering of client communication is important and for which is it not.
- Companies should note where there are increasing numbers of women among their clients. Where this is so, they should undertake research on what roles women prefer in seeking information, and whether they are different from, or similar to, those adopted by men.
- As one outcome of this research, advisor-training could continue to focus on a 'neutered' advice style or to show trainees how to note the gender elements that are important to advising success when they occur, and how to respond to them.
- With respect to menu priorities, advisory providers should note whether there are different priorities for men and for women and, if so, bring this into their decision making about menu priorities.
- Telephones may soon be able to recognize the gender of the client (McLean, 2001) and this could lead to menu variation where significant gender differences are found in that service's client base.
- On a more micro-level, advisors should be trained to note any signs of gendered communication change as the event progresses and change their style to fit.
- And, as times and clients change, the advice providers and their trainers should not just concentrate on the style of advisors, but should also note where client improvements in presentation are occurring and which faults are still prevalent, and adjust the training accordingly.
- Again at a micro-level, for example, some advisors offer running commentaries on what they are doing if the advice can only slowly be produced; and this is perceived as better by the client who can often feel neglected in long silences (this is true of both telephone and face-to-face events). In this respect, a useful tactic can be to utilize the possibilities that computers can provide. For example, the University of Queensland Library enquiry counter increases the affiliative element and at the same time improves efficiency for both parties by the simple move of having staff swivel their computer monitor so that they and the client can read it simultaneously – creating a situation in which both parties have access to the same information and where either party can efficiently raise relevant issues, without the need to explain or describe their referent, since both can see it on screen.

# References

Antaki, C. (ed.) (1988), *Analysing Everyday Explanation: A Casebook of Methods*. London: Sage.

Baker, M. A. (1991), 'Gender and verbal communication in professional settings: A review of research', *Management Communication Quarterly*, **5**(1): 36–63.

Belenky, M. F., Clinchy, B. M., Goldberger, N. R. and Tarule, J. M. (1986), *Women's Ways of Knowing: The Development of Self, Voice, and Mind*. New York: Basic Books.

Borisoff, D. and Merrill, L. (1985), *The Power to Communicate: Gender Differences as Barriers*. Prospect Heights IL: Waveland.

Drew, P. and Heritage, J. (eds) (1992), *Talk at Work: Interaction in Institutional Settings*. Cambridge: Cambridge University Press.

Fairclough, N. (1994), 'Conversationalisation of public discourse and the authority of the consumer', in R. Kent, N. Whiteley and N. Abercrombie (eds), *The Authority of the Consumer*. London: Routledge. pp. 253–68.

Firth, A. (ed.) (1995), *The Discourse of Negotiation*. Oxford: Pergamon.

Game, A. and Pringle, R. (1983), *Gender at Work*. Sydney: George Allen and Unwin.

Garfinkel, H. (1967), *Studies in Ethnomethodology*. Englewood Cliffs, NJ: Prentice-Hall.

Goddard, A. and Patterson, L. M. (2000), *Language and Gender*. London: Routledge.

Gumperz, J. (1982), *Discourse Strategies*. Cambridge: Cambridge University Press.

Harper, N. and Hirokawa, R. (1988), 'A comparison of persuasive strategies used by female and male managers', *Management Communication Quarterly*, **4**: 30–50.

Hatcher, C. (2001), 'Affairs of the heart: The alliances of gender and business that matter to good business communication', *Australian Journal of Communication*, **28**(3): 55–72.

Lakoff, R. (1973), 'Language and woman's place', *Language in Society*, **2**: 45–79.

Lay, M. (1994), 'The value of gender studies to professional communication research', *Journal of Business and Technical Communication*, **8**(1): 58–90.

McLean, C. (2001), 'Voice recognition comes of age', *Banking and Financial Services*, **115**(4): 26–7.

Mulholland, J. (1991), *The Language of Negotiation*. London: Routledge.

Mulholland, J. (1994), *Handbook of Persuasive Tactics*. London: Routledge.

Pringle, R. (1988), *Secretaries Talk: Sexuality, Power and Work*. Sydney: Allen and Unwin.

Schegloff, E. (1997), 'Whose text ? Whose context ?' *Discourse and Society*, **8**(2): 165–87.

Stokoe, E. H. and Smithson, J. (2001), 'Making gender relevant: Conversation analysis and gender categories in interaction', *Discourse and Society*, **12**(2): 217–44.

Tannen, D. (1990), *You Just Don't Understand*. New York: William Morrow.

Tannen, D. (1994), *Talking from 9 to 5*. New York: William Morrow.

Tebeaux, E. (1990), 'Toward an understanding of gender differences in written communications', *Journal of Business and Technical Communication*, **4**(1): 25–43.

Tracy, K. (1998), 'Analysing context: Framing the discussion', *Research in Language and Social Interaction*, **31**(1): 1–28.

Tymson, C. (2001), 'Business communication: How to bridge the gender gap', *Banking and Financial Services*, **115**(3): 18–25.

Van Den Broek, D. (2004), 'Call centre capital: Gender, culture and work identity', *Labour and Industry*, **14**(3): 59–75.

West, C. and Zimmerman, D. H. (1987), 'Doing gender', *Gender and Society*, **9**(1): 125–51.

Wierzbicka, A. (1987), *English Speech Act Verbs: A Semantic Dictionary*. Sydney: Academic Press.

Wodak, R. (ed.) (1997), *Gender and Discourse*. London: Sage.

## Chapter 7

# Gender, Communication and International Business

Beverly D. Metcalfe

## Introduction

The aim of this chapter is to explore developments in gender and communication research in the international business arena. The discussion considers gender and communication issues in two different socio-cultural regions, the Middle East and Eastern Europe, in order to highlight the fluidity and variety in the nature and style of communication strategies. The importance of gender and communication is also discussed in international organizations and assignments. The discussion links together gender and performative theory (identity), communities of practice (context) and critical discourse analysis (ideology) as a way of capturing the complexity of gender and communication studies in international research fields. The chapter concludes by suggesting that globalization processes and an increasing interest in cross-cultural management research open out the field of gender and communication inquiry that has previously been uncharted.

## Overview of Current Research

As is evidenced throughout this book, research into gender and communication in the workplace is now quite considerable and spans 30 years (for example Cameron, 1996; Holmes and Marra, 2004; Lakoff, 1975; Tannen, 1990). Since the early 1970s, traditional gender roles in the workplace have been under challenge, specifically at the managerial level (Davidson and Cooper, 1992; Davidson and Burke, 1994). There are now more females entering the workplace in managerial and professional roles and statistics suggest that this will continue. Indeed, the increase of women in the labour market is a global phenomenon (Wirth, 2001). Women's entry into senior professional roles, however, has been limited when compared to their male counterparts. Consequently, a great deal of research has examined how language and communication strategies in the workplace may act as barriers to women's advancement.

Research on gender and communication in international business, however, is uncovered ground – something which is surprising on account of women's advancements in organizations worldwide, as well as their more modest achievements gained in international management assignments (see Adler, 2005; Davidson and Burke, 2004; Taylor et al., 2002). Similarly, there is very limited scholarship that examines gender within international human resource management studies. Globalization, global feminism(s) and developments in transnational organization relations have spearheaded a critical interest in cross-cultural communication and distinct business and managerial practices associated with specific regions (Carney, 2003; Hearn et al., 2005). This chapter contributes to this limited research field. The next section summarizes research on gender and communication which is largely positioned within western economies. A methodological framework is then proposed linking together gender and identity positioning and the social context, based on communities of practice (CofP) and critical discourse analysis (CDA). It is suggested that this multi-layered framework will provide a useful lens through which to examine gender and language in the international business context. A brief analysis of gender and language and implications for business practices is then undertaken for the Middle East and Eastern Europe.

## Gender and Communication Debates in the West

Scholars have investigated how speech strategies such as assertion, paying compliments and accepting proposals have gender constructions and effects (Bergvall, 1999; Coates, 1999; Elgin, 1993). Studies have also explored how language defines gender identities and roles in organizations. Differences in language highlight the formation and reformation of gendered power relations and result in 'miscommunication' or what Rosener (1997) calls 'sexual static'. 'Miscommunication' arising from different speech structures affects personal relationships and career development opportunities and strategies for men and women (Holmes et al., 2003).

A great deal of gender and communication research literature has sought to explain how the communication styles of women managers have created barriers to their advancement, especially in relation to promotion decisions and perceived performance and managerial competences (for example Holmes, 1990; West, 1995). The majority of these accounts however, rely on discussions of organization and managerial practices in the West, in particular the United States, Australia and the UK (for example, Elgin, 1993; Holmes, 1990).

The way in which communication strategies are gendered is reflected by the limited representation of women at middle management and senior management levels in private and public organizations and in politics, although it is fair to say it has improved in the last decade (Adler, 2005; Davidson and Burke, 2004). The limited advancement of women in decision-making and executive roles is a global phenomenon (Wirth, 2001). In every region, whether the United States, Europe, Africa, Middle East and Asia, men outnumber women in senior roles in organizations and as political representatives in governments and public bodies (Wirth, 2001). The only exceptions are some of the former communist countries in Central and Eastern Europe, Lithuania and Estonia, which have 60 per cent and 70 per cent of women in managerial and technical occupations respectively, although evidence has shown that women's professional roles are being reduced in number (Metcalfe and Afanassieva, 2005a, in press; Wirth, 2001). Thus, although women have been entering the labour market in increasing numbers over the last 30 years, there are still barriers that limit their career progression.

A common assertion (illustrated by other contributors to this book) is that, for women to succeed in the business arena, they need to develop language styles like those of men. Indeed, this position underpins managerial and leadership stereotypes that equate managerial and leadership effectiveness with masculinity (see Rosener, 1997) and it suggests that ambitious women need to adopt powerful modes of speaking associated with men (Barrett, 2004).

Despite the view that there are fixed male and female differences in speech patterns, research studies have questioned this reasoning. Debates on gender and communication research have been classically held between two paradigms: *gender difference* (for example, Tannen, 1990) and *gender dominance* (for example, Zimmerman and West, 1975). The difference approach stresses that men and women speak differently due to differences that are implemented during the socialization process. The dominance approach highlights how the considerable economic power that men have over women in society permeates into language, resulting in male domination in spoken interaction. Both approaches rely on an acceptance of 'essential' differences between the sexes. For example, a great deal of research focuses on the way in which feminine speech and style has advantages for women in certain business situations (Rosener, 1990). The common view that emerges is to view female speech strategies as exhibiting collaborative and supportive communication styles, whereas men use language strategies that challenge and are combative. This approach reinforces gender stereotypes, and, it is argued, has not advanced women in the organizational sphere, because these paradigms create and sustain gender/language hierarchies and view the feminine as 'lesser valued' and 'lesser than' (Irigaray, 2002). Critics of the approaches have also highlighted how the diversity of speech patterns in groups of men and women are overlooked (see Barrett, 2004; Bergvall et al., 1996; Cameron, 1996; Holmes et al., 2003).

These critiques are highly relevant to the study of gender and communication in international business. The dominance and difference perspectives ignore cultural differences that may be the result of other social variables, for example, race, ethnicity, age, religion and sexuality. Gender is but one of the many relevant social identities we construct and perform in the workplace. Given that communication and business research is predominantly based in western countries, we need an approach that takes into account different socio-cultural contexts and within-group differences. As Holmes et al. (2003) suggest, it is misleading to assume that: 'the [western] workplace is a monolithic, social context, unmodified by different objectives, participants and networks, not to mention physical settings and institutional culture' (p. 415).

A way forward is to consider gender and communication in international business on a number of multi-layered levels. Critical communication scholars now acknowledge the fluidity and variety of language strategies and suggest that 'interaction in the workplace can be productively viewed as social practice in action' (Holmes et al., 2003, p. 415; see also Holmes and Marra, 2004). This social constructionist perspective acknowledges a move away from fixed notions of gender and language styles to one that is subject to ongoing change. Citing McConnell-Ginet (2000), Holmes et al. (2003), argue: 'Whether a particular person's talk and other actions affect many or a few, it is the unfolding over time of a structured totality of situated acts that creates meaning in, and for, society' (p. 415).

## Developments in Gender and Communication Research: An International Perspective

Before the multi-layered model is outlined, it is important to map the existing terrain of international business and gender and communication research. First, investigations of international business research can incorporate an examination of communication strategies and practices in a multinational organization. Management research in this area focuses on the skills of international managers, especially their cultural sensitivity, adaptability and aptitude for managing global development change (Scullion and Lineham, 2005). Gender and communication scholarly inquiry is entirely absent from this literature and only a small amount of research has considered women's role in international management assignments (for example Taylor et al., 2002). The communication styles of international male and female managers is thus an important area for future investigation. Alternatively, international business investigations can explore the socio-cultural context in which diverse business operations occur. This field of study examines the cultural and social values specific to a country or region and evaluates their impact on organizational and managerial practice (Scullion and Lineham, 2005). As already highlighted, there is a wealth of gender and management literature, although it tends to derive from western economies. Gender research is a growing area in Asia, but it tends to focus on the different skills of men and women and does not incorporate detailed communication approaches (for example Cooke, 2003). There is a need, therefore, within the field of international business and human resource management to unravel the socio-cultural variables that may shape language styles and consider their implications for women's managerial roles and advancement.

A useful starting point is to consider developments in gender theorizing outside the discipline. These include the 'constructionist turn' in language and explanations of sex and gender that move away from binary categories (Fraser, 1995). These developments have highlighted that gender and communication research is more complex than gender dominance and gender difference approaches imply. Mullany (2000) has proposed an integrated approach that is based on her examination of gender identity and discourse in professional communication. Promoting a social constructionist perspective, she argues that gender should be viewed as 'performative' at the individual identity level (Butler, 1990, 1993; see also Barrett, 2004). Individuals, however, also come together and perform their gendered identity in specific contexts or CofP. CofP are also shaped at a broader ideological level, where individual linguistic behaviours may be constrained by forces at a wider societal level. This multi-layered framework and its suitability for international business research is explained in the sections that follow.

## Gender and Identity

Across the social sciences, gender scholars have acknowledged that gender cannot be viewed as fixed or as a stable category, since this would be universalizing the experiences of men and women. Global feminism has highlighted how the everyday lives of women and men are highly variable and influenced by a myriad of social features (Carney, 2003; Hearn et al., 2005). Communication scholars in particular (for example Bergvall et al., 1996; Cameron, 1996) have drawn on Judith Butler's influential work (1990, 1993) which stresses gender as a performative social construct. She states that gender should be understood as a performance of stylized acts (Butler, 1990). Gender then is understood as something that is fluid and constantly in process. As Cameron (1996) has suggested, men and women do not learn and then mechanically reproduce ways of speaking that are appropriate to their own sex, rather, individuals employ a range of linguistic repertoires.

## Communities of Practice

Studies of language and gender have been criticized for ignoring the social and cultural practices in which talk is produced. Authors such as Lave and Wenger (1991) and Eckert and McConnell-Ginet (1992) suggest CofP can assist understanding of gender dynamics in language. Drawing on Lave and Wenger's model, Eckert and McConnell-Ginet suggest CofP can be described as a form of 'mutual engagement', where people can identify with 'ways of doing things, ways of talking, beliefs, values, power relations – in short practices' (Eckert and McConnell-Ginet, 1992, p. 464; see also Wenger, 1999). The notion of a CofP is particularly important for thinking about the fluid nature of an individual's gender identity, because it is clear that individuals belong to a wide range of different communities with different norms and values, and they will have different identity positions within these groups, both dominant and marginal. Thus, rather than describing a single gender, it is possible to analyse multiple gendered identities that will be activated and used strategically within particular CofPs. Eckert and McConnell-Ginet stress that individuals and CofP change consistently, resulting in multiple masculinities and femininities and new and transformative gender relations.

This constructionist model of gender makes it more difficult to make global statements about women's or men's language, since it allows for variations within the categories 'men' and 'women' and allows for the possibility of contestation and change. The application would therefore be of particular relevance for researching diverse business cultures. As Eckert and McConnell-Ginet state:

An emphasis on talk as constitutive of gender draws attention away from a more serious investigation of the relations among language, gender and other components of social identity: it ignores the ways difference (or beliefs therein) function in constructing dominance relations. Gender can be thought of as a sex-based way of experiencing other social attributes like class, ethnicity or age (and also less obviously social qualities like ambition, athleticism and musicality (Eckert and McConnell-Ginet, 1992, pp. 488-9).

Certain activities within those communities of practice may also be coded or recognized as stereotypically masculine or feminine and thus certain types of linguistic activity may be considered by males and females as appropriate or inappropriate within interaction and sanctioned by the group as a whole. In a recent work, Eckert and McConnell-Ginet (1999) also point out that CofP techniques could extend to 'global communities' such as 'academic fields' and 'religions', although this is being debated (Mullany, 2000; see also Wenger, 1999). The Islamic community, which unites many individuals globally, could possibly be identified here.

Bergvall (1999) points out that the CofP approach is an extremely beneficial way to examine contexts where gender roles are in flux or under challenge. In particular, gender roles are both in flux and under challenge in international business. Globalization and the diversification of business have created tremendous challenges for organizations seeking to develop management systems across borders, as well as attempting to recruit and train staff to deal with global management assignments (Scullion and Lineham, 2005). Taylor et al. (2002) have argued that global management careers reflect men's working career stages. Further, managerial skills are often perceived as reflecting masculinist speech and behaviour (Rosener, 1997), although there are now concerted efforts by multinational corporations to tackle the dynamics of cross-cultural language and diversity through extensive training and this is resulting in the numbers of women slowly growing in international assignments (Adler, 2005). It is suggested that the global glass ceiling has some cracks, but it will be some time before it is shattered.

Bergvall (1999, p. 279) goes on to argue that the CofP approach is also of value where participants may be constructing different practices in response to different social opportunities and settings, such as work within non-traditional fields. This is highly relevant to the position of women in Middle East and Eastern European economies. These economic environments are undergoing significant social and political change. Women's increasing participation in the workforce, especially at the professional level, is seen as a central feature of this ongoing change.

Bergvall (1999) also suggests that a focus on the local ignores gender norms at the global level of hegemony and ideology. This is also important in terms of wider social and political discourses that shape gender roles such as those in the Middle East and Eastern Europe. In the Middle East there are strong gender differences culturally communicated via Islamic discourses and a clear demarcation of gender roles advocated. In contrast, in Eastern Europe, a dominant discourse defining aspects of identity (albeit changing in the context of transition) is communist ideology. Bergvall (1999, p. 288) states: 'without the broader studies of ideologies at the textual and global levels we cannot understand how interpretations of gender by gate-keeping elites are generated or spread'.

## Critical Discourse Analysis

CDA focuses on the way in which language creates and sustains gendered power relations. CDA, an approach attributed to Fairclough (1995), highlights how text, discourse practice and socio-cultural practice all assist in the formation of gender identities. The approach has been influential in feminist theory and organization studies, because it can reveal the way in which everyday managerial discourses are constructed and how feminine or masculine texts reproduce power relations. Fairclough argues that the discourse of 'social institutions' should be analysed instead of casual conversations, as this enables discussion of issues surrounding the role that institutional discourse plays in producing and maintaining a society's power structure (see also Holmes and Marra, 2004). CDA thus appears to be an extremely useful tool to examine institutionalized gender norms in the workplace that have been established prior to the performance of gender identity (Mullany, 2000).

The foregoing discussion has highlighted a framework that could be adopted in international research into gender and communication in a business context. The plethora of gender and communication studies that is rooted in western paradigms of management poses problems for those wanting to undertake cross-cultural research and assess gender and language in diverse international settings and global assignments. It cannot be assumed that communication styles and interventions will be interpreted and coded in the same way in different geographical locations, nor can we assume that there are two universal categories, men and women. A multi-layered approach, therefore, that considers the formation of gendered identities and speech acts, the individual's positioning and the management of a language repertoire, together with an examination of the broader discourses that shape social institutions, can all provide a fruitful contribution to theoretical perspectives in language and gender research in the global sphere. The following discussions of the Middle East and Eastern Europe use this approach to focus on broader discourses and communities of practice.

## Gender and Communication in the Middle East

The growth in female labour-market participation is a significant aspect of social and economic change in the Middle East (Metcalfe, 2006; UNDP, 2003). Influenced by the increase in women's educational opportunities and attainment and a decline in the fertility rate, the percentage growth in female labour participation overall for the Middle East and North Africa (MENA) between 1960 and 2000 is 47 per cent, although women's labour-market participation in MENA still remains the lowest in world (World Bank, 2003, p. 49). This masks the dramatic increases in certain regions: Bahrain has seen women's labour-market participation increase over this period by 668 per cent, Kuwait by 486 per cent and the United Arab Emirates by

548 per cent, while Yemen's female labour participation increased only 15 per cent (World Bank, 2003, p. 59). Total female labour participation for Bahrain was 25.8 per cent in 2001, and for Jordan 27.8 per cent (World Bank, 2003). While employment still remains strongly gender segregated in all MENA regions, the employment of women has increased by 50 per cent in political, economic and law professions between 1991 and 2001 (Wirth, 2001). Bahrain, along with Jordan and Kuwait, has also seen a sizeable increase in entrepreneurial development and self-employment among women (UNDP, 2003). The growth in female employment has also been facilitated by increased political representation (World Bank, 2003).

There is limited research that reviews management styles and communication strategies in Middle East organizational contexts. Gender research has been concerned with social and health policy dimensions (UNDP, 2003) rather than aspects of management and organizational communication. However, the limited research that exists paints a different picture of organizational life and managerial styles than that associated with western accounts of business practice. The majority of Middle East states are constitutionally Islamic and the dominant discourses (Fairclough, 1995) of this social institution have a significant bearing on business communication processes. Islamic discourse constructs rigid gender roles by reference to Sharia law and in some countries discourages the free mixing of men and women through the creation of segregated work environments (Metcalfe, 2006; see also Ahmed, 1998). This undoubtedly has implications for the professional and managerial roles that women can occupy as well as having an impact upon their career progression.

Islamic worship can be viewed as a CofP where members mutually interact within prescribed understandings of doing things, ways of talking, beliefs, values and power relations. In essence, this relates to a shared repertoire for negotiating meaning (Holmes et al., 2003). In sustained mutual relationships there are shared ways of engaging in doing things together, a knowledge of knowing what others know, what they can do and how they can contribute to an enterprise. It must be stressed that Islamic discourse is an overarching aspect that constructs individual identity and meaning in both the home and work sphere (Ahmed, 1998). The characteristics of a devout Muslim's identity are relevant both in the public and private domains. Above all, there is an emphasis on humility, benevolence and in maintaining balance and equilibrium (*adl*) in life and thus in human interaction. This emphasizes the importance of establishing close and collaborative relationships with family and work colleagues. Through *watsa* (personal connections), business planning and projects are mutually secured.

Assertiveness, directive questioning, hedging and interruption tactics are therefore not culturally part of the language repertoire that would be linked with effective communication behaviours, for either men or women. Combative dialogue is not valued as a communication style. Interpersonal exchanges that emphasize respect and recognize the value of others' opinions and nurture cooperativeness are encouraged. Participants in business meetings, although formally arranged and executed, would respect the authority of the chair and interruptions and staging would seem inappropriate and impolite.

The importance of humility in establishing personal and close relations is emphasized by Weir's (2002) account of Arab management styles. Drawing on Hofstede's cultural model, Weir describes Arab countries as moderately 'feminine'. Engaging in behaviours that are self-promoting such as those that described by Tannen (1996) would be perceived as disrespecting Allah's own humility. The nature of effective business communication therefore does not adhere to dominant modes of speech patterns that emphasize masculinist language styles as necessary for success and as being associated with men's talk. Rather, culturally, language signifiers that would be read as feminine (and less successful) in western social contexts would be coded as language style patterns that both men and women would adopt. The implications for business are that to be successful in management negotiations in the Middle East one would be advised to adopt communication styles that are feminine rather than masculine. This reaffirms the socially constructed nature of speech patterns.

While managerial communication exchanges would more likely be described in stereotypically feminine terms, it is also important to appreciate the gendered structures governing organization and social relations, specifically the social context within which talk is produced. In Iran, Jordan, Saudi Arabia and Bahrain, for example, countries that follow a strict adherence to Sharia law, it is common for a woman to have to ask for permission to work from her husband and this permission will be obtained prior to marriage (Metcalfe, 2006). In addition, men and women in both social gatherings and in business settings are not permitted to shake hands. This cultural practice is followed as Sharia law argues that women's sexuality must be protected and the touching of a woman's hand by someone other than her husband can be construed as an intimate gesture. Underpinning Islamic philosophy is the concept of *qiwama* or protection and welfare.

Some business environments are also sexually segregated (especially Saudi Arabia and Qatar) and this is especially the case in financial and banking services, which tend to provide separate facilities for men and women. Metcalfe (2006) has argued that western corporations wishing to expand in Middle East regions should recognize that women managers are a source of advantage as they can develop business relations with both men and women, whereas men can only establish work contacts and relations through, and with, men. The positioning of women within certain social structures shapes women's opportunity to engage in business development and dialogue. The point is important since it points to the need to adopt a multi-layered approach to gender and communication studies. Language formations and interactions are socially constituted. It is not just what is said in exchanges, but also the social and political context within which language is positioned. Within Islamic contexts, therefore, communication patterns are also embedded within prescribed gender structures and relationships.

*Gender and Communication in Eastern Europe*

While business opportunities are expanding rapidly in the Middle East, another region that has experienced recent growth and development is comprised of the former post-communist states in Central and Eastern Europe (CEE) (Pollert, 2003; Zimney, 2002). The study of gender in this socio-cultural region is an important and topical field of research, since under communist ideology women's status was considered equal to men's in the public and private spheres and equality was enshrined in constitutional frameworks. The USSR constitution stated that: 'a woman is afforded equal rights in all areas of economic, civil, and cultural and socio-political life (USSR Constitution, 1936, Article 122; see also Metcalfe and Afanassieva, 2005b).

Consequently, women's participation in managerial, professional and political roles has historically been high in CEE states (Metcalfe and Afanassieva, 2005a; see also Wirth, 2001). However, the reality of equality for women in communist systems has recently been questioned by gender scholars, since socialist planning systems created hidden gender inequalities. Women were often in lower-level political roles, and managerial and decision making positions in production were primarily reserved for men. Women were also paid less than men. The communist political administration system did not record these employment differences.

There is evidence to suggest that the transition from a planned to market economy is exacerbating these inequalities. For example, in the USSR (later the Russian Federation), until 1999 women accounted for 38 per cent of political representatives – a figure to be envied by most European countries, and also by Australia and the USA (Pollert, 2003). Since 1999 the number of women in politics (now only 7.8 per cent) has reduced significantly, as Putin has replaced them with male intelligentsia and defence officials (Metcalfe and Afanassieva, 2005b).

Similar to the Middle East, there has been limited research on gender and management research in CEE states (an exception is Metcalfe and Afanassieva, 2005a, in press and 2005b, in press). Indeed, gender research has been largely absent from the transition literature as a whole. This is largely attributable to the belief that communist political ideology and work systems had solved the 'woman question'. Since all citizens were considered equal, gender analysis was deemed unnecessary (Metcalfe and Afanassieva, 2005b). Nevertheless, public discourse promoted 'essentialist' gender roles while at the same time suggesting that gender issues were not important in social and economic policy.

The 'worker-mother' discourse shaped women's work and social identities. Communist ideology promoted the importance of all citizens in contributing to the economic collective and permitted women to participate fully in the economic sphere through the provision of extensive child support services or 'children's institutions', flexible work arrangements and generous maternity leave entitlements. Responsibility for childcare was politically and socially acknowledged as women's. As Eckert and McConnell-Ginet (1992) emphasize, the strength of a CofP is that people mutually engage in the production of these practices and help constitute its power effects. And as Fairclough (1995) highlights, CDA foregrounds the link between social practice and language. The dominant worker mother discourse produced and consumed within communist political systems shapes socio-cultural practices and gender relations. The combination of home, work and political activism were thus all defining aspects of women's gender identity. This triple burden resulted in women's gender identity being promoted in western society as a *baba*, a superwoman. A *baba* was presented as having strength, determination, power and resilience, although the Soviet gender order established prescribed roles for men and women based on a patriarchal logic.

The collapse of communism in 1991 is transforming gender relations (Pollert, 2003). New political discourses are helping constitute the formation of new work and social identities. Privatization and the development of a free market economy have resulted in the dismantling of childcare programmes. The movement of childcare responsibility from the state to the family is affecting women's career options and opportunities. Market restructuring has seen large-scale lay-offs and a reduction in salaries and women have been disproportionately affected. Transition has had profound gender effects, but this is not acknowledged in market reform processes.

A dominant discourse that exists within post-socialist states is the 'irrelevant' and 'dangerous' aspect of feminist research. This is related to the ideological legacy of communist systems that, as noted earlier, suggested that the 'woman question' had been solved. Feminist modes of investigation are those that identify women as a category of social analysis. In Moscow University, for example, in 2002, the Academy of Economic Sciences organized a series of research seminars entitled 'What is dangerous in feminism?', which was intended to reinforce the inappropriateness of western feminist ideas to transition states. Another example is the reluctance of employment specialists to devise policies that pay special attention to gender issues, for example in training and development. Neo-liberal reform agendas stress the importance of individualism and market competition and to privilege one sex above another would be seen to be working against market systems.

However, it is important to note, as Fairclough (1995) highlights, that there are multiple competing discourses at play that help shape power structures and relations. Both discourse and CofP approaches emphasize people's 'active engagement in the reproduction of, or resistance to, gender arrangements in their communities' (Eckert and McConnell-Ginet, 1992, p. 466). Women's activism is now resisting the dominant *baba* image of a working woman with a masculinized face. In the West, personal grooming has been an important aspect of professionalism, but there is ambivalence towards the view that sexuality be commodified as part of a working repertoire. In Eastern Europe, the construction of an overtly feminine and highly sexualized professional persona is perceived as an important part of women's liberation and formation of a gender identity not controlled by communist ideals. This is evidenced by the growth in women's organizations (Metcalfe and Afanassieva, 2005b) that provide training and guidance on etiquette and 'feminine professionalism'.

While political discourse is promoting an apparent gender neutrality, there are CofPs that are embedded within business culture that have implications for how men and women 'do gender' in the workplace (Zimmerman and West, 1975). As with Middle East business cultures, there is little research that has examined gender and management in transition states (with the exception of Metcalfe and Afanassieva, 2005a, in press and 2005b, in press). Research on management styles in communist systems has highlighted the aggressive communication styles prevalent in business relations. Directness, abruptness and assertiveness are commonplace behaviours for both men and women. There is little emphasis on developing collaborative and inclusive interactions and business meetings are characterized by frequent hedging and interruptions. Ways of talking and business values thus constitute a stereotypical masculinist communication repertoire.

This masculinist cultural environment, it is argued in western economies, has provided barriers to women's progress. It is suggested that women in authority face a double bind regarding professionalism and femininity. Lakoff argues:

> When a woman is placed in a position in which being assertive and forceful is necessary, she is faced with a paradox. She can be a good woman but a bad executive or professional, or vice versa. To do both is impossible (Lakoff, cited in Kendall and Tannen, 1997, p. 92).

Within CEE business culture, this statement would have been difficult to conceptualize, since identity was shaped through political allegiance not sex/ gender. Sex/gender was not seen as significant: individuals were party workers and masculinist communication styles were culturally embedded in work practices. This gender-neutral social discourse (though underpinned by a masculinist logic) is now being transformed as communist regimes have been dismantled. Women are constructing what in the West would be perceived as a stereotypical feminine business image while at the same time remaining committed to a masculine communication repertoire.

The foregoing discussion provides support for a multi-layered approach to gender and language research within the international business arena. Viewing text and talk within social context opens out the field of gender and communication inquiry and helps us appreciate the variety of communication exchanges within different business regions of the world and of the multiplicity of gender relations and communities.

## Conclusion

Deborah Cameron argues that:

> because language and gender studies, like other subfields within sociolinguistics, has tended to neglect its 'socio' side (in this instance, gender) and because of a lack of interdisciplinarity in gender research, linguists are cut off from insights that would be relevant to their work (1996, p. 33).

Eckert and McConnell-Ginet (1992) argue that in order to make reasonable and justifiable claims about language and gender, integration of research from a variety of fields is required. The same argument can be applied to research that focuses on gender and communication in the international arena. As gender and communication scholars now argue, variations in language styles and speech practices are part of globalization processes (Carney, 2003; Wethearall, 1998). The language of feminism, and specifically its relationship to policy and organization development within different contexts, is crucial to unravelling how and why gendered inequalities exist and how languages structures contribute to these inequalities. There is a need to acknowledge, therefore, where appropriate, that dominant western paradigms, and western managerial research may not be the most useful lens through which to explore cultural and global diversity. The examples of the Middle East and Eastern Europe suggest strongly that gender and communication is a multi-faceted research terrain and requires an understanding of the social context in which talk is enacted and an understanding of the discourses at the societal level. The advent of globalization, incorporating the internationalization of product and management strategies, the development of subsidiary operations across all continents, global women's movements and global feminisms, as evidenced by feminist reform agendas primarily in developing nations (Hearn et al., 2005; Metcalfe and Afanassieva, 2005a; UNDP, 2003; World Bank; 2003), all provide opportunities to advance gender and communication research.

Clearly the terrain of gender and communication inquiry is in an important state of theoretical development. This chapter has proposed an integrative model of gender and communication investigation relevant to the diversity of international business developments. This 'revisioning' approach (Wethearall, 1998) links gender identity, CofPs and discourse analysis. The growth of international business and globalization processes reinforces the need to move away from the gender dominance and gender difference approaches in order to capture the cultural relativity of gender and language styles/structures.

In addition, there are subtle differences in communication approaches for both genders in diverse geographic regions, as evidenced by communications in the Middle East and Eastern Europe. In the Middle East, a stereotypically feminine communication style that emphasizes less interruptive tactics, and collaborative language repertoires would be the preferred communication style by both men and women. In contrast, in Eastern Europe assertive and direct, or stereotypically masculinist communication styles would be encouraged.

It is also evident that masculinity and femininity are not opposites, but mutually overlapping constructs giving rise to multiple masculinities and femininities (Holmes et al., 2003). The linking of gender and communication research with constructionist and post-structuralist approaches to gender represents an exciting avenue of opportunity to further explore the nuances and subtleties of gender and language, and the implications for women's role and status in organizations and their career development (Holmes and Marra, 2004).

## Future Research

There is obviously a need for future research in order to advance critical understandings of international business and communication studies, especially where this has implications for career advancement and promotion for women and men in the global arena. In particular this will involve:

- examination of language strategies of men and women in multinational corporations and international assignments;
- relatedly, a focus on the nature and content of international diversity policies of multinational corporations;
- a focus on gender and cross-cultural communication and language styles within specific geographic business locations; and
- a move towards multi-disciplinary approaches in gender and communication research in order to advance understandings of how gender, language and work relations are socially constituted.

## References

Adler, N. (2005), 'Leadership in the 21st century', in H. Scullion and M. Lineham (eds), *International HRM, A Critical Text*. Basingstoke: Palgrave.

Ahmed, A. S. (1998), *Islam Today*. London: I. B. Tauris.

Barrett, M. (2004), 'Should they learn to interrupt? Workplace communication strategies Australian women managers forecast as effective', *Women in Management Review*, **19**(8): 391–403.

Bergvall, V. (1999), 'Towards a comprehensive theory of language and gender', *Language in Society*, **28**(2): 273–93.

Bergvall, V., Bing, J. and Freed, A. (eds) (1996), *Rethinking Language and Gender Research: Theory and Practice*. New York: Longman.

Butler, J. (1990), *Gender Trouble*. New York: Routledge.

Butler, J. (1993), *Bodies that Matter*. New York: Routledge.

Cameron, D. (1996), 'The language–gender interface: Challenging co-optation', in V. Bergvall, J. Bing and A. Freed (eds), *Rethinking Language and Gender Research: Theory and Practice*. New York: Longman.

Carney, G. (2003), 'Communicating or just talking? Gender mainstreaming and the communication of global feminism', *Women and Language* **26**(1): 52–61.

Coates, J. (1999), 'Women behaving badly: Female speakers backstage', *Journal of Sociolinguistics*, **3**: 65–80.

Cooke, F. L. (2003), 'Equal opportunities: Women's careers in government organizations in China', *International Journal of HRM*, **14**(2): 317–33.

Davidson, M. and Burke, R. J. (1994), *Women in Management: Current Research Issues*. London: Paul Chapman.

Davidson, M. and Burke, R. J. (2004), *Women in Management Worldwide: Facts, Figures and Analysis*. London: Ashgate.

Davidson, M. and Cooper, C. (1992), *Shattering the Glass Ceiling: The Woman Manager*. London: Paul Chapman.

Eckert, P. and McConnell-Ginet, S. (1992), 'Think practically look locally: Language and gender as community based practice', *Annual Review of Anthropology*, **21**: 461–90.

Eckert, P. and McConnell-Ginet, S. (1999), 'New generalizations and explanations in language and gender research', *Language in Society*, **28**(2): 185–201.

Elgin, S. H. (1993), *Genderspeak, Men, Women and the Gentle Art of Self-Defence*. New York: Wiley.

Fairclough, N. (1995), *Critical Discourse Analysis: The Critical Study of Language*. New York: Longman.

Fraser, N. (1995), 'Pragmatism, feminism and the linguistic turn', in S. Benhabib, J. Butler, D. Cornell and N. Fraser (eds), *Feminist Contentions: A Philosophical Exchange*. New York: Routledge. pp. 141–75.

Hearn, J., Metcalfe, B. and Piekerri, R. (2005), 'Gender and international HRM', in I. Bjorkman and G. Stahl, G. (eds), *Handbook of Research on International HRM*. Cheltenham: Edward Elgar. pp. 502–11.

Holmes, J. (1990), 'Hedges and boosters in women's and men's speech', *Language and Communication*, **10**(3): 185–205.

Holmes, J., Burns, L., Marra, M., Stubbe, M. and Vine, B. (2003), 'Women managing discourse in the workplace', *Women in Management Review*, **18**(8): 414–24.

Holmes, J. and Marra, M. (2004), 'Relational practice in the workplace: Women's talk or gendered discourse?', *Language in Society*, **33**: 377–98.

Irigaray, Luce (2002), *To Speak is Never Neutral*, trans. Gail Schwab. New York: Routledge.

Kendall, S. and Tannen, D. (1997), 'Gender and language in the workplace', in R. Wodak (ed.), *Gender and Discourse*. London: Sage. pp. 81–105.

Lakoff, R. (1975), *Language and Women's Place*. New York: Harper and Row.

Lave, J. and Wenger, E. (1991), *Situated Learning: Legitimate Peripheral Participation*, Cambridge: Cambridge University Press.

McConnell-Ginet, S. (2000), 'Breaking through the glass ceiling: Can linguistic awareness help?', in J. Holmes (ed.), *Gendered Speech in Social Context: Perspectives from Gown to Town*. Wellington: Victoria University Press. pp. 259–82.

Metcalfe, B. D. (2006), 'Exploring cultural dimensions of gender and management in the Middle East', *Thunderbird International Business Review*, **48**(1): 93–109.

Metcalfe, B. D. and Afanassieva, M. (2005a), 'Gender, work and equal opportunities in Central and Eastern Europe', *Women in Management Review* **20**(6): 397–411.

Metcalfe, B. D. and Afanassieva, M. (2005b), 'The woman question? A critical review of gender and management in the Russian Federation', *Women in Management Review*, **20**(6): 429–45.

Mullany, L. (2000), 'The application of current language and gender theory to managerial meeting discourse', *Nottingham Linguistic Circular*, **15**: 1–16.

Pollert, A. (2003), 'Women, work and equal opportunities', *Work Employment and Society*, **17**(2): 331–57.

Rosener, J. (1990), 'Ways women lead', *Harvard Business Review*, **68**(November–December): 119–25.

Rosener, J. (1997), 'Sexual static', in K. Grint (ed.), *Leadership: Classical, Contemporary and Critical Approaches*. Oxford: Oxford University Press. pp. 211–23.

Scullion, H. and Lineham, M. (eds) (2005), *International Human Resource Management: A Critical Text*. Basingstoke: Palgrave Macmillan.

Tannen, D. (1990), *You Just Don't Understand: Women and Men in Conversation*. New York: William Morrow.

Taylor, S., Napier, N. K. and Mayrhofer, W. (2002), 'Women in global business: An introduction', *International Journal of Human Resource Management*, **13**(5): 739–42.

UNDP (United Nations Development Program) (2003), *Arab Human Development Report*. New York: United Nations Publications.

USSR Constitution (1936). Retrieved June 19, 2005 from www.politicsforum.org/documents/constitution_ussr_1936.php.

Weir, David. (2002), 'Management in the Arab world: A fourth paradigm?', in A. Al-Shamali and J. Denton (eds), *Arab Business: The Globalization Imperative*. Bristol: Kogan Page.

Wenger, E. (1999), *Communities of Practice*. Cambridge: Cambridge University Press.

West, C. (1995), 'Women's competence in conversation', *Discourse and Society*, **6**: 107–31.

Wethearall, A. (1998), 'Revisioning language and gender research', *Women and Language*, **21**: 1–9.

Wirth, L. (2001), *Shattering the Glass Ceiling*. Geneva: International Labour Organization.

World Bank (2003), *Gender and Development in the Middle East and North Africa: Women in the Public Sphere*. Washington: World Bank.

Zimmerman, D. and West, C. (1975), 'Sex roles, interruptions and silences in conversation', in B. Thorne and N. Henley (eds), *Language and Sex: Difference and Dominance*. Rowley MA: Newbury House.

Zimney, E. W. (2002), *Gender Aspects of Changes in the Labour Markets in Transition Economies*. Geneva: United Nations Economic Commission for Europe.

## Chapter 8

# Gender, Violation and Communication at Work

Jeff Hearn and Wendy Parkin

## Introduction

Communication is often seen axiomatically as a 'good thing'. Problems, at work as at home and elsewhere, are frequently understood as arising from poor or insufficient communication. Indeed communication is sometimes seen as the very 'stuff of life'. The MacBride Report (1980, cited in Crookall and Saunders, 1989) stated:

> Communication maintains and animates life. It is also the motor and expression of civilization … it creates a common pool of ideas, strengthens the feeling of togetherness through exchange of messages and translates thought into action, reflecting every emotion and need from the humblest tasks of human survival to supreme manifestations of creativity – or destruction. Communication integrates knowledge, organization and power and runs as a thread linking the earliest memory of man [sic] to his noblest aspirations. (p. 6)

Yet communication is itself neither good nor bad. It is a process that can convey almost any possible message or meaning imaginable, positive or negative, verbal or non-verbal, facilitative or violating. It is not itself beyond discourse. It involves both 'din' and 'silence'. Indeed it cannot be emphasized too strongly that silence, gendered silence, is part of communication (Harlow et al., 1995).

We examine here some of the connections between communication and violation at work, with particular emphasis on gender relations. The idea that communication can somehow be gender neutral is widespread but generally flawed. Communication in organizations, including communication which forms part of violations such as harassment, bullying and even physical violence, is usually gendered, sometimes overwhelmingly so, often through men's power. Whilst the focus on gender relations is necessary and urgent, gender does not operate in isolation from other social divisions and differences. It is never present in 'pure' form, but mediates and is mediated by other divisions and differences, such as age, class and ethnicity.

There are many ways in which violation and communication at work interconnect with gender relations. We continue in the next section with a discussion on silence and din. Next, we examine how violations, gendered violations, can be understood as forms of communication and how the social processes of harassment, bullying and physical violence are subject to complex processes of recognition and communication as violations. Third, the processes and practices of organization violations are reviewed. Finally, contemporary social changes in communication, gender and violation are examined, with special attention to globalization, multinational corporations (MNCs) and information and communication technologies (ICTs).

## Overview and Implications of Current Research

### Communication, Silence and Din

Gendered communication can involve both din and silence, both literally and metaphorically (Harlow et al., 1995; Hearn and Parkin, 2001). Gendered communication proceeds partly in and through the *presence* of words, symbols and noise – din – and partly in and through their *absence* – silence: '(s)ilence might mean the absence of noise but it can at the same time be full of significantly meaningful content' (Harlow et al., 1995, p. 91). Dins and silences operate at several communication levels of: broadly, macro, meso and micro. They include gendered domains of organizations, gendered organizational structures, and gendered interactions and constructions of the individual subject.

Silence as a form of communication can indicate both *power* and/or *powerlessness* (Hearn, 2004). It can represent the silence of the relatively *powerful*: he, or occasionally she, who does need to speak to justify their actions or who does not need, or does not think they need, to give feedback – the authoritarian manager, chairperson or main shareholder. It can also represent the relative *powerlessness* of those who are subjugated in silence, such as those who do not dare to speak for fear of further isolation, threat, violation or expulsion from organizations or management. This can be a common form of silence, especially in the uncertainties of the gender restructurings of the 'flexible economy' (Lavikka, 2004). More generally, organizations can be thought of as arenas or keepers of different kinds of silence, in protecting their interests as collective actors, maintaining business secrets, and so on.

Organizations sometimes also bring people together *to silence them*. In the most extreme case this can be to eliminate them (Harlow et al., 1995, p. 95). There is now a considerable literature on the organization of the holocaust as a metaphor of modern organization (Bauman, 1989; Burrell, 1999; Hearn and Parkin, 2001). 'To silence' can indeed be a euphemism for 'to put to death'. These actions have historically been perpetrated overwhelmingly by men; they are terrifyingly gendered.

A more common form of organizational silencing is simply through exclusion: those outside are silent and silenced through their absence. These silenced ones need much more study, whether they are not allowed in in the first place (as when organizations are men-only), are marginalized (as with those in temporary or casualized employment) or leave of their own decision (for 'push' or 'pull' reasons) (Husu, 2001).

Silence can also mean the silence of unresolved tensions, arguments or resentments. For example, a management group may meet with 'everyone knowing about x' but colluding in not talking about it. Groupthink, where group members in seeking to achieve unanimous agreement fail to consider realistic alternative courses of action, can hide many gendered 'elephants in the room'. Alternatively, silence may suggest *peace and harmony*, as when work in a workgroup or team is proceeding so well that words are not needed. The idea of 'flow' that takes place in intense work concentration may be resonant here (Csikszentmihalyi, 1990).

And then there are *new* forms of silence – if someone does not speak to you in the corridor or in a meeting, you usually have a good idea of what is happening and whether it is important. In some organizations this (that is, not speaking) is indeed quite normal. On the other hand, if you not do hear from someone by email, you do not know what is happening; again such virtual non-communications can be clearly gendered. Silence within virtuality is problematic, and is becoming an increasingly important issue in virtual organizing and managing.

*Sexual Harassment, Bullying and Physical Violence*

We now look at sexual harassment, bullying and physical violence – three phenomena that are usually considered as separate forms of violation of the person. All three are violations through or of communication, and all can be considered as forms of communication.

Of these three, sexual harassment is the most obviously gendered, though none can be understood outside gendered power relations. It is recognized that definitions of what constitutes harassment include how the behaviour is perceived and received by the individual; it is harassment if it is felt to be such by the recipient. Rubenstein defines it as 'unwanted conduct of a sexual nature or conduct based on sex which is offensive to the recipient' (1992, p. 2). Sexual harassment has long been understood as a function of male power (MacKinnon, 1979). Sexual harassment communicates a lack of respect for the integrity, the gender and sexual integrity, of the violated person. It also communicates sexist, often heterosexist, and oppressive practice, attitudes and values, and may often, but not always, be a part of a wider communicative gendered 'community' or 'culture' with similar practices, attitudes and values in and around the workplace concerned (Hearn and Parkin, 1995). Quine (1999) suggests that:

> most definitions of workplace bullying share three elements that are influenced by case law definitions in the related areas of racial and sexual harassment. First, bullying is defined in terms of its effect on the recipient not the intention of the bully; thus it is subject to variations in personal perception. Second, there must be a negative effect on the victim. Third, the bullying behaviour must be persistent. (p. 229)

Field (1996, pp. 41–46) lists six pages of bullying behaviours. Bullying communicates disrespect for others in the organization; it shows a preference for *power over* and oppression rather than *power with*, empowerment and more equal relations. It is hierarchical and anti-democratic in perspective.

The gendered nature of bullying may often not be as apparent as it is for sexual harassment and some sources. Cardy (1992) and Field (2005) deny that gendering is an issue in bullying, as women as well as men bully. It is also the case that women are more likely to report incidences of bullying. Men can find it difficult to report bullying, as this may communicate messages of inadequacy and shame, so bullying becomes something to be hidden. Bullying is typically individualized, even though bullying cultures are recognized. Bullying, though not obviously gendered, arises in the context of organizational cultures that are clearly gendered (Gregory and Lees, 1999). There can be a fine line between managers taking a 'strong managerial line' and bullying (Andrea Adams Trust, n.d.). Corporate pride in strong management including bullying can be part of company culture emphasizing high levels of productivity. Bullying thrives where it is common behaviour across management hierarchies, especially in highly competitive environments where individuals regularly use bullying to motivate staff. It may thus become seen as natural and increasingly taken for granted. The theme of management failure to act or management participation remains central.

Physical violence can range from high-profile violence, such as school shootings and armed robbery, to assaults on professionals in the course of their duties. It often has its own policies and practices to deal with it, sometimes set within a health and safety framework. It can attract wide sympathetic publicity compared with bullying and harassment and its victims are more likely to be identified as crime victims than organizational members. Physical violence communicates the valuing of force and coercion, especially bodily force and coercion, over other modes of communication, including discussion, dialogue and negotiation. It reproduces hierarchy and oppression over more equal relations.

The predominant discourse around physical violence focuses on violence by employees or users rather than managers or external agents (for example Poyner and Warne, 1986). This deflects attention from other organizational violations, including bullying and harassment and the effects of working in harmful environments. According to the International Labour Organization, 1.1 million people, including 12,000 children, are killed at work every year. Developing countries have especially high figures, with the death rate in the construction industry over 10 times that in industrialized countries. International Labour Organization (ILO) estimates suggest 160 million people develop occupational diseases and 250 million suffer workplace injuries every year (Chappell and Di Martino, 2000).

*The Recognition of Harassment, Bullying and Physical Violence as Complex Processes of Communication*

Many recognition struggles have been characterized by the formation of collective groupings of those in similar situations, which in turn opens up communication and leads to the possibility of change through political processes. With harassment, this has been difficult: it often occurs in isolation and despite women speaking out, going to tribunals, press coverage, preventive organizational policies, it remains a feature of many organizations. Sexual harassment, and communication on it has been recognized on organizational agendas since the mid-1970s, though the problem clearly has a much longer history. In recent decades, there has been growing dialogue on the issue. What is less known is how many women are prevented from communicating this violation and dare not speak out. As there have been successful cases taken to tribunals and courts, it could be assumed that this further opens up communication on harassment with more possibility of redress. However, a deterrent to speaking out is the knowledge that in some cases the people who would be the first line of communication for a complaint are the perpetrators themselves, who often hold powerful positions in the hierarchy (Hearn and Parkin, 2001, pp. 53–4).

The processes of harassment, bullying and physical violence have appeared on organizational agendas at different historical times, with physical violence being the most recent. While bullying has been long recognized as a problem in schools, it has only recently been recognized as a feature of adult organizations, with increasing reports of bullying there. The recognition of bullying and physical violence has been through various channels, such as media reports, trade union campaigns, tribunals, personal experience reported through websites, for example, Bully Online (www.bullyonline.org) (TUC, 1998a, 1998b, 1999).

All three processes are generally individualized in the sense that each has its own discourse with its own forms of communication, policies and practices. This makes it difficult to see the connections and facilitate communication between them. A way of opening communication is to perceive them all as violations of the person, whether through physical attack or the ongoing traumatic effects of bullying and harassment. Accordingly, the concept of 'organization violations' encapsulates all these forms of violence to, and violation of, the person. In indicating that each form of 'violence' violates and damages the person, the concept of organization violation contradicts any presumed linearity.

It would be too simple to suggest that harassment, bullying and physical violence are 'failures in communication'. The process of the recognition of harassment, bullying and violence is complex and communicated at different levels at different times. To see them as failures of communication simplifies complex power issues which prevent people from speaking out. We see them as part of the male domination of organizations.

There are at least five ways in which this male domination operates (Hearn and Parkin, 2004). First, there is the perpetration of sexual harassment, bullying and physical violence by men, individually, in groups, or more collectively. Second, we can point to male domination in the nature of men's reactions to sexual harassment, bullying and physical violence, whether formally in policies, or more informally in terms of collusion, avoidance or other responses. Third is the dominant male presence throughout organizations and their hierarchies, such as business, governments, the police, the judiciary, the church, armed forces, and so on.

Fourth, there are many organizations and professions seen as predominantly female that still have male management either directly or at a distance. Moreover, just because an organization is not obviously male dominated does not mean that men's power is not being exercised. There are clear gendered hierarchies of occupations, professions and whole or parts of organizations, such as doctors over nurses, lawyers over social workers, and so on. These are relevant to both the contextualization and practice of harassment, bullying and physical violence, facilitating some forms of behaviour and constraining others.

Fifth, and more subtly, there are powerful assumptions about what constitutes management with the emphasis on 'strong', 'macho' environments still being seen as desirable (Collinson, 1988; Einarsen and Raknes, 1997). Whatever the gender, such a culture of management is imposed on personnel regardless of their gender, but with women having to comply in order to progress and men having to comply to avoid being seen as 'soft' or 'feminine'.

Additionally, some men's reluctance to complain about bullying can be perceived as their unwillingness to present other than a so-called 'macho' coping image. Some men accept the 'all's fair in business' culture so much that they suppress their reactions and refuse to label negative experiences as bullying or violation in case it is seen as a sign of weakness (Wright and Smye, 1997). On the other hand, there can be 'weak' management and leadership regimes where harassment, bullying and even physical violence may not be intervened against (Einarsen et al., 1994). As Brodsky (1976, p. 83, cited in Salin, 2003) noted, 'for harassment to occur, harassment elements must exist within a culture that permits and rewards harassment.' Accordingly, Salin (2003, pp. 1220-21) suggests that:

> If there is no policy against bullying, no monitoring policy, and no punishments for those who engage in bullying, it might be interpreted as if the organization accepts it, and a possible perpetrator will perceive the costs and dangers of bullying as very low.

## *The Processes and Practices of Organization Violations*

Processes of communication are important not only in the recognition of violence and violations, but also in the development and enactment of those violences and violations. In this way organizational communication and organization violations, both intensely gendered, are intimately interconnected with broader organizational macro-locations, meso-structures and micro-processes. Macro-organizational domains and orientations, and meso-patterns of organizational structure and function are very significant in providing the main contours of organizational life, but they do not necessarily determine the local complexities of communications and violations within organizations and workplaces. To do this involves attending to micro-processes of organizational communication and organization violations.

Organizational processes of communication are immensely important in considering organization violations, and especially their temporal aspects. Organizations can be understood as social processes, as sites of organizing and as accumulations of organizational practices and communication, rather than as fixed organizational structures. Such social communicative processes include small group interaction processes, management styles of control, flows of information and the reproduction of organizational cultures over time. These communicative processes may contribute to, or undermine, the formal goals and tasks of workplaces and other organizations.

There are complex links between these levels of analysis, such as between organizational structures, policies, occupational constructions of violence/violation, relations with those who have been violent, and organizational communication processes and practices. It is likely that the greater the violence/violation, and the more immediate the contact with violence/violation, the greater the likely range of communicative and coping strategies used by staff. This often entails stress and anxiety for the violent and the violated, for managers, staff and service users (Hearn and Parkin, 2001).

Another kind of interconnection is between violence by organizations, violence in organizations and organizational responses to violence. While conceptually distinct, in practice, these may be simultaneous and overlapping. Organizational responses to violence may be part of organizational goals, including the extent to which restraint is used. Furthermore, all these aspects of the relations of organizations and violations may be contested. This is most easily seen in contestation around communication on, and talking about, violence and violation, for indeed talking about violence and violation may be a means of further violation.

Interconnections also occur in the form that organizations take and the kinds of organizational worlds created. For example, within whole institutions, the interrelations of coercion, violence, abuse and confinement, and thus communication patterns, are important (Johnson, 1986). Such organizations are frequently, perhaps characteristically, bound in a profound paradox whereby they are separated from the rest of society for specific purposes and yet that separation creates the conditions for other purposes, and indeed counter patterns of communication, to be pursued there. This may mean that societal or official purposes of violence may be subverted, or official purposes of non-violence may be subverted so that violence is enacted. These issues are especially significant where the residents are not there voluntarily. Such organizational arrangements are often clearly gendered, as when institutions are single-sex or strictly segregated on gender lines.

In these and other ways, organizations are engaged in processes of reproducing, contesting, constructing and defining violence and violation. These practices and processes apply to violence/violation by organizations, violence/violation in organizations, and organizational responses to violence/violation. All three aspects are in part cultural constructions and contribute to the cultural construction of violence/violation. Such cultural constructions of violence/violation contribute to the reproduction of masculinities and femininities in organizations and elsewhere. For example, masculinity may be defined through the performance of violence, the potential for violence, the emulation of others' violence, the denial of violence, or even sometimes opposition to violence and violation.

Gendered managerial and organizational processes have various effects on the reproduction and construction of gendered violence and violation. These include the detrimental effects on employees of management control systems (Leidner, 1993) in 'dangerous working environments' (Jermier et al., 1989) and with particular technologies (Zuboff, 1989). Management's power and control, characteristically gendered, can often be reconceptualized as violence/violation or tending to increase violence/violation. While managerial control and motivation systems might not be intended to generate directly harmful or violating effects, they may contribute to organizational cultures that in turn increase tensions, vulnerabilities and intentionally harmful behaviours in the workplace. Wright and Smye (1996) have identified three kinds of corporate abuse: extremely competitive, 'win/lose' corporate cultures, in which people strive against their colleagues rather than with them; blaming cultures, in which people are frightened to step out of line; and sacrifice and overwork cultures, which involve people putting their jobs and their work above their personal and social lives and well-being to the extent that they become ill (Johnson, 1986). Such processes and practices are all gendered and may be exacerbated where there are distinct 'front' and 'back' regions, for example, in restaurants and commercial kitchens.

Micro-violations include labour processes that can be violent/violating or likely to lead to violence/violation. This may be through monotony of work (Appelberg, 1996), the rigidity of organizational hierarchies and task allocation, and work intensification and work pressure. A number of sectors and factors appear to present particular risks of physical violence, such as handling money and/or valuable goods, those in authority, lone workers, providers of care, advice, education and service, and those working with potentially violent people and in 'dangerous work'. These organizational arrangements are also often gendered. The local organizational construction of time and space can have specific implications for productions of violence. Similar effects may result from increasing pressures on employees to work longer hours as part of the '24-hour-a-day economy'. Late night opening of retail outlets can render employees, especially women workers, vulnerable to intentionally harmful behaviour, as with robberies and sexual attack. Lone workers, such as taxi drivers, who are often but not always men, often ethnic minority men, may be vulnerable to violence and attack (Cardy, 1992; Hearn and Parkin, 2001; Poyner and Warne, 1988; Woods et al., 1993).

Specific factors that may increase violation include restructuring crises and other organizational changes (Salin, 2003). Such organizational changes include customer care initiatives, work intensification, subcontracting and internal markets, quality initiatives, business process re-engineering, technological innovations, restructuring and downsizing, surveillance and new forms of managerial control. Organizational crisis, work stress, strong internal competition and time pressures may be associated with bullying, the search for scapegoats and other violations (Einarsen et al., 1994; Vartia, 1996). Teamworking can generate conflict between co-workers where intense pressure to meet deadlines leads to aggression towards employees who have difficulty complying with required production levels, especially where increased work pressures impinge on group cohesion (Klein, 1996).

Micro-communications may be intensely patriarchal in form, with particular groups of men routinely producing violations, for example, through the perpetuation of men's dominant cultures in organizations. The form of violent/violating, usually but not necessarily masculine, organizational cultures that reproduce violent, bullying, harassing and conflictual behaviours and experiences is crucial here (Parkin and Maddock, 1994). Organizational responses to violence are also significant in this respect. Inadequate managerial responses to sexual harassment can reinforce rather than resolve claims of sexual harassment (Collinson and Collinson, 1996), and may be related to the gender profile of management (Collinson and Hearn, 1996).

Patriarchal organizational violations interlink closely with other micro-cultural and ethnic violations involving local organizational exclusions of 'outsiders'. 'Motivating factors' (Salin, 2003) towards violation include the nature of the reward system and expected benefits, the presence of very high or very low performing colleagues or subordinates, as well as changes in workgroups leading to dominant subgroups resisting them. Violence may also follow perceived injustice (for either subordinate or dominant groups) within or from organizations (Folger and Baron, 1996).

The details of how violation episodes develop over time, and how organizational life is lived and experienced by organizational members in relation to violence remains a key research area. The qualitative dynamics of such organizational situations may develop over long time periods and take complex forms. Leymann (1992) has looked at the developmental processes of bullying episodes in workplaces and how they often move through various stages: from conflicts and unethical communication, targeting of individuals by psychological violence, violating responses by personnel staff, to expulsion. Standing and Nicolini's (1997) work on scenarios is valuable in distinguishing different kinds of relationships between participants. Gwartney-Gibbs and Lach (1994) have examined gender and workplace disputes, stressing the gendered origins, processes and outcomes of such disputes; in each phase they emphasize the importance of the patterning of gender roles, sex segregation in jobs, and institutionalized work structures.

In the most extreme form, a small number of sacked employees, virtually always men and particularly in the United States, have responded by shooting their superiors and/or colleagues. Violence may also be targeted against oneself, as in drug abuse. Where usually gendered workplace cultures are characterized by heavy drinking and/or intense competition between employees within or between organizations, violence is more likely to occur (Bennett and Lehman, 1996). Heavy drinking can occur as a means of workers dealing with feelings of intense conflict, guilt or shame (Johnson, 1986, p. 196) – in extreme cases in the military, death camps and other organizations specializing in violence.

Organizations provide huge social and communicative resources for the reproduction of mundane violation processes and individual psychologies of violation. These include processes of rationalization, distancing, following organizational 'role' authority, trivialization and humour. Bomber pilots and crew may adopt trivializing, casual, ironic and supposedly humorous language, such as 'There goes the cookie', in continuing their bombing without too much direct thought for the impact of their bombs (Johnson, 1986; Smith, 1993). This is an extreme case of routines of organizational defence found in more peaceful organizations (Menzies, 1960).

*Contemporary Social Change in Communication, Gender and Violation*

It is important to address some broad organizational changes bearing on the changing relations of communication, gender and violation. We briefly consider three such interconnected elements: globalization (or glocalization), MNCs, and ICTs.

There is huge contemporary interest in globalization. However, globalization is not new: it has been part of the world story since the beginnings of exploration. The contemporary era has brought intensification, with the advancement of technologies of transport, communication, refrigeration, mass production, information, and media. Through these social and technical processes, place and space have new meanings. Indeed Waters (1995, p. 3) defines globalization as a 'social process in which the constraints of geography on social and cultural arrangements recede and in which people become increasingly aware that they are receding'.

Most globalization literature has been ungendered, presented as 'gender neutral', reproducing an implicit male narrative, let alone making explicit gendered violation. There is a strong need to gender globalization, as there are many gendered aspects of that process, such as patterns of migration, global symbolic systems, and male-dominated transnational polities and governances. In many such processes, it is particular groups of men who are the main purveyors of power (Hearn, 1996). Sexuality is also strongly affected by global change, through trafficking in women, global pornography, computer sex and technological developments in computer imaging. Another example is the link between the European and US imperialism and militarism, mass prostitution and sex tourism in South East Asia (Enloe, 1983).

Many of the social relations within globalization narratives involve violence and violation. Global political economic developments and connections are not 'without' violence and violation; they may involve slavery, indentured labour, child labour, trafficked labour, and other exploitative practices and human rights violations. Many legitimate global economic institutional arrangements depend for their reproduction on violence and violation. These violations may be institutionally embedded in the exploitative economic and political arrangements between those with very unequal power, whether nations, companies, owners, employers or workers. Sometimes this is a matter of the specific and persistent use of physical and other violences by those with the power to do so 'legitimately', that is, with few repercussions for them.

Within globalizing processes, the dominance of local and national bureaucracies and nation-states are problematized by the growth of transnational corporations, as part of powerful globalizing processes. The nation-state is no longer necessarily the most important political economic unit. MNCs constitute collective social actors that may transcend the nation, being in some cases larger than individual nations. The gross national product (GNP) of some nation-states is exceeded by the assets of many supranational corporations (Bauman, 1995, p. 152). Five hundred companies now control 42 per cent of the world's wealth. Furthermore, 'The world's 500 largest industrial corporations, which employ only five hundredths of 1 per cent of the world's population, control 25 per cent of the world's economic output' (Korten, 1998, p. 4). Of the 100 largest economies, half are corporations, half are countries.

The ten biggest companies turn over more money than the 100 smallest countries. The top ten companies account for 11.7 per cent of the total revenues of the top 500, 15 per cent of profits, and 13.6 per cent of employment. Multinational corporations not only have economic effects on national economies via investment strategies, stock markets, market development and management methods, they also have socio-cultural effects on gendered practices and wider gender relations.

The size, concentration of wealth and associated power of some MNCs means they are able to marshal huge resources transcending national borders and legal controls. Contemporary MNCs have had a special place in the organization of violence, cutting across the lines and responsibilities of nation-states and sometimes leading to large-scale destruction of human and natural environments. Their violating effects can be obscured through the complexity of their corporate organization, including subcontracting to local companies for the performance of direct organization violations. In some cases, these lead to major campaigns, for example, that against alleged environmental and human rights violations by Union Oil Company of California (Unocal). This includes: 'ecocide, environmental devastation', 'unfair and unethical treatment of workers', 'aiding the oppression of women', 'aiding oppression of homosexuals', 'enslavement and forced labour', 'forced relocation of Burmese villages and villagers', 'killings, torture and rape', 'complicity in gradual cultural genocide of tribal and indigenous peoples', 'usurpation of political power', and 'deception of the courts, shareholders and the public'. Some of these allegations stem from close business ties with the Burma and Taliban military regimes, with their own human rights violations (Benson, 1999).

On the other hand, MNCs are not necessarily violent. There is growing debate on not just 'ethical investment', but 'ethical global corporations'. Some MNCs have produced positive corporate policies against violence. The third annual Work to End Domestic Violence Day, October 1, 1998, involved the participation of hundreds of US businesses and other organizations. Such initiatives intersect with growing awareness of business, working life and other economic costs of violence (de Vylder, 2004; NOW Legal Defense and Education Fund, 1996; Yodanis and Godenzi, 2000).

ICTs are of growing importance, economically and materially. ICTs involve the use of multiple complex technologies. Such technologies are not just texts, but exist within and create material social relations. They are ever-changing and expanding, becoming cheaper and more widespread, though still beyond the reach of many. They contribute to major change in the form and process of organizational communication. ICTs raise complex issues around control and communication, with potential for both decentralized temporary autonomous zones, and centralization and surveillance. ICTs can be both 'free-space', unfettered by moral codes, and the social arena most subject to surveillance yet (Shields, 1996).

The use and misuse of communication via email and the Internet, by both employees and management, are matters of growing legal, policy and social concern for MNCs, in terms of company time and resources, sexual, racial or other offences, such as pornography use, and cyberliability. Derogatory remarks can lead to suing from individuals or companies. In May 1998, the US Justice Department anti-trust lawsuit filed against Microsoft involved emails from Bill Gates and others as crucial evidence of attempts to exclude Netscape from the market: 'Screw Sun ... Let's move on and steal the Java language' (Kehoe, 1998). Companies have disciplined or sacked employees for sexist and racist email use, have been sued by workers for allowing harassing workplaces, and are increasingly carrying out surveillance of email and Internet use.

The extension of global technologies of 'communication' can also be seen through the eyes of violation. Global models of persons, images and cultural artefacts can constitute violation to local symbols and meanings. They are not innocent; they may comprise cultural violence and violation. ICTs are not only gendered, they are also structured or have meaning in terms of sexuality or violence. The Internet, initially developed in the military, universities, hospitals, government and business, is now a major site for changing forms of sexuality, violence and sexual violence. ICTs provide major communication channels for sexuality and violence, as in the sex trade. They can be used to form communities of users either for or against particular forms of sexuality and violence. The Internet and ICTs can be and are used for the delivery of sexuality, sexual performance, sexualized violence, violence and violation, as in the promotion of racist hatred and racial violence, or opposition to them as in the formation of anti-bullying networks. More novel is the production of both blatantly sexist and increasingly ambiguous sexual messages in advertising, their diffusion through the Internet and multimedia, and easy availability globally. Increasingly complex intersections of local and global sexual meanings occur in 'glocalized sexualization'.

## Conclusions and Recommendations

Communication is not gender neutral, and nor is it separate from violation. In this chapter we have sought to show some of the key connections between gender, communication and violation at work – harassment, bullying and physical violence, in both macro-structures and more mundane violating practices and processes. A central theme throughout has been the persistence of gendered hierarchical and managerial power. As men still dominate management, their opportunities to exercise power in negative, violating ways are greater than those of women, as is their ability to silence complaints. Some women are accessing higher positions, bringing opportunities to exercise power negatively, as suggested in some bullying surveys. Powerful male cultures may lead to difficulties for women (Collinson and Hearn, 1996; French, 1995). The masculinization of workplaces sets the norms by which women who seek to join must behave, as reflected in the phrase 'becoming one of the boys' (Wajcman, 1998). This may be necessary to survive in an environment where the greatest insult to a man would be to be seen in any way 'soft' or 'like a woman'. For men, to point the finger at women who bully can divert attention from their responsibilities and masculinist environments.

Moreover, there are major contemporary changes in workplaces. Often defined in terms of a fixed place, work organizations have become increasingly diffuse in time and space, as they have expanded and changed in character. This involves complex patterns of communication and probably increasing difficulties in creating violation-free organizations, a project which, in the face of all this, may seem idealistic and utopian. Nevertheless, we see the creation of violation-free organizations as a necessary state to work towards long term.

The phenomenon of communication and the huge variety of forms of communication in and around organizations are not intrinsically benevolent or beneficent. Developing policies on communication and practices of communication that reduce and abolish forms of violation is the main challenge and our main recommendation. This is part of the development of more equal gendered communication between and among genders.

Recognizing that communication is not beyond discourse and not outside violation, but rather integrally gendered and power laden, particularly as exercised by men in organizations, is a way of starting to work towards more violation-free organizations.

## References

Andrea Adams Trust Factsheet (n.d.), *Workplace Bullying*. Hove: Andrea Adams Trust.

Appelberg, K. (1996), *Interpersonal Conflicts at Work: Impact on Health Behavior, Psychiatric Morbidity and Work Disability*. Helsinki: Finnish Institute of Occupational Health.

Bauman, Z. (1989), *Modernity and the Holocaust*. Cambridge: Polity: Oxford: Blackwell.

Bauman, Z. (1995), 'Searching for a centre that holds', in M. Featherstone, S. Lash and R. Robertson, R. (eds), *Global Modernities*. London: Sage. pp. 140–54.

Bennett J. B. and Lehman, W. E. K. (1996), 'Alcohol, antagonism, and witnessing violence in the workplace: Drinking climates and social alienation–integration', in G. R. VandenBos and E. Q. Bulatao (eds), *Violence on the Job: Identifying Risks and Developing Solutions*. Washington, DC: American Psychological Association. pp. 105–52.

Benson, R. W. (1999), *Challenging Corporate Rule*. New York: Apex Press.

Burrell, G. (1999), 'Normal science, paradigms, metaphors, discourses and genealogies of analysis', in S. R. Clegg and C. Hardy (eds), *Studying Organizations: Theory and Method*. London: Sage. pp. 388–404.

Cardy, C. (1992 ), *Training for Personal Safety at Work*. Aldershot: Gower.

Chappell, D. and Di Martino, V. (2000), *Violence at Work*. Geneva: International Labour Office.

Collinson, D. L. (1998), ' "Engineering humour": Masculinity, joking and conflict in shopfloor relations', *Organization Studies*, **9**(2): 181–99.

Collinson, D. L. and Hearn, J. (eds) (1996), *Men as Managers, Managers as Men: Critical Perspectives on Men, Masculinities and Managements*. London: Sage.

Collinson, M. and Collinson, D. L. (1996), '"It's only Dick ...": The sexual harassment of women managers in insurance sales', *Work, Employment and Society*, **10**(1): 29–56.

Crookall, D. and Saunders, D. (1989), 'Towards an integration of communication and simulation', in D. Crookall and D. Saunders (eds), *Communication and Simulation: From Two Fields to One Theme*. Clevedon: Multilingual Matters. pp. 3–29.

Csikszentmihalyi, M. (1990), *Flow: The Psychology of Optimal Experience*. New York: Harper and Row.

de Vylder, S. (2004), 'Costs of male violence', in H. Ferguson, J. Hearn, Ø. G. Holter, L. Jalmert, M. Immel, J. Lang, R. Morrell (eds), *Ending Gender-based Violence: A Call for Global Action to Involve Men*. Stockholm: Swedish International Development Cooperation Agency (SIDA). pp. 62–125. Retrieved February 7, 2005 from www.sida.se/content/1/c6/02/47/27/SVI34602.pdf.

Einarsen, S. and Raknes, B. I. (1997), 'Harassment in the workplace and the victimization of men', *Violence and Victims*, **12**: 247–63.

Einarsen, S., Raknes, B. I. and Mathieson, S. B. (1994), 'Bullying and harassment at work and their relationships to work environment quality: An exploratory study', *European Work and Organizational Psychologist*, **4**(4): 381–401.

Enloe, C. (1983), *Does Khaki Become You? The Militarization of Women's Lives*, Boston, MA: South End Press; London: Pluto.

Field, T. (1996), *Bully in Sight: How to Predict, Resist, Challenge and Combat Workplace Bullying*. Didcot: Success Unlimited.

Field, T. (2005), *Bullying at Work: Those Who Can, Do. Those Who Can't, Bully*. Retrieved 19 December, 2005 from www.bullyonline.org/workbully/faq.htm.

Folger, R. and Baron, R. A. (1996), 'Violence and hostility at work: A model of reactions to perceived injustice', in G. R. VandenBos and E. Q. Bulatao (eds), *Violence on the Job: Identifying Risks and Developing Solutions*. Washington, DC: American Psychological Association. pp. 51–81.

French, K. (1995), 'Men and locations of power: Why move over?', in C. Itzin and J. Newman (eds), *Gender, Culture and Organizational Change: Putting Theory into Practice*. London and New York: Routledge. pp. 54–67.

Gregory, J. and Lees, S. (1999), *Policing Sexual Assault*. London and New York: Routledge.

Gwartney-Gibbs, P. A. and Lach, D. H. (1994), 'Gender and workplace dispute resolution: A conceptual and theoretical model', *Law and Society Review*, **23**(1): 265–96.

Harlow, E., Hearn, J. and Parkin, W. (1995), 'Gendered noise: Organizations and the silence and din of domination', in C. Itzin and J. Newman (eds), *Gender, Culture and Organizational Change*. London: Routledge. pp. 89–105.

Hearn, J. (1996), 'Deconstructing the dominant: Making the one(s) the other(s)', *Organization*, 3(4): 611–26.

Hearn, J. (2004), ' "Silence is golden": Silences and sciences in organisations and management', *Ekonomiska Samfundets Tidskrift*, 56(1–2): 63–70.

Hearn, J. and Parkin, W. (1995), *'Sex' at 'Work': The Power and Paradox of Organization Sexuality*, rev. edn. Hemel Hempstead: Prentice Hall/Harvester Wheatsheaf.

Hearn, J. and Parkin, W. (2001), *Gender, Sexuality and Violence in Organizations: The Unspoken Forces of Organization Violations*. London and Thousand Oaks, CA: Sage.

Hearn, J. and Parkin, W. (2004), 'Recognizing sexual harassment, bullying and violence at work: The move to organization violations', in J. Gruber and P. Morgan (eds), *In the Company of Men: Male Domination and Sexual Harassment*. Ithaca, NY: Northeastern University Press. pp. 92–116.

Husu, L. (2001), *Sexism, Support and Survival in Academia*. Helsinki: Social Psychological Studies, University of Helsinki.

Jermier, J. M., Gaines, J. and McIntosh, N. J. (1989), 'Reactions to physically dangerous work: A conceptual and empirical analysis', *Journal of Organizational Behavior*, 10: 15–33.

Johnson, R. (1986), 'Institutions and the promotion of violence', in A. Campbell and J. J. Gibbs (eds), *Violent Transactions*, Oxford: Blackwell. pp. 181–205.

Kehoe, L. (1998), 'Think before you send that e-mail', *Financial Times*, 'Weekend', May 30/31: 7.

Klein, S. (1996), 'A longitudinal study of the impact of work pressures on group cohesive behaviors', *International Journal of Management*, 13(1): 68–75.

Korten, D. (1998), *Taming the giants*. Retrieved February 7, 2005 from http://www.geocities.com/RainForest/3621/KORTEN.HTM.

Lavikka, R. (2004), 'Fulfillment or slavery? The changing sense of self at work', in T. Heiskanen and J. Hearn (eds), *Information Society and the Workplace*. London: Routledge. pp. 143–77.

Leidner, R. (1993), *Fast Food, Fast Talk: Service Work and the Routinization of Everyday Life*. Berkeley, CA: University of California Press.

Leymann, H. (1992), *Från mobbning till utslagning i arbetslivet* (From bullying to expulsion from work life). Stockholm: Publica.

MacKinnon, C. A. (1979), *The Sexual Harassment of Working Women*. New Haven, CT: Yale University Press.

Menzies, I. E. P. (1960), 'A case study in the functioning of social systems as a defense against anxiety: A report of a study of the nursing service of a general hospital', *Human Relations*, 13(2): 95–121.

NOW Legal Defense and Education Fund (1996), *The Impact of Violence in the Lives of Working Women: Creating Solutions – Creating Change*. New York: NOW Legal Defense and Education Fund.

Parkin, D. and Maddock, S. (1994), 'A gender typology of organizational culture', in C. Itzin and J. Newman (eds), *Gender and Organizational Change: Putting Theory into Practice*. London: Routledge. pp. 68–80.

Poyner, B. and Warne, C. (1986), *Violence to Staff: A Basis for Assessment and Prevention*. London: Tavistock Institute of Human Relations/Health and Safety Executive.

Poyner, B. and Warne, C. (1988). *Preventing Violence to Staff*. London: Tavistock Institute of Human Relations/Health and Safety Executive.

Quine, L. (1999), 'Workplace bullying in NHS Community Trust: Staff questionnaire survey', *British Medical Journal*, 3(18): January 23: 228–32.

Rubenstein, M. (1992), *Preventing and Remedying Sexual Harassment at Work: A Resource Manual*, 2nd edn. London: Eclipse.

Salin, D. (2003), 'Ways of explaining workplace bullying: A review of enabling, motivating and precipitating structures and processes in the work environment', *Human Relations*, 56(10): 1213–32.

Shields, R. (ed.) (1996), *Cultures of the Internet: Virtual Spaces, Histories, Living Bodies*. London: Sage.

Smith, J. (1993), *Misogynies*. London: Faber and Faber.

Standing, H. and Nicolini, D. (1997), *Review of Workplace-related Violence*, Contract Research Report 143/1997. London: Health and Safety Executive.

TUC (1998a), *Beat Bullying at Work: A Guide for Trade Union Representatives and Personnel Managers*. London: Trades Union Congress.

TUC (1998b), *Bullied at Work? Don't Suffer in Silence: Your Guide to Tackling Workplace Bullying*. London: Trades Union Congress.

TUC (1999), *Violent Times: Preventing Violence at Work*. London: Trades Union Congress.

Vartia, M. (1996), 'The sources of bullying – psychological work environment and organizational climate', *European Journal of Work and Organizational Psychology*, 5(2): 203–14.

Wajcman, J. (1998), *Managing Like a Man: Women and Men in Corporate Management*. Cambridge: Polity.

Waters, M. (1995), *Globalization*. London: Routledge.

Woods, M. and Whitehead, J. with Lamplugh, D. (1993), *Working Alone: Surviving and Thriving*. London: IPM/Pitman.

Wright, L. and Smye, M. (1996), *Corporate Abuse*. New York: Simon and Schuster.

Yodanis, C. and Godenzi, A. (2000), 'Male violence: the economic costs. A methodological review', in *Men and Violence Against Women Seminar 7–8 October 1999: Proceedings*, EG/SEM/VIO (99) 21. Strasbourg: Council of Europe. pp. 117–28.

Zuboff, S. (1989), *In the Age of the Smart Machine*. New York: Basic Books.

# PART III
# Gender and Communication Channels in Special Workplace Environments

## Chapter 9

# Communication Channels and Gender Structures at Work

Catherine W. Ng and Laura Byra

## Introduction

At the beginning of the twenty-first century, a wide variety of communication channels are being used by workers all over the world. Although the conventional face-to-face communication format is still considered to be the most direct and to contain the richest information (Lind, 2001; Rowley, 1999; Spangler, 1995), there has been a surge in the use of other communication channels. Computer-mediated communication (CMC) systems have been studied quite extensively in the past decades with the advent of telecommunication technologies (for example, Kerr and Hiltz, 1982; Mayer, 1999; Riva, 2002; Walters, 1995). More recently, it has been proposed that information systems (IS) also form part of organizational communication (Rice and Gattiker, 2001). CMC and IS together form computer-mediated communication and information systems (CIS), which contain the four components of:

- computing;
- telecommunication networks;
- information or communication resources ranging from databases to communities of potential participants; and
- digitization of contents.

In most organizations today, CISs include communication and information technologies such as personal computers, phones and pagers, facsimiles and data communication networks. The Internet, the World Wide Web (WWW), videoconferencing, computer bulletin boards, email, voicemail and teletext are examples of widely used non-face-to-face communication media.

The increase in the number of communication technologies, systems, media and channels over the past few decades has generated a lot of research interest. The focus of scientific studies is logically on technological developments, while that of sociological studies is on how social attitudes, values, identities and cultures might affect, and might be affected by, CISs (for example, Frissen 1992; Taylor, 1999).

Fewer studies, however, examine how gender relates to the use of communication channels and how the various communication channels, especially CISs, construct gender in organizations. Through an extensive literature review, Rice and Gattiker (2001) illustrate how social structures such as culture and social pressure influence the adoption and implementation of CIS and face-to-face communications, and how the latter influence social structures in organizations, such as power and communication participation. Social structures include structures of meaning, such as norms and perceptions and structures of relations including social networks and social influences. In other words, there is a dialectic relationship between communication means and social structure. In their publication, Rice and Gattiker (2001) make only brief mention of gender and its role in power relations and social structure. In this chapter, we aim to expand on the gender theme and focus on the relationship between communication channels and gendered social structures at work.

## Overview of Current Research

### Gender and Communication Patterns

As evidenced throughout this book, much research has been done on the differences in women and men's communication styles. Both Bernard's 'expressive talk' (1969) and Lakoff's 'request talk' (1975) describe how women are more consensus seeking (rather than high authority) in their communications, and how women's communications put greater emphasis on relationship building and affective responses than on factual information. In 1973, Hirschman (1994) delivered research results on how women and men interact in conversations, showing that 'females tend to talk more about their own experiences and feelings, while males tend to generalize and talk rather abstractly' (p. 434). Gilligan (1982) argues that men speak the language of 'rights, ethic of justice' on the premise of equality (everyone should be treated the same), while women, the language of 'responsibilities, ethic of care' on the premise of non-violence (no one is to be hurt). Tannen (1990) argues that women are more comfortable with 'rapport talk', which seeks to build relationships, while men use 'report talk', which is one of their survival skills. Studies of gender differences in communication styles have led many to believe that women focus on shared feelings and men on shared activities in their communications.

Other researchers (Herrick 1999; Ng, 1998; Walker, 1994), however, have contested these essentialist theories of communication differences based on gender. In a meta-analysis of 25 studies on the effects of gender on managerial communication, Wilkins and Anderson (1991) found no statistically significant differences in women and men's communication behaviours based on current quantitative findings. They did, however, find that self-reports were more likely to show gender differences; that is, individuals were more likely to use gender differences to explain their own behaviour. A study of 114 upper-level university students participating in two electronic boards – one using pseudonyms, one not – found that men's discourse changed more than women's when using a pseudonym (Jaffe et al., 1999). The male participants exhibited more social interdependence and less traditional independence when using pseudonyms. The researchers speculated that social interdependence may be the more basic human style of discourse when the restrictions of social pressure to be masculine are removed.

Walker's 1994 study of 52 women and men of working- and middle-class backgrounds showed similar results. When talking in general terms, both women and men tend to describe their communications with friends according to stereotypical feminine and masculine norms; that is, women reported sharing more intimate details about their lives and emotions than men did. But when asked to describe specific friendships, working-class men recalled having many conversations with their friends about emotions and relationships. Conversely, several middle-class women in the study described having relationships in which they did not share intimate feelings or problems with friends. Walker (1994) concluded that social class is a more significant factor than gender in the degree of intimacy and the extent of feeling sharing in conversations. For both women and men, the middle class have less time to build relationships and are more guarded in sharing feelings than the working class. It seems that even if communication patterns are found to be gendered, the gender difference is largely socially constructed.

Tannen (1994) argues that women's communication patterns contribute to their being less effective in gaining recognition and as negotiators. However, through narratives gathered in an ethnographic study of an organization, and through the stories of two women working in a male-dominated environment, Herrick (1999) convincingly refutes the argument that women's language and speech styles render them powerless because they are 'in a double bind of being perceived as either likeable but weak and ineffective or as unlikeable but competent and professional' (p. 275). She instead shows that communication at work is situated in the wider context of gender-role expectations, employee relations, physical office locations and other micro-practices of everyday organizational life. The study is illuminating.

We argue, similarly, that the relationship between communication channels and gender is mediated by situational specifics. In this chapter, we delve deeper into gender constructions at work, focusing in particular on how women professionals perceive and use different communication channels. This should prove useful in enriching Herrick's (1999) argument, as well as in furthering the shift from a universalistic to a multiplicity paradigm in the study of women's issues (Ng, 1999).

*The Influence of Gender on Communication Channel*

Researchers into managerial use of communication media have found that task characteristics and equivocality of the message have the greatest impact on the choice of communication media (Trevino et al., 1990). Highly equivocal communications, that is, those that involve lots of ambiguity, necessitate a richer communication medium; for example, a performance review or a salary negotiation must be carried out face-to-face and not via email. Individual differences only come into play when equivocality is low. For example, managers can choose to inform their staff of the time and venue for a meeting face-to-face by walking around the office, or through email or in a memo. The choice of medium will be based on the individual manager's personality and preferences. Thus, for tasks that allow a choice of communications media, gender differences may be one of the personal factors that influence communication channel usage.

A common perception is that women exhibit more non-verbal cues in conversation than men do (Spangler, 1995). They are also perceived to pay more attention to non-verbal communication and to be more adept at, and even prefer, face-to-face communications (Mitchell, 2000). This may lead to the assumption that women are less willing to use CIS communication channels and are less skilled in their use. Schumacher and Morahan-Martin (2001), in a study carried out in 1989–90 and a follow-up study in 1997, found higher levels of computer confidence and competence among male university students than among their female counterparts. Male students were more experienced in writing computer programs and in playing computer games and 79 per cent of male students, as opposed to 59 per cent of female students, in the 1997 study, owned a computer. Male students also used the Internet more often. Women have also been found to show more negative attitudes towards new technology. Schottenbauer et al. (2004) found that women had experienced greater Year 2000 (Y2K) anxiety than men. These results support the common perception of women being less skilled in, and more anxious about, the use of computer technology.

However, these gender differences in attitude and competence in using computers, when they exist, may be due to disadvantages women face in acquiring computer skills rather than underlying gender differences in communication style or preference. Acker (1990) and Gutek (1994) argue that typically women predominate in lower-paid clerical jobs; decisions about the implementation of CISs are made mostly by higher-ranking men. Female clerical workers are often not consulted by male managers, who see women workers as women first, workers second. The implementation strategy often results in an increase of the manager's influence and power and a tightening of control on female workers, 'who are perceived (probably incorrectly) as tending toward dependency, passivity, [with] little leadership ability and little mechanical aptitude or interest' (Gutek, 1994, p. 220). Furthermore, it has been found that women tend to receive less training required for skill upgrading than men (Murray, 1994; Pazy, 1994). In other words, differences, if any, found on the use of CIS and face-to-face communications among women and men might be less related to gender, but more to gender stereotypes and unequal job and training opportunities.

This hypothesis is supported by Hoxmeier et al.'s (2000) research. They found that gender difference in the level of confidence in using email exists only among less-experienced computer users. Walsh et al. (2000) studied 333 female and male US scientists and found little difference in email use between the two genders. Parry and Wharton's (1994) study, based on a sample of faculty from a mid-sized comprehensive university, also concludes that when the contextual factors of occupational field, training and experience are taken into consideration, gender differences in using CISs disappear. Moreover, some researchers have obtained results that show women favouring CMCs over other forms of communication (Lind, 2001; Walsh et al., 2000). Lind (2001), in a survey of professionals in the telecommunications sector, found that women use email more than men. She speculates that the reason for this might be that women simply have better keyboarding skills. Keyboarding skills are not gender neutral. They have long been considered as 'women's skills', used mostly by clerical and secretarial staff.

## *The Influence of Communication Channel on Gender Construction*

The debate about the impact of gender on the selection and effectiveness of communication channels at work centres around whether gender is an independent variable explaining the communication patterns of women and men. The focus of the debate about the influence of communication channels on gender construction at work, on the other hand, is on social and power relations. This, we feel, is an important discussion, because it has been argued that breaking the glass ceiling (Morrison et al., 1987) has persistently been difficult for women professionals because strategies to overcome sex discrimination at work are more about 'gaining power, not changing it' (Cockburn, 1989, p. 217). Although it is commonly perceived that women are better at face-to-face communication, women who exhibit male body language are judged more harshly than men who exhibit female body language (Spangler, 1995). If this is true, it appears that face-to-face communications, especially non-verbal messages sent and received, are as much a product of social norms as an important tool to shape perceptions of femininity and masculinity.

Furthermore, it has been shown that women and men use email in ways that replicate gender roles and communication style differences in other forms of communication (Boneva et al., 2001). Because of its anonymity, online communication may be more uninhibited. This may in turn lead to more, rather than fewer, gender-based stereotypical comments. A study of a free public electronic networking system in the United States shows that some female users found some remarks posted by male users so offensive that they soon decided to stop participating in the e-forum (Collins-Jarvis, 1993). Herring's (1999) analysis of postings to electronic forums led her to conclude that male users as a group tend toward more adversarial behaviours and female users as a group tend toward more attenuated and supportive behaviours. As a consequence, cyberspace is perceived as more hostile and less hospitable by women than by men, thus discouraging female participation, possibly rendering women more silent in mixed-sex forums and potentially limiting their active participation to women-centred groups. A related issue is online sexual harassment, which also can lead some women to drop out of, or never join, or self-censor (out of fear) e-discussions (Brail, 1996).

Other studies also indicate that CIS communications perpetuated problems women found with other media. Takayoshi (1994) found that women users in academia reported that once they had learned the system it gave them more connections within their profession, but they also faced harassment and problems with accessibility. Women felt that they did not receive adequate support in learning the system and women who did begin using the system received unwanted attention from male users. This may explain why women may have more of a tendency to communicate with other women, even in a computer-mediated environment (Belanger, 1999). On the whole, then, the evidence suggests that both face-to-face and CIS communications are gender construction sites, whereby gender norms are adhered to and reinforced.

However, there are research findings that support the contention that CISs are helping to level the playing field between women and men managers and professionals. Far from putting women at a disadvantage, CISs may help to level barriers women face in the workplace. Several studies show that women have been quick to perceive the benefits of email usage on their careers. For example, the women scientists in Walsh et al.'s (2000) study reported experiencing more positive effects from email use than did men. They reported significantly greater effects for contact with scholars at other institutions and receiving information about grants. The results suggest that email may have the potential to overcome some of the disadvantages that women traditionally experience in scientific communities. Through email, women scientists may become more integrated into scientific communities. They may be able to use electronic communications to both overcome the effect of gendered style difference in communications with men in the workplace and also to build networks with women at other institutions.

In Lind's (2001) study, not only were women more frequent users of email, but they were more satisfied with their access to communication channels when email was provided. Part of women's satisfaction with email may be due to their greater emphasis on consensus and relationship building in general. Women may transfer better skills and greater satisfaction with relationship building over to the new medium. In fact, when both women and men are trained in computer-mediated communication, female-only groups score highest on group development and group satisfaction. Male-only groups show the lowest level of participation (Savicki et al., 2002). Lind (2001) speculates that the 'facelessness' of email may have an equalizing effect on communications between genders. Studies conducted among students and in laboratory settings suggest that in early stages of group development, there is a negative relationship between CIS communications and domination by a few members; in other words, participation is usually less unequal in CIS communications compared to face-to-face communications (Hiltz and Turoff, 1993; Kraemer and Pinsonneault, 1990). This is due, first, to the increased technological ability to enter comments at any time, rather than waiting for a turn to speak; and second, to the decreased influence of the non-verbal cues of an informal loquacious leader on members who might tend to defer to the dominant speaker (Rice, 1984). Thus, email communications seem well suited to a consensus-building, rather than a power-seeking, communication style.

However, Lind (2001) is less positive than Walsh et al. (2000) on the empowering effects of email, questioning if over-reliance on email deprives women of important face-to-face networking opportunities. It should be noted, though, that it has been shown that in face-to-face communications women and men also follow different patterns, possibly to the detriment of women's ability to build a power base. In a study of 55 bank managers, female managers were found to communicate more within their own departments. Women were more likely to communicate one to one, whereas male managers were more likely to communicate in groups of seven to ten people (Macleod et al., 1992). It is therefore not altogether conclusive whether face-to-face or CIS communications are more effective for women in establishing power and influence in work organizations.

## Implications

A review of current research indicates that new communication technologies can be used in ways that are empowering or disempowering to women in the workplace. Situational factors including work setting, type and culture of organization, workers' skill and knowledge of the communications system and proportion of each gender in the workplace affect the way gender may be related to communication media. It seems that when the technology is well supported, CISs do help women professionally, especially in establishing external professional networks. Internally, CISs could just be another communication channel through which the gender construction patterns found in face-to-face communications are replicated. This is particularly true when members of an organization know each other so well that they 'talk' via faceless communication channels just as they do face to face. Organizations need to be sensitive to the problems women experience, especially when they are in the minority in positions of power; problems such as tokenism, sexual harassment, difficulties in being fully recognized and being promoted (Alvesson and Billing, 1997; Kanter, 1977). Women face these problems irrespective of the type of the communication channels used, since gendered power structures remain the same.

However, faceless communication may have more potential to break gender stereotypes than face-to-face communication channels because there is less likelihood of public sanctions of non-stereotypical behaviours in the former type. Some situational factors may also be helpful. For example, when communication goes on via CISs more so than via face-to-face communications and when non-stereotypical behaviours are supported, CISs may serve to deconstruct stereotypes. It seems that whether CISs help equalize gender power depends on how they are implemented in the organization.

An organization aiming to be women-friendly needs to first of all ensure that women are given quality training and support in using CISs. But this is a necessary but not sufficient condition for developing organizational women-friendliness. In addition to women having equal access and attaining proficiency in using CISs, organizations need leaders who are sensitive to gender issues and who take initiatives to break gender stereotypes via all kinds of communication channels used in the workplace. CISs form part of gendered organizational life (Alvesson and Billing, 1997; Mills and Tancred, 1992), and are, therefore, women-friendly only when the organizations using them as channels of communication take active steps to break down stereotypes and traditional gendered power relations.

## Conclusions

The concerns about communication channels as sites of gender construction and power relations need to be further studied. Current research shows that women often lag behind men in acquiring the skills to use CISs. When training and technical support is available, women perceive the advantages of using CISs and are able to use them to their benefit. However, the faceless nature of CISs and the convenience they might offer in group communications have not always encouraged more women to speak up. When power relations in an organization are already established, CISs may be no different from face-to-face communications in maintaining an unequal balance of power. In other words, CISs seem to be as much a site for gender construction as face-to-face communication channels. It appears that whether CIS or face-to-face communications are beneficial to women is situation specific. One direction for further research would be to examine in which organizational contexts CISs are especially beneficial to women.

## Recommendations

### Further Research

All of the research we reviewed on the relationship between communication channels and gender has been conducted in the West. Further research could look at how access to CISs may affect women workers in societies in Asia. For example, in Hong Kong the number of mobile phone subscribers to the total population is 96 per cent. This is the second highest penetration rate in Asia (van der Kamp, 2003). Sixty-eight per cent of Hong Kong households have a personal computer (*HK Magazine*, 2004). Email, voice mail, computers and fax machines are standard equipment in the Hong Kong workplace. Yet Hong Kong remains a fairly gender-stereotypical society. For example, in a survey commissioned by the Equal Opportunities Commission (EOC) to understand the population's gender concepts, it was found that 21.6 per cent of the respondents agreed that daughters should do more housework than sons, and only 18.6 per cent endorsed that women should not have to do housework when they have jobs in the daytime (EOC, 1997). It would be interesting to study whether and in what ways CISs influence gender construction processes at work in Hong Kong, a place that, while technologically advanced and highly computer literate, has entrenched gender stereotypes.

Furthermore, access to 'faceless' communication channels may play a different role in societies with different cultural dimensions (Hofstede, 1994). For example, in less individualistic, higher power-distance societies, self-expression may be a less important factor in workplace satisfaction and power building.

Another area for further research would be the interaction between gender and other diversity factors, such as race, on the impact of communication channels. Hoffman (1985) has found that the increasing race ratio in a group is associated with increasing organizational-level communication but decreasing within-team communication. Tsui and Gutek (1999) agree that increasing the proportion of a racial minority serves to heighten inter-group distinction and to polarize racial differences in an organization. Research could focus on determining under what circumstances gender is a more powerful determinant of communication patterns than race and under what circumstances the reverse is true.

## Organizations

In planning the introduction of new CISs, organizations should consider how changes in communication channels may affect social structures and power relations within the organization. In particular, planning should include a consideration of the training and support necessary for the implementation of CISs at different levels and by staff of different genders, ages and backgrounds.

## Managers

Managers should take the lead to break down gender stereotypes via all kinds of communication channels. They should also reflect on how they and their subordinates use communication channels. Are communication channels appropriate for the content of the messages being sent? Could CISs and other communication channels be used more effectively to include the voices of women and other minorities? Special care should be taken that 'faceless' communication channels do not become sites for harassment.

## Women

Walsh et al. (2000) have discussed how women academics found using CISs beneficial in building external professional networks. Women who are minorities within their own organizations may benefit from the use of CISs to build external contacts within their field. Women may also need to advocate for greater technical support and training in using CISs, or to take outside opportunities to become knowledgeable about their use. CISs such as email not only give women a chance to get their voices heard, but also allow them to keep a record of their contributions or of sensitive communications. As with other communication channels, women must use them strategically to build empowering networks within and outside their organizations.

# References

Acker, Joan (1990), 'Hierarchies, jobs, bodies: A theory of gendered organizations', *Gender and Society*, **4**(2): 139–58.

Alvesson, Mats and Billing, Yvonne D. (1997), *Understanding Gender and Organizations*. London: Sage.

Belanger, France (1999), 'Communication patterns in distributed work groups: A network analysis', *IEEE Transactions on Professional Communication*, **42**(4): 261–75.

Bernard, J. (1969), *The Sex Game*. London: Leslie Frewin.

Boneva, Bonka, Kraut, Robert and Frohlich, David (2001), 'Using e-mail for personal relationships: The difference gender makes', *The American Behavioral Scientist*, **45**(3): 530–50.

Brail, Stephanie (1996), 'The price of admission: Harassment and free speech in the Wild, Wild West', in L. Cherny and E. Weise (eds), *Wired-Women: Gender and New Realities in Cyberspace*. Seattle, WA: Seal. pp. 141–57.

Cockburn, Cynthia (1989), 'Equal opportunities: The short and long agenda', *Industrial Relations Journal*, **20**(3): 213–25.

Collins-Jarvis, Lori A. (1993), 'Gender representation in an electronic city hall: Female adoption of Santa Monica's PEN system', *Journal of Broadcasting and Electronic Media*, **37**(1): 49–65.

EOC (1997), *A Baseline Survey of Equal Opportunities on the Basis of Gender in Hong Kong 1996–1997*. Hong Kong: Equal Opportunities Commission.

Frissen, Valerie (1992), 'Trapped in electronic cages? Gender and new information technologies in the public and private domain: an overview of research', *Media, Culture and Society*, **14**: 31–49.

Gilligan, Carol (1982), *In a Different Voice: Psychological Theory and Women's Development*. Cambridge, MA: Harvard University Press.

Gutek, Barbara A. (1994), 'Clerical work and information technology: Implications of managerial assumptions', in Urs E. Gattiker (ed.), *Technology Innovation and Human Resources Vol. 4: Women and Technology*, Berlin: Walter de Gruyter. pp. 205–26.

Herrick, Jeanne Weiland (1999), '"And then she said": Office stories and what they tell us about gender in the workplace', *Journal of Business and Technical Communication*, **13**(3): 274–96.

Herring, Susan (1999), 'Posting in a different voice: Gender and ethics in computer-mediated communication', in Paul A. Mayer (ed.), *Computer Media and Communication: A Reader*. New York: Oxford University Press. pp. 241–65.

Hiltz, S. R. and Turoff, M. (1993), *The Network Nation: Human Communication via Computer*, 2nd edn. Reading, MA: Addison-Wesley.

Hirschman, L. (1994), 'Female–male differences in conversational interaction', *Language in Society*, **23**: 427–42.

*HK Magazine* (2004), *Numerology: Online Community*, April 16: 6

Hoffman, E. (1985), 'The effect of race ratio composition on the frequency of organizational communication', *Social Psychology Quarterly*, **48**(1): 17–26.

Hofstede, Geert (1994), *Cultures and Organizations*. London: Harper Collins.

Hoxmeier, John A., Nie, Winter and Purvis, G. Thomas (2000), 'The impact of gender and experience on user confidence in electronic mail', *Journal of End User Computing*, **12**(4): 11–20.

Jaffe, J. Michael, Lee, Young-Eum, Huang, Li-Ning and Oshagan, Hayg (1999), 'Gender identification, interdependence and pseudonyms in CMC: language patterns in an electronic conference', *The Information Society*, **12**, 221–34.

Kanter, R. M. (1977), *Men and Women of the Corporation*. New York: Basic Books.

Kerr, Elaine B. and Hiltz, Starr Roxanne (1982), *Computer-Mediated Communication Systems: Status and Evaluation*. New York: Academic Press.

Kraemer, Kenneth L. and Pinsonneault, Alain (1990), 'Technology and Groups: Assessment of the Empirical Research', in J. Galegher, R. Kraut and Egido, C. (eds), *Intellectual Teamwork: Social and Technological Foundations of Cooperative Work*. Hillsdale, NJ: Lawrence Erlbaum Associates. pp. 375–405.

Lakoff, R. (1973), 'Language and women's place', *Language in Society*, **2**: 45–80.

Lind, Mary R. (2001), 'An exploration of communication channel usage by gender', *Work Study*, **50**(6/7): 234–41.

Macleod, Laura, Scriven, Jolene and Wayne, F. Stanford (1992), 'Gender and management level difference in the oral communication patterns of bank managers', *The Journal of Business Communication*, **29**(4): 343–65.

Mayer, Paul A. (ed.) (1999), *Computer Media and Communication: A Reader*. New York: Oxford University Press.

Mills, A. and Tancred, P. (eds) (1992), *Gendering Organizational Analysis*. London: Sage.

Mitchell, Mary Stewart (2000), 'When actions speak louder than words between the sexes', *Law Practice Management*, **26**(5): 57–9.

Morrison, Ann M., White, Randall P., van Velsor, Ellen and the Center for Creative Leadership (1987), *Breaking the Glass Ceiling: Can Women Reach the Top of America's Largest Corporations?* Reading, MA: Addison-Wesley.

Murray, Lee (1994), 'Women in Science Occupations: Some Impacts of Technological Change', in Urs E. Gattiker (ed.), *Technology Innovation and Human Resources Vol. 4: Women and Technology*, Berlin: Walter de Gruyter. pp. 93–129.

Ng, Catherine W. (1998), 'Do women and men communicate differently at work? An empirical study in Hong Kong', *Women in Management Review*, **13**(1): 3–10.

Ng, Catherine W. (1999), 'A multiplicity model of oppression/liberation of working women', unpublished PhD dissertation, University of Kent at Canterbury.

Parry, Linda E. and Wharton, Robert R. (1994), 'Networking in the workplace: The role of gender in electronic communications', in Urs E. Gattiker (ed.), *Technology Innovation and Human Resources Vol. 4: Women and Technology*, Berlin: Walter de Gruyter. pp. 65–91.

Pazy, A. (1994), 'Trying to combat professional obsolescence: The experience of women in technical careers', in Urs E. Gattiker (ed.), *Technology Innovation and*

*Human Resources Vol. 4: Women and Technology*, Berlin: Walter de Gruyter. pp. 65–91.

Rice, Ronald E. (1984), 'Mediated group communication', in R. E. Rice and Associates, *The New Media: Communication, Research and Technology*. Beverly Hills, CA: Sage. pp. 129–54.

Rice, Ronald and Gattiker, Urs E. (2001), 'New media and organizational structuring', in Fredric M. Jablin and Linda L. Putnam (eds), *The New Handbook of Organizational Communication: Advances in Theory Research, and Methods*, Thousand Oaks, CA: Sage. pp. 544–81.

Riva, Giuseppe (2002), 'Communicating in CMC: Making order out of miscommunication', in Luigi Anolli, Rita Ciceri and Giuseppe Riva (eds), *Say not to Say: New Perspectives on Miscommunications*, Amsterdam: IOS Press. pp. 197–227.

Rowley, Jennifer (1999), 'Computer mediated communication – is it good for organizations?', *Industrial and Commercial Training*, 31(2): 72–4.

Savicki, Victor, Kelley, Merle and Ammon, Benjamin (2002), 'Effects of training on computer-mediated communication in single or mixed gender small task groups', *Computers in Human Behavior*, 18(3): 257–69.

Schottenbauer, Michele A., Rodriguez, Benjamin F., Glass, Carol R. and Arnkoff, Diane B. (2004), 'Computers, anxiety, and gender: An analysis of reactions to the Y2K computer problem', *Computers in Human Behavior*, 20: 67–83.

Schumacher, P. and Morahan-Martin, J. (2001), 'Gender, Internet and computer attitudes and experiences', *Computers in Human Behavior*, 17(1): 95–110.

Spangler, Lori (1995), 'Gender-specific non-verbal communication: Impact for speaker effectiveness', *Human Resource Development Quarterly*, 6(4): 409–19.

Takayoshi, Pamela (1994), 'Building new networks from the old: Women's experiences with electronic communications', *Computers and Composition*, 11, 21–35.

Tannen, Deborah (1990), *You Just Don't Understand: Women and Men in Conversation*. New York: Ballantine Books.

Tannen, Deborah (1994), *Talking from 9 to 5*. New York: William Morrow.

Taylor, Jacqueline (1999), 'Electronic mail, communication and social identity: A social psychological analysis of computer-mediated group interaction', in Lyn Pemberton and Simon Shurville (eds), *Words on the Web: Computer Mediated Communication*. Portland, OR: Intellect. pp. 96–105.

Trevino, Linda Klebe, Lengel, Robert H., Bodensteiner, Wayne D., Gerloff, Edwin A. and Muir, Nan Kanoff (1990), 'The richness imperative and cognitive style: The role of individual differences in media choice behavior', *Management Communication Quarterly*, 4(2): 176–97.

Tsui, Anne S. and Gutek, Barbara A. (1999), *Demographic Differences in Organizations: Current Research and Future Directions*. Lanham, MD: Lexington Books.

van der Kamp, Jake (2003), 'Expect full spectrum of excuses on 2G fees', *South China Morning Post*, September 23: B20.

Walker, Karen (1994), 'Men, women, and friendship: What they say, what they do', *Gender and Society*, **8**(2): 246–65.

Walsh, John P., Kucker, Stephanie, Maloney, Nancy G. and Gabbay, Shaul (2000), 'Connecting minds: Computer-mediated communication and scientific work', *Journal of the American Society for Information Science*, **51**(14): 1295–305.

Walters, Rob (1995), *Computer-Mediated Communications: Multimedia Applications*. Boston, MA: Artech House.

Wilkins, Brenda M. and Anderson, Peter A. (1991), 'Gender differences and similarities in management communication: A meta-analysis', *Management Communication Quarterly*, **5** (1), August, 6–35.

Chapter 10

# Women's Work: The Language Use of Call Centre Representatives

Margaret Franken and Catherine Wallace

## Introduction

The huge rise in service sector jobs has seen a resulting growth in call centres. Anton (2000) and Feinberg et al. (2000) write about the call centres of today evolving into the customer access centres of the future, with these providing the new competitive basis for many organizations. While call centres are seen as customer service portals or service centres, the emphasis on control and efficiency is reported at the expense of employee stress and turnover, customer orientation and service priorities (Knights and McCabe, 1998; Taylor and Bain, 1999; Wallace et al., 2000). Findings from these and other call centre studies, including those of the authors, suggest it is difficult for front-line staff to be customer oriented with the tension that exists between serving the customer and 'doing the business', whether this takes the form of outbounding (calling clients or potential clients to build rapport, get feedback, resolve conflicts, generate sales, and so on), responding to customer inquiries, or selling various products and services.

The rhetoric of serving the customer and the language used for achieving this form the basis for this chapter. We discuss the ways in which women are seen to be particularly well matched to call centre practices that require them to be 'aesthetic labour' (Warhurst et al., 2000, p. 12), and to be able to be aesthetically trained and monitored in the area of language use. We explore situation-specific issues of the call centre environment, identify the research issues and address various perspectives regarding the analysis of women's call centre language. We follow this by looking at language prescriptions, typical patterns and the nature of communication as a commodity. The chapter concludes with some implications for researchers and call centre managers.

**Overview of Current Research**

*The Call Centre Phenomenon*

According to Taylor and Bain (1999, p. 101), 'academic studies of the call centre phenomenon remain limited in both number and scope, particularly in the fields of the employment relationship and the labour process'. Belt et al. (2000) also draw attention to the fact that little research has specifically looked at the role of women in this relatively new industry. Given the fact that women constitute the largest proportion of employees – some 70 to 75 per cent of the workforce in a number of western economies, such as the UK and New Zealand (Belt et al., 2000, p 367; Belt, 2002; Singh and Pandey, 2005, Snyder, 2001) – this is somewhat surprising. Taylor and Bain (1999) maintain that this paucity of research is due to two main factors: the rapid growth in the sector and confusions about what constitutes a call centre.

Call centres are 'customer contact centres' that provide dedicated customer support for their respective companies or undertake projects on behalf of other companies by handling their customer-related queries. In order to handle these queries and provide the necessary assistance to customers, the call centres employ customer support officers (CSOs). In some countries these are referred to as customer service representatives (CSRs) (the latter being the term we use in this chapter).

Taylor and Bain (1999, p. 102) define a call centre as 'a dedicated operation in which computer-utilizing employees receive inbound – or make outbound – telephone calls, with those calls processed and controlled either by an Automatic Call Distribution (ACD) or predictive dialling system'. The main distinction between inbound and outbound call centres is that in an inbound call centre, the customer calls an agent or customer support representative and seeks information about, for example, a bank balance or concert tickets, while in an outbound call centre this is reversed, as in 'cold calling' customers to sell products or services (Taylor and Bain, 1999). In summary, a call centre can be defined as:

> a work environment in which the main business is mediated by computer and telephone-based technologies that enable the efficient distribution of incoming calls (or allocation of outgoing calls) to available staff, and permit customer-employee interaction to occur simultaneously with the use of display screen equipment and the instant access to, and inputting of, information. This includes parts of companies dedicated to this activity, as well as the whole company (Holman, 2003, p. 124).

Taylor and Bain (1999) propose that while technological developments are central to the operation of the call centre, the reason for their rapid growth is related to organizations' adoption of vigorous, direct-selling techniques and by expected dramatic savings in costs and overheads coming from centralizing back-office customer service functions. Banks, telemarketers and mail-order catalogue companies realized in the late 1960s that a single point of customer contact would have a significant impact on their revenues and improve their customer relations (Zemke, 2003), eventually leading to the establishment of call centres during the early part of the 1980s. The advent of globalization and major advancements in the field of Internet have also made it possible for companies to outsource their call centre operations to cheaper locations, enabling them to cut costs without compromising on quality (Kirkpatrick, 2003). Call centres have become a strategic asset to a company by delivering targeted customer service and have therefore changed the ways in which companies interact with their customers (Miciak and Desmarais, 2001).

The growth in call centre transactions and business benefits are much lauded with many predicting future developments including web-based call centres and avatars. New Zealand figures indicate that the call centre industry grew at 15 per cent in 2001 and had a value of NZ $1.7 billion (ACA Research Pty Ltd, 2003).

As staffing costs typically represent 60–75 per cent of call centre budgets (Genesys, 2003), the impetus is on managers to constantly seek improvements in the efficient use of human resources. The human resources are most typically women. This may largely be attributed to the fact that the work is often part time or shift work compatible with other aspects of women's lives. With this in mind, we consider the view of one prominent consultant in his statement that call centres were the new 'dark satanic mills' (Income Data Services, 1997, p. 13).

While we may think of call centre work as requiring some degree of technical competence with the technology, a large part of what is required is social or aesthetic. Thompson et al. (2000) list a number of somewhat elusive social or aesthetic skills required of CSRs, such as empathy, trust, socializing abilities, quest for success, adaptability and sense of humour, as essential skills that are sought by the call centre management during recruitment. Many of these have been thought to be more characteristic of women than men. While some skills, mostly technical, required for call centre work are seen to be able to be developed after employment, aesthetic and social skills are considered to be natural. Thompson et al. (2000) term these skills 'embodied capacities'. People who possess these skills are referred to as 'aesthetic labour' – labour that has the inherent qualities and abilities at the time of employment.

*Language, Gender and the Telephone*

Call centre representatives (CSRs) can be considered part of organizations whose aim is primarily to sell goods and services. The goals of the organization are achieved by means of interaction mainly, but not exclusively, through the medium of the telephone. In this chapter, the focus is on telephone interaction. The medium of the telephone constrains interaction in time and restricts interaction to the use of voice. The telephone also allows the achievement of goals to be monitored in a specific and analytical way by others in the organization. This suggests that the language that CSRs use in interactions with customers is constrained in a way that it is not for members of other types of organizations, who interact more freely with each other and with their customers.

Early work by linguists in the area of communicative acts and telephone communication tried to analyse stretches of telephone interaction in terms of principles or functions of particular moves. Schegloff (1979), for instance, recognized that some series of moves by speakers in telephone interaction seem to follow a predictable form, and involve formulaic language. However, the unpredictable middle section of most telephone conversations precluded this type of interaction from being considered a genre in its own right. (See Swales, 1990 for a further discussion of genre status.) While our own study (Franken and Wallace, 2000) sought to analyse the functions of selected CSRs' utterances, in no way could we say that the utterances represented a generic pattern or sequence. Rather, utterances were seen to reflect the use of somewhat recursive strategies, such as affirming customer choice or selection, or minimizing the effort required by the CSR to carry out a customer request.

As mentioned above, the majority of CSRs are women. Jobs in call centres for women (and the small number of men) call for 'politeness, indirection, attention to affect, and other features of interactional style that have been essentialized as female' (Eckert and McConnell-Ginet, 1999, p. 194). Cameron likewise suggests that these features of interactional style are 'symbolic markers of feminine gender' (2000, p. 324). 'Styles ... which have been experientially very important to individuals in their previous histories, may be carried into interactions with strangers', or into new contexts such as call centres (Eckert and McConnell-Ginet, 1999, p. 189).

This means that gender has been institutionalized in the discourse of CSRs (Eckert and McConnell-Ginet, 1999, p. 189). Therefore the challenge for researchers interested in gender and call centre language is to account for 'the difference gender makes' (Holmes and Meyerhoff, 1999). Keeping this perspective in mind and the fact that interaction is constrained greatly by the medium of the telephone and by organization prescription, we carried out research investigating a number of perspectives on the analysis of, and theoretical orientations on, language and discourse that may be potentially useful. These findings are discussed in the next section. However, initially we need to acknowledge a number of constraints that operate in the research of call centre language use and interaction.

*Research Issues Associated with Call Centre Language Use and Interaction*

While there are clearly rich areas to investigate in call centres, specifically in the area of the language use of CSRs and interaction between CSRs and customers, the research is constrained by a number of factors. The major constraint is the limited access to data of actual language use and this is reported in a number of studies (for example Cameron, 2000).

While management may declare their support of research of CSRs' language, they often place constraints on or limit access to particular kinds of data. In our experience, this often happens after the research is underway – aspects of the research are sought to be renegotiated by management. For example, in one of our research studies (Franken and Wallace, 2000; Wallace and Franken, 2000), management in one call centre claimed to have the customers' interests and confidentiality at heart in their decision to provide access only to a limited and selected number of tapes of CSRs and customers. They also sought to monitor our interpretation of data by requesting that they too, in addition to carefully selected CSRs, be given an opportunity to evaluate a number of phrases taken from our data; and sought to be informed of our interpretation of the evaluations. In other cases, management chose to restrict discussion to the general workings of the call centre (such as wait time) rather than focus on language per se.

Many researchers consequently focus on analysis of training manuals and other textual materials. Some researchers resort to interviewing employees off site – because there are time constraints and, as Cameron identifies, 'reticence engendered by the culture of surveillance' (2000, p. 329). In our own research, we became aware of this in discussion with a small number of CSRs personally known to us. One in particular was keen to talk further with us in her own home so that she could explain to us her response to her employer's prescription. When asked for her evaluation of a number of phrases identified from our data, she noted that several of them were 'too [company name]!'.

*Perspectives Guiding the Analysis and Interpretation of Call Centre Language Data*

Organizational discourse studies approach analysis primarily from a linguistic-discursive perspective. In other words, studies most often record and attempt to analyse stretches of interaction between participants within an organizational community, or between members of that organizational community and others. This approach has been variously described as discourse analysis or conversation analysis. Schegloff (1999) clarifies the purpose of such analysis in his statement regarding conversation analysis: 'CA deals with relatively short stretches of interaction and holds these to be revelatory and representative of interactional and organizational principles'. While the tools and the units of analysis are relatively unproblematic in studies of organizational discourse, it is the interpretation of the language or discourse data, guided by different theoretical frameworks, that may be at issue.

Much of research into organizational discourse is framed by a communities of practice (CofP) paradigm. Holmes and Meyerhoff (1999, p. 177) outline the perspectives such a paradigm can bring to understanding the dynamics and discourse of organizations. A CofP framework captures the notion of community and the notion of shared and mutually understood practices that are sustained over a period of time. Eckert and McConnell-Ginet (1999, p. 185) define a CofP as 'a group whose joint engagement in some activity or enterprise is sufficiently intensive to give rise over time to a repertoire of shared practices'. Stressing the enduring nature of discourse use in a CofP, Eckert and McConnell-Ginet, (1999, p. 190) state that 'It is the PRACTICE component of the CofP that makes it such a useful construct for language and gender analysis …'.

While the CofP framework may provide insights for the analysis of discourse between CSRs as a community, it cannot account for the discourse between CSRs and customers for a number of reasons. First, while interactions between CSRs and customers are a negotiated enterprise, the extent to which there is mutual engagement is debatable. Call centre language and practices are not generated by participants. Rather they are imposed by the company. Arguably, language that is primed and scripted, driven by the goal of achieving a sale, is indicative of a lack of genuine engagement and it cannot be considered as a negotiable resource. The particular nature of the call centre is that interactions are with strangers, are quick and not sustained over time.

However, the very features that make call centre discourse fall outside a CofP framework make it of interest to organizational discourse researchers. In particular:

- There is arguably a community of sorts made up of both management and CSRs. They have a shared sense of group, consolidated by the overt goal of working for the company and the possibly more covert goals of sales and/or keeping the customer satisfied.
- The interactions are perceived as a way of dealing with 'outsiders' on behalf of 'the group' or the company.
- While knowledge of acceptable interactional practices is shared as a result of training and compliance, the practices are not engaged in or performed together; CSRs are communicating with others, not with each other, to consolidate their group goals.
- CSRs need to 'buy into' these practices themselves before they can hope to get customers sold on them.

These features of CSR and customer interaction lead us to consider a more useful theoretical paradigm, that of social identity theory. This 'holds that individuals' social behaviour is a joint function of (a) their affiliation to a particular group identity that is salient at that moment in the interaction, and (b) their interpretation of the relationship of one's ingroup to salient outgroups' (Holmes and Meyerhoff, 1999, p. 177). Social identity theory leads to interesting areas for consideration in call centre language use and interaction:

- language prescription and monitoring as a way of maintaining ingroup identity, but also as a way of bridging the gap between the ingroup and the outgroup;
- the competing claims on membership of respective groups as evidenced by particular politeness strategies that serve to both reduce the social distance between CSR and customer and also impose a social distance or tone of respect for the customer.

*Language Prescription*

A company's reputation and worth is perpetually under scrutiny with every customer a CSR comes in contact with, making the CSR the mouthpiece or 'voice of the company' (Doyle and Carolan, 1998). The way in which organizations seek to prescribe the way in which CSRs are to speak to customers is evidenced in the organizations' training manuals. As mentioned above, many researchers find this a more productive source of data than actual language use. In some call centres, the moves of a CSR are tightly scripted, while in others, organizations guide the use of moves more by suggestion (description of possible utterances, or prompts) than by prescription. Clearly, prescription by scripting utterances of CSRs has the purpose of 'reducing optional variation in performance' (Cameron, 2000, p. 324). The ultimate goal of such practices is, in Cameron's view, 'to subordinate individuals to a corporate norm' (Cameron, 2000, p. 324).

In a training manual for a university call centre that we studied (TARPnz, 1999, p. 70), such scripting was achieved by means of prompts such as 'Extend an appropriate Verbal Handshake', followed by 'State the company or your divisional name', and 'Introduce yourself, offer your name'. These prompts guided CSRs for the call opening moves. The 'core of a telephone call' was less supported by prompts. The moves involved in call closing were again heavily guided by prompts. For instance, CSRs are prompted to control the closing moves by beginning 'to shut the door', achieved by summarizing the call and identifying further action. Another important move is that of showing appreciation for a customer's call, by thanking them for calling.

Tolerance of variation related to regional or non-standard varieties of English is variable in different organizations. Some organizations value such features in terms of the way in which they reduce the distance between the CSR and the customer. For instance, one university call centre recruited students for the purpose of conducting outbound calls to enquire whether former students were interested in re-enrolling. They welcomed the rather informal register these CSRs used and a number (but not too many) of the age-related non-standard features associated with younger speakers of English, such as slang. The training manual for the CSRs in this call centre explicitly encouraged CSRs to accommodate to the voice of the customer, by stating, 'Mirroring or matching someone's voice speed, pauses, language, and ultimately their breathing is the final stage to truly establishing rapport' (TARPnz, 1999, p. 15).

In other call centres with a different customer base, there is often much less tolerance. In these organizations, training manuals have been seen to contain some 'folklinguistic myths' and pejorative attitudes towards regional varieties of English and their effect on listeners. The training manual used for a university call centre contained erroneous descriptions of New Zealand English features, such as:

> There is a huge set of muscles in the jaw. Some Kiwis lock these when talking ... Kiwis naturally talk about 190 words per minute – to be heard and understood on the telephone the ideal speech speed is between 140-160 words per minute ... By not opening our mouths vowel sounds come out flat and uninteresting (TARPnz, 1999, p. 36).

It is not only a consideration of what one must say, but also of what one must not say that features in prescriptions. For example, use of certain words such as 'sorry' and 'significantly', was found to have a negative influence on the customer and hence those words were considered as forbidden, Rest In Peace (RIP) words in

Sturdy's (2002) study. They were replaced by use of positive sounding words like 'rest assured', 'immediate' and 'great'.

As well as prescriptions for what is said (or should not be said), prescriptions also control or 'style' how utterances are performed (Cameron, 2000, p. 330). Warhurst et al. (2000) suggest that an organization's major concern is the acoustic experience of the customer, especially their reaction towards the CSRs' accent and speech modulation. Cameron includes 'prosody, voice quality, and the way in which particular speech acts are performed' (Cameron, 2000, p. 324).

Overwhelmingly, though, the energy and enthusiasm of the call centre operative is seen as a primary means by which customer satisfaction is guaranteed. Energy and enthusiasm are seen to be transmitted to the customer by the 'smile in the voice' (G. Wiggins, personal communication, May 24, 2001). Other writers have likewise identified the 'smile down the phone' (see, for example, Cameron, 2000; Richardson and Marshall, 1996; Thompson et al., 2000). The ubiquitous smile metaphor suggests that the overriding relationship to be achieved between the CSR and the customer is one of friendliness, in which the social distance between the two interlocutors is reduced. Friendliness is also sometimes represented as rapport (TARPnz, 1999, p. 15). In this document, rapport is firstly defined as 'a sympathetic relationship or common understanding', and achieved by 'smiling or thinking positive thoughts'. This aspect of call centre language is discussed in the following section. As noted by Warhurst et al. (2000), this aesthetic aspect of the job links closely to the fact that women are often seen as particularly suited to call centre work.

A great deal of effort is put into 'training' employees, both new and ongoing, on what to say and how to say it, with reference to training manuals. In terms of new staff, there is often a training period in which employees are put through a programme of learning and careful monitoring before they become fully fledged CSRs. The programme of learning often involves not just the learning of prescribed language forms, but also a received and sometimes erroneous view of the function of different types of language forms – therefore not just linguistic information but metalinguistic information. Following this, there is ongoing monitoring so that adherence to standards prescribed in the manuals and through the training courses is maintained. Zemke's (2003) study found that a successful call centre spends double the amount of money on initial and follow-up training of customer representatives than an average call centre, with initial training taking an average of 15 days.

*Politeness Strategies*

There is an inherent tension between closing a sale or securing a deal and serving the customer. A good CSR is seen as a person who can retain a level of 'call control' to maximize the effectiveness in handling. A good CSR is also seen as a person who simultaneously treats every customer as being of utmost importance (Baker, 2002). The latter appears to be achieved by means of two types of politeness strategies: those that seek to reduce the social distance between CSR and customer and those that impose a level of formality or distance in the interaction. Franken and Wallace

(2000) identify the following functions associated with politeness strategies in the language of CSRs: establish affiliation with the customer, establish the customer as special, establish oneself, the CSR, as professional, minimize effort on the CSR's part. So, for instance, to establish affiliation with the customer, social distance is reduced by such strategies as naming the customer by their first name, or by letting the customer into the process by such utterances as 'Let's have a look'. Strategies that appear to impose some social distance and a degree of respect on the part of the CSR are achieved by, for example, minimizing effort by using utterances such as 'That's not a problem for us'.

Given the lack of a genuine relationship between CSR and customer, positive politeness strategies that seek to reduce social distance may be deemed not to be genuine. Customer representatives who establish friendly relationships with customers by using 'positive politeness strategies' must be genuine and trustworthy in their approach towards customers (Wallace and Franken, 2000). Some studies have suggested that a good CSR can transcend this problem if they possess the feminine attribute of natural empathy for others (Baker, 2002; Korczynski, 2001; Thompson et al. 2000; Wallace and Franken, 2000), or are naturally 'socially confident' (Baker, 2002). If this is difficult, Freemantle, a management consultant, recommends some vital 'emotional labour' tactics for service sector employees, which can be applied in the call centre industry (Freemantle, 1998). One of these is the advice that, 'By drawing on your feelings and emotions to fine-tune the way you use your voice, you will be much better able to connect emotionally with customers and become someone they really like' (1998, p. 109).

Sturdy (2002) also suggests that we move beyond language prescription to include the skill of active listening. At this point we can say that the relationship between the CSR and customer may be one of interactional reciprocity.

**Conclusions and Recommendations**

Organizational discourse analysis concerns itself with the nature of discourse practices within an organization or a sector such as call centres. The discourse practices that govern call centres are captured by Sturdy's (2002) term 'the rhetoric of serving the customer'. This chapter has pointed out that rather than actual interactional discourse being studied, much of what we understand about call centre language use and interaction is gleaned from studying the prescriptions embodied in training manuals.

While call centres vary, in general, the prescription of the language used by CSRs to both initiate interaction and to respond to the initiations of customers serves as a method of controlling the language they use and the way they speak. It also serves to present the distinct identity of the company. In essence, while CSRs are encouraged to think of themselves as a team or a group and part of the company, they operate as mouthpieces for the company in the realization of the company's goals. Given the degree of prescription, we offer the following recommendations for further research and change in institutional practices.

- We propose that more research should focus on the way in which CSRs reconcile their personal identities with that imposed as part of the company/group. The literature on aesthetic and emotional labour, especially as undertaken by women, will be helpful in this task. As we have indicated, little research about call centres and their operations manages to connect with CSRs, much less give them a voice to express their individual personality within the confines of the prescribed format.
- Another perceived gap in the research is the study of the effect of particular communication strategies used by CSRs with customers. Trainers and managers who assume that there is only one way to speak and that this is the best way, will be in danger of making faulty assumptions about their customers' preferences and tolerances.
- In management terms, many call centres are hierarchically organized with team leaders mediating between management and CSRs. It would seem that much could be gained by making use of the expertise of successful CSRs. Mentoring, rather than prescription and enforcement, may provide CSRs with a more socially satisfying experience of learning, and may alleviate some of the problems associated with low employee retention rates.
- While current research approaches focus on documenting and understanding particular sites, researchers need to develop more general understandings of particular types of call centres such as those offering banking services, those associated with selling insurance, and also more general understandings of nationally and internationally based call centres. The latter, in particular, offer interesting understandings of intercultural communication.

It would seem that call centres will continue to proliferate. However, changing forms of technology may well enable new forms of communication that rely less on the social and aesthetic. These are also worthy of further study, and doing so may throw light on the operation of more traditional call centres.

## References

ACA Research Pty Ltd, (2003), *Home: Delivering Knowledge*. Retrieved August 6, 2005 from: www.callcentres.net/ACA/LIVE/me.get?site.home.

Anton, J. (2000), 'The past, present and future of customer access centers', *International Journal of Service Industry Management*, **11**(2): 120–30.

Baker, G. (2002), Heroes in headsets, *NZ Business*, **16**(4): 35–7.

Belt, V. (2002) 'A female ghetto? Women's careers in call centres', *Human Resource Management Journal*, **12**(4): 51–66.

Belt, V., Richardson, R. and Webster, J. (2000), 'Women's work in the information economy: The case of telephone call centres', *Information, Communication and Society*, **3**(3): 366–85.

Brodsky, C. M. (1976), *The Harassed Worker*. Toronto: Lexington Books, D. C. Heath and Company.

Cameron, D. (2000), 'Styling the worker: Gender and the commodification of language in the globalized service economy', *Journal of Sociolinguistics*, **4**: 323–47.

Demaret, L., Quinn, P. and Grumiau, S. (1999), *Call Centres – The New Assembly Lines*. UK: International Confederation of Trade Unions, Labournet.

Doyle, J. C. and Carolan, M. D. (1998), 'Calling all trainers', *Training and Development*, **52**(1): 53–68.

Eckert, P. and McConnell-Ginet, S. (1999), 'New generalizations and explanations in language and gender research', *Language in Society*, **28**: 185–201.

Feinberg, R. A., Kim, I. S., Hokama, L., de Ruyter, K. and Keen, C. (2000), 'Operational determinants of caller satisfaction in the call center', *International Journal of Service Industry Management*, **11**(2): 131–41.

Franken, M. and Wallace, C. (2000), 'Buying in or opting out: The commodification of call centre language', paper presented at the 7th Language and Society Conference, Auckland, June.

Freemantle, D. (1998), *What Customers Like About You: Adding Emotional Value for Service Excellence and Competitive Advantage*. London and Santa Rosa, CA: Nicholas Brealey.

Genesys (2003), *Contact Centre Realities: Managing Agent Satisfaction for Better Customer Satisfaction*. Sydney: Genesys Laboratories Australasia.

Holman, D. (2003), 'Phoning in sick? An overview of employee stress in call centres', *Journal of Leadership and Organization Development*, **24**(3): 123–30.

Holmes, J. and Meyerhoff, M. (1999), 'The Community of Practice: Theories and methodologies in language and gender research', *Language in Society*, **28**: 173–83.

Income Data Services (1997), *Pay and Conditions in Call Centres*. London: IDS.

Kirkpatrick, D. (2003), 'The net makes it all easier – including exporting US jobs', *Fortune*, **147**(10): 146.

Knights, D. and McCabe, D. (1998), 'What happens when the phone goes wild? Staff, stress and spaces for escape in a BPR telephone banking regime', *Journal of Management Studies*, **35**(2): 163–94.

Korczynski, M. (2001), 'The contradictions of service work: The call centre as customer-oriented bureaucracy' in A. Sturdy, I. Grugulis and H. Wilmott (eds), *Customer Service – Control, Colonisation and Contradictions*. London: Macmillan. pp. 79–101.

MacBride Report (1980), *Many Voices, One World: Towards a New, More Just, and More Efficient World, Information and Communication Order*. Paris: UNESCO; London: Kogan Page; New York: Unipub.

Miciak, A. and Desmarais, M. (2001), 'Benchmarking service quality performance at business-to-business and business-to-consumer call centres', *The Journal of Business and Industrial Marketing*, **16**(5): 340–53.

Richardson, R. and Marshall, J. N. (1996), 'The growth of telephone call centres in peripheral areas of Britain: Evidence from Tyneside and Wear', *Area*, **28**(3): 308–17.

Schegloff, E. A. (1979), 'Identification and recognition in telephone conversation openings', in G. Psathas (ed.), *Everyday Language: Studies in Ethnomethodology*. New York: Irvington. pp. 23–78.

Schegloff, E. A. (1999), 'Discourse, pragmatics, conversation, analysis', *Discourse Studies*, **1**(4): 405–35.

Singh, P. and Pandey, A. (2005) 'Women in call centres', *Economic and Political Weekly*, February: 684–8. Retrieved January 2, 2006 from: www.eldis.org/static/DOC19087.htm.

Snyder, N. (2001) 'Women in call centres. A Canadian gender and development issue?', *Women in Development* (York University, Canada). Retrieved January 2, 2006 from: www.goodgirl.ca/Nikko%20Snyder%20Call%20Centre.pdf.

Sturdy, A. J. (2002), 'Front line diffusion – The production and negotiation of knowledge through training interactions', in T. Clark and R. Fincham (eds), *Critical Consulting: Perspectives on the Management Advice Industry*. Oxford: Blackwell. pp. 130–51.

Swales, J. M. (1990), *Genre Analysis: English in Academic and Research Settings*. Cambridge: Cambridge University Press.

TARPnz (1999), *Telephone Customer Service Training Programme*. New Zealand: Call Centre Dynamics.

Taylor, P. and Bain, P. (1999), '"An assembly line in the head": Work and employee relations in the call centre', *Industrial Relations Journal*, **30**(2): 101–17.

Thompson, P., Warhurst, C. and Callaghan, G. (2000), 'Human capital or capitalising on humanity? Knowledge, skills and competencies in interactive service work', in C. Prichard, R. Hull, M. Chumer and H. Wilmott (eds), *Managing Knowledge: Critical Investigations of Work and Learning*. Basingstoke: Macmillan Business. pp. 122–40.

Wallace, C. and Franken, M. (2000), 'Call girls and phonies: Synthetic and subversive language in a call centre context', paper presented at the Australian and New Zealand Communication Association Conference, Ballina, July.

Wallace, C. M., Eagleson, G. and Waldersee, R. (2000), 'The sacrificial HR strategy in call centres', *International Journal of Service Industry Management*, **11**(2): 174–84.

Warhurst, C., Nickson, D., Witz, A. and Cullen, A. M. (2000), 'Aesthetic labour in interactive service work: Some case study evidence from the 'new' Glasgow', *Services Industries Journal*, **20**(3): 1–18.

Zemke, R. (2003), 'Action center or afterthought: Tremendous growth in the call center industry also brings a number of training challenges', *Training*, **40**(4): 38–42.

Chapter 11

# Putting Gender in its Place: A Case Study on Constructing Speaker Identities in a Management Meeting

Judith Baxter

## Introduction

How important is gender for constructing the spoken interactions of senior managers in formal meetings? What part does gender play alongside other salient aspects of a speaker's identity? Have feminists overplayed the gender card in their desire to understand communication issues at work?

This chapter seeks to ground its exploration of these wider questions within the context of a small-scale ethnographic case study of a successful British dotcom company. This study specifically examined the spoken interactions of a management board during a series of formal meetings over a period of 3 months. The author was particularly interested in investigating the minority position in meetings of 'Sarah', the only female member of an otherwise all-male board of seven directors, and wanted to find out more about the language women use to construct themselves as senior managers and leaders. Clearly, while no generalizations can be made from a single case study of this type, Sarah's minority position within the team is quite typical of the national pattern of female board directorships. In the UK, only 7.2 per cent of FTSE 100 directorships are held by women according to Singh et al. (2001).

The chapter aims to contribute to the broader discussion of gender and communication issues at work in this book by offering a post-structuralist perspective of the role of gender (for example Butler, 1991) in constructing the 'speaker identities' of senior managers in top-level meetings. The concept of 'speaker identities' refers to the ways in which speakers are being continuously positioned and 'constructed' by institutional discourses within their organization, but yet have some agency to negotiate their own roles as communicators (for example Cameron, 1997; Bucholtz et al., 1999). More specifically, this chapter has three aims, as follows:

- To contest traditional language and gender literature, which attributes a binary and polarized discursive framework to the formation of speaker identities. The 'dominance' view (for example Lakoff, 1975; Spender, 1980) – that females have acquired more submissive and compliant speech styles and males more powerful and authoritative speech styles – is challenged. The author also questions the more positive 'difference' view that males and females have been socialized (by same-sex friendship groups during childhood) into separately gendered subcultures, thus making their speech styles 'different but equal' (for example Coates, 1995; Holmes, 1992; Tannen, 1996).

- To demonstrate a form of discourse analysis that reveals how speaker identities are actively negotiated or constructed 'live' during the course of a management meeting, in order to examine the salience of gender alongside other aspects of identity.
- To consider more broadly what insights a post-structuralist perspective can contribute to the subject of gender, communication and leadership in organizations.

The following section now explores in more detail what is meant by a 'post-structuralist perspective' on the salience of gender in constructing the speaker identities of senior managers in business meetings.

## Overview of Current Research: A Post-structuralist Perspective

As Paechter (2001, p. 41) has noted, 'there are a wide variety of post-structuralisms just as there are a wide variety of feminisms, but there are a number of features that are common to most approaches'. This section will focus upon four post-structuralist features that are considered useful to the field of discourse analysis, and in particular to the interpretation of spoken interactions in institutional settings.

### Discourse as Social/Ideological Practice

First is the post-structuralist conception of discourse as a form of social/ideological practice. According to Foucault (1972, p. 49), discourse*s* are used in the plural sense to denote 'practices that systematically form the objects of which they speak'. So, discourses are forms of knowledge, sets of assumptions, expectations, values and ways of explaining the world that govern mainstream cultural practices, including those within organizations. An example of a dominant discourse on gender would be that of *gender differentiation*. Not only is gender considered to be a polarized construct in common-sense thinking, as reflected in recent popular bestsellers on the subject (for example Gray, 1992; Pease and Pease, 2001; Tannen, 1996), but also in mainstream language and gender research literature (quoted above). Furthermore, Foucauldian notions of discourse (1984, p. 61) are always inextricably linked with concepts of *power*, not as a negative, repressive force but as something that constitutes and energizes all social relations. Accordingly, 'power is not a possession in somebody's hands, but a net-like organization which weaves itself discursively through social structures, meanings, relations, and the construction of speakers' identities' (Baxter, 2003). Thus, a post-structuralist perspective considers that all interactions between speakers are interwoven with a web of social and institutional discourses, which act as a means of organizing power relations between these speakers. In terms of conducting a discourse analysis of a given stretch of speech, analysts can look at the way different discourses work to position speakers as variously powerful or powerless, according to their shifting subject positions within these different discourses. This principle is illustrated more fully in the section that follows.

### Incredulity towards Meta-narratives

The second feature of the post-structuralist perspective is a 'stance of incredulity towards meta-narratives' (Lyotard, 1984, p. xxiv) or towards any all-embracing theory, explanation, wisdom or 'truth' that tends to locate power within particular structures, groups or people. While meta-narratives are favoured by Enlightenment thought, post-structuralism focuses upon 'small, local stories about specific discourses and power relations' (Paechter, 2001, p. 44). In other words, a post-structuralist perspective on spoken interactions at work is concerned to deconstruct power relations within small-scale, localized and temporary settings. It wishes to avoid making sweeping theorizations about causes and effects, but rather to locate and describe what is happening on the ground at given, precise moments.

### Multiplicity of Human Identity

The third feature of the post-structuralist perspective is a belief in the multiplicity of human identity. The dominant, common-sense view of female and male identity in many cultures is that gender is a key, if not predominant, distinguishing feature. Males and females are perceived to inhabit rather different subcultures in terms of their dress, appearance, use of language, lifestyles, behaviours, skills and abilities, which often lead to miscommunication between the sexes within both personal and professional relationships (for example Gray, 1992; Pease and Pease, 2001; Tannen, 1996). Underlying the 'dominance' version of gender differentiation is a power relationship: historically at least, males are regarded as holding the balance of power. In contrast, the post-structuralist perspective posits that people's identity comprises a complex mix of gender, age, class, ethnicity, education, language, personality, and so on. Women, for example, are regarded as multi-dimensional, rather than primarily defined by feminine constructs or narrow stereotypes, and are thus able to accommodate to plural and sometimes contradictory positions in their lives: as workers, colleagues, partners, friends, mothers, daughters, sportspeople, and so on.

*Identity in Process*

The fourth feature of the post-structuralist perspective, which moves it decisively away from any resemblance to 'sex-role socialization theory' as applied to work contexts (for example Singh et al., 2002), is the notion of identity in process. Within any single speech event, both male and female speakers are constantly negotiating their subject positions within interwoven and often competing institutional discourses, as discussed above. While speakers may be positioned as relatively powerful within one discourse, they may be relatively powerless within another, often shifting between subject positions in a matter of moments. In other words, speakers are never wholly powerful or powerless all of the time. Thus, the post-structuralist approach to discourse analysis is concerned with the *fluidity* of speaker identities, looking at the way these are actively negotiated or constructed *live* within the span of a single stretch of speech.

To sum up, within any single spoken interaction such as a management meeting, there are likely to be a number of 'discursive practices' that are not necessarily gendered. While it might be argued that gendered discourses operate within almost any work setting, these are always interwoven with, and interacting with other institutional discourses. The author's own study shows that there are 'gendered moments' when Sarah, the sole female director, is positioned as relatively powerless in relation to her male colleagues, and other moments when she can access more powerful subject positions within alternative discourses. She is certainly no victim, as the following analysis of one extract from a management meeting will demonstrate.

## Exploration of the Issues: An Analysis of a Management Meeting

Four institutional 'discourses' – or sets of expectations/values governing the ways in which spoken interactions were routinely negotiated in these management board meetings – were identified in this ethnographic research study. These discourses became evident in the course of observing a number of management meetings over a period of 3 months and by conducting individual interviews with the research participants. These were:

- *Competing specialisms*: overt competition between directors in terms of who was considered to have the most important job on the management board. Sarah's responsibility over the highly technical area of Operations gave her considerable prestige in this company.
- *Historical legacy*: a strong cachet around length of job experience in the company. There was a notable hierarchy of who was appointed before whom on the senior team.
- *Open dialogue*: a company culture formally recognizing the value of an 'open' exchange of ideas and information. There were supposed to be no secrets

between members of the management board.
- Masculinization: the only obviously gendered discourse among the four, this means the way in which communication often manifested stereotypically male speech patterns such as cross-questioning, interruptions, emphatic speech and topic control (see Thornborrow, 2002).

The meeting featured in the following extract lasted for just over an hour and took place in a private meeting room in the company offices. Falling under the heading of 'Bogs and Boilers', the meeting was largely concerned with non-confidential, day-to-day issues. Five members of the management board were present on this occasion. These were: the Chief Executive Officer (CEO), 'Keith', who also chaired the meeting; 'Sarah', Operations Director; 'Jack', Sales and Marketing Director; 'Richard', Product Director; and 'Pete', the Finance Director.

The author's method of textual analysis has been described fully elsewhere (see Baxter, 2002; 2003). Accordingly, in the first section below, there is a detailed, *denotative* description of the verbal and non-verbal interactions of the key participants within both extracts. The second section supplies a *connotative* analysis – that is, a more wide-ranging, interpretative account of the ways in which speakers' identities are constructed 'live' by interwoven and competing institutional discourses.

Just before this extract began, Sarah had given a lengthy and technical explanation of a short-term, yet serious problem that was affecting the company at the time of the meeting – the company's website was 'down' and therefore unavailable to both employees and customers. Jack's first question to Sarah (turn 01 below) implicitly opens up the floor to all the participants of the meeting.

01    **Jack**: Does everyone in the company know that the system was down?
02    **Sarah**: Yes.
03    **Jack**: And single node was what it was on yesterday which meant that …
04    **Sarah**: No, it was … it's really, really complex. I'm sorry, I can't explain it any simpler.
05    **Jack**: OK, then, the question really is …
06    **Sarah**: [overlapping] No, no … I really can't explain it.
07    **Jack**: Is … is the way that it comes up going to mean that performance is less than …
08    **Sarah**: [interrupting] The way … no.
09    **Jack**: So yesterday was …
10    **Sarah**: [interrupting] We are aiming … we are aiming that it will come up on the database server with 12          CPUs on it, rather than the standard six anyway.
11    **Jack**: Right, so it won't mean that …
12    **Sarah**: [interrupting] Last night, it was screaming, it was screaming through.
13    **Jack**: So when it really does come up, it won't be performance issues, it's just that it's going to be …
14    **Sarah**: [interrupting] We had different issues yesterday afternoon as I said, in that we had, one, a database issue which shouldn't have affected performance at all. But we had a problem with the networks falling over, and it's hard to correlate the two. I can't guarantee …

15 **Jack**: [interrupting] No, no, no ... all I'm concerned about is that, when an email is sent out that says, 'Hurrah, it's back up' that if necessary we say, 'It's back up but at the same time there will be some performance issues, so if you're talking to customers and you are taking people through the site, that they may well experience difficulties.

16 **Keith**: There's a sort of user interpretation of 'back up' and a technical interpretation. Yesterday afternoon I thought it was down because I couldn't get to it but there was a different reason, I understand that.

17 **Sarah**: I didn't understand you were having those experiences, and I sit next to you. [laughs] I knew what we were doing, I knew we were having issues, but I did not understand that user issues were absolutely appalling. [with emphasis] Nobody told me.

18 [Silence among whole meeting for several seconds.]

19 **Jack**: Well, I just thought the site was down all day you see ...

20 **Sarah**: [interrupting] We did communicate to everybody when it was back up.

21 **Keith**: Could we have some way of making sure when the site is back up ...

22 **Sarah**: Yeah, well, the guys upstairs would have been aware, but I'm just saying that I wasn't. It isn't as if they would get it back up and ignore it. You know, get it back up and just walk away, it doesn't work that way.

23 **Jack**: That's why I just assumed that if the guys upstairs ... If they were having problems with it, they ...

24 **Sarah**: [interrupting and overlapping] The guys upstairs understand it but you're asking ... [continuing to talk over the others] you're asking for a different interpretation to different people, which is fine, but I need to be aware of that and this discussion is absolutely fine.

25 [Silence among the whole meeting for several seconds.]

*Denotative Analysis*

During this extract, Jack takes on an interrogative stance by subjecting Sarah to a series of testing questions. His second question (turn 03) appears to indicate that he hasn't quite assimilated the earlier technical explanation. At the same time, he is keen to show that he shares her technical knowledge and is therefore on her wavelength by using technical jargon ('single node', turn 03). However, he seems concerned to establish that there may still be less technical but substantive 'performance issues' affecting colleagues and customers that Sarah has not fully considered. Jack's interrogative stance is indicated by his more or less complete dominance of the floor as questioner (until turn 16); his use of definite question markers at the start of sentences such as 'so', 'right' and 'OK', and his attempts to demystify Sarah's more technical explanations by translating them into more down-to-earth language (turns 13 and 15). The only other speaker to contribute to this part of the discussion is Keith, the CEO. Both his contributions (turns 16 and 21) appear to be in keeping with his role as the meeting's Chair. His first comment merely clarifies a possible confusion by contributing a point of information to Jack and Sarah's discussion and his second is an attempt at producing 'an action' from the discussion of a problematic issue; he does not obviously take sides.

Sarah's responses to Jack in turns 04 and 06, where she flatly refuses to explain further and apologizes for her inability to do so, may indicate some irritation that she is being forced to defend her actions. After this point, she repeatedly interrupts and speaks over Jack when he continues to question her about what happened, to the extent that he rarely completes a sentence (for example turns 07, 09, 11, 13). Her emphasis is not upon what went *wrong*, but on what she has been doing to put the matter *right* (turns 10, 12) She resists the position of 'scapegoat' not simply by defending her own actions, but by criticizing those of her colleagues. For example, she indicates that other people must take some responsibility for the consequences of the operations failure. In turn 18, she admonishes her colleagues for a contributing factor: their inability to communicate their experience of the problem to her ('Nobody told me.'). Indeed, she causes the meeting to fall silent for a significant few seconds on two occasions during this extract (turns 18 and 25). This might either indicate an embarrassed acceptance on the part of her colleagues of some of the blame, or, in line with Zimmerman and West's (1975) research on delayed responses in mixed-sex settings, might signify a sense of withdrawal or lack of support from her male colleagues. There is a hint that Sarah feels that she may have alienated her colleagues by over-reacting to Jack's questions when she says meta-analytically, 'I need to be aware of that and this discussion is absolutely fine' (turn 24).

*Connotative Analysis*

It is evident in this extract that there is a sense of increasing tension between the two most voluble speakers, Sarah and Jack. Sarah can be seen as progressively more dominant in relation to Jack according to an interplay of all four identified discourses, but not unambiguously so. With regard to *historical legacy*, the interview data revealed that the company was originally Sarah's 'brain-child' and that she was single-handedly responsible for founding it. Until Keith was appointed as CEO, she had widespread responsibility for almost all areas of its work: the design and implementation of the technology, the day-to-day operations of the website, and for all sales and marketing functions, as she says below:

> all the day-to-day work, I was more or less a one-woman band ... I will admit that because of this, I have found it very difficult letting go of certain areas of the business, because I am still actively interested in everything. But it is something I am working on. I see it is as one of my greatest challenges.

One of the areas of the business Sarah has had to 'let go' is that of sales and marketing. While Jack is considered a founder member in so far as he was appointed at an early stage in the company's short history, he nonetheless inherits the legacy of Sarah's knowledge of, and original responsibility for his job role. However, it must remain speculative whether the tension that emerges between them in this extract is a result of Sarah's powerful position in terms of historical legacy. Certainly, the way in which she repeatedly cuts in and talks over Jack (over five times in this extract), and the corresponding way in which he accedes to her interruptions, are linguistic manifestations of her dominance (for example Fishman, 1980; Thornborrow, 2002; Zimmerman and West, 1975) that indicate an exercise of authority on her part and a deferral to authority on his. Of course, language and gender literature, quoted above, has traditionally attributed such speech strategies to the male dominance of women. The fact that there is a role reversal in this case points to the anti-essentialist explanation that a variety of competing discourses are governing Sarah's shifting subject position as a speaker.

Thus, Jack's deferral to Sarah in this context might also be explained by her apparent empowerment within the discourses of *masculinization* and *competing specialisms*, which seem to work together here. However, there are two features of Sarah's use of language that suggest her powerful subject position is a somewhat ambiguous one. First, she signifies her highly specialized, technical knowledge of computer operations – an area traditionally associated with masculine expertise – by using an abstruse, technical jargon. At the start of the extract, for example, Jack makes several tentative attempts to demystify her specialist language in order to spell out the implications of the technical problem:

03   Jack: And single node was what it was on yesterday which meant that it was …
07   Jack: Is … is the way that it comes up going to mean that performance is less …

Sarah's subsequent refusal to explain the technical problem any further in lay-person's terms reinforces the general awareness that she has exclusive access to a specialist knowledge within the company that is fundamental to its entire operation. While this imbues her with real authority as a speaker at this meeting because she can determine how much knowledge to make available, it simultaneously appears to expose her expertise to challenge and contestation. There are at least three possible readings of Jack's need to cross-question Sarah in this extract:

- He feels he has a duty to interrogate Sarah's competing specialism on behalf of the company's espoused culture of open dialogue in order to democratize her knowledge for the benefit of the others. In other words, the sharing of knowledge would help to equalize the power relationship between different specialisms: between Sarah as technical expert and her less technical colleagues.
- Again, in terms of competing specialisms, Jack's sense of exclusion from an area of knowledge that has implications for his sales and marketing responsibilities is perceived as a professional threat – he may feel he is unable to explain to clients why the website is experiencing difficulties.
- Jack is unwilling to place his trust in Sarah's professional judgement because there is a lack of trust between them, according to Richard, Product Director:

Sarah and Jack have an element in their relationship [to do with trust] but it is more Jack drilling Sarah than the other way round. Jack pushes for more information, because he isn't entirely comfortable with what is happening … with that relationship, Sarah would say, 'I am sorry the site is down' and he would say, 'that's not good enough, tell me what's happening.' If there was a level of trust, you would say, 'you must be having a shit time there', but that's not what happens.

Richard makes no explicit suggestion that this lack of trust has chauvinist or sexist connotations, although the use of phallic imagery ('drilling'; 'pushing') is somewhat indexical. However, Richard *does* imply that Jack's refusal to sympathize with Sarah's plight is a masculinized response, out of tune with the company culture of open dialogue.

Ironically, the second feature of Sarah's language that suggests that she adopts an ambiguously powerful subject position, is her own use of a masculinized speech style (for example use of interruptions, lengthy turns, talking over others, blocking statements, refusals to comply, bald assertions). This is because she is herself subject to, and partially disempowered by, this discourse of masculinization. Sarah's partial disempowerment is a result of the masculinized style of engagement that symbolically constructs any pair of speakers, male or female, as opponents in a fight. In the interview data, several participants described the discussion between Sarah and Jack using metaphors of fighting and aggression, drawing on the boxing ring, target practice and the battlefield. With its implications of male physicality, this is a metaphorical construction that is inherently gendered. Thus, there is little question that when this imagery is applied by male colleagues to Sarah, there are obvious sexist connotations:

Richard: Sarah, under pressure, becomes very defensive at which point you don't get any more information out of her because she is just *defending her territory*, not able to reason at this stage ... [emphasis added]

Pete: Jack will back down very quickly when pushed by Keith, but *will attack quite hard when he has Sarah on the ropes*. He's comfortable with *pushing* her. He's not beyond *sniping* at anyone but he's cautious who his *targets* are. He doesn't try to *play that game with me* ... [emphasis added]

Overall, Sarah appears to be a persuasive and influential speaker relative to Jack during this extract, largely because of her ascendant subject positions within the discourses of historical legacy and competing specialisms. But this ascendancy is contested and undermined by a discourse of masculinization that has appropriated the meeting's terms of engagement (in the official company rhetoric, one of open dialogue), and cast Jack as 'goal attack' and Sarah as 'goal defence'. It seems that Sarah's ability to resist verbal attack is an ambiguous achievement. When interviewed, she explained that she felt compelled to adopt a masculinized style of engagement in order to survive in what she called the 'boysy' culture, while making it clear that she was far from comfortable with it:

I've noticed recently that the dynamics of the management board have changed enormously over the last year, and I think this has made me more defensive than I used to be. Before last year, there used to be two women on the board and this gave us a combined position of strength. Since then, I've noticed that the atmosphere in the team has become very 'boysy'.

To sum up, Sarah at first glance appears to be assimilated within the 'boysy culture' of the management board, evidenced by her colleagues' deference to her subject position as a technical expert and her dominant and masculinized style of interaction. However, Sarah's lack of ease with her own show of dominance is indicated both in her interview comments, and in her need to meta-analyse her own performance at the end of the extract ('I need to be aware of that and this discussion is absolutely fine.' turn 24). It seems that Sarah is adopting competing subject positions in the meeting with the effect that she is both assimilated within, and separated from, the 'boysy culture' or masculinized discourse she has identified. This possibility is signalled in the extract by the way her show of dominance produces a strained silence among her colleagues at this meeting, tolerated but perhaps resented.

## Conclusion

The data analysed from this single transcript of speech can only give a snapshot of the complex interactions between male and female directors recorded over a 3-month period. But such a snapshot is useful in questioning the modernist feminist presumption that discourses of gender will necessarily override the impact of other discourses in constructing mixed-sex spoken interactions.

This chapter has aimed to show that speakers' identities, and the ways in which these are negotiated within meetings, are governed by a complex mix of competing and interwoven discourses. The construction of Sarah's speaker identity in this extract cannot be explained simply by the 'gender difference' view (for example Coates, 1995; Holmes, 1992) that females prefer a more cooperative, supportive speech style. Nor can her spoken interactions be readily explained by the 'dominance' view (for example Spender, 1980) that males in a patriarchal society have evolved ways of silencing and controlling females' talk. In order to make clear sense of the degree of ambiguity attached to Sarah's shifting identity as a speaker, a more fluid, open-ended and multi-dimensional means of interpretation is required. This is offered by the post-structuralist perspective that would view Sarah's dominant manner as multiply constructed by her relatively powerful subject positions within and across the four context-bound discourses identified by my research: historical legacy, open dialogue, masculinization and competing specialisms. In more concrete terms, her authority is derived from her speech and actions as the founder member of the company; her espousal of the company's philosophy of open dialogue; her readiness to use a stereotypically masculinized style of engagement when needed; and finally from the high corporate value placed upon her information and communication technology (ICT) expertise. However, it has been argued that Sarah's position of authority proved a mixed blessing in the long run. While there were no obvious signs of a discourse of gender differentiation governing the talk and behaviour of this board of directors, there *were* gendered undercurrents. Sarah's views were frequently contested and subjected to scrutiny, and her unstereotypical use of a masculinized speech style seemed to construct her asymmetrically as 'fair game' for verbal attack.

So while Sarah was no obvious victim of gendered practices on the management board, she was constantly being called upon to renegotiate the terms of her position of authority in public meetings. To sum up, the post-structuralist perspective would primarily view Sarah as a multi-faceted *individual* constituted by different sets of power relations, while recognizing that her minority position as a *woman* within the 'boysy' culture of an otherwise all-male team would continue to proscribe the range of identities to which she has access as a speaker.

### Recommendations

The results of this study were fed back to the management board via a 'discourse map' that provided a set of insights into how the company culture might be perceived, as well as guiding principles for understanding where and how possible sources of conflict between individual managers might take place in their organization.

　　In terms of wider application, the insights raised by this case study could be of real, practical benefit to service providers, management consultants and management boards themselves, by increasing an awareness of the discursive effects of spoken interactions, and, as a consequence, helping organizations to challenge and review their management practices. For now, researchers in the field are recommended to conduct further research into:

- the value of post-structuralist approaches for identifying the impact of competing institutional discourses upon management practices; and
- methods of translating concepts of post-structuralist theory into practical, jargon-free strategies for use in management development programmes.

### References

Baxter, J. (2002), 'Competing discourses in the classroom: A post-structuralist analysis of girls' and boys' speech in public contexts', *Discourse and Society*, **13**(6): 827–42.

Baxter, J. (2003), *Positioning Discourse in Gender: A Feminist Methodology*. Basingstoke: Palgrave Macmillan.

Bucholtz, M., Liang, A. C. and Sutton, L. (eds) (1999), *Reinventing Identities: The Gendered Self in Discourse*. New York: Oxford University Press.

Butler, J. (1991), *Gender Trouble: Feminism and the Subversion of Identity*. New York: Routledge.

Cameron, D. (1997), 'Performing gender identity: Young men's talk and the construction of heterosexual identity', in S. Johnson and U. H. Meinhof (eds), *Language and Masculinity*. London: Blackwell. pp. 47–64.

Coates, J. (1995), 'Language, gender and career', in S. Mills (ed.), *Language and Gender: Interdisciplinary Perspectives*. London: Longman. pp. 13–30.

Fishman, P. (1980), 'Conversational insecurity', in D. Cameron (ed.), *The Feminist Critique of Language: A Reader*. London: Routledge. pp. 234–41.

Foucault, M. (1972), *The Archaeology of Knowledge and the Discourse on Language*. New York: Pantheon.

Foucault, M. (1984), 'What is enlightenment?', in P. Rabinow (ed.), *The Foucault Reader*. Hamondsworth: Penguin. pp. 32–50.

Gray, J. (1992), *Men are from Mars, Women are from Venus*. London: Thorsons.

Holmes, J. (1992), 'Women's speech in public contexts', *Discourse and Society*, **3**(2), 131–50.

Lakoff, R. (1975), *Language and Women's Place*. New York: Harper Row.

Lyotard, J. (1984), *The Post-modern Condition*. Manchester: Manchester University Press.

Paechter, C. (2001), 'Using post-structuralist ideas in gender theory and research', in B. Francis and C. Skelton (eds), *Investigating Gender: Contemporary Perspectives in Education*. Buckingham: Open University Press. pp. 41–51.

Pease, A. and Pease, B. (2001), *Why Men don't Listen and Women can't Read Maps*. London: Orion Books.

Singh, V., Kumra, S. and Vinnicombe, S. (2002), 'Gender and impression management: playing the promotion game', *Journal of Business Ethics*, **37**: 77–89.

Singh, V., Vinnicombe, S. and Johnson, P. (2001), 'Women directors on top UK boards', *Corporate Governance: An International Review*, **9**(3): 206–16.

Spender, D. (1980*)*, *Man-made Language*. London: Pandora.

Tannen, D. (1996), *Talking from 9 to 5*. London: Virago.

Thornborrow, J. (2002), *Power Talk: Language and Interaction in Institutional Discourse*. London: Longman.

Zimmerman, D. and West, C. (1975), 'Sex roles, interruptions and silences in conversation', in B. Thorne and N. Henley (eds), *Language, Gender and Society*. Cambridge: Newbury House Publishers. pp. 105–29.

Chapter 12

# Communication and Gender Issues in an Italian Medical Emergency Control Room: A Case Study

Isabella Paoletti

## Introduction

Control rooms in underground and railway stations, airports, emergency numbers, power plants, and so on, are places saturated with technology, in particular communication technology. Studies have described the specific interactional practices that characterize these work settings (Heath et al., 2000; Heath and Luff, 2000; Hutchby, 2001; Suchman, 1987). This chapter presents a case study based on a research project on control rooms of the medical emergency number, 118, in Italy. The study highlights some of the main communication issues in the control room and looks in particular at gender issues, focusing on a discussion between a call operator, a woman, and a doctor in a helicopter team, a man. The discussion is about the call operator's decision to have the helicopter intervene in that particular case, to rescue a person who, it later turned out, was already dead. As we shall see, communication issues that are quite typical in an emergency call are at the base of the quarrel, as well as what could be defined as a sexist remark. The case study will allow us to draw useful conclusions with implications for training of control room personnel and for finding strategies to challenge sexism.

Recent research developments in language and gender studies show an increasing interest, in particular among feminist scholars, in the use of discourse analysis and conversation analysis to explore the social construction of gender (for example Cameron, 1998; Kotthoff and Wodack, 1997; Miller and Metcalfe, 1998; Stokoe, 1998; Wodack, 1997). Particularly interesting in this respect is the debate between feminist scholars and conversation analysts carried out in the journal *Discourse and Society* with a special issue devoted to the topic of language and gender (Stokoe and Weatherall, 2002). Gender is a pervasive organizing instrument of members' knowledge and practices; that is, a members' category device (Sacks, 1992). Gendering work, doing gender and gender identification work, are all established topics of ethnomethodological research (Edwards, 1998; Garfinkel, 1967; Jayyusi, 1984; Nilan, 1994; Paoletti, 1998, 2001, 2002; Stokoe and Smithson, 2001, 2002;

Stokoe and Weatherall, 2002). According to these studies, being a woman, or being a man, takes work, and this can be shown in detail by analysing ordinary instances of interaction. It is clear that understanding 'the mechanics' of how gender identities and practices are produced can be very useful if one wishes to change some features of those identities and practices. However, one needs to question whether this detailed understanding of gendering work is being applied to the study of workplaces, in particular those with a significant use of IT.

There is a growing field of research – workplace studies – and in particular, computer supported cooperative work (CSCW), that is focused on studying work practices that are supported by IT. As Heath and Luff (2000, p. 8) point out: 'work practices do not necessarily change to make systems work', that is, the introduction of complex IT systems is not guaranteed to work. Sophisticated communication technology systems have to be included in living social environments, that is, actual workplaces, and major failures have forcefully shown that this process is often problematic (Heath et al., 2000). Moreover, new approaches to system design, namely, 'cooperative design' and 'participatory design', stress the relevance of the 'central and abiding concern for direct and continuous interaction with those who are the ultimate arbiters of system adequacy, namely, those who will use the technology in their everyday lives and work' (Suchman, 1993, p. vii). Ethnomethodological studies have made a major contribution to these fields of research, detailing specific interactional procedures typical of these workplaces, but without a specific interest in describing gendering practices within these social environments.

Studies of the impact of technology on women's work are quite a recent endeavour. In 1994, Gattiker could write: 'Women and technology has not garnered much attention so far' (1994, p. 251). Feminist scholars have shown that 'workplaces are infused with gender' (Yancey Martin, 2003, p. 343) and have highlighted specific mechanisms that discriminate against women, such as 'general cultural tendencies to devaluate the work of women [which] lead to lower earnings for typically female work' (Tomaskovic-Devey and Skaggs, 2002, p. 103) and the double standard for competence: 'Women either have to perform better than men, or they have to exhibit additional qualities above those required of men, before both sexes exert comparable levels of influence' (Foschi, 1992, p. 198). In line with these studies, the research on women and technology shows a gender hierarchy within communication technology-mediated work (Stanworth, 2000; Tijdens, 1999; Yancey Martin, 1992). As Yancey Martin (1992, pp. 211–12) says, 'computer work is stratified internally into men's work and women's work. Men perform head work – computer scientist and programmer – and women do the routine work – data entry and computer equipment operator'. This is closely combined with a lack of involvement of women in education and training in relation to IT (Dunkle, 1994; Stanworth, 2000). In particular, Stanworth (2000, p. 24) points out that 'employers tend to invest less in the short-term and non-standard workforce, where many women are located'.

Gender differences in attitudes towards technology and in the impact of the introduction of technology on work practices have also been the object of studies.

The general prejudice of women's dislike of technology and their inability to use communication technology has been criticized. Gattiker (1994) says in this regard:

> Women in powerful positions must eradicate and signal their dislike of gender-based technology bias. Unless women take it upon themselves to make change happen, gender based technology bias and rational discrimination is here to stay, much to society's disadvantage and women's detriment. (p. 282)

The research results on gender differences in attitudes toward IT appear controversial, or rather, they describe a situation that is rapidly evolving (Gattiker, 1994; Kirkup and Smith-Keller, 1992; Webster, 1996; Stanworth, 2000). Dunkle (1994) reports women's more positive attitude towards the introduction of IT compared to the male colleagues in her study of white collar workers in the United States. In particular, Dunkle (1994, p. 54) points out that 'the manager should not assume that male workers are the most appropriate initial targets for innovations involving information technology.' In her study of Dutch female office workers, Tijdens (1999) reports that most women use computers nowadays; and Zauchner and her colleagues in Vienna point out in their study that 'no gender-related effects of IT implementations were found' (Zauchner et al., 2000, p. 126). Stanworth, (2000, p. 24) describes UK women as 'severely disadvantaged in terms of IT occupations', but the situation is rapidly changing, with 'a growing number of UK women highly qualified' (Stanworth, 2000, p. 24).

In the analysis presented in this chapter, emphasis will be given to specific communication problems in the control room, with particular attention to gender issues. Calls to emergency numbers have been the object of studies for some time (Tracy, 1997; Wakin and Zimmerman, 1999; Watson, 1984; Whalen and Zimmerman, 1987, 1998; Zimmerman, 1992a, 1992b). A number of differences between the structure of ordinary calls and that of calls to an emergency number have been highlighted; for example, Whalen and Zimmerman (1987) point out that: 'Recognitionals, greetings, and "howareyous" are ... routinely *absent* in emergency and other types of service calls' (p. 177). A typical five-step structure characterizes emergency calls and includes: (1) identification; (2) reason for the call; (3) interrogative series; (4) the response to the request for help; and (5) closing (Whalen and Zimmerman, 1987). Moreover, studies have highlighted the relevance of emotions and emotional labour in such calls (Imbens-Bailey and McCabe, 2000; Tracy and Tracy, 1998a, 1998b; Whalen and Zimmerman, 1998; Whalen et al.,1988). A problem of framing has been also described. Tracy (1997, p. 316) observes that 'Citizens ... frequently bring a 'customer service' frame to the exchange, whereas emergency call takers assume what I have labelled a 'public service' frame'. That is, callers ask for the provision of an ambulance as they would ask for a taxi or a pizza, while the call taker needs to have details on the condition of the person in need of help in order to send the appropriate means for assistance; the questioning sequence is often perceived by callers as inappropriate and a way of delaying assistance. The communication problems addressed in the data analysed here are in fact related precisely to this problem of framing.

## The Study

In Italy, since the introduction of the centralized medical emergency number in 1992, the idea itself of emergency assistance has radically changed. Before this, the patient was brought to the hospital; now the hospital is brought to the street, to the person in need of help. Some ambulances are miniaturized hospitals; they are provided with equipment and drugs that allow interventions on the street similar to those carried out in hospital emergency departments. Moreover, at times the call operator of the medical emergency control room is engaged in actual rescue activity via the phone, giving detailed instructions to family members or immediate helpers in order to provide first aid. In cases, for example, of heart attacks, choking or massive bleeding, it is the immediate helper who saves lives. In this respect, the call operators carry out an intensive educational and training activity in schools and non-governmental organizations, the aim of which is to inform the public about how to use the emergency service correctly and to teach the basics of first aid.

The call takers in the medical emergency control room in the Italian town of Trento are mainly professional nurses with paramedic training, and only a few are former ambulance drivers who are not trained nurses. They have shifts comprising both work in the control room and in the ambulance, and only a few of them are also part of the helicopter teams. On a regular basis, they have to attend in-service courses on various specialized aspects of first aid assistance. In the control room in Trento, there are three computer consoles located in different boxes that deal with incoming calls: from the city of Trento (called box 4), from the province (called box 3), and in relation to planned or routine transportation (as in the case of dialysis) of patients to or between hospitals. The boxes are equipped with a computer console, through which incoming calls are queued and dealt with and the data of all cases is registered, a radio, and a telephone. Two operators work in each box. The task of the call taker is not only to send the most appropriate means of assistance in the shortest time to an emergency, but also to manage scarce resources; that is, to send the most appropriate means of help in the light of the possibility that other emergencies, possibly more serious, might occur. In particular, one of the priorities of call takers is not to leave an area 'uncovered', that is, without an ambulance in the vicinity, ready to intervene if an emergency occurs.

On entering the control room, the first impression is that gender division of work is not an issue: men and women work together at the console, showing a high level of mastery of the job in both comfortably using the equipment and managing complex tasks and stressful situations, very often with lightness and humour, creating a pleasant working environment. Looking at the hierarchy within the emergency department, the head of the department is a male doctor and the head of the control room is a male nurse, but the head of 36 male ambulance drivers is a female nurse and the head of all the province ambulance stations and nurses is also a female nurse.

The data presented in this study refers to the management of a specific case, an accident at a paper factory, in which communication problems arose. This case is particularly useful, not only because it illustrates very clearly some of the most common communication problems that arise in emergency calls, but also as an example of 'good practice' in terms of training. In fact, the call taker who managed the case decided to focus her degree thesis on this work experience that was particularly difficult and stressful for her. The decision itself to make this case the subject of her thesis seemed an act of strength and resistance; this way, a difficult working experience was turned into a very useful training experience.

The data analysed in this chapter are part of a wider corpus collected in an ongoing research project on language and technology carried out by the Department of Communication Sciences of the University of Bologna and the Sociology Department of the University of Trento, Italy. The transcripts reported are taken from the tape recordings of the calls to and from the control room in relation to an emergency in a paper factory, and the interview with the call operator who dealt with that case. The data are investigated through a detailed conversation analysis within an ethnomethodological framework (Garfinkel, 1967; Sacks, 1992) in order to highlight not only specific communication problems that might arise in a control room, but also gender issues in this particular work setting.

*The Initial Call*

In this first call, the problem of the 'frame' (Tracy, 1997) is immediately evident. The caller is clearly asking for an ambulance, just as he would order a pizza. The call taker is attempting to elicit information from the caller on the condition of the person in need of help in order to send the most appropriate means to deal with the emergency. But let us look closely at the actual interaction. The transcript starts a few seconds after the beginning of the call; that is, when the caller is put on to the territorially relevant operator in relation to the place where the event is taking place. (Transcript notational conventions are set out in Table 12.1. In the transcript below, O3 is the call taker; C1 is the first caller from the paper factory; A is the ambulance driver.)

**Call no. 1: from the paper factory; time 11:38:36**
01   O3:   118? ((the call taker of box 3 answers))
02   C1:   118 it's the paper factory of Villalagarina=
03   O3:   = yes (.) what happen[ed?]
04   C1:                       [an a]mbulance is urgently needed a boy's hurt himself =
05   O3:   =tell me what happened to him
06   C1:   well no: no I can't tell you (.) he is on the ground unconscious
07   O3:   is he on the ground unconscious do you see him breathing?
08   C1:   eh now (you see the cal[ls)]
09   O3:                         [but ]he didn't hurt himself sir you must tell me precisely what happened because if necessary I'll send the helicopter too
10   C1:   hh (.) eh hold on a second
11   (3.1)
12   O3:   attention Rovereto from headquarters ((time 11.39.02: by radio the call taker calls Rovereto post while waiting for further information from the paper factory))

13 (2.3)
14 A: (a moment/go ahead) [( )]
15 O3:                                    [leave] for the paper factory a fainting fit then I'll tell you
more later (.)Villalagarina paper factory.
16 A: (fine)=
17 O3: um? (1.5) ( your) yes I see (and now) I'll explain what I've said
18 C1: (hallo pardon)
19 O3: yes tell[me?]
20 C1:          [but] send the helicopter I don't I don't know
21 O3: no listen you don't have to tell me what I have to send
22 O3: [you tell] me the person's condition =
23 C1: [( )]          =well there is a boy who is unwell here =
24 O3: = well is he breathing?
25 C1: hh (1.4) it seems he isn't it seems fuck!
26 O3: please give me your number (.) hallo? ((the caller hangs up))

**Table 12.1 Transcript notational conventions**

| | | | |
|---|---|---|---|
| (.) | Stop or pause in the rhythm of the conversation | ... | Part of the transcript has been omitted |
| [ | Overlapping utterances at this point | ? | Rising intonation |
| = | No gaps in the flow of conversation | ! | Excited tone |
| | | ::::: | Elongation |
| ( ) | Word(s) spoken, but not intelligible | hh | audible aspiration |
| | | (0.4) | Pause timed in seconds |
| (dog) | Word(s) not clearly intelligible | ((laugh)) | Transcriber description |

The opening of the call is characterized by self-identification, precisely institutional self-identifications in both cases, the emergency service on one hand, *'118?'*, on the other, a factory, *'it's the paper factory of Villalagarina'*. The form of the exchange communicates urgency, especially on the part of the operator. All the operators answer with *'118?'*. It would be impossible to produce a shorter institutional self-identification. The rising intonation – 118 is pronounced with the intonation of a question – immediately represents an elicitation of the reason for the call; as if to say: *'Yes you have reached 118, what do you want from us? Hurry up, tell us.'* Brevity communicates urgency. In fact, in many cases the caller's self-identification is immediately followed by the reason for the call. But not in this case; therefore the operator explicitly solicits the reason for the call, *'yes, what happened?'*

Here is the first formulation of the reason for the call: *'an ambulance is urgently needed a boy's hurt himself'*. From this type of formulation it is possible to infer that some kind of accident has happened; being in a factory, the immediate thought is a work accident. The interrogation series starts at this point, and the operator asks the caller to tell the story of what happened: *'tell me what happened to him'*. The caller first expresses a difficulty in relation to describing what happened, *'well no: no I can't tell you'*, then adds, *'he is on the ground unconscious'*. This is a very different formulation from the previous one; here a fainting fit is inferable.

There is a 'prescribed' sequence of questions that call takers have to ask in order to ascertain the condition of the person in need of help and consequently send the most appropriate means of help. Ascertaining the condition of vital functions, such as breathing, is one of the main parts of the questioning series: *'is he on the ground unconscious do you see him breathing?'* The caller's answer is unclear, (see line 08). He is probably calling from a place different from that of the accident. The operator's question implies that the caller is able to see the injured person while he is calling, but the caller may not have seen the injured person himself at all. He may have just been sent in a hurry to make the call, to ask for the ambulance. This seems to be his frame.

The call taker at this point solicits a clarification between the two versions so far, accident versus fainting fit: *'but he didn't hurt himself'*. Again she solicits more information: *'Sir, you must tell me precisely what happened.'* She states the reason for the necessity for more information, that is, the sending of the most appropriate means of help: *'because if necessary I'll send the helicopter too'*. In a subsequent interview between the call taker and the author, the call taker said that she considered this formulation a mistake when she analysed it afterwards. She felt that she shifted on to the caller the responsibility of choosing the means of rescue. But her intention was to motivate him to cooperate, because she felt him *'like slipping away'*.

The caller at this point asks the operator to hold the line. He is probably inquiring about what happened: *'hh (.) eh hold on a second'*. In the few seconds of interruption, the operator calls the closest ambulance station to the factory and sends an ambulance. Notice the form of her communication: *'leave for the paper factory a fainting fit then I'll tell you more later (.) Villalagarina paper factory'*. Again brevity communicates urgency. It is probable that the ambulance left at high speed and with sirens wailing, although she does not say anything to her colleagues in this regard. In the interview, she mentions explicitly that the form of the communication is sufficient to communicate to the colleagues the type of code, a red code in this case; that is, maximum urgency.

The communication is resumed; the different frames problem becomes very evident at this point, and causes the interruption of the communication. The caller is not aware that the ambulance has been sent. He perceives the questioning as a delay to his urgent request for help. He has done his duty: he has asked for the ambulance. Why aren't they sending it? Why do they keep asking questions instead of coming here? When he says, *'but send the helicopter I don't I don't know'* he is conveying that it is not his job to say what is necessary. There is a crescendo, the operator feels annoyed because the caller is not cooperating in the expected way, giving the necessary information: *'no listen you don't have to tell me what I have to send, you tell me the person's condition'*. The several speech overlaps communicate the agitation, haste and annoyance in the interchange at this point. The caller again produces a very generic statement about the young man being unwell; in fact, he probably does not actually know what happened, or he is so shocked that he is not able to tell: *'Well there is a boy who is unwell here.'* The operator again solicits a precise description: *'well is he breathing?'* The caller gives vent to his fear, anger and frustration. He curses, saying *'hh (1.4) it seems he isn't it seems fuck!'*, and hangs up. This type of interrupted call is not uncommon in communication in the control room, nor are cursing, rudeness and face attacks (Tracy and Tracy, 1998a; Whalen and Zimmerman, 1998).

The call taker is left with an unclear idea of the nature of the young man's problems. There are three subsequent calls with the paper factory. In the third one, the caller says that the boy is breathing, is still alive. Then the ambulance arrives and the driver tells the call taker that the boy is dead, that he is under the engine. But he does not specify the dynamics of the accident, that the young man actually passed through the rollers and was completely crushed. Probably for the ambulance driver it was so evident that he was dead that he just said it, without explaining it. He was probably shocked too. The call taker at this point decides to send the helicopter. She had received contradictory reports on the accident and, in fact, a 'dead' person – that is, a person who appears to be dead – can sometimes be reanimated. Moreover there was no doctor at the scene of the accident. According to institutional regulations she cannot accept an ambulance driver's report of a person's death, unless the person is beheaded or is burnt to ashes.

After the event, the doctor of the helicopter team called her and complained about her sending the helicopter when the person was obviously dead. In the interview, the call taker said that she felt offended and angry because of that call; she felt she was treated and judged unjustly by the doctor. During the call she tried unsuccessfully to explain to him that she did the right thing in relation to the information she had. This call in fact was one of the reasons why she decided to study that particular case in her thesis. The following brief passage from that call has been chosen as being significant because it contains what could be defined by some as a sexist remark.

At this point it is important to specify a methodological position. In conversation analysis, the explicatory strength of the analysis is based on the mutual understanding that is shown by participants in the development of the conversation; that is, in the sequential organization of the talk. Unless a particular interpretation of the interaction is shown and made available by participants, it is not sustainable in the analysis, but there is no overall agreement on this point. For example Speer and Potter (2000) in their article on heterosexist talk say:

> it is important not to mix up the two analytic levels: on the one hand, what the participants take the interaction to mean (as derogatory and offensive, or perfectly acceptable, for example), and on the other hand, what we, as analysts, choose to make of that piece of interaction, over and above, or regardless of what its status is for the participants (p. 563).

There are no signs in the interaction that the remark has been understood or meant as sexist by either party to the conversation. It is the analyst who is interpreting it as such.

*The Problem with the Intensive Care Doctor: Is There A Gender Issue?*

The passage reported below occurs towards the end of the call. The doctor and the call taker had been talking for some time, the doctor was arguing that the call taker should not have sent the helicopter for a code four, that is, a dead person. The call taker was explaining that she had had contradictory information and that she had judged it safest to send the helicopter anyway. The discussion is getting quite heated, when the doctor asks the call taker to calm down. (See below for transcript notational conventions; O3 is the call taker; D is the doctor in the helicopter team.)

**Call no. 21: second call of the intensive care doctor from Mattarello airport to Trento 118; the first call taker (O3) answers; time 13:53:48**

01    D:   excuse me a moment keep calm nothing is
           happen[ing in particular, if you need some tranquilli[zer

02    O3:   [well                               [no, I don't need any
           tranquillizer [but since you told me

03    D:          [(well well) I am telling you that the man declared that he explicitly
           stated (.) that it was a code four (.) he said very clearly a code four and that you
           said that you were going to send me anyway then this (.) version is different from
           yours [(I )

04    O3:   [(no I'll) explain it to you

To talk of women as 'neurotic' and 'over reacting' is quite a common sexist remark. The agitation of the passage is visible from the several overlapping turns. An apparently reassuring remark, *'excuse me a moment keep calm nothing is happening in particular'*, is followed by a clear face attack: *'if you need some tranquillizer'*. This is countered decisively by the call taker, *'no, I don't need any tranquillizer'*, and she probably starts an explanation about why she is getting angry, *'but since you told me'*. The doctor regains the turn, talking over her and states his position. The discussion continues.

When the author asked the call taker about this passage in the subsequent interview, she said that she felt offended and angry in particular because she felt treated: *'like an anxious neurotic and (1.3) and who didn't do her job well sending him around for nothing (.) Instead from my point of view this was not true.'* Apparently the comment on her agitation during the conversation had extended to the quality of her work, or rather it was combined with the doctors' criticism of her decisions. That is, the call taker felt it as an attack on her self-esteem, as control room operator. This is what the author would define as a sexist remark; that is, an attack on one's self-esteem as a person, or a devaluation of what one does, based on gender stereotypes. In the interview, she was also explicitly asked if she thought that: *'if you need some tranquillizer'* was a sexist remark. She did not. She explained that she saw it strictly in a professional light: a doctor criticizing her work. In the control room there is a very unusual institutional twist in the hierarchy: doctors are told what to do by nurses and they have to do it. They can complain afterwards, as in this case, but during the emergency, the control room operator has the power to decide what means to mobilize. The call taker explicitly expressed that the doctor's remark did not leave her cold, even if she thought it unjust, precisely because he was a doctor, she said: *'I want him to think of me (.) eh:::: that I was an operator who acted rightly and well.'*

## Implications

For women to recognize sexism is certainly healthy for their self-esteem, but then, ignoring it, or rather, not confronting it directly, can also be at times a winning strategy (Yancey-Martin, 2003). Here is a passage from an interview with one of the women in a managing position in the emergency department, discussing gender relationships within the department personnel:

> with males there is the initial underestimation because anyway she is just a woman ... I have had to manage this aspect very much because there was an attitude 'I can handle her because she is a woman', therefore I initially let this be the approach and then bit by bit I regain my role ... I let them think in this way then in the actual fact (I fix them up).

The use of a gender stereotype could particularly hinder the female operator's confidence in operating in a complex communication technology environment, that it is often considered a 'male province'. But in fact, the call taker did not acknowledge the sexist nature of the remark even to herself. She acted in a way that was quite empowering for her in the end, turning a negative work experience into a very useful training experience. In particular, she pointed out in the interview that through the transcription process and the analysis of the data, she came to realize that she had wrongly decided at the beginning of the call that it was a fainting fit and not an accident. She learnt that it is important to leave open your interpretation of what is actually going on at the scene; that is to treat your interpretation as hypothetical. She says: *'with hindsight eh:: I would have analysed that as being sick I would not have (.) decided that it was a fainting fit'*. No lecture, instruction, or injunction could have produced this powerful and extremely useful realization for a call taker in a medical emergency control room – the awareness of one's own mental constructions of what was happening at the scene – except the critical reflection on one's own work experience, through the careful inspection of the actual interaction.

## Conclusion

In this chapter, some communication problems in a medical emergency control room have been presented, together with an instance of sexist communication. IT-supported work is becoming increasingly common in a vast variety of work settings. The careful inspection of communication and practices in these work settings, with a particular interest in gender issues, can be very useful not only in understanding the mechanism through which sexism and gender division of work is reproduced, but also how they are resisted. In fact, as Hollander (2002, p. 491) points out: 'Gender is not monolithic or stable in its construction; innovation and resistance exist alongside more conventional expressions that reproduce the gender status quo.' A list of specific recommendations follows in relation to contrasting sexism and the gender division of labour in communication technology-supported work sites.

## Recommendations

- Women, particularly those in powerful positions, must express forcefully their dislike of, and the unacceptability of, gender-based technology bias.
- Managers should not assume that male workers are the most appropriate initial targets for innovations involving IT.
- Employers and governmental agencies should invest more in terms of communication technology training in the short-term and non-standard workforce, where many women are located.
- Managers of control rooms of medical emergency numbers should include in the training of the operators the possibility for systematic reflection on communication practices, particularly of problematic cases.
- Women should learn to recognize sexism in ordinary talk and practices, that is, ways that undermine their self-esteem as persons and their value professionally, based on gender stereotypes.
- Women should be aware that indirect ways of fighting sexism can be as effective, or even more effective, than direct confrontation.

## Acknowledgements

I would like to thank all the personnel in the 118 control room in Trento for their patience and cooperation during the data collection, in particular the call taker who let me use some of her recorded data, and Professor Giolo Fele for the interesting discussions on the data.

## References

Cameron, D. (1998), '"Is there any ketchup, Vera?" Gender, power and pragmatics', *Discourse and Society*, **9**(4): 437–55.

Dunkle, D. E. (1994), 'Women, men, and information technology: A gender based comparison of the impacts of computing experienced by white collar workers', in U. E. Gattiker (ed.), *Women and Technology*. Berlin: Gruyter. pp. 31–63.

Edwards, D. (1998), 'The relevant thing about her: Social identity categories in use', in C. Antaki and S. Widdicombe, S. (eds), *Identities in Talk*. London: Sage. pp. 15–33.

Foschi, M. (1992), 'Gender and double standards for competence', in C. L. Ridgeway (ed.), *Gender, Interaction, and Inequality*. New York: Springer-Verlag. pp. 181–207.

Garfinkel, H. (1967), *Studies in Ethnomethodology*. Englewood Cliffs, NJ: Prentice-Hall.

Gattiker, U. E. (1994), 'Where Do We Go from Here? Directions for Future Research and Managers', in U. E. Gattiker, U. E. (ed.), *Women and Technology*. Berlin: Gruyter. pp. 245–86.

Heath, C. and Luff, P. (2000), *Technology in Action*. Cambridge: Cambridge University Press.

Heath, C., Knoblauch, H. and Luff, P. (2000), 'Technology and social interaction: The emergence of workplace studies', *British Journal of Sociology*, **51**(2): 299–320.

Hollander, J. A. (2002), 'Resisting vulnerability: The social reconstruction of gender in interaction', *Social Problems*, **49**(4): 474–96.

Hutchby, I. (2001), *Conversation and Technology*. Cambridge: Polity.

Imbens-Bailey, A. and McCabe, A. (2000), 'The discourse of distress: A narrative analysis of emergency calls to 911', *Language and Communication*, **20**(3): 275–96.

Jayyusi, L. (1984), *Categorization and the Moral Order*. London: Routledge and Kegan Paul.

Kirkup, G. and Smith Keller, L. (eds) (1992), *Inventing Women: Science, Technology and Gender*. Cambridge: The Open University Press.

Kotthoff, H. and Wodak, R. (eds) (1997), *Communicating Gender in Context*. Amsterdam: John Benjamins.

Miller, L. J. and Metcalfe, J. (1998), 'Strategically speaking: the problem of essentializing terms in feminist theory and feminist organizational talk', *Human Studies*, **21**(3): 235–57.

Nilan, P. (1994), 'Gender as positioned identity maintenance in every discourse', *Social Semiotics*, **4**(1–2): 139–62.

Paoletti, I. (1998), 'Handling "incoherence" according to the speaker's on-sight categorization', in C. Antaki and S. Widdicombe (eds), *Identities in Talk*. London: Sage. pp. 171–90.

Paoletti, I. (2001), 'Membership categorization and time appraisal in interviews with family carers of disabled elderly', *Human Studies*, **24**(3): 293–325.

Paoletti, I. (2002), 'Caring for older people: A gendered practice', *Discourse and Society*, **13**(6): 805–17.

Sacks, H. (1992), *Lectures on Conversation*, Vols I and II, Oxford: Blackwell.

Speer, S. A. and Potter, J. (2000), 'The management of heterosexist talk: Conversational resources and prejudiced claims', *Discourse and Society*, **11**(4): 543–72.

Stanworth, C. (2000), 'Women and work in the information age', *Gender, Work and Organization*, **7**(1): 20–32.

Stokoe, E. H. (1998), 'Talking about gender: The conversational construction of gender categories in academic discourse', *Discourse and Society*, **9**(2): 217–40.

Stokoe, E. H. and Smithson J. (2001), 'Making gender relevant: Conversational analysis and gender categories in interaction', *Discourse and Society*, **12**(2): 217–44.

Stokoe, E. H. and Smithson J. (2002), 'Gender and sexuality in talk-in-interaction: Considering conversation analytic perspectives', in P. Mcllvenny (ed.), *Talking Gender and Sexuality: Conversation, Performativity and Discourse in Interaction*. Amsterdam: John Benjamins.

Stokoe, E. H. and Weatherall, A. (2002), 'Gender, language, conversation analysis and feminism', *Discourse and Society*, **13**(6): 707–13.

Suchman, L. (1987), *Plans and situated actions: The problem of human–machine communication*. Cambridge: Cambridge University Press.

Suchman, L. (1993), 'Foreword', in D. Shuler and A. Namioka (eds), *Participatory Design: Principles and Practices*, Hillsdale, NJ: Lawrence Erlbaum Associates.

Tijdens, K. G. (1999), 'Behind the screens: The foreseen and unforeseen impact of computerization on female office workers' jobs', *Gender, Work and Organization*, **6**(1): 47–57.

Tomaskovic-Devey, D. and Skaggs, S. (2002), 'Sex segregation, labor process organization, and gender earnings inequality', *American Journal of Sociology*, **108**(1): 102–28.

Tracy, K. (1997), 'Interactional trouble in emergency services requests: A problem of frames'. *Research on Language and Social Interaction*, **30**(4): 315–43.

Tracy, K. and Tracy, S. J. (1998a), 'Rudeness at 911: Reconceptualizing face and face attack', *Human Communication Research*, **25**(2): 225–51.

Tracy, K. and Tracy, S. J. (1998b), 'Emotion labor at 911: A case study and theoretical critique', *Journal of Applied Communication Research*, **26**(4): 390–411.

Wakin, M. A. and Zimmerman, D. H. (1999), 'Reduction and specialization in emergency and directory assistance calls', *Research on Language and Social Interaction*, **32**(4): 409–37.

Watson, R. D. (1984), 'Doing the organization's work: An examination of aspects of the operation of a crisis intervention center', in S. Fisher and A. D. Todd (eds), *Discourse and Institutional Authority: Medicine, Education and Law*, Norwood, NJ: Ablex. pp. 91–120.

Webster, J. (1996), *Shaping Women's Work: Gender, Employment and Information Technology*. London: Longman.

Whalen, J. and Zimmerman, D. H. (1998), 'Observation on the display and management of emotions in natural occurring activities: The case of "hysteria" in calls to 9-1-1', *Social Psychology Quarterly*, **61**(2): 141–59.

Whalen, J., Zimmerman, D. H. and Whalen, M. R. (1988), 'When words fail: A single case analysis', *Social Problems*, **35**(4): 335–62.

Whalen, M. R. and Zimmerman, D. H. (1987), 'Sequential and institutional contexts in calls for help', *Social Psychology Quarterly*, **50**(2): 172–85.

Wodak, R. (1997), '"I know, we won't revolutionize the world with it, but ...": Styles of female leadership in institutions', in H. Kotthoff and R. Wodak (eds), *Communicating Gender in Context*. Amsterdam: John Benjamins. pp. 335–70.

Yancey Martin, P. (1992), 'Gender, interaction and inequality in organizations', in C. L. Ridgeway (ed.), *Gender, Interaction and Inequality*. New York: Springer-Verlag. pp. 208–31.

Yancey Martin, P. (2003), '"Said and done" versus "saying and doing": Gendering practices, practising gender at work', *Gender and Society*, **17**(3): 342–66.

Zauchner, S., Korunka, C., Weiss, A. and Kafka-Lützow, A. (2000), 'Gender-related effects of information technology implementation', *Gender, Work and Organization*, **7** (2), 119–32.

Zimmerman, D. H. (1992a), 'The interactional organization of calls for emergency assistance', in P. Drew and J. Heritage (eds), *Talk at Work*. Cambridge: Cambridge University Press. pp. 418–69.

Zimmerman, D. H. (1992b), 'Achieving context: Openings in emergency calls', in G. Watson and R. M. Seiler (eds), *Text in Context*. Newbury Park, CA: Sage. pp. 35–51.

# PART IV
# Communicating to Get Things Done

# Chapter 13

# Gender, Leadership and Communication

Leonie V. Still

## Introduction

The paucity of women in leadership positions has emerged as a characteristic of the workforce in most Western industrialized countries in recent times. Despite almost 35 years of rapid social change for women, their improved higher education attainments, their increased numbers in management and their 'credentialling' for leadership by way of experience, line management, networking and other such activities, relatively few are attaining executive management or board positions.

Three recent Australian surveys (Equal Opportunity in the Workplace Agency and Catalyst, 2002, 2003, 2004) of the numbers of women in senior management and on the boards of the nation's top 200 companies who represent 90 per cent of Australia's market capitalization, give ample evidence of this. The findings revealed that women held only 10.2 per cent of executive management positions (compared to 8.4 per cent in 2002) and 8.6 per cent of board directorships (8.2 per cent in 2002). Just over 42 per cent of the companies had no women executive managers in 2004, while 47 per cent had no women directors. Only four women held a CEO position in the 200 companies, while only two women chaired boards. The numbers of women in line positions, the traditional recruitment area for top positions, amounted to 6.5 per cent in 2004 (up from 4.7 per cent in 2003).

The little incremental change in the leadership attainments of women both in Australia and overseas (Davidson and Burke, 2004; Wirth, 2001) gives added impetus to determining why this is so. It has been known for some time that a lack of line management and profit centre experience have been major drawbacks to aspiring and ambitious women (Sheridan and Milgate, 2003; Vinnicombe and Singh, 2003). Other explanations for the paucity of women in leadership positions include the prescriptive nature of stereotypes; many women's lack of ambition or fear of assault on their 'authenticity' (Saunders, 1996); women's preference for support, rather than line management, roles because of the nature of the work; the difficulties of accommodating work and family; the male managerial culture; women's lack of mentors and networks; and their difficulty in adjusting to, and operating within, certain organizational cultures.

However, while all these aspects have often restricted career opportunities for women, the issue of women as leaders and associated gender differences in communication and/or linguistic styles are also important factors. Although these issues have also been examined over time, both individually and collectively, and in both the popular and academic literature, it is timely to review them to determine just how the interplay between these factors prevents more women from moving into leadership roles. According to Claes (1999), gender and language (communication) are social constructs, while Sinclair (1998) believes the same can be said of leadership. Hence, the way these social constructs combine and interact in the workplace in particular, and society in general, can have an enormous impact on the number of women in leadership positions. The following discussion examines these factors from a managerial, rather than a sociological or socio-psychological, perspective, while using the leadership lens as the focus to examine the issues.

## Overview of Current Research

Most of the research into women in leadership and the interplay with communication can be categorized into three distinct areas. First, there is the issue of women as leaders and whether they are acceptable candidates for such roles given the 'heroic' models of leadership (Lucas, 2003; Merrill-Sands and Kolb, 2001; Sinclair, 1998). Second, there is the issue of gender differences in management/leadership 'styles' (Applebaum and Shapiro, 1993; Bartol et al., 2003; Claes, 1999; Eagly and Johannesen-Schmidt, 2001; Eagly and Johnson, 1990; Eagly et al., 1992; Kabacoff, 2000; Oshagbemi and Gill, 2003; Rosener, 1990; Stelter, 2002; Van Engen et al., 2001). Third, and related to the second category, is the aspect of gender-related communication/linguistic 'styles' or how men and women communicate in the workplace (Case, 1994; Claes, 1999; Tannen, 1994; Zanetic and Jeffery, 1999). Each of these areas is now discussed in turn.

*Women as Leaders*

Research on women in leadership has revolved mainly around the employment status of women and their representation in management and on boards (for example, Burton, 1997; Equal Opportunity for Women in the Workplace Agency and Catalyst, 2002, 2003, 2004; Still, 2004); the issue of the glass ceiling and how it curtails the ambitions of women at a certain hierarchical level (for example, Meyerson and Fletcher, 2000; Powell, 2000; Still, 1997; Wirth, 2001); and the shift of women into self-employment and entrepreneurial activities because of the glass ceiling and the difficulties involved in adjusting to the corporate world (Carter and Anderson, 2001; Carter et al., 2001; Centre for Women's Business Research, 2001; Korn/Ferry International, 2001; Still and Timms, 2000; Still and Walker, 2003).

However, despite the advances made by women in the past 35 years, the term leadership is not normally associated with them (Sinclair, 1998). In fact, women's lack of acceptance in the corridors of power can be traced directly to the development of the first leadership theories and concepts of power.

Philosophers originally thought personal characteristics were important for leadership and proposed the 'great man' theory, which later evolved into the trait theory of leadership. Leadership was assumed to be the property of the individual, such as having superior genes or a certain personality. Aspiring women were kept from gaining prominence because it was assumed they lacked the necessary traits to become leaders.

Despite theoretical advances in leadership theory since this stage, attitudes towards women assuming authority roles are still locked in the 'great man' time warp. Investigating the Australian corporate culture, Sinclair (1994, 1998) found that the 'great man' or 'hero' still dominated criteria for leadership positions. Anyone embarking on a quest for membership of the executive culture was considered to be on 'a Ulysses-like journey: full of grand-scale trials of endurance and tests of strength – the modern day equivalent of the heroic quest!' (1994, p. 15). This type of stereotypical thinking is confirmed by Kim Campbell, the only woman Prime Minster of Canada, who stated that the greatest obstacle she encountered was the deeply rooted belief that women were not competent and could not lead. People found her natural inclination towards consensus building, as well as being communal, expressive and nurturing, to be disturbing. 'A woman wasn't supposed to be prime minister. I wasn't entitled to be there' (Campbell, 2002, p. 20).

According to Apfelbaum and Hadley (1986), women have become leaders in four main ways:

- through charismatic leadership: the unique example being Joan of Arc;
- through inherited leadership positions: examples include women who become heads of family businesses or queens of kingdoms;
- through the achievement of professional eminence: women who become leading figures in their disciplines because of their professional and/or scientific achievements: examples include Madame Curie, Margaret Mead;
- through becoming a selected leader – that is, elected, appointed or nominated to important public offices such as prime minister, senator: examples include Margaret Thatcher, Hillary Clinton and Kim Campbell.

A fifth path to leadership, *selection by merit*, has arisen recently through the adoption of equal opportunity laws in many countries. The interpretation of merit depends largely on the assumptions, perceptions and values of the people and organizations applying the principle, but one particular view sees it as the relationship between a person's job-related qualities and those genuinely required for performance in particular positions (Burton et al., 1994). Where non-merit prevails, the 'old boy's club', a person's school or military service, and whether or not the person 'fits in' to the culture, image or environment become selection criteria. Women gain under a merit interpretation, and lose under the non-merit one.

Despite this advance, however, Sinclair (1994, 1998) and Merrill-Sands and Kolb (2001) maintain that the concept of leadership remains a masculine notion defined by subtle and deeply rooted cultural norms and values in organizations. Although several studies (Kabacoff, 2000; Posner and Kouzes, 1993) have shown that when assessed on specific skills that are considered important for effective leadership in today's world, women are perceived to do as well as men or even outperform them, Merrill-Sands and Kolb (2001) conclude that the specific skills and competencies identified as being important for effective leadership do not mirror the assumptions and images people hold of effective leaders. Instead, unrecognized, cultural assumptions persist that 'good leaders are heroic, autonomous, disciplined, emotionally constrained, command-and-control figures' (p. 2). The result is a paradox: women are rated as having the required skills, but are not seen culturally as leaders in comparison to men.

Even the concept of post-heroic leadership or shared leadership (Huey and Sookdeo, 1994) does not advance women's interests according to Fletcher (2002). Because the traits associated with post-heroic leadership – empathy, capacity for listening, relational ability – are socially ascribed to women, it was felt that this shift would create a 'female advantage' and lead to more leadership positions for women. Fletcher believes that this will not occur because the 'transformational call of the new leadership' (p. 3) has already been incorporated into the mainstream discourse according to the rules of the old paradigm. 'The result is yet another idealized image of heroic leadership – post-heroic heroes' (p. 4).

Finally, Sinclair (1995) adds a further neglected dimension when she highlights the relevancy and importance of 'sexuality' to masculine forms of leadership. Given these circumstances, a woman's sexuality, in comparison, is thus neither culturally acceptable nor seen as appropriate in leadership roles.

## Gender Differences in Leadership Styles

The perceived inability of women to communicate themselves to others as possessing the attributes, capabilities and virtues of the 'heroic' leader, the 'preferred form' of leadership in many organizations, also applies to their leadership style. A number of reviews have examined gender differences in leadership behaviour (for example Eagly and Johnson, 1990; Kabacoff, 2000; Van Engen and Willemsen, 2000; Vinkenburg et al., 2000) in an attempt to resolve some of these assumptions and stereotypes. While few gender differences have been found in the analyses, Rosener (1990) called this conclusion into question with her assertion that women were essentially 'transformational' leaders, and men 'transactional' leaders. A 'transformational' leader was seen as one who was able to get subordinates to transform their own self-interest into the interest of the group through concern for a broader goal. A 'transactional' leader, in contrast, was one who viewed job performance as a series of transactions with subordinates – exchanging rewards for services rendered or punishment for inadequate performance.

While the finding of 'transformational' versus 'transactional' styles captured both researchers and women alike because many women felt both uncomfortable and unnatural in following the traditional male managerial style of command and control, further research by Alimo-Metcalf (1995), Bass et al. (1996), Burke and

Collins (2001), Carless (1998) and others on this issue was not conclusive. Van Engen and Willemsen (2000) have since argued that gender differences in leadership styles are largely a consequence of the context in which male and female leaders work, a finding also supported by Becker et al. (2002), Van Engen et al. (2001) and Eagly and Johnson (1990).

Despite these findings, many subordinates believe that women are not as able culturally as men to obtain resources for departments, divisions and employees because they are usually locked out of the decision-making 'elites'. Bryson (1987), looking at public sector reforms in Australia, found that a woman's 'cooperative' management style was less favoured at promotion time in contrast to a man's 'corporate management' style when it came to a consideration of outcomes and measurement of performance.

## Leadership and Communication

The gendered notions of leaders and leadership and leadership/management styles also affect notions of acceptable forms of gender communication in the workplace. Iteratively, these notions also impact back on women's supposed unsuitability as leaders. According to Case (1994), leadership has typically been linked with:

> masculine models of communication – assertion, independence, competitiveness and confidence. Deference, inclusivity, collaboration and cooperation, prioritized in women's speech communities, have been linked with subordinate roles rather than leadership. (p. 161)

Spender (1980) and Claes (1999) concur, stating that male speech and conversation strategies are usually taken as the norm, with female speech being assessed in relation to male speech. Consequently, female language is defined as polite and insecure and male language as assertive and direct. Oakley (2000) asserts that the less aggressive and assertive forms of communication associated with females may be particularly unacceptable ways to communicate in the upper echelons of most corporations. Linguistic style can be a key factor in the ability to negotiate with authority.

Several popular writers (Tannen, 1994; Zanetic and Jeffery, 1999) point out that men more often than women engage in behaviours that get them recognized by those in power. If women wish to succeed, then, they are almost forced to change their linguistic style to a more command-oriented form in order to be perceived as strong, decisive and in control. However, this can lead to them being perceived as being 'too aggressive' by males. This double-bind of leadership for women is what Jamieson (1995) calls the femininity/competence bind.

How do gender differences in communication impact on leadership? Claes (1999) maintains that language plays critical roles in creating and perpetuating gendered identities and social patterns in interaction. For women, this translates into using communication as a means to establish and maintain relationships with one another, to share things about themselves and to learn about others (Case, 1994). Conversations are viewed as negotiations of hierarchies of friendship for closeness

(Tannen, 1994, p. 25). Because equality of people is generally considered important in women's communication, women build a participatory mode of interaction in which communicators respond to and build on each other's ideas. Simultaneous speech and co-conversations may occur that allow for multi-layered development of topics. There is little competition for 'turns' as in men's speech communities. The result is that most people are able to contribute and the result is often a jointly negotiated whole. Research also indicates that women show support for others in their language rituals, and little emphasis is placed on dominance or hierarchy. Case (1994, p. 150) asserts that there is 'an orientation towards collaboration and support with groups actively discouraging the establishment of leaders'.

Apart from showing support for others, six other features of women's speech style are recognized by Case (1994) , Tannen (1994) and others. These features are minimal responses (such as 'um'), which are inserted throughout streams of talk to indicate attention and interest (and which are misunderstood by men as agreement); a focus on feelings and the relationship between communicators rather than on the content of the message; efforts to sustain conversation by inviting others to speak and by prompting them to elaborate on their experiences; the establishment of rapport through displaying similarities and matching experiences; displaying tentativeness, which leaves open the door for others to respond and express their opinions; and use of personal experiences rather than authority when they try to convince others to their point of view. For Case, women are more concerned about interaction and relationships in their communications than information.

Unfortunately, most of these features of women's speech/communication style are not associated with normal stereotypes or views of leadership. In fact, these features can lead others to interpret them as reflecting uncertainty, deference, powerlessness and lack of authority. Women are not given credit for involving others and for enabling and facilitating 'real' communication and involvement as opposed to merely giving orders (the 'command' situation).

Gender differences in communication styles become more obvious when men's speech communities are considered. According to Case (1994), 'the goals of men's talk involve exerting control, preserving independence, and enhancing status. Conversation is an arena for proving oneself and negotiating prestige'. Consequently, men use talk to establish and defend their personal status and ideas. They also support each other by not interrupting or criticizing.

Other features of men's speech include instrumentality (telling people what to do to solve problems); conversational dominance (for example holding the floor in meetings, diverting the conversation or interrupting others while they are talking); expressing themselves in assertive, absolute ways; not being highly responsive to others on a relationship level of communication; and communicating abstractly rather than at a personal level (Case, 1994; Tannen, 1994). Case considers that most of the latter orientation comes from the public and impersonal contexts in which men operate, such as business and management.

These gender differences in speech patterns and style can cause misunderstandings and miscommunications at both a public and private level. However, for women there is a double impact. Not only are they not considered to be as good at communicating as men (they ramble more, are less direct and appear emotional in comparison), but also they do not exhibit the 'accepted' qualities of a leader in their speech patterns. Thus, women's way of talking acts against them by reinforcing already existing stereotypes that they would be less effective in a leadership role.

## Implications

### Communication Strategies

From the foregoing review, gender differences in communication styles and patterns of conversation appear to play a major role in reinforcing men and women's perceptions and stereotypes of whether or not women are able to be effective leaders. In fact, communication issues are also an intricate part of perceptions of men's and women's leadership styles. Given that this is so, what can be done about this devaluing of women's abilities because they do not meet a culturally accepted standard? Several communication strategies spring to mind.

First, men and women need to appreciate that they have different 'ways of speaking'. Although popularized by Gray (1992, 2002) in his series on *Men are from Mars, Women are from Venus* themes, most managerial cultures have not awakened to this fact or acknowledged that the use of words may have different gendered cultural meanings because of different socialization. It is assumed that because everyone speaks English, the accepted business language, that they are speaking the same language. Similar miscommunications arise when management and unions negotiate: words have different meanings in different cultural contexts.

Second, once the awareness has been awakened, both men and women need to understand the varying gender cultural contexts to appreciate the base points of the communicator. Unless the cultural understanding goes hand in hand with the language variations, no real progress will be made.

Third, women need to learn 'leadership speak'. Although feminists and other progressives may object to this strategy, believing it to devalue women's skills, capabilities and uniqueness, it is a cultural fact that the vast majority of the workplace expects 'leadership speak' from their leaders. Leadership itself demands a certain language and linguistic style – just listen to any politician or business leader!

Fourth, just as managers and employees are expected to be multi-faceted and multi-skilled in today's changing workplace, so they should be able to communicate appropriately for many roles, either work or non-work. Women already speak the languages of a wife, mother, daughter, friend, subordinate and boss. They should also become versatile in the linguistic styles of as many managerial roles as possible, as well as executive-type positions in the public arena. By doing so they will gain greater acceptance for leadership positions when the opportunity arises.

Finally, all communicators need to be able to 'sell' themselves to their audiences. The above-mentioned strategies will assist in this process, but the element of 'salesmanship' needs to be added. Just listen to the persuasive powers of Hillary Clinton and other prominent women: all had to learn these skills to become effective. These women serve as good role models for any woman having communication difficulty.

*Implications for the Workplace*

Women have for a long time been endeavouring to secure better equity in the workplace. The above review has portrayed communication skills and style as being a significant barrier to achieving that equity. However, many women believe that the workplace should change to accommodate their particular skills, abilities and style rather than women being, once again, the ones to change. As already pointed out, many women are uncomfortable with the male managerial culture and its various dimensions, including linguistic styles. Many women are also labelled 'aggressive' when they adopt male communication styles. The above communication strategies would thus create certain tensions, if adopted, among groups of women in the workplace.

Second, men themselves would be unlikely to see the value in seeking to understand another 'system' or 'style' when the system they already work in is comfortable for them and is accepted as favouring them. The decision makers may not be prepared to invest the time, energy and resources into investigating what is considered to be a 'soft' issue both managerially and financially. Hence, suggestions to examine such matters may find little support. In the meantime, however, women will still face a continued battle to overcome the side-effects of the language barriers and will continue to exit corporate structures to create their own more accommodating workplaces. While it cannot be said that communication is the sole reason behind the 'brain drain' of women into small business, it is possible that it is more important than has previously been suspected.

**Conclusion**

In all the research into women in leadership and their lack of an equitable representation in the annals of power and decision making, the impact of communication ability, style and effectiveness has not been given sufficient prominence. While it has been investigated from an interpersonal perspective – that is, how both genders interrelate in the workplace, the impact on leadership opportunities for women has been a neglected issue. It is time more thought was given to this aspect to determine if it has validity and, if so, to devise strategies and processes so that equity can be achieved by all.

## Recommendations for Change and Further Research

As foreshadowed above, further research needs to be undertaken into the varying gender linguistic styles in the workplace to determine if their impact is impeding the progress of women into leadership positions. Second, both men and women need to be made aware that such differences exist in order to improve communication in the workplace. This awareness can be created by appropriate programmes or by observers evaluating meeting processes to ensure active participation by all. And finally, organizations need to examine whether communication aspects may be underpinning many of their termination issues, industrial conflicts, inter-generational tensions and other such workplace disparities. If a few of these recommendations were implemented, the outcome may be less gender division in a range of workplace behaviours and more opportunities for women to emerge as leaders.

## References

Alimo-Metcalf, B. (1995), 'An investigation of female and male constructs of leadership and empowerment', *Women in Management Review*, **10**(2): 3–8.

Apfelbaum, E. and Hadley, M. (1986), 'Leadership Ms-qualified: 11. Reflections on initial case study investigation of contemporary women leaders', in C. F. Graumann and S. Moscovici, S. (eds), *Changing Conceptions of Leadership*. New York: Springer-Verlag. pp. 199–221.

Applebaum, S. and Shapiro, B. (1993), 'Why can't men lead like women?', *Leadership and Organisation Development Journal*, **14**(7): 28–34.

Bartol, K. M., Martin, D. C. and Kromkowski, J. A. (2003), 'Leadership and the glass ceiling: Gender and ethnic group influences on leader behaviours at middle and executive managerial levels', *The Journal of Leadership and Organizational Studies*, **9**(3): 8–19.

Bass, B. M., Avolio, B. J. and Atwater, L. (1996), 'The transformational and transactional leadership of men and women', *Applied Psychology: An International Review*, **45**(1): 5–34.

Becker, J., Ayman, R. and Korabik, K. (2002), 'Discrepancies in self/subordinates' perceptions of leadership behaviour', *Group and Organisation Management*, **27**(2): 226–44.

Bryson, L. (1987), 'Women and Management in the Public Sector', *Australian Journal of Public Administration*, **46**(3): 259–72.

Burke, S. and Collins, K. M. (2001), 'Gender differences in leadership styles and management skills', *Women in Management Review*, **16**(5): 244–56.

Burton, C. (1997), 'Women's representation on Commonwealth and private sector boards', research paper, Office for Status Women, Department of Family and Community Affairs, Government of Australia. Retrieved February 2, 2005 from ofw.facs.gov.au/publications/clareburton97.htm.

Burton, C., Ryall, C. and Todd, C. (1994), 'Managing for diversity', in Industry Task Force on Leadership and Management Skills, *Enterprising Nation: Renewing*

*Australia's Managers to Meet the Challenges of the Asia-Pacific Century* (The Karpin Report), Research Report, Vol. 2. Canberra: Australian Government Publishing Service. pp. 765–814.

Campbell, K. (2002), 'Conversation: The emancipated organisation: Insights on gender, leadership and power formed over 25 years on the front line', *Harvard Business Review*, **80**(9): 20–21.

Carless, S. A. (1998), 'Gender differences in transformational leadership: An examination of superior, leader and subordinate perspectives', *Sex Roles*, **39**(11–12): 887–902.

Carter, S. and Anderson, S. (2001), *On the Move: Women and Men Business Owners in the United Kingdom.* Washington: National Foundation for Women Business Owners. Retrieved February 2, 2005 from www.womensbusinessresearch.org/pressreleases/2-28-2001/executivereport.pdf.

Carter, S., Anderson, S. and Shaw, E. (2001), *Women's Business Ownership: A Review of the Academic, Popular and Internet Literature*, report to the Small Business Service. Glasgow: University of Strathclyde.

Case, S. S. (1994), 'Gender Differences in communication and behaviour in organisations', in M. J. Davidson and R. J. Burke, R. J. (eds), *Women in Management: Current Research Issues*. London: Paul Chapman. pp. 144–67.

Centre for Women's Business Research (2001), *The New Generation of Women Business Owners: An Executive Report*. Retrieved February 2, 2005 from http://www.womensbusinessresearch.org/pressreleases/8-21-2001/NewGenerationExecutiveReport.pdf.

Claes, M. T. (1999), 'Women, men and management styles', *International Labour Review*, **138**(4): 431–46.

Davidson, M. J. and Burke, R. J. (eds) (2004), *Women in Management Worldwide: Progress and Prospects*. London: Paul Chapman.

Eagly, A. and Johannesen-Schmidt, M. (2001), 'The leadership style of women and men', *Journal of Social Issues*, **57**: 781–97.

Eagly, A. and Johnson, B. (1990), 'Gender and leadership style: A meta-analysis', *Psychological Bulletin*, **108** (2): 233–56.

Eagly, A., Makhijani, M. and Klonsky, B. (1992), 'Gender and the evaluation of leaders: A meta-analysis', *Psychological Bulletin*, **111**(1): 3–22.

Equal Opportunity for Women in the Workplace Agency and Catalyst (2002, November), *Australian Census of Women Executive Managers and Women Board Directors*. Sydney: EOWA.

Equal Opportunity in the Workplace Agency and Catalyst (2003, October), *Australian Census of Women Executive Managers and Women Board Directors*. Sydney: EOWA.

Equal Opportunity in the Workplace Agency and Catalyst (2004, October), *Australian Census of Women Executive Managers and Women Board Directors*. Sydney: EOWA.

Fletcher, J. (2002), *The Greatly Exaggerated Demise of Heroic Leadership: Gender, Power and the Myth of the Female Advantage*, CGO Insights No. 13. Boston, MA: Centre for Gender in Organisations, Simmons School of Management.

Gray, J. (1992), *Men are from Mars, Women are from Venus*. New York: HarperCollins.

Gray, J. (2002), *Mars and Venus in the Workplace*. Sydney: Macmillan.

Huey, J. and Sookdeo, R. (1994), 'The new post-*heroic* leadership', *Fortune*, **129**(4): 42–6.

Jamieson, K. H. (1995), *Beyond the Double Bind: Women and Leadership*. New York: Oxford University Press.

Kabacoff, R. K. (2000), 'Gender and leadership in the corporate boardroom', paper presented at the 108th Annual Convention of the American Psychological Association, Washington DC, August.

Korn/Ferry International (2001), *What Women Want in Business: A Survey of Executives and Entrepreneurs*. Korn/Ferry International in collaboration with Columbia Business School and the Duran Group. Retrieved February 2, 2005 from www.kornferry.com/Library/Process.asp?P=PUB_004.

Lucas, J. W. (2003), 'Status processes and the institutionalisation of women as leaders', *American Sociological Review*, **68**(3): 464–80.

Merrill-Sands, D. and Kolb, D. (2001), *Women as Leaders: The Paradox of Success*, CGO Insights No. 9. Boston, MA: Centre for Gender in Organisations, Simmons School of Management.

Meyerson, D. E. and Fletcher, J. K. (2000), 'A modest manifesto for shattering the glass ceiling', *Harvard Business Review*, **78**: 127–36.

Oakley, J. (2000), 'Gender-based barriers to senior management positions: Understanding the scarcity of female CEOs', *Journal of Business Ethics*, **27**(4): 321–34.

Oshagbemi, T. and Gill, R. (2003), 'Gender differences and similarities in the leadership styles and behaviour of UK managers, *Women in Management Review*, **18**(6): 288–98.

Posner, B. and Kouzes, J. (1993), 'Psychometric properties of the leadership practices inventory – updated', *Educational and Psychological Measurement*, **53**: 191–9.

Powell, G. N. (2000), 'The glass ceiling: Explaining the good and the bad news', in M. J. Davidson and R. J. Burke (eds), *Women in Management: Current Research Issues Vol. 2*. London: Sage, 236–49.

Rosener, J. (1990), 'Ways women lead', *Harvard Business Review*, **68**(November–December): 119–25.

Saunders, H. (1996), *Acts of Courage? Public Sector CEOs on Men, Women and Work*, Issues Paper No. 4. Public Sector Standards Commission: Director of Equal Opportunity in Public Employment.

Sheridan, A. and Milgate, G. (2003), 'Accessing board positions: A comparison of women's and men's views', Discussion Paper No. 6, Centre for Women and Business, Graduate School of Management, The University of Western Australia.

Sinclair, A. (1994), *Trials at the Top: Chief Executives Talk About Men and Women and the Australian Executive Culture*. Parkville Victoria: The Australia Centre, University of Melbourne.

Sinclair, A. (1995), 'Sexuality in leadership', *International Review of Women and Leadership*, **1**(2): 25–38.

Sinclair, A. (1998), *Doing Leadership Differently: Gender, Power and Sexuality in a Changing Business Culture*. Victoria: Melbourne University Press.

Spender, D. (1980), *Man-made Language*. London: Routledge and Kegan Paul.

Stelter, N. (2002), 'Gender differences in leadership: Current social issues and future organizational implications', *The Journal of Leadership Studies*, **8**(4): 88–99.

Still, L. V. (1997), *Glass Ceilings and Sticky Floors: Barriers to the Careers of Women in the Australian Finance Industry*. Sydney: Human Rights and Equal Opportunity Commission.

Still, L. V. (2004), 'Women in management in Australia', in M. J. Davidson and R. J. Burke (eds), *Women in Management Worldwide: Progress and Prospects*. pp. 225–42.

Still, L. V. and Timms, W. (2000), 'Women's business: The flexible alternative workstyle for women', *Women in Management Review*, **15**(5/6): 272–82.

Still, L. V. and Walker, E. A. (2003), 'Women's business: Towards a new paradigm?', research report, Centre for Women and Business, Graduate School of Management, The University of Western Australia.

Tannen, D. (1994), *Talking from 9 to 5*. New York: William Morrow.

Van Engen, M. and Willemsen, T. M. (2000), *Gender and Leadership Styles: A Review of the Past Decade*, WORC paper 00.10.09. The Netherlands: Tilburg University.

Van Engen, M., Van der Leeden, R. and Willemsen, T. M. (2001), 'Gender, context and leadership styles: A field study', *Journal of Occupational and Organizational Psychology*, **74**(5): 581–98.

Vinkenburg, C. J., Jansen, P. G. and Koopman, P. L. (2000), 'Feminine leadership: A review of gender differences in managerial behaviour and effectiveness', in M. J. Davidson and R. J. Burke (eds), *Women in Management: Current Research Issues, Vol. 2*. London: Sage, 120–37.

Vinnicombe, S. and Singh, V. (2003), 'Locks and keys to the boardroom', *Women in Management Review*, **18**(6): 325–33.

Wirth, L. (2001), *Breaking Through the Glass Ceiling: Women in Management*. Geneva: International Labour Office.

Zanetic, S. and Jeffery, C. (1999), *Me Jane, You Tarzan: Resolving the Battle of the Sexes in the Corporate Jungle*. Sydney: HarperCollins.

## Chapter 14

# 'We Don't Need Another Hero!': Organizational Storytelling as a Vehicle for Communicating a Female Archetype of Workplace Leadership

Su Olsson

### Introduction: Organizational Myths and Storytelling as Communication Management

Organizational myths and stories are vehicles of communication management, which shore up official goals, values and role models within the organization, while promoting public images of corporate success (Kaye, 1995; Olsson, 2000a, 2002). More specifically, official organizational stories continue to represent the executive or senior manager as hero (Clark and Salaman, 1998; Handy, 1995; Jackson and Parry, 2001; Kaye, 1996; Olsson, 2000a, 2000b, 2002), despite critics who argue that the heroic model reinforces a hierarchical and masculinist paradigm of leadership that has become obsolete in contemporary organizations (Halford and Leonard, 2001; Sinclair, 1998). Such depictions of 'the senior manager as heroic and transformational leader' (Clark and Salaman, 1998, p. 137) have drawn on subconscious images of leadership by aligning executives with specific mythical heroes. These heroes include Ulysses/Odysseus and his epic quest, Theseus killing the Minotaur and Mercury the winged messenger (Handy, 1995; Kaye, 1996; Morong, 1994; Sinclair, 1994, 1998). Nirenberg (2001, p. 3) argues that the notion of the hero manager has stimulated the public imagination and escalated into a 'cult of personality perpetrated by the press and massive public relations campaigns by large organizations'. In his 'practitioner's' survey of leadership literature, Nirenberg claims that the 'cultural mindset of leadership as a heroic act' is created not only by the news, entertainment and advertising media, but also by the business press and leadership literature: 'With only a rare exception or two, the leadership literature … reinforces the idea of the heroic CEO' (p. 8). He points out that this depiction has little to do with best practice or effectiveness. At the same time, the internal and public images of the executive as hero communicate masculine images of the executive that marginalize women in management positions.

Paradoxically, organizational storytelling that currently supports executive male norms also provides a means to break through the dominant masculinist appropriation of leadership and to communicate a female archetype of leadership in the workplace. This chapter examines women executives' self-representations of identity within the context of organizational storytelling. Most immediately, this chapter examines the persuasive power of leadership as archetype and how it has been 'operationalized' in the business context to communicate and reinforce male norms (Olsson, 2000a, 2000b, 2002; Steyrer, 1998). The research that has sought to communicate a female leadership paradigm and to reclaim a female archetype is discussed together with its limitations. In contrast to the heroic archetype as exampled by the Ulysses epic, the warrior princess Xena is argued to provide a paradigm to represent the way women in management reconfigure and communicate an evolving and modern female archetype of leadership through the stories they tell other women. In the women executives' stories included in this chapter, their 'heroic' qualities and competencies are a given, and humour is often used to deconstruct masculinist assumptions of dominant organizational models and to 'slay the monsters' of women's corporate experiences. These narratives involve the sharing of experiences through the interactive process of storytelling that provides inspirations, role models and sometimes cautionary tales (Olsson, 2000a, 2000b). It is argued that the process of storytelling for these women is one of 'breaking through the silences' and finding 'forms of communication which express women's voices and allow them to create and articulate their own meanings' (Marshall, 1995, p. 8). The chapter concludes by suggesting that organizational storytelling as a vehicle of communication management needs to acknowledge and to celebrate a female archetype of leadership present in women's stories of the workplace.

## Overview of Current Research

### Of Heroes and Archetypes

The persistent power of the 'global "hero manager" phenomenon' (Jackson and Parry, 2001, p. 21) lies in its harnessing of cultural archetypes of leadership. The concept of archetypes goes back to Jung (Carr, 2002; Matthews, 2002; Sinclair, 1998). Archetypes are primordial patterns common to all human beings across all cultures and they give rise to archetypal images, 'universal symbols, myths and motifs – such as the shadow, the anima, the animus, the wise man, the hero, the father, the self' (Matthews, 2002, p. 426). These archetypes operate at a subconscious level within cultural myths and stories. Abrams (1998, p. 201) describes archetypes as 'narrative designs, character types, or images', which occur in a wide diversity of phenomena from works of literature to modes of social behaviour: 'The archetypal similarities within these diverse phenomena are held to reflect a set of universal, primitive, elemental patterns, whose effective embodiment in a literary work evokes a profound response in the reader'. Sinclair (1998, p. 31) emphasizes the collaborative, social constructionist dimensions of such stories: 'An archetype of leadership is not a style, which is a reflection of an individual personality, but a social construction'. Understanding leadership as archetype reveals the power of narrative to contain images and patterns within the representations of a particular character, which seem to be elemental and universal to the nature of leaders, but which are instead collaborative, social constructions. Thus, the construct of leadership as archetype situates stories of the hero manager within the wider social and discursive history of social narrative, reinforcing the persuasive power of images of executive leadership through the continual reclaiming and honouring of past and present leaders, mythical and actual, within the ongoing stories of executive identity (Olsson, 2002).

At the same time, such organizational stories reiterate a masculinist paradigm of leadership as archetype. Steyrer (1998, p. 817), for instance, points out that charisma is 'operationalized' in the context of business organizations through the four 'decidedly masculine' archetypes of father, hero, saviour and king. Within the official rhetoric of organizations, these archetypes of leadership are 'both inscriptions of past performances and scripts and staging instructions for future performances' (Czarniawska, 1988, p. 20). Steyrer (1998), for example, states that the hero provides a symbol of career success. Zanetti (2002, p. 525) claims that for people in organizations 'the identity of the "ideal" employee is fueled by the myth of the heroic individual'. In this sense, organizational myths not only shape the image of the executive, but function as exemplars or models (Kaye, 1995, 1996) and can be seen as a form of communication management that attempts to 'control' and 'homogenize' executive identity (Salzer-Morling, 1998, p. 112). For instance, Maier (1999, p. 71) points out that while there are many masculinities, organizations foster and reward what he calls 'corporate masculinity'. Sinclair (1998, pp. 50–51) adopts the term 'heroic masculinism' to argue that 'the intertwining ideologies of masculinity and leadership serve the important purposes of maintaining the *status quo*, the privilege of an *elite*, and of perpetuating assumed assessments of "who looks like leadership material"'.

Whatever the criteria for effective executive leadership, and however well men and women meet these criteria, organizational and business press representations of heroic leadership involve an active process of gendering that reinforces a masculinist paradigm, while leaving female leadership as absence or other. In the process of executive celebrity making, women feature either as honorary males or as a few, exceptional women. McConnell-Ginet (2000, p. 272) states that 'so long as they [women leaders] remain a few exceptional women the glass ceiling will remain in place'.

*The Quest for a Female Archetype of Leadership*

Attempts to negate the power of heroic masculinism have met with limited success, partly because they fail to counter the social constructionist, collaborative dimensions of leadership as archetype. Thus neither the research that repeatedly establishes the similarities of styles, competencies, and aspirations of men and women in management (Butterfield and Grinnel, 1999; Wilson, 2003), nor that which argues for the special contribution to management of women's differences (Tannen, 1994; Wilson, 2003) has dislodged the prevalence not only of 'think manager/think male', but also of 'think leadership/think male' notions. Indeed, Steyrer (1998, p. 824) raises the question of 'whether leadership and charisma only emerge by means of masculine forms of self-representation' and suggests that this 'might be one of the reasons why access to leadership positions is still more difficult for women'. Yet, as the author has argued previously, what women lack is neither leadership nor charisma, but rather an archetypal profile as leaders (Olsson, 2000a, 2000b, 2002).

A number of traditional images of women in history and mythology have already been suggested as the basis for reclaiming a female archetype of leadership (Marshall, 1984, 1995). Athena, for example, is portrayed as the inspiration for career women (Handy, 1995). Halford and Leonard (2001) suggest that female figures offering images for women's identity include Luna (the moon), Lila (playfulness), Athena (career) and Medusa (the abyss of transformation). Steyrer (1998, p. 824) refers to several types of female leadership, for example, 'Great Mother, Amazone, Daughter, Jeanne d'Arc'.

One of the problems of reclaiming these female archetypes is that 'the social connotations connected with the concept of "leadership" are to a large extent influenced by patriarchy' (Steyrer, 1998, p. 824). Moi (1985, p. 116) describes how patriarchal binary thought consists of an opposition of man/woman where each binary opposition 'can be analysed as a hierarchy where the "feminine" side is always seen as the negative, powerless instance'. Traditional female archetypes have been constituted within a patriarchal binary context. For example, in the Sun (male)/Moon (female) opposition, the sun is the source of light, whereas the moon or Luna is 'passive' in that it only reflects the sun's light. Athena can be said to embody the public/private split that has disadvantaged women because although she is both the goddess of war and of peace, she is also the goddess of handicrafts who 'gave the peasant his plough, to women she gave the loom' (Lurker, 1988, p. 45). Amazone has negative connotations representing a lack of femininity: *amazon* is a Greek word meaning 'without breasts' and in Greek mythology refers to a race of female warriors who had no men in their nation 'but any sons born of their union with neighbours were killed or sent to their fathers ... The term is now applied to any strong, brawny women of masculine habits' (Brewer, 1974, p. 29). Jeanne d'Arc was successful when she presented as a man, but burned at the stake as a woman. In an account of the wounding or negative connotations associated by patriarchy with the feminine, Zanetti (2002, p. 530) makes the point that, while we live in the cultural context of patriarchy, 'the archetype that causes most fear and anxiety is that of the mother, not the father'. In other words, it is not only a matter of acknowledging and reclaiming female archetypes, it is a matter of reconfiguring and rewriting in order to communicate a modern female archetype of leadership.

This reconfiguring is part of the dynamic and changing dimensions of archetypes. Matthews (2002, p. 462) states: 'Archetypes are dynamic, they are capable of evolution through *inner* and *outer* dynamics ... through their diversity of forms ...

and their interaction with one another in a network of relations'. There are a number of examples of this process. Morong (1994) describes how the entrepreneur has become the real hero in capitalist society. Matthews (2002) analyses the evolution of archetypal images within the competitive-based system of capitalism. Jackson and Parry (2001, p. 21) trace the rise of the hero manager to the emergence of 'guru theory' and the 'hero manager gurus' in the 1980s and 1990s. The evolving nature of archetypes in these examples is particularly pertinent to women in executive leadership positions. Halford and Leonard (2001) point out that we are now in a period of social revolution where an increasing number of women, as well as men, hold substantial positions of power. While gender remains a continuing given of social constructions and interactions (Olsson, 2002), gender content evolves and changes. The time is ripe for the claiming and reconfiguring of female archetypes of leadership arising out of women's experiences.

Myth-making and storytelling in organizations that currently reinforce a masculinist paradigm of leadership also provide a means for women in management to reconfigure and communicate an archetypal profile. Marshall (1995, p. 8) describes this process for women as 'breaking through the silences' by finding 'forms of communication which express women's voices and allow them to create and articulate their own meanings'. More specifically, stories include discourse strategies that position the professional persona or identity. McConnell-Ginet (2000, p. 269) states: 'Speaking and having your contributions recognized are part of constructing engagement, of positioning yourself and being positioned in the discourse'. Just as stories of the manager have constituted male leadership as archetype, so women executives' narratives can be seen to provide a distinctive female archetype of women as leaders, which needs to be acknowledged and celebrated.

The stories from women managers in this chapter demonstrate that an untapped, distinctive, female subculture of storytelling exists in the stories women tell other women about the workplace. In these stories women managers' 'heroic' qualities and competencies are a given, and humour is often used to deconstruct masculinist assumptions of dominant organizational models and to 'slay the monsters' of women's corporate experiences. These narratives involve the sharing of experiences through the interactive process of storytelling that provides inspiration, role models and sometimes cautionary tales. Thus, these stories construct an archetype of leadership for women in management, which is compared to the 'battlefields' of Xena, warrior princess.

This present chapter brings together material from articles about executive managers that the author has published over the past four years.[1] These articles involve three main studies: a qualitative study of narratives of gender in the workplace that consisted of 96 collected stories, 29 of which were from women managers (Olsson, 2000a, 2000b[2]); a study of male executives' career identities (Olsson, 2000c, 2002); an ongoing major study of the career identities of senior women managers that, to date, comprises 30 interviews with executive women (Olsson, 2002; Olsson and Pringle, 2004; Olsson and Walker, 2003; Olsson and Walker, 2004; Pringle and Olsson, 2002). In addition to these publications, this chapter also draws upon some previously unused material from these interviews. In all three studies, material was given a simple numerical code and names of participants and their organizations changed to ensure confidentiality.

*Reconfiguring Leadership as Archetype: Ulysses and Xena*

Cash (1997, p. 160) states that all forms of narrative, from epic to cartoon, 'need the "other" or hidden story set up in the mind of the listener to have their effect'. In line with Sinclair's (1994, 1998) discussions of heroic masculinism and in the author's previous studies of executive identity referred to above, the Ulysses (Odysseus) ten-year epic quest was used to represent male leadership as archetype. Ulysses, a mythical king of Ithaca, sets out on his journey, leaving his faithful wife Penelope at home. He faces many life-threatening disasters, he battles with giants and monsters, and he withstands the temptations of those who would seduce him from his quest, for instance, the Lotus Eaters and the Sirens (Brewer, 1974). The Ulysses myth provides the archetypal images for the battles, feats and triumphs for the career journey of the present-day male executive (Sinclair, 1994, 1998; Olsson, 2000c).

In place of Ulysses, the author has previously proposed Xena as a mythical figure who breaks into the male appropriation of leadership. Xena has been chosen for the following reasons. First, the name Xena is the feminine of the Greek word *xenos* meaning a stranger, suggesting a woman who has existed for some time but, like the woman executive, is not recognized by the dominant culture as one of them. Second, the Xena character is an entirely modern invention of the entertainment industry, who is nevertheless depicted as a classical leader of an often disparate band of women who equal men in their heroic exploits while providing a quintessentially female form and image. In this respect, Xena can be seen as a dynamic and evolving archetype of female leadership (Olsson, 2000a, 2000b, 2002).

Sinclair (1998) reminds us that archetypes are ongoing social constructions. Such is the power of the media-created character to tap into subconscious images of women as leaders, that despite possible views that the series is a further Hollywood-type exploitation of women's sexuality, Xena has entered the popular consciousness and even achieved cult following in parts of the United States. Similarly, in Greece, the popularity of Xena among young people resulted in the attempt by some educationalists to have the programme banned, as they saw it as corrupting the purity of their classical mythology and teachings (Olsson, 2000a).

Finally, since the author first proposed Xena as a female archetype of leadership, Morreale's (1998) fascinating article on Xena: Warrior Princess as Feminist Camp has had new influence. Morreale points out that the Xena programme was 'the first television series to place a woman in the role of archetypal hero on a quest' (p. 79). She argues that the show parodies gender roles through masquerade, sometimes with men disguised as women, but more often with Xena called upon to disguise herself as a traditional woman and so subvert female stereotypes by highlighting their constructed nature: 'Gender parody becomes a critical tool, a way of initiating change in sex and gender roles' (p. 83). In this chapter, a comparable process of gender parody often occurs in many of the stories women tell other women. The stories are grouped under four interrelated headings: emotion, stereotypes, sexuality and leadership.

## Emotion

Maier (1999, p. 4) claims that two major themes of masculinist management are 'No Sissy Stuff: The Stigma of Anything Vaguely Feminine' and 'Give 'Em Hell'. Certainly, women are aware of an injunction against displays of so-called feminine emotions in the workplace. In a parodic description of male behaviours, one woman states, 'You can scream and yell and you can slam the door and kick a desk, but apart from that you wouldn't show any other emotion'. Another senior executive claims that women have been brought up to express strong feelings through tears so it is natural for them to cry, but she does so in her car or in private. A leading public sector executive describes an incident from her younger days as a prison officer, when she was called up before the Chief and blamed for something that was not her concern. She explains that when she is really angry she cries.

The meeting is terminated and the Chief avoids the woman for the next few days. Then she is asked to report again to his office and told she can't do that if she wants to do well in the prison service: 'I'm unsure exactly what it is I can't do ... so I ask. His response was to leave me speechless and even to this day provokes a smile: "You can't cry when you don't get your own way"' (Olsson, 2000a).

Sinclair (1998) points out that what is seen as heroic toughness in a man is evaluated negatively in a woman. A number of executive women speak of using humour to deal with males in conflict situations. At the same time, Xena women acknowledge that 'there are times when you have to fight for it' (Olsson, 2002). A CEO provides a parodic account not only of rudeness, but of negative evaluation when she engaged in a 'battle' for funding:

> I got there and I was put through a Spanish Inquisition of unbelievable rudeness about – you know, 'Oh, for goodness sake!' and 'Why on earth should we fund public xxx?' Things like that. So I got stuck in the end. You can only push someone so far. But it was reported back to me that it had been described to the Prime Minister's department as emotive and defensive behaviour. And I was very angry because I suppose in some ways it was. Why not? But in a man it would have been, 'Spoke his mind, was forthright, etc.' And it actually made me even more determined and angry and in the end I suppose you could say we won. But at great cost.

One theme to emerge is that women CEOs are no longer prepared to tolerate aggressive male behaviours (Olsson, 2002; Olsson and Walker, 2004). A CEO describes how she dealt with the confrontation and political game playing of executives in her organization:

> It was very male dominated and it was very much the old boys' network. And they just seemed to spend all their time fighting and putting out fires. Since I've come along I just

say, 'I'm not going to get into that crap. We don't do it like that. We don't play party politics. We don't play people off against one another.' And I made those rules pretty straight, pretty clear from the beginning.

The Xena executive voices a passion and energy for what she is doing, together with a belief in directness and a rejection of people with hidden agendas. A senior manager in corporate banking states: 'What aggravates me is the extent of the boys' regime in the place and, you know, the bullshit that comes with that which is around internal politics' (Olsson and Walker, 2004). Perhaps what is most noticeable is that Xena women are now seeing their passion and directness as a deliberate choice, in contrast to male indirectness and politicking:

I've been exposed. I've poured my heart out. I used to get upset about a lot of things five years ago. I'm more – I'm hardened to the fact that this is my style and I'm not going to modify it because of you [the men] because my story is based on that openness, not on being closed. And if I start modifying too much, then I could end up like one of you guys!

In these ways Xena women reconfigure and communicate a female archetype of leadership.

*Stereotypes*

A growing consensus among executive women is that the last 20 years have seen major changes and a greater acceptance of women in business (Olsson and Walker, 2003, 2004). Only a few mentioned stereotyped attitudes that they had encountered from some people at times in their career journeys and these attitudes were more likely to be towards women in male-dominated industries. A general manager in the manufacturing industry states: 'I think there are still a few limiting views out there where people don't expect a woman to be running a manufacturing company'. Similarly, a senior manager in the computing industry, who acknowledges all of her peers are men, states:

A lot of men don't view it as a natural thing for a woman to be in senior management. They're quite surprised initially at the role you're doing but then they accept it pretty quickly … . I still think there's a lot of, you know, 'the woman should be in the kitchen' …. You prove your worth by performing and delivering and I've just had a survey done by my staff and I got 100 per cent in 21 categories, which was the most outstanding in all the management here in the company. I just get on and do it (Olsson and Walker, 2003).

Most of the lingering stereotypes seem to arise around expectations of women's behaviour. A woman executive in one of Australasia's largest manufacturing industries describes returning to a key supplier a parcel of gifts which included three toffees implying this 'tough' woman needed to sweeten up: 'The supplier has since described me as "having balls" and now ensures he is always accompanied by his wife when meeting me' (Olsson, 2000b). One executive feels it comes down to 'the perception thing' and relates a situation that illustrates the 'the double-edged sword' for women in authority over men, where it is harder for the male to take criticism from a woman than from another 'bloke':

> There was a situation a couple of years ago when I really felt this chief executive had let the company down. I was quite blunt about it … . What was the word he used? He said he thought that I was quite intimidating. When I talked about it with my daughters that night, they said, 'Well, frankly, Mum, if I was in business, I'd rather be intimidating than a bloody wimp.' I thought that's absolutely right (Olsson and Walker, 2003).

As with emotion, then, Xena women are reconfiguring a female archetype of leadership by claiming their right to directness and authority. As a senior manager states: 'Women don't have to put up with rubbish any more'. A CEO goes further to suggest that although male executives often engage in stereotyped behaviours, 'I think women are lucky because we can do it differently [from men]. We don't have to be the [male] stereotypes' (Olsson and Walker, 2004).

*Sexuality*

In the Ulysses myth, women are depicted as either temptress or faithful supporter, a classical rendering of the whore/madonna split that underlies issues around sexuality for women in the workplace (Olsson, 2000b). The Xena woman challenges such images by asserting her femininity: 'We can't deny our femininity. It's what we are' (Olsson and Walker, 2004). Moreover, sexuality is seen as part of this femininity: 'I've always been proud of being a woman. I'm never not proud. I'm a package. I think my talents are part of that, of who I am, which is part of sexuality. You can't park something at the door. That's like saying my home is my life so that the lessons I learn being a good partner or mother aren't lessons I should bring to work. Rubbish'.

Nor is ageism an issue for executive women. As one senior women states, 'From my experience – women just get better as they get older.' Some younger women executives, however, express frustration when they are seen primarily in terms of their physical attractiveness: 'I get incredibly frustrated with people who decide to look at the package, instead of look at who I am or what I bring … I'm a woman not a dolly bird'. There is also a strong rejection of women who use their sexuality to try to gain advantages in the workplace. This is seen as something that impacts negatively on other women (Olsson and Walker, 2004).

With one exception (Olsson, 2000b), none of the women had experienced sexual harassment in the workplace. While expressing sympathy for women who did experience such harassment, it was suggested by one executive that some women send out the wrong signals, instead of earning respect. Xena women are not prepared to tolerate such behaviour: 'I've never had any sexual harassment. I'd chop someone's balls off before I'd put up with anything like that. They kind of know that about you anyway, they know not to do it.'

Motherhood also seems to have diminished as a reason for attitudes that disadvantage women in the workplace. Executive women with children speak of the difficulties of the balancing act they engage in and those with younger children see a nanny as essential to survival in senior management (Olsson, 2002). While family is their first priority, their career is something they do for themselves, and many suggest that they feel they are better mothers because they feel fulfilled and spend quality time with their children. One senior manager states that when she is introducing herself in corporate groups she includes the statement, 'I am George's mother', an assertion of pride in her womanhood.

One problematic area concerns lesbians. A senior manager in the health sector suggests that she finds it necessary to stem derogatory remarks that can occur about gay women:

> I've seen men make those derogatory remarks about, oh you know, 'she's real butch' or 'she couldn't be more butch if she tried'. What I do, I will just say to them, "Well, you know, I suppose that's better than being in the closet still and being homophobic.' That does stop it. It stops it for them then and there. I'm not saying that it changes any attitudes, but makes it known that that's not acceptable.

Thus, Xena women are prepared not only to celebrate, but to defend women's sexuality as part of their overall presence in the workplace. The author found these attitudes represented a shift from the first study of women managers' stories in which attitudes to aspects of women's sexuality in the workplace were often described as problematic for the women concerned (Olsson, 2000b) to the interviews with senior women executives in which sexuality, though not to be 'used to gain advantages', was described as an essential aspect of 'femininity' (Olsson, 2002; Olsson and Walker, 2004).

*Leadership*

Xena executives construct a distinctive archetype of leadership. Key factors are passion, energy, credibility, communication skills, overachieving, the motivation of others, vision, and the ability to view change as challenging and rewarding. A number of women mention the importance of teams and the need to create a sense of shared enterprise rather than hierarchy (Pringle and Olsson, 2002; Olsson, 2002; Olsson and Walker, 2004). One of the skills of leadership is to know your own weaknesses and ensure you have people to access for that particular skill. This ability is often contrasted to the entrenched positions men take up where such behaviour is seen as a failure (Olsson and Walker, 2003). A CEO encapsulates these views:

> Leadership is not about strutting about. I think it's important that the chief executive should not feel threatened by other people's talent. And I think that in the past that has been a problem. I think that often male behaviours, and I'm no rabid feminist in this – but men like to win the point, whereas I was fairly humble from the outset. So if someone says to me in a meeting, 'Why don't we try it this way?' and it makes sense to me, as it

frequently does, then you know I look good and feel good. And what the hell, I've had a glorious run. And I'm not threatened by the next generation coming through.

What is perhaps new within women's experience of executive culture is their acknowledgement and enjoyment of power: 'There is no doubt about it, the power thing is good for you. You shouldn't admit that you get a buzz out of it. But in actual fact you do' (Olsson and Pringle, 2004). Part of this power comes from being recognized in their own right as female leaders: 'My career's been very important to me. I came very early on, I mean, I'm going back 15, 20 years. I was aware that as a woman I was somebody's wife, somebody's mother. And the biggest thrill to me was when I was recognized in my own right.'

Linked to this excitement in achievement and recognition is a concern to assist others to reach their personal potential. One CEO constructs an image of 'lighting the flame' in others. Another defines leadership in these terms, 'Taking someone to a place that they wouldn't have got there on their own. To me that's a mind change' (Pringle and Olsson, 2002; Olsson and Pringle, 2004). In reconfiguring a female archetype of leadership, women executives are also contributing to a wider change in the social construction of women in business. As a senior executive points out, 'Women are in more persuasive and more power positions than they've ever been before. Also relationships have altered'. Xena has come of age. The archetype has evolved.

On one level, the female archetype of leadership is about being able to deliver the vision and to engage in strategic planning and thinking, rather than focus solely on short-term financial gain. But even more importantly it is about investing in people and making the workplace an enjoyable place to be:

> I love to see people succeeding and doing well and having fun. Like they're enjoying their work. And I love to see them being successful. Their success is my success. That's the thing that gives me a buzz, is seeing a happy, successful team (Olsson, 2002).

A recurrent theme among women executives is the need to be natural and to celebrate achievements as a means to promoting their staff's full and satisfying engagement in the shared enterprise:

> I try to be completely natural so, you know, if I'm excited about something I'm liable to run up and down the corridor and go 'Yay! Isn't that great!' It's important that people are able to feel, 'Oh, the CEO's being completely herself. It's okay for me to be like that!' I think people work better when they're comfortable in the environment that they're working in … Behind my resolve is that I want 100 per cent, no 110 per cent activity from the people I'm managing and from my point of view that's been a much more effective way of getting that than fear or dominance.

In a parodic summation, a CEO provides an image of the newness of the female archetype of leadership in what used to be referred to as the male domain of executive culture:

Inside, of course, you're still 18 and you think, as a lot of women feel apparently, that you'll be caught out one day. One day burly men will appear in the door and point out that this has been a terrible mistake and you shouldn't be within a bull's roar of 21 million dollars let alone 250 staff.

One of the ways of affirming change, of making it happen, is by women telling their stories, as these women have done. In so doing, they are also 'breaking through the silences' and finding 'forms of communication which express women's voices and allow them to create and articulate their own meanings' (Marshall, 1995, p. 8).

## Implications

The process of 'breaking through the silences' has important implications both for women executives and for women in the wider workforce. Most immediately, the executive women's stories in this chapter constitute an archetypal profile of women in leadership and decision-making positions that strengthens and communicates an emerging culture of women in business (Olsson and Walker, 2003, 2004). At the level of official organizational storytelling, this female archetypal profile challenges the norms of 'corporate masculinity', which maintain the 'privilege of an *elite*' and perpetuate assumed assessments of 'who looks like leadership material' (Sinclair, 1998, p. 51), by communicating distinctive images of women leaders arising out of their expressed voices. In turn, the communication of these women's voices positions their professional personae or identities within executive culture to challenge the glass ceiling by representing them neither as honorary males nor as a few exceptional women (McConnell-Ginet, 2000) but rather as distinctively female leaders, whose archetypal profile suggests that they bring approaches, understandings and values to the processes of executive leadership that are different from those of many of their colleagues who pursue the model of 'corporate masculinity'. Equally importantly, by speaking out and expressing female leadership, these women provide role models for other women. Their voices not only challenge traditional and masculinist assumptions about leadership, but also attitudes surrounding the expression of emotion, female sexuality, ageism and motherhood that have often disadvantaged women in the workplace. Their example may encourage a more widespread expression of women's voices in all areas of the workforce.

## Conclusions

Heroic masculinism or the 'manager as hero' plays upon subconscious archetypes of leadership that reinforce a male paradigm of leadership, while leaving female leadership as either absence or other. To dismiss the hero manager as obsolete to contemporary organizations is to fail to recognize the power of archetypes in the ongoing social construction of leadership. It is not a matter of women being accorded the status of honorary male heroes, as this does not overcome patriarchal binary oppositions that reinforce women as the passive or negative force. This chapter has also suggested that while female archetypes of leadership can be reclaimed from mythical and historical female figures, these traditional archetypes have been constructed within the cultural context of patriarchy (Zanetti, 2001) and may retain some traditional and stereotyped, negative associations. At the same time, archetypes are dynamic and evolving. We live in a time of social revolution where women increasingly hold positions of substantial power. The executive women's stories in this chapter give voice to women's dynamic and evolving experiences to reconfigure a female archetype of leadership, which has been compared in this chapter to the modern myth of Xena. Other archetypes, including classical figures, could equally well be reconfigured to overcome possible traditional, negative associations so that they provide 'forms of communication' that express women's current leadership experiences and meanings.

This process of honouring the past within the ongoing stories of the present allows for both women and men to do leadership differently, since archetypes are social constructions rather than reflections of particular styles or personalities (Sinclair, 1998). To date, however, male myths and stories have dominated executive culture to appropriate leadership as archetype. Five years ago when the author began her research with women managers, she sought to trace the 'heroic' qualities of women's experiences and argued that they enact a distinctive but comparable paradigm of leadership to that of men. She also recognized that women have traditionally honoured their past and their ongoing experiences in the stories they tell other women. In working with these women's voices, the author has come to the conclusion that 'we don't need another hero'. These stories break through the constraints of heroic masculinism to reconfigure a distinctive female archetype of leadership for women in management. This view is not meant to deny the material oppression and other continuing issues for many women within the workplace. But as one woman executive said: 'If no-one's speaking out and showing how things are progressing then we'll never get anywhere. I think people need to be outspoken about things for change to occur.' Part of this process of change is to recognize, communicate and celebrate a female archetype of leadership by providing both forums and forms for the expression of women's voices.

## Recommendations

The following recommendations arise from this chapter:

- There should be further scholarship to examine female leadership and the emerging culture of women in business.
- Scholarship should be published that explores and expresses women's voices in mainstream management and academic journals.
- Organizational forums and forms for the expression of women's voices are needed.

- Official organizational stories that express women's voices are needed.
- Communication management models should include women's values, goals and experiences.
- Public communication of corporate successes should include the expression of female archetypes of leadership.
- The business press and leadership literature should celebrate female voices and female archetypes of leadership.

## Notes

1. The author thanks Emerald Group Publishing Ltd for permission to draw on material from the five articles she has published in Emerald journals, all of which are listed in the final references. © Emerald Publishing Group Ltd http://www.emeraldinsight.com/wimr.htm.

2. The author thanks Victoria University Press for permission to draw on material from her article (2000b) 'The Xena paradigm: Women's narratives of gender in the workplace', in J. Holmes (ed.), *Gendered Speech in Social Context*. Wellington, NZ: Victoria University Press.

## References

Abrams, M. H. (1988), *A Glossary of Literary Terms*, 5th edn. London: Holt, Reinhart and Winston.

Brewer, E. (1974), *Brewer's Dictionary of Phrase and Fable: Centenary Edition*. London: Cassell.

Butterfield, D. A. and Grinnell, J. P. (1999), 'Re-viewing gender, leadership and managerial behavior: Do three decades of research tell us anything?', in G. N. Powell (ed.), *Gender and Work*. Newbury Park, CA: Sage. pp. 223–38.

Carr, A. (2002), 'Jung, archetypes and mirroring in organizational change management: Lessons from a longitudinal case study', *Journal of Organizational Change Management*, **15**(5): 477–89.

Cash, M. (1997), 'Stories within a story: parables from "The New Zealand Experiment"', *The Learning Organisation*, **4**(4): 159–67.

Clark, T. and Salaman, G. (1998), 'Telling tales: Management gurus' narratives and constructions of managerial identity', *Journal of Management Studies*, **35**(2): 137–61.

Czarniawska, B. (1988), *A Narrative Approach to Organization Studies*. London: Sage.

Halford, S. and Leonard, P. (2001), *Gender, Power and Organisations*. London: Palgrave.

Handy, C. (1995), *Gods of Management*. London: Arrow.

Jackson, B. G. and Parry, Ken (2001), *The Hero Manager: Learning from New Zealand's Top Chief Executives*. Auckland: Penguin.

Kaye, M. (1995), 'Organizational myths and storytelling as communication management', *Journal of the Australian and New Zealand Academy of Management*, **1**(2): 1–13.

Kaye, M. (1996), *Myth Makers and Story-tellers*. Sydney: Business and Professional Publishing.

Lurker, M. (1988), *Gods and Goddesses, Devils and Demons*. London: Routledge.

Maier, M. (1999), 'On the gendered substructure of organization: Dimensions and dilemmas of corporate masculinity', in Gary Powell (ed.), *Handbook of Gender and Work*. London: Sage. pp. 69–94.

Marshall, J. (1984), *Women Managers: Travellers in a Male World*. Chichester: Wiley.

Marshall, J. (1995), 'Researching women and leadership: Some comments on challenges and opportunities', *International Review of Women and Leadership*, **1**(1): 1–10.

Matthews, R. (2002), 'Competition archetypes and creative imagination', *Journal of Organizational Change Management*, **15**(5): 461–76.

McConnell-Ginet, S. (2000), 'Breaking through the "glass ceiling": Can linguistic awareness help?' in Janet Holmes (ed.), *Gendered Speech in Social Context: Perspectives from Gown and Town*. Wellington, NZ: Victoria University Press. pp. 259–82.

Moi, T. (1985), *Sexual/Textual Politics*. London: Methuen.

Morong, C. (1994), 'Mythology, Joseph Campbell, and the socio-economic conflict', *Journal of Socio-Economics*, **23**(4): 363–73.

Morreale, J. (1998), 'Xena: Warrior princess as feminist camp', *Journal of Popular Culture*, **32**(2): 79–86.

Nirenberg, J. (2001), 'Leadership: A practitioner's perspective on the literature', *Singapore Management Review*, **23**(1): 1–34.

Olsson, S. (2000a), 'Acknowledging the female archetype: Women managers' narratives of gender', *Women in Management Review*, **15**(5/6): 296–302.

Olsson, S. (2000b), 'The Xena paradigm: Women's narratives of gender in the workplace', in Janet Holmes (ed.), *Gendered Speech in Social Context: Perspectives from Gown and Town*. Wellington, NZ: Victoria University Press. pp. 178–91.

Olsson, S. (2000c), 'Tall tales and true? New Zealand male executives' self-representations of career identity', paper presented at the Australia and New Zealand Communication Association (ANZCA) Conference, Ballina, Lismore, 3–5 July.

Olsson, S. (2002), 'Gendered heroes: Male and female representations of executive identity', *Women in Management Review*, **17**(3/4): 142–50.

Olsson S. and Pringle, J. (2004), 'Women executives: Public and private sectors as sites of advancement?', *Women in Management Review*, **19**(1): 29–39.

Olsson, S. and Walker, R. (2003), 'Through a gendered lens? Male and female executives' representations of one another', *Leadership and Organization Development Journal*, **24**(7): 387–96.

Olsson, S. and Walker, R. (2004), '"The women and the boys": Patterns of identification and differentiation in senior women executives' representations of career identity', *Women in Management Review*, **19**(5): 244–51.

Pringle, J. and Olsson, S. (2002), *Sites of Hope and Success? A Cross-perceptual Study of Executive Women in the New Zealand Public and Private Sectors*, New Zealand Centre for Women and Leadership Working Paper Series 02/3. Palmerston North, NZ: Massey University.

Salzer-Morling, M. (1998), 'As god created the earth: A saga that makes sense?' in D. Grant, T. Keenoy and C. Oswick (eds), *Discourse and Organization*. London: Sage. pp. 104–18.

Sinclair, A. (1994), 'The Australian executive culture: Heroes and women', in P. Carrol (ed.), *Feminine Forces: Redefining the Workplace: Women and Leadership 1994 National Conference Proceedings*. Perth: Edith Cowan University. pp. 180–93.

Sinclair, A. (1998), *Doing Leadership Differently: Gender, Power and Sexuality in a Changing Business Culture*. Melbourne: Melbourne University Press.

Steyrer, J. (1998), 'Charisma and archetypes of leadership', *Organization Studies*, **19**(5): 807–28.

Tannen, D. (1994), *Talking from 9 to 5*. New York: William Morrow.

Wilson, F. (2003), *Organizational Behaviour and Gender*. New York: McGraw-Hill.

Zanetti, L. A. (2002), 'Leaving our father's house: Micrologies, archetypes and barriers to conscious femininity in organizational contexts', *Journal of Organizational Change Management*, **15**(5): 52–37.

## Chapter 15

# Negotiating while Female: Research and Implications

Alice F. Stuhlmacher and Rebecca B. Winkler

## Introduction

In the workplace, negotiation is a fundamental tool for resolving big conflicts as well as little differences of opinion. It is so important, that one source estimates that negotiation consumes 20 per cent of a manager's time (Baron, 1989). Negotiation brings to mind images of adversaries, antagonism, deception and lies; in reality, however, workplace negotiation is a complex mix of a social interaction with perceived incompatibilities, interdependence, and ongoing cooperation and competition existing within a relationship (Putnam and Kolb, 2000).

This chapter, which considers gender and workplace negotiation, has three primary aims. First, in an overview of major research findings, we examine the differences in outcomes, behaviours and perceptions that occur when males and females negotiate. Second, we examine possible theoretical explanations for these differing effects. Finally, we contemplate the implications of the literature and offer recommendations for researchers, negotiators and organizations.

## Overview of Current Research: Empirical Findings

Although the evidence of gender differences between men and women in negotiation may strike some as mixed or inconsequential (Menkel-Meadow, 2000; Rubin and Brown, 1975; Ruble and Schneer, 1994; Wall and Blum, 1991), we believe that it consistently points to important concerns. For example, Stuhlmacher and Walters (1999), after examining studies on the profits earned by male and female negotiators under similar conditions, found that men earned a small but significantly higher amount of profit than did women. In a controlled set of experimental investigations (Ayres, 1991, 1995; Ayres and Siegelman, 1995), female car buyers were consistently offered a higher price for a car than male car buyers trained to use the exact same negotiating strategies. These experiments carefully controlled for factors such as occupation, attire, attractiveness, economic status, and script. Even the addresses of the car buyers were identical. In short, while women can be successful negotiators, the outcomes of their negotiations seem to be limited by significant barriers.

One barrier may be the negotiation behaviours of men and women. A meta-analysis of negotiation behaviours found small but significant differences for gender (Walters et al., 1998). Across 62 studies of negotiation that measured competition or cooperation (for example, demand level, concession rate, threats and put downs), women exhibited significantly more cooperative behaviours during negotiation than men exhibited. Research also suggests differences in how likely men and women are to approach or avoid negotiations. Gwartney-Gibbs and Lach (1991) found that women were less likely to resolve their workplace conflicts using formal dispute resolution procedures and were instead more likely to pursue informal mechanisms such as transferring out of the department. In their recent book, Babcock and Laschever (2003) argue that women, unlike men, consistently do not ask for things they want and are less likely to initiate a negotiation. A woman's reluctance to promote her own interests has profound implications for gender differences in resource allocation, opportunities, status and workload within organizations.

In addition to outcomes and behaviours, evidence suggests that male and female negotiators are perceived differently (Morrissett and Stuhlmacher, 2004). Differing perceptions of male and female negotiators may remain the most pervasive barrier in negotiations. When negotiators believe their negotiating partner is female, they perceive the partner to be more cooperative than if they believe the partner to be male (Matheson, 1991). Others (DeRiemer et al., 1982) suggest that women are perceived as having less bargaining power than men, despite identical situations.

## Theoretical Frameworks

Explanations for the influence of gender in negotiation are found in several theoretical perspectives. We consider theories from four areas: task and relationship orientation, gender stereotypes, stereotype threat and the situational/power perspective. The predictions of each of these perspectives may appear similar, but differences exist in the potential mediating and moderating mechanisms (see Figure 15.1).

### Task and Relationship Orientation

An initial framework to explain gender differences in negotiation was advanced by Rubin and Brown (1975). They suggested that in negotiations, women are more relationship oriented while males are more performance oriented. Thus, women are more aware of interpersonal cues than focused on profit and outcomes. The Dual Concern Model in negotiation (Pruitt and Rubin, 1986; Rahim and Bonoma, 1979) labels a task orientation as *concern for self* (CS) and a relationship orientation as *concern for other* (CO). A strong CS combined with a strong CO is believed to result in integrating, problem solving and effective negotiations. Higher joint negotiation outcomes result when a negotiator has both high CS and high CO; lower joint outcomes are found when either CS or CO is low (for example Ben-Yoav and Pruitt, 1984a, 1984b; Ruble and Thomas, 1976). Calhoun and Smith (1999) found that men and women did not differ in negotiation outcomes when CS was high. However, when CS was low, women tended to negotiate poorer outcomes than men and tended to yield to the other party. These findings imply that unless a woman is highly concerned for her own outcomes, chances are that she will negotiate a poorer outcome than a man. Task versus relationship orientation may also explain why women, compared to men, consistently allocate fewer resources to themselves when dividing outcomes or rewards (Major, 1987). This lack of a sense of entitlement suggests that women may value a relationship more than the outcome. This would appear as high CO and low CS.

*Gender Stereotypes*

Gender stereotypes also explain negotiation differences, particularly relating to the perceptions of men and women in negotiation. Traditional sex-role stereotypes suggest that men in negotiation will be tougher and more competitive than women. Women may be perceived as less effective negotiators compared to men because workplace social roles (such as supervisor or negotiator) are not congruent with sex-typical roles. Social role theory (Eagly, 1987) posits that the activities, or roles, within a society influence how individuals in those roles are perceived. In most societies, men and women have different social roles and then are expected to have the skills to fulfil these roles. In addition to being perceived as having the skills to fulfil various roles, individuals may accommodate to the roles. For example, Eagly and Wood (1999) discuss that women may acquire relationship or domestic skills from being in a caretaker role, while men may accommodate to employment roles and incorporate qualities like assertiveness or dominance. Gender-typical roles would then drive expectations and gender norms. While changes in social roles are expected as society and the workforce change, these stereotypes may be slow to change. Indeed, examining studies over time has not found evidence of reduced gender differences in behaviours or outcomes of negotiation (Stuhlmacher and Walters, 1999; Walters et al., 1998).

Social-role theory suggests that certain situations make gender roles more or less salient. In particular, the saliency of gender roles may be influenced by such things as the negotiation group's composition, communication form, communication style and type of task (for example workplace versus child care).

*Stereotype Threat*

Gender differences in negotiation have also been explained with the phenomenon of stereotype threat. Initially conceptualized by Steele and Aronson (Steele, 1997; Steele and Aronson, 1995), stereotype threat can be defined as the fear one has of confirming a negative stereotype about one's group, which in turn leads to performance decrements. For women, simply being aware of the stereotype that men perform better in negotiations (for example, when buying a car) could be enough to trigger a fear of confirming that stereotype when entering a negotiation situation (Kray et al.,

2002). This leads to a self-fulfilling prophecy in that this fear of underperforming actually leads to poorer outcomes.

Typically, the poor negotiation performance is only believed to occur when the situation is presented as being diagnostic of ability, as this is enough to *implicitly* activate the stereotype (Kray et al., 2002). However, negative effects on performance can be mitigated by tying the stereotyped group's traits to high performance (for example, telling participants that people with feminine traits do better in negotiation situations) or by giving individuals a chance to self-affirm their abilities before the negotiation situation (Galinsky et al., 2003; Kray et al., 2002). Interestingly, if the stereotype is explicitly activated, women may make a concerted effort to resist that stereotype by outperforming men in negotiation situations (Kray et al., 2001). Women may react against the stereotype of 'poor negotiator', but other pervasive stereotypes of women in negotiation may be relevant in relation to performance and behaviour. For example, women may react against a stereotype of being 'domineering' or pushy for pursuing self-interests. If this stereotype is activated, perhaps then a woman would be more relationship focused or show increased concern for the other party than if the stereotype is not salient.

To understand how stereotype threat works to diminish performance, researchers have investigated what forces mediate the process. It appears that lowered performance expectations (in the form of less challenging goals) lead to underperformance (Kray et al., 2002). Consider the case of a woman entering a salary negotiation situation. Stereotype threat would predict that her salary goal would be significantly less than the salary goal of a man, leading to her being paid less than that man for the exact same work. Indeed, empirical results have found support for goal-level mediating expectations (Kray et al., 2002).

*Situational Power/Context*

Despite the predictions of stereotype threat, social-role theory and orientation differences, it may be simply that being in a particular role (irrespective of gender) corresponds to low performance expectations or low positional power. For example, Galinsky et al. (2003) have shown that non-gendered roles can influence negotiation outcomes. In role-playing a recruiter and job candidate, recruiters were typically seen as possessing more situational power than a job candidate. When the negotiation situation was manipulated as being diagnostic of ability, recruiters significantly outperformed the candidate. However, when the situation was manipulated as not diagnostic of ability, the candidate performed significantly better in negotiating the same issues, such as salary and benefits. In this situation, it seems as if the performance expectation was based on context-driven power differences.

Watson (1994a, 1994b) also suggests gender differences in negotiation arise from contextual or power differences rather than inherent differences between the genders. Gender might co-vary with the factors in the context or situation to influence the likelihood of negotiation, the process and the outcome. Indeed, research has shown that organizational norms and culture have a stronger influence than gender on the negotiation strategies that individuals choose to use in resolving a conflict (Gayle, 1991), while others have found rank and experience to predict style more than gender (Chusmir and Mills, 1989). Major et al. (1984) propose that information differences may limit opportunities. Women may have a limited frame of reference compared to men. So, for example, if a woman compares herself to other underpaid individuals (like other women) she may be less likely to seek out additional salary or benefits in a negotiation.

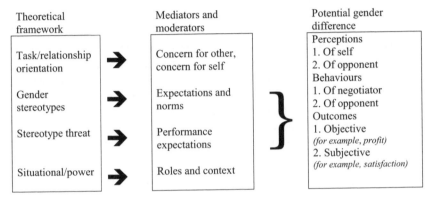

**Figure 15.1  Mediating and moderating mechanisms**

## Implications

The theoretical explanations and extent of gender differences in negotiation have important implications for women. Specifically, these differences have practical effects on how women deal with conflict, how they are paid, and what opportunities are open to them.

One implication is that differences between men and women in negotiation contribute to unequal employment opportunities and gender pay inequity. For example, given that pay increases are often based on a percentage of current salary, any inequity between men and women in starting salary would be perpetuated (and increased) over time. In addition, Stuhlmacher and Walters (1999) suggest that negotiation outcomes are a factor contributing to women gaining access to status and outcomes in organizations. Recognizing that an employee may be involved in multiple negotiations throughout the workday, the cumulative disparities from negotiations may be particularly striking. Indeed, Martell et al. (1996) simulated the cumulative effect of small biases (1 to 5 per cent bias for males) in performance ratings. Results showed that even with this small bias, women would be extremely under-represented in senior management levels through reduced opportunities for merit-based promotion.

In addition, the literature suggests that some situations may enhance gender differences. For example, the sex-type of the job interacts with gender in predicting negotiation strategies and outcomes. Specifically, Gwartney-Gibbs and Lach (1991) found that tokens (for example females in male-typed jobs) experience different conflict origins and use different strategies to resolve them than individuals not in a token role. Tokens experienced more harassment and discrimination, and they were more likely to deal with the problem on their own and forego the use of formal dispute resolution processes. Another situation that influences negotiation is the mode of the exchange. Walters et al. (1998) found that gender differences were reversed (women were more competitive than men) in negotiations that involved prisoner dilemma/matrix games compared to face-to-face negotiations. Matrix games involve less communication, less relationship building, and less possible face-to-face contact than explicit negotiations. In another meta-analysis comparing face-to-face negotiations to virtual negotiations (for example email, telephone), Stuhlmacher and Citera (2005) found that women engaged in less hostile behaviour in face-to-face negotiations than when negotiating by text, email, or telephone. Surprisingly, women made more profit when they were not face-to-face than face-to-face. For men, the hostile behaviours and the amount of profit were not influenced by the negotiation mode.

## Conclusions and Recommendations

The discussion above suggests caution before concluding that gender is *not* important in negotiation. It also suggests that more than one theoretical perspective needs to be brought to the table to predict and describe the empirical results. None of the theories at this point completely explains the complexity of gender issues in negotiation. As a set, however, recommendations can be made to researchers, negotiators and organizations to more fully understand the theories, research, and implications. These are set out in Table 15.1.

**Table 15.1    Recommendations for research, negotiators and organizations**

| Research | Negotiators | Organizations |
|---|---|---|
| • Increase attention to construct definition and measurement<br>• Include diverse research participants and tasks<br>• Use longitudinal, archival, or observational research in the workplace | • Get realistic and varied comparison information<br>• Set challenging goals for negotiation<br>• Participate in training programmes that increase goal-setting, self-efficacy, and perceived control in negotiation | • Recognize how negotiation may disadvantage women<br>• Pay attention to formal and informal conflict resolution mechanisms<br>• Implement organizational interventions such as mentoring to increase fairness and equity |

*Research Recommendations*

Several methodological issues are important for future research. First, detecting significant effects may be difficult. Meta-analytic results suggest that gender differences in negotiation are very small (Stuhlmacher and Walters, 1999; Walters et al., 1998). A large number of participants would be required to provide sufficient statistical power to detect significant differences. Statistical power tables (Cohen, 1992) would suggest a sample size of 393 participants per cell in a two-group ANOVA (analysis of variance) to detect a correlation of 0.10 (a small effect size). It is a rare negotiation study with a large enough sample to adequately test for gender differences.

Second, the assortment of measures concerning the styles, tactics and outcomes between men and women in negotiation creates confusion about gender differences in negotiation. For example, negotiation *success* has been defined in objective terms (for example, profit, money earned) but the subjective component (for example, satisfaction, perceptions of opponent, desire for future interactions) could also be a measure of success. Likewise, negotiator behaviour has been conceptualized with measures such as the amount of first offers, threats, lies, information exchange, concession frequency, and even ratings of one's own strategy. These disparate measures are difficult to compare and even more challenging to interpret the motivations and implications behind the behaviours. Measurement tools shape results. For example, Gayle (1991) found only 17 per cent overlap in responses when using a checklist of negotiation behaviours versus an open-ended question for the same sample of individuals. Similar measurement issues exist in other workplace conflicts involving gender, such as sexual harassment. Sexual harassment in the workplace is a clear example of a conflict with perceived incompatibilities and at least some perceived interdependence between parties. The reported prevalence of sexual harassment is influenced by how frequency is assessed (Ilies et al., 2003). When women were asked if they had experienced sexual harassment, less harassment was reported than when women used checklists to indicate exposure to behaviours that constitute harassment behaviours (35 per cent versus 62 per cent). More attention needs to be directed to the definition of constructs and the measurements of conflict and negotiation variables.

Finally, before making sweeping pronouncements on gender differences in negotiation, we must seriously assess whether existing research captures the range and reality of negotiation experiences of both men and women. More work is needed to understand the generalizability of theories and findings across broader samples of negotiators. Many negotiation studies rely on predominantly white, middle-class and young college students in the United States. Research such as Ayres (1995) suggests that race and gender interact to influence the negotiation process and we have substantial reasons to believe differences may exist as well for age, class and national culture. Further, Putnam and Kolb (2000) discuss how there are many ways parties may come to an agreement, but experimental negotiation tasks have focused on 'trade and transaction' rather than more complex situations. Frequently, the experimental situation minimizes relationships and produces very strong situations. Kolb (2000) notes that concern for long-term relationships (leading to increased levels of CO in negotiation situations) should not be considered maladaptive. Rather, she contends that collaboration is indeed a desirable characteristic if negotiation is an ongoing part of the relationship. One research approach may be through increased use of real-life negotiations, perhaps through archival or observational research in the workplace (Stuhlmacher and Walters, 1999). A broader variety of research paradigms could better capture the complexity of negotiation.

*Recommendations for Negotiators*

Like the Dual Concern Model, Watson (1994b) encourages women to look out for their own interests while sustaining good relations with the other negotiating party. While Watson suggests that both men and women would benefit from these negotiating skills, 'women may need these skills more than men because of the conflicting expectations they face when negotiating. Whereas men may be able to get away with competitive tactics some of the time, women may not' (Watson, 1994b, p. 125).

Training programmes for negotiation may be particularly useful for women. Specifically, in the case of negotiation, strengthening a woman's belief in her ability to obtain a successful outcome could increase performance. Self-efficacy is a belief in, or judgment about, one's ability to meet task demands (Wood and Bandura, 1989). In studies on training negotiation skills (Gist et al., 1991; Stevens and Gist, 1997), pre-training self-efficacy was significantly related to negotiation performance and negotiation skill maintenance. Self-efficacy is important in part because it influences the goals that are set for the negotiation (Stevens and Gist, 1997) and negotiation goals lead to higher profits (Zetik and Stuhlmacher, 2002). Self-management training (Gist et al., 1991) and perceived control (Stevens et al., 1993) also enhance goal setting and performance in negotiation.

As discussed in conjunction with stereotype threat, entitlement, self-efficacy and self-management training, goals seem to play an important part in the outcomes of negotiation. Even within the orientation framework, CS is affected by variables such as the flexibility of one's goals and boundaries (Rahim and Bonoma, 1979). Zetik and Stuhlmacher (2002) found that entering a negotiation with a specific and challenging goal had about six times the impact on the profit as the impact of gender differences. Thus, attention to negotiation goals seems particularly important for women.

*Recommendations for Organizations*

As suggested at the outset of the chapter, many organizational activities can be characterized as negotiation; that is, a social interaction with perceived incompatibilities, interdependence, and ongoing cooperation and competition in the relationship. Our review suggests that negotiation, or certain factors in the situation, may disadvantage women. On the positive side, women (because of factors such as a relationship or interpersonal orientation) actually have extremely valuable skills and abilities to offer in a negotiation (Kolb and Williams, 2000). The question then becomes how organizations can value and develop women in the workplace. We suggest that organization members:

- recognize situations in negotiations that may disadvantage women or other low power organizational members;
- consider appropriate conflict resolution mechanisms; and
- implement organizational interventions that increase equity.

As organizational leaders take steps to develop and promote women, they must recognize that negotiation and conflict can perpetuate the gap between the genders. We have discussed this already in relation to pay, but there are other disparities in the workplace. For sexual harassment victims in the workplace, resolving harassment is a trying situation at best. Behaviours may be interpreted to the detriment of women. A non-assertive coping style of enduring sexual harassment is usually seen as consenting to the treatment, when in fact the victim of harassment may be motivated by the necessity of a steady income. Further, because harassers tend to hold a higher job position than targets (for example O'Connell and Korabik, 2000), women are more likely to be on the losing end of any negotiation, because women are rarely in a position of power when being harassed.

Organizations need well thought out grievance and conflict resolution policies. This is particularly important given that significant differences in organizational outcomes are found to be related to the gender of the dyad involved in grievance proceedings (for example Dalton and Todor, 1985; Dalton et al., 1985). Many women do not consider formal grievance policies to be adequately suited to reconcile the type of conflicts (for example, over personality) they have at work (Gwartney-Gibbs and Lach, 1991). These findings might have negative long-term implications for women who choose to resolve conflict by informal methods (such as transferring out of their departments), which disadvantage women in terms of chances for promotions or advanced job assignments. Women's preference for informal processes may be due to gender-role socialization, lack of supervisor support or a lack of trust in the formal processes, but suggests that increased attention to the negotiation processes is warranted.

Similarly, other proactive organizational interventions should be considered. For example, mentoring may broaden the frame of reference for women, clarify goals, and move beyond some gender-stereotyped activities that women are less likely to participate in. Mentoring affects many different things, including one's perceptions of organizational justice (Scandura, 1997), perceived job alternatives (Baugh et al., 1996), and even self-esteem (Scandura, 1998). Even bottom-line business results can be affected by mentoring relationships within the organization. Mentored individuals have lower role ambiguity, increased job satisfaction and lower desire to quit, which leads to decreased turnover (Lankau and Scandura, 2002). More specific to the individual protégé, a successful mentoring relationship can lead to career development and psychological support, which have far-reaching consequences for one's career path through adulthood (Kram, 1983) and income (Dreher and Cox, 1996). Given the concrete benefits that mentoring is capable of producing, mentoring is increasingly important for dismantling the 'glass ceiling' and increasing diversity in leadership and employees' organizational experiences.

In short, our chapter suggests that gender issues are critical in workplace negotiation. Indeed, gender issues need clarification because of the inequality that may result if women are consistently underachieving or are perceived as ineffective negotiators. Although gender differences in negotiation appear small when any single negotiation is considered, when aggregated, these differences take a significant toll on women and those relying on women. Our discussion offers significant information for researchers, negotiators and organizations interested in increasing equity and fairness in outcomes and opportunities for women in negotiations.

### Acknowledgement

We thank Maryalice Citera and Anthony Winkler for helpful comments on a previous version of this chapter.

### References

Ayres, Ian (1991), 'Fair driving: Gender and race discrimination in retail car negotiations', *Harvard Law Review*, **104**(4): 817–72.

Ayres, Ian (1995), 'Further evidence of discrimination in new car negotiations and estimates of its cause', *Michigan Law Review*, **94**(109): 109–47.

Ayres, Ian and Siegelman, Peter (1995), 'Race and gender discrimination in bargaining for a new car', *The American Economic Review*, **85**(3): 304–21.

Babcock, Linda and Laschever, Sara, (2003), *Women don't ask: Negotiation and the gender divide*. Princeton, NJ: Princeton University Press.

Baron, Robert A. (1989), 'Personality and organizational conflict: Effects of the Type A behaviour pattern and self-monitoring', *Organizational Behaviour and Human Decision Processes*, **41**: 111–27.

Baugh, S. Gayle, Lankau, Melenie J. and Scandura, Terri A. (1996), 'An investigation of the effects of protégé gender on responses to mentoring', *Journal of Vocational Behaviour*, **49**: 309–23.

Ben-Yoav, Orly and Pruitt, Dean G. (1984a), 'Accountability to constituents: A two-edged sword', *Organizational Behaviour and Human Decision Processes*, **34**: 282–95.

Ben-Yoav, Orly and Pruitt, Dean G. (1984b), 'Resistance to yielding and expectation of cooperative future interaction in negotiation', *Journal of Experimental Social Psychology*, **20**: 323–53.

Calhoun, Patrick S. and Smith, William P. (1999), 'Integrative bargaining: Does gender make a difference?', *International Journal of Conflict Management*, **10**(3): 203–25.

Chusmir, Leonard H. and Mills, Joan (1989), 'Gender differences in conflict resolution styles of managers: At work and at home', *Sex Roles*, **20**(3): 149–63.

Cohen, Jacob (1992), 'A power primer', *Psychological Bulletin*, **112**: 155–9.

Dalton, Dan R. and Todor, William D. (1985), 'Composition of dyads as a factor in the outcome of workplace justice', *Academy of Management Journal*, **28**: 704–12.

Dalton, Dan R., Todor, William D. and Owen, Crystal L. (1985), 'Sex effects in workplace justice outcomes: A field assessment', *Journal of Applied Psychology*, **72**: 156–9.

DeRiemer, Cynthia, Quarles, Dan R. and Temple, Charles M. (1982), 'The success rate of personal salary negotiations: A further investigation of academic pay differentials by sex', *Research in Higher Education*, **16**(2): 139–54.

Dreher, George F. and Cox, Taylor H. (1996), 'Race, gender, and opportunity: A study of compensation attainment and the establishment of mentoring relationships', *Journal of Applied Psychology*, **81**(3): 297–308.

Eagly, Alice H. (1987), *Sex Differences in Social Behaviour: A Social-role Interpretation*. Hillsdale, NJ: Lawrence Erlbaum Associates.

Eagly, Alice H. and Wood, Wendy (1999), 'The origins of sex differences in human behaviour: Evolved dispositions versus social roles', *American Psychologist*, **54**: 408–23.

Galinsky, Adam, Thompson, Leigh and Kray, Laura (2003), 'Taking stereotypes out of stereotype threat: The effect of role-based expectations', unpublished manuscript, Northwestern University.

Gayle, Barbara Mae (1991), 'Sex equity in workplace conflict management', *Journal of Applied Communication Research*, **19**: 152–69.

Gist, Marilyn E., Stevens, Cynthia K. and Bavetta, Anna G. (1991), 'Effects of self-efficacy and post-training intervention on the acquisition and maintenance of complex interpersonal skills', *Personnel Psychology*, **44**: 837–61.

Gwartney-Gibbs, Patricia A. and Lach, Denise H. (1991), 'Workplace dispute resolution and gender inequality', *Negotiation Journal*, **7**(2): 187–200.

Ilies, Remus, Hauserman, Nancy, Schwochau, Susan and Stibal, John (2003), 'Reported incidence rates of work-related sexual harassment in the United States: Using meta-analysis to explain reported rate disparities', *Personnel Psychology*, **56**: 607–31.

Kolb, Deborah M. (2000), 'More than just a footnote: Constructing a theoretical framework for teaching about gender in negotiation', *Negotiation Journal*, **16**(4): 347–56.

Kolb, Deborah M. and Williams, Judith (2000), *The Shadow Negotiator: How Women Can Master the Hidden Agendas that Determine Bargaining Success*. New York: Simon and Schuster.

Kram, Kathy E. (1983), 'Phases of the mentor relationship', *Academy of Management Journal*, **26**(4): 608–25.

Kray, Laura J., Galinsky, Adam D. and Thompson, Leigh (2002), 'Reversing the gender gap in negotiations: An exploration of stereotype regeneration', *Organizational Behaviour and Human Decision Processes*, **87**(2): 386–409.

Kray, Laura J., Thompson, Leigh and Galinsky, Adam (2001), 'Battle of the sexes: Gender stereotype confirmation and reactance in negotiations', *Journal of Personality and Social Psychology*, **80**(6): 942–58.

Lankau, Melenie J. and Scandura, Terri A. (2002), 'An investigation of personal learning in mentoring relationships: Content, antecedents and consequences', *Academy of Management Journal*, **45**(4): 779–90.

Major, Brenda (1987), 'Gender, justice, and the psychology of entitlement', in Phillip Shaver and Clyde Hendrick (eds), *Review of personality and social psychology: Sex and gender, Vol. 7*. Newbury Park, CA: Sage. pp 124–48.

Major, Brenda, McFarlin, Dean B. and Gagnon, Diana (1984), 'Overworked and underpaid: On the nature of gender differences in personal entitlement', *Journal of Personality and Social Psychology*, **47**: 1399–412.

Martell, Richard F., Lane, David M. and Emrich, Cynthia (1996), 'Male–female differences: A computer simulation', *American Psychologist*, **51**(2): 157–8.

Matheson, Kimberly (1991), 'Social cues in computer-mediated negotiations: Gender makes a difference', *Computers in Human Behaviour*, **7**: 137–45.

Menkel-Meadow, Carrie (2000), 'Teaching about gender and negotiation: Sex, truths and videotape', *Negotiation Journal*, **16**(4): 357–75.

Morrissett, Melissa and Stuhlmacher, Alice F. (2004), 'Men and women as mediators: Disputant perceptions', unpublished manuscript, DePaul University.

O'Connell, Colleen E. and Korabik, Karen (2000), 'Sexual harassment: The relationship of personal vulnerability, work context, perpetrator status, and type of harassment to outcomes', *Journal of Vocational Behaviour*, **56**: 299–329.

Pruitt, Dean G. and Rubin, Jeffrey Z. (1986), *Social conflict: Escalation, stalemate, and Settlement*. New York: McGraw-Hill.

Putnam, Linda L. and Kolb, Deborah M. (2000), 'Rethinking negotiation: Feminist views of communication and exchange', in Patrice Buzzanell (ed.), *Rethinking organizational communication from feminist perspectives*. Newbury Park, CA: Sage. pp 76–104.

Rahim, Afzalur and Bonoma, Thomas V. (1979), 'Managing organizational conflict: A model for diagnosis and intervention', *Psychological Reports*, **44**: 1323–44.

Rubin, Jeffrey Z. and Brown, Bert R. (1975), *The Social Psychology of Bargaining and Negotiation*. New York: Academic Press.

Ruble, Thomas L. and Thomas, Kenneth W. (1976), 'Support for a two-dimensional model of conflict behaviour', *Organizational Behaviour and Human Performance*, **16**: 143–55.

Ruble, Thomas L. and Schneer, Joy A. (1994), 'Gender differences in conflict-handling styles: Less than meets the eye?', in A. Taylor and J. Beinstein Miller (eds), *Conflict and Gender*. Cresskill, NJ: Hampton Press. pp 155–66.

Scandura, Terri A. (1997), 'Mentoring and organizational justice: An empirical investigation', *Journal of Vocational Behaviour*, **51**: 58–69.

Scandura, Terri A. (1998), 'Dysfunctional mentoring relationships and outcomes', *Journal of Management*, **24**(3): 449–67.

Steele, Claude M. (1997), 'A threat in the air: How stereotypes shape intellectual identity and performance', *American Psychologist*, **52**(6): 613–29.

Steele, Claude M. and Aronson, Joshua (1995), 'Stereotype threat and women's math performance', *Journal of Personality and Social Psychology*, **69**: 797–811.

Stevens, Cynthia K. and Gist, Marilyn E. (1997), 'Effects of self-efficacy and goal-orientation training on negotiation skill mechanisms: What are the mechanisms?', *Personnel Psychology*, **50**: 955–78.

Stevens, Cynthia K., Bavetta, Anna G. and Gist, Marilyn E. (1993), 'Gender differences in the acquisition of salary negotiation skills: The role of goals, self-efficacy, and perceived control', *Journal of Applied Psychology*, **78**: 723–35.

Stuhlmacher, Alice F. and Citera, Maryalice (2005), 'Hostile behaviour and profit in virtual negotiations: A meta-analysis', *Journal of Business and Psychology*, **20**(1): 69–93.

Stuhlmacher, Alice F. and Walters, Amy E. (1999), 'Gender differences in negotiation outcome: A meta-analysis', *Personnel Psychology*, **52**: 653–77.

Wall, J. A. and Blum, M. W. (1991), 'Negotiation', *Journal of Management*, **17**: 272–303.

Walters, Amy E., Stuhlmacher, Alice F. and Meyer, Lia L. (1998), 'Gender and negotiator competitiveness', *Organizational Behaviour and Human Decision Processes*, **76**: 1–29.

Watson, Carol (1994a), 'Gender differences in negotiating behaviour and outcomes: Fact or artifact?', in A. Taylor and J. Beinstein Miller (eds), *Conflict and Gender*. Cresskill, NJ: Hampton Press. pp 191–210.

Watson, Carol (1994b), 'Gender versus power as a predictor of negotiation behaviour and outcomes', *Negotiation Journal*, **10**: 117–27.

Wood, Robert E. and Bandura, Albert (1989), 'Impact of conceptions of ability on self-regulatory mechanisms and complex decision making', *Journal of Personality and Social Psychology*, **56**: 407–15.

Zetik, Deborah C. and Stuhlmacher, Alice F. (2002), 'Goal setting and negotiation performance: A meta-analysis', *Group Processes and Interpersonal Relations*, 5: 35–52.

# Chapter 16

# Gender and the Expression of Emotion in Organizations

Theresa A. Domagalski

## Introduction

Emotions are fundamental to the human experience. They are a necessary ingredient in many elements of everyday organizational life. Successful leadership, for one, turns on the ability to articulate a strategic vision and to mobilize commitment among employees. Effective leaders are known to inspire others through emotional and impassioned appeals (Ashforth and Humphrey, 1995). Yet, despite a long tradition of examination in such fields as philosophy and psychology, the dominance of rationality as a governing principle for organizations has consigned emotions to a marginalized position in the management literature (Domagalski, 1999; Fineman, 1993a; Putnam and Mumby, 1993). Emotions are perceived as the antithesis of efficiency, as disruptive forces to be restrained in the interest of attaining organizational outcomes and confined instead to the private domain where women's work was performed. During the past two decades, however, emotions have gained legitimacy as a subject of academic inquiry. This shift in position is evidenced by the emergence of conferences on emotions in organizations, published books (Ashkanasy et al., 2000; Ashkanasy et al., 2002; Fineman, 1993b, 2000; Lord et al., 2002) and special issues of scholarly journals devoted specifically to emotion themes (Fisher and Ashkanasy, 2000).

Organizational researchers have taken varying directions in their study of emotions. Perhaps most widely acknowledged as the seminal contribution in this area is the work of Hochschild (1983), who examined how organizational practices are used to manage the felt and displayed emotions of flight attendants. Her contention that employee emotions are commodified in the interest of pursuing corporate profit imperatives laid the foundation for further research on the emotional labour requirements of certain occupations, such as theme park ride operators (Van Maanen and Kunda, 1989), bill collectors (Sutton, 1991) and convenience store clerks (Rafaeli and Sutton, 1989). This body of work on emotional labour, and a scholarly interest in the emotional features of organizations more generally, has illuminated the socially constituted nature of emotions. In contrast to other, biologically determined theories that have emphasized the bodily features of emotion, the social and relational nature of emotions has gained prominence with this line of inquiry and the communicative function of emotions is now more apparent in the organizational literature.

This chapter will address the gendered nature of emotional expression in the context of work organizations. First, a discussion of gender stereotypes as they relate to emotions, including conventional associations of gender with discrete emotions such as anger and sadness is presented. Next, a fuller treatment of the concept of emotional labour that was foreshadowed above is provided, giving particular emphasis to the way that emotional labour research has linked this concept to traditional gender role expectations. This is followed by a review of how issues of power and status intertwine with sex differences in emotional expression. Finally, the practical implications of this line of inquiry are discussed along with conclusions offering directions for future research.

**Overview of Current Research**

One of the more enduring stereotypes about gender is that males and females differ in their emotionality (Brody and Hall, 2000). Females in western cultures have traditionally been assigned the status of the emotional sex in that they are believed to experience emotions with greater intensity and to also be more emotionally expressive (Hess et al., 2000). Implicit in this stereotype is that males, as less emotional, are rational, controlled and focused on instrumental concerns, attributes that are generally associated with organizational success. To a degree, the persistence of gender-differentiated generalizations about emotion may reflect reality, since they may signify the potency of societal norms and expectations (Brody, 2000). Studies have confirmed that the socialization of normatively appropriate emotions differs along gender lines (for reviews, see Brody, 2000; Gray and Heatherington, 2003). Boys, for example, are taught to remain tough and keep a stiff upper lip in the face of adversity, whereas girls are permitted to express feelings of vulnerability (Levant and Kopecky, 1995; Maccoby, 1998). When gender distinctions such as this are reinforced in early childhood and beyond, they assume normative properties that carry social consequences when violated.

Such universal generalizations on the basis of gender are nonetheless somewhat misleading, for they obscure the impact of cultural distinctions, situational factors and individual differences (Brody, 2000; Brody and Hall, 2000; Hutson-Comeaux and Kelly, 2002). Yet another factor is the influence of methodological choice as a potential explanatory variable in findings pertaining to sex differences in emotionality (Brody and Hall, 2000; Kelly and Hutson-Comeaux, 1999). In fact, methodological differences have yielded disparate results about gender and emotion. Findings based upon the use of self-report measures assert that males and females differ in the experience of emotion, whereas those that have used physiological and experiential measures report fewer differences (Kelly and Hutson-Comeaux, 1999; Shields, 2002). This suggests that research participants invoke gender stereotypes of emotions when they are asked to provide retrospective accounts of emotional experiences (Crawford et al., 1992; Hess et al., 2000). However, emotions that are experienced in real time and identified by diary reports and measures of physiological arousal, tell a different story, one in which males and females are reportedly quite congruent. Similarly, with respect to specific emotions, such as that of anger, the experience of anger has been found to be undifferentiated for males and females (Averill, 1982).

When examining gender stereotypes related to emotion, it is important to distinguish between the expression of emotion and the experience of emotion (Brody and Hall, 2000). The findings above concern the manner in which males and females either experience emotions or report experiencing emotions. Greater consistency across methodological approaches is noted when the variable of interest is the expression of emotions. In this case, studies that examine emotional expression in a general sense routinely find sex differences in how emotions are expressed between males and females (Allen and Haccoun, 1976; Hess et al., 2000). When specific events or situations are introduced, however, the findings become more complex. The social context in which emotions are experienced and expressed offers additional edification concerning the validity of gender stereotypes. As Shields (2002, p. 27) notes, 'gender similarities are the rule; that said, the more that social context is embedded in the research question, the more likely we will find gender differences'. For example, the target to whom emotion is being expressed figures prominently. Relational intimacy, power and status asymmetries, and the sex of each interactant are all pertinent to emotional expression (Allen and Haccoun, 1976; Brody and Hall, 2000). Both males and females, for instance, have been found to express emotions more freely in the presence of those with whom they are familiar (Brody and Hall, 2000). Furthermore, gender stereotypes differ for achievement-oriented contexts as compared to relational contexts. Expressions of anger and pride are rated as more acceptable when displayed by males, particularly in achievement-oriented situations, whereas sadness, fear and happiness, all emotions that are stereotypically associated with females, are considered more appropriate in intimate or relational contexts (Kelly and Hutson-Comeaux, 1999). In addition, when males are in the presence of others who are emotionally expressive, particularly other males, they demonstrate a greater willingness to express themselves emotionally, even when the emotion in question, sadness, is typically associated with females (Gray and Heatherington, 2003). When the medium of expression is investigated, some research reports that males are more likely to internalize anger by experiencing it physiologically, whereas females have shown a pattern of external expression without a concomitant physiological manifestation (Brody and Hall, 2000). Although in one sense this may seem counterintuitive because anger is usually regarded as a male emotion, it nonetheless reinforces the axiom that males maintain control over their emotions and females are emotionally expressive.

This line of research suggests that gender stereotypes concerning emotions are oversimplified and imprecise when they neglect to include a consideration of social context or individual differences. The nature of the relationship and personal characteristics of the parties, the context in which interaction occurs – whether achievement or personal in orientation – the emotional expressivity of others and the medium of expression are factors to address when attempting to understand whether and when males and females express or suppress the display of particular emotions (Brody and Hall, 2000). Stated somewhat differently, variations in the expression of emotions by gender may be a function of social influences that reinforce gender role expectations.

Thus far, we have reviewed the relationship between emotions and gender stereotypes that emanate from societal norms and formative socialization processes. Early experiences, however pronounced, offer a partial understanding of the relationship between gender and emotion. To more fully understand the differences in emotional displays across gender lines requires an understanding of how other social contexts beyond those of societal norms inculcated in familial and peer group settings mould emotional display rules. The indoctrination that occurs during occupational training and from organizational directives assumes prominence among adults and is explored next.

*Emotional Labour*

> Different work organizations will inherit the wider emotion rules of the society of which they are a part, but they also adapt them to create their own codes of emotion propriety – such as what is 'right' for the medical doctor, the social worker, the hamburger salesperson, accountant or police officer. (Fineman, 2000)

Academic interest in organizationally specific emotion norms emerged with the publication of Hochschild's (1983) study on the emotional labour requirements of flight attendants. Hochschild used the term 'emotional labour' to describe the mental and emotional efforts required of employees to produce the display of organizationally desired emotions or suppress emotions that are not desired by the organization. Sometimes likened to the exchange relationship between wages and physical labour, emotional labour comprises the practices invoked by organizations to commodify the emotions of employees in an effort to attain organizational goals, such as repeat customers and profit maximization. Organizations create initiatives, such as selection practices, training programmes, rewards and sanctions, to teach employees how and when to regulate emotions, both felt and expressed, in their dealings with clients and customers. Hochschild adopted the dramaturgical concepts of deep and surface acting to explain how emotional labour is enacted (Goffman, 1959). Surface acting refers to the effort engaged by employees to feign desired emotions when in the presence of passengers (or customers, more generally) in order to induce desired states among those whom an organization services, whereas deep acting is concerned with techniques adopted to invoke required emotions in an effort to genuinely feel them when dealing with the public.

Since Hochschild, others have contributed to the discourse by examining the organizational practices involved in the management of emotional labour for theme park operators (Van Maanen and Kunda, 1989), convenience store employees (Sutton and Rafaeli, 1988), nurses (James, 1993; Steinberg and Figart, 1999), bill collectors

(Sutton, 1991), call centre employees (Callaghan and Thompson, 2002), lawyers (Harris, 2002) and police officers (Steinberg and Figart, 1999). Much of the research has focused on occupations in the service sector and those involved in front-line service to the public, because it is here that displayed emotions have an exchange value. It is estimated that some type of emotional labour, whether faking emotions that are not felt or suppressing those that are felt but prohibited by the organization, occurs in two-thirds of workplace communication (Mann, 1999).

Hochschild (1983) took as axiomatic that emotional labour requirements had a negative impact on those who were subjected to feeling and display rules. She assumed that the necessity of feigning emotions that were not authentically felt would leave employees feeling alienated and exploited, despite the organizational advantages. However, if gender stereotypes that proclaim that females are more emotionally expressive and males are more emotionally reserved are correct, this would suggest that workplace emotion rules that conform to these stereotypes would have no such negative consequences among employees. In fact, the conviction that emotional labour is harmful to employees has been challenged by some who point to the potential congruence between required emotional labour on the job and the emotional demands of home life, particularly for females who perform most of the emotion work on the home front (Wharton, 1993; Wharton and Erickson, 1993). To the degree that emotion requirements in different contexts are congruent, the dissonance between authentic and organizationally required emotions may be minimized. Likewise, careful selection practices may identify new hires whose personality characteristics are aligned with the emotional labour demands of the job and result in mutual benefits for the organization and the employee (Grandey, 2000; Wharton, 1993). Individuals who identify strongly with their occupational role are less likely to feel inauthentic when engaging in emotional impression management (Ashforth and Tomiuk, 2000).

Exploration of the possible congruence between job-related emotional labour requirements and gendered expectations of emotional expression necessitates a consideration of how role requirements differ across diverse occupations. For instance, if females are socialized to smile and display happiness, be compassionate with others, control their anger and convey vulnerability, would this imply that females will perform the role requirements of occupations such as customer service, nursing and airline cabin service more effectively than males? Similarly, if males are socialized to be dispassionate and emotionally reserved, and to display anger and pride, will they be more successful in occupations such as law enforcement, management, medicine and bill collecting, which reinforce these emotional reactions? What of an employee who displays organizationally required emotions that are inconsistent with gender stereotypes? Also, which emotion rules assume priority when someone of one sex enters an occupation that is dominated by the opposite sex?

Interestingly, there is a limited understanding of these questions since the literature on emotional labour has given scant attention to sex differences or gender role identities. When gender effects have been investigated, the findings have been discordant. In one examination by Rafaeli (1989), female sales clerks were shown to express positive emotions more than males. Likewise, a study of barristers concluded that gender stereotypes concerning emotions were overly simplistic, because male barristers were found to display emotions in their everyday work, whereas females appeared to experience greater negative effects from the emotional labour demands of the profession (Harris, 2002). By contrast, there were no differences in the emotional reactions of male and female technicians in a telecommunications company concerning company lay-off decisions (Armstrong-Stassen, 1998). And, in an investigation of nurses and law enforcement personnel, significant differences for emotional labour were found within occupations rather than between occupations (Steinberg and Figart, 1999). More specifically, the emotional requirements varied among clinical nurses, public health nurses and those employed in nursing homes more than they did between police officers and public health nurses, for example. One inference to be made from these findings is that the duties and responsibilities of jobs must be considered before conclusions may be offered concerning the relationship between gender and the emotional demands of occupations (Steinberg and Figart, 1999).

The significance of analysing job requirements is informed by an investigation of human resources professionals. Although differences along gender lines were observed, the source of differences in emotional labour behaviours for men and women was found to be disjunctive job requirements (Simpson and Lenoir, 2003). Close examination of the data revealed that females conformed to gender stereotypes for emotional expression because they were more represented in jobs that involved employee welfare functions, whereas males demonstrated stereotypically male forms of emotional labour, since they more often engaged in labour relations duties that required addressing adversarial and conflictual relationships between management and labour. Yet, these gender distinctions disappeared when the job duties of females consisted of performing labour relations tasks or when males performed in a caretaking human resources function. These findings lend support to Steinberg and Figart's (1999) exhortation to analyse job content for the particular emotional requirements of given jobs, since variation exists within occupational groups and may have widely disparate emotional labour demands.

'Are there gender differences in emotion? Of course there are. What is interesting about these differences, however, is that they are far more context dependent than the prevailing emotion stereotype leads us to expect' (Shields, 2002). The findings from the emotional labour literature raise an interesting issue, specifically, whether occupational and organizational norms have a more potent influence on emotion display rules than societal norms do, at least in organizational contexts. It may be that the social consequences of violating organizational directives for emotional expression are so formidable that males and females adhere to organizationally prescribed practices, even when doing so violates more general societal gender stereotypes for emotional expression. To know whether this is the case will require further research, since, as mentioned previously, little effort has been made to understand the relationship between gender and emotional labour on the job.

*Sex, Status and Emotion*

To this point, we have considered whether males and females play by the same rules of emotion expression when these rules are mediated by societal expectations of what is gender-appropriate, and also, when regulated by organizational and occupational imperatives. Despite the hegemony of rationality as a driving force in the construction of organizations, workplaces are infused with emotionality. Organizational power holders actively manage the emotional expressions of their members when doing so serves corporate interests. Moreover, members bring gender identities imbued with emotion stereotypes to the workplace. Power and status act upon emotions to sustain power relationships, and emotions in turn serve to reinforce the status hierarchy (Hearn, 1993).

Such is the case even when the dominant precept calls for emotional neutrality (Hearn, 1993; Kramer and Hess, 2002). Management as an occupation may be seen as a kind of emotional labour in that management is concerned with controlling others and with maintaining self-control (Hearn, 1993). Since males continue to outnumber females in high status positions within organizational hierarchies, discourses of control and emotional neutrality enable those with power (who are predominantly male), to sustain their power. Even when females adopt emotional behaviours that are similar to males, they may nonetheless be perceived differently and rendered ineffective. Tannen (1994) describes how gender stereotypes may be in conflict with occupational norms in the story of a male physician whose detached and brusque demeanour met with compliance from nursing staff, but resistance from the same staff when these same emotions were exhibited by a female physician. Here, obtaining cooperation from lower-status members required occupational norms to be suspended and replaced with a degree of feminine emotionality. When females express emotion in accord with gender stereotypes, what impact does this have on their status? Are they perceived as lacking in impulse control, being overly emotional, and thus given lower status? What does the expression of emotions by males signify in terms of their place in the organizational hierarchy? How does the acceptance of anger expression as prototypically male affect perceptions of males and their status?

Some researchers postulate that anger and power are closely intertwined in that anger is a means of asserting and sustaining power (Shields, 2002; Tiedens, 2000). Anger is apt to be shifted downward toward the powerless and used strategically to maintain power. Tiedens (2000) contends that a cyclical relationship exists among perceptions that those of high status are competent, that those who are angry are competent and that angry people are of higher status. She qualifies this by acknowledging that gender differences have not been considered in this conceptualization. Anger may be used by power holders in a deliberate attempt to intimidate lower-status organization members by conveying the capacity to impose negative costs on others (Gibson and Schroeder, 2002).

The relationship between gender and workplace expressions of anger, independent of status, has been studied empirically. In support of Averill's (1982) findings on anger, a recent study reported the absence of gender differences in both the experience and expression of workplace anger (Gianakos, 2002). Furthermore, control strategies were reported to be the dominant mode of handling anger on the job. Paradoxically, in another investigation of sex differences, although the control of anger expression was also the most frequently identified anger-coping strategy by males and females, gender differences were observed nonetheless (Domagalski and Steelman, 2004). Males were significantly more likely to report using verbally or physically aggressive forms of anger expression and females adopted a greater range of expressive forms, including avoidance, aphasia and tears. Inasmuch as workplace social rules may dictate a controlled posture when angry on the job, the inconsistent results from these studies signal the need to exercise caution when relying upon self-report measures of anger expression.

Less well understood is what influence positive emotions may have on the status of females and males in organizational environments. Females are encouraged by cultural display rules to express happiness, warmth and empathy, and to exhibit more smiling behaviour (Brody, 2000). When they do, existing power and status imbalances within the culture are sustained, and often to the disadvantage of females, who generally possess less power within cultures. Yet, evidence points to the deliberate use of positive emotions among power holders in organizations as a strategy to engage lower-status members (Gibson and Schroeder, 2002). Charismatic leaders are apt to summon their passion, energy and enthusiasm as they seek to evoke commitment and loyalty from their members and to gain acceptance of their corporate visions. To be sure, there are female leaders who invoke positive emotions to successful ends and hence maintain a privileged location in the status hierarchy (Martin et al., 2000). This would suggest that factors other than gender are necessary to explain the correspondence between emotional expression and organizational status and power. Taken as a whole, it seems that the role of gender in the expression of emotion within the context of organizations offers numerous research possibilities.

**Implications**

We are all emotional beings. That cultures shape the ways that emotions are experienced and how they are expressed is understood. Furthermore, the overtones of emotional expression carry different rules for males and females. Socialization of gender-appropriate emotional displays begins at an early age and is reinforced in play groups (Tannen, 1994), families (Brody, 2000) and elsewhere. Among working adults, the rules of emotional engagement become complicated. Emotional expectations vary according to occupation. Norms for the display of emotions are forged by socialization processes that occur during the course of occupational training. They are also instilled through organizational requirements, where they may become part of the wage effort bargain.

Occupational and organizational norms may not be in harmony with societal norms and gender stereotypes. When emotion norms are incongruent, there may be undesirable consequences for employees, for organizations or both. Employees who violate the emotion norms of their occupations or organizations face the possibility of diminished status and job-related sanctions. When they fail to adhere to gender stereotypes, employees may risk the loss of cooperation from others and experience a sense of alienation. When occupational precepts and personal obligations have considerable emotional demands, employees may experience role conflicts and tenuous social identities (Wharton, 1993). For organizations, breach of emotional labour requirements by employees may result in the failure to attain corporate objectives.

It is important for decision makers and power holders in organizations to recognize that societal gender stereotypes and organizational demands may not be compatible. When organizational display rules are congruent with the gender stereotypes of one sex, but are performed by an employee of the opposite sex, these same emotional behaviours may be perceived differently. An occupation that requires detachment and neutrality, for example, may be labelled as 'professional' when exhibited by a male, yet be designated as cold, unfeminine or worse when employed by a female. Not only do organizations face the possibility of legal repercussions, such as employment discrimination, when applying different standards to males and females, they also miss valuable opportunities to capitalize on the benefits of talented employees who neglect to conform to narrow expectations of what is gender appropriate versus what is organizationally appropriate.

Among academics, a mere two decades of research on the emotional facets of work organizations suggests that this line of inquiry is in its infancy. It is an excellent time for organizational and management scholars to advance the knowledge on the topic of emotions. Numerous investigations on emotional labour have informed our understanding of how employees' emotions are strategically managed for corporate benefit. Missing from this literature is the interplay between organizational expectations and culturally shaped gender stereotypes. Additional research is needed to better understand the intersection of organizational and societal norms and expectations. Similarly, further investigation is warranted on the correspondence between emotions and power relations. Specifically, we require a more complete understanding of how emotions work to establish power and how emotions are used to maintain power and status. As a corollary, it will be important to determine which emotions are implicated in power relations and the way that gender comes into play.

## Conclusion

The principal aim of this chapter was to explore the relationship between gender and the expression of emotions within the context of work environments. Three distinct themes were introduced. The first of these concerned prevailing gender stereotypes related to emotions. An attempt was made to elucidate the complexity of typecasting emotions in gender terms by pointing to the socially determined nature of stereotypes and the importance of social context to understanding gender-based emotion stereotypes. An informed understanding of emotion norms requires that individual differences and situational circumstances be taken into account, along with awareness of the distinction between the experience of emotion and emotion expression. An examination of organizational norms pertaining to emotional expression adopted a narrower lens to explicate how organizations shape desired forms of emotional expression among employees with the concept of emotional labour. It was observed that the organizational context adds a layer of complexity to the understanding of gender and emotion, since organizational display rules are not necessarily congruent with societal norms. As such, understanding the relative contributions of organizational and societal norms to emotional expression by males and females is problematic. The final theme addressed was the association among emotions, gender and status relations. Emotions are sometimes used to assert and to affirm organizational status. Anger is one emotion that has been identified with power holders as a method of maintaining a privileged location in organizational hierarchies. However, it is also regarded as a male emotion, and, as such, the correspondence between anger and power for females remains obfuscated. Despite a profusion of research on the socialization of gender-appropriate emotions and culturally bound stereotypes of male and female emotional expressivity, there is much that remains unknown about emotional expression in work organizations along gendered lines.

## Recommendations

The following recommendations arise from the discussion in this chapter.

- Managers and those with responsibilities for directing employees should be alerted to the tensions that may exist between societal norms and organizational norms as they relate to gender and emotions. The potentially incongruous expectations may have adverse consequences for employees in terms of performance evaluations, prospects for upward mobility, the conferral of status and other organizational rewards.
- Researchers interested in gender studies, communication and organizational scholarship are challenged to take up the gaps in knowledge identified in this chapter by incorporating the investigation of gender and emotion in organizational contexts into their research programmes.
- Female employees are cautioned to take heed of their precarious situation as they negotiate the incompatibilities between culturally constituted gender stereotypes and display rules engendered by occupational and organizational imperatives for the expression of emotion. The disparities between societal and organizational norms have potential significance for the bestowal of status and power, as well as cooperation or resistance garnered from other members of the organization with whom female employees engage in the performance of their duties.

# References

Allen, J. and Haccoun, D. (1976), 'Sex differences in emotionality: A multidimensional approach', *Human Relations*, **29**(8): 711–22.

Armstrong-Stassen, M. (1998), 'The effect of gender and organizational level on how survivors appraise and cope with organizational downsizing', *The Journal of Applied Behavioral Science*, **34**(2): 125–42.

Ashforth, B. and Humphrey, R. (1995), 'Emotion in the workplace: A reappraisal', *Human Relations*, **48**: 97–125.

Ashforth, B. and Tomiuk, M. (2000), 'Emotional labour and authenticity: Views from service agents', in S. Fineman (ed.), *Emotion in Organizations*, 2nd edn. London: Sage. pp. 184–203.

Ashkanasy, N., Hartel, C. and Zerbe, W. (eds) (2000), *Emotions in the Workplace: Research, Theory and Practice*. Connecticut: Quorum Books.

Ashkanasy, N., Zerbe, W. and Hartel, C. (eds) (2002), *Managing Emotions in the Workplace*. New York: M. E. Sharpe.

Averill, J. (1982), *Anger and Aggression: An Essay on Emotion*. New York: Springer-Verlag.

Brody, L. (2000), 'The socialization of gender differences in emotional expression: Display rules, infant temperament and differentiation', in A. Fischer (ed.), *Gender and Emotion: Social Psychological Perspectives*. Cambridge: Cambridge University Press. pp. 24–47.

Brody, L. and Hall, J. (2000), 'Gender, emotion, and expression', in M. Lewis and J. Haviland-Jones (eds), *Handbook of Emotions*, 2nd edn. New York: The Guilford Press. pp. 338–49.

Callaghan, G. and Thompson, P. (2002), 'We recruit attitude: The selection and shaping of routine call centre labour', *Journal of Management Studies*, **39**(2): 233–54.

Crawford, J., Kippax, S., Onyx, J., Gault, U. and Benton, P. (1992), *Emotion and Gender: Constructing Meaning from Memory*. London: Sage.

Domagalski, T. A. (1999), 'Emotion in organizations', *Human Relations*, **52**(6), 833–52.

Domagalski, T. A. and Steelman, L. (2004), 'Differences in workplace anger expression on the basis of sex and status', unpublished manuscript.

Fineman, S. (1993a), 'Organizations as emotional arenas', in S. Fineman (ed.), *Emotion in Organizations*. London: Sage. pp. 9–35.

Fineman, S. (ed.) (1993b), *Emotion in Organizations*. London: Sage.

Fineman, S. (ed.) (2000), *Emotion in Organizations*, 2nd edn. London: Sage.

Fisher, C. and Ashkanasy, N. (eds) (2000), *Journal of Organizational Behavior*, special issue: 'Emotions in organizations', **21**(2).

Gianakos, I. (2002), 'Issues of anger in the workplace: Do gender and gender roles matter?', *The Career Development Quarterly*, **51**, 155–71.

Gibson, D. and Schroeder, S. (2002), 'Grinning, frowning, and emotionless: Agent perceptions of power and their effect on felt and displayed emotions in influence attempts, in N. Ashkanasy, W. Zerbe and C. Hartel (eds), *Managing Emotions in the Workplace*. New York: M. E. Sharpe. pp. 184–211.

Goffman, E. (1959), *The Presentation of Self in Everyday Life*. New York: Doubleday Anchor.

Grandey, A. (2000), 'Emotion regulation in the workplace: A new way to conceptualise emotional labour', *Journal of Occupational Health Psychology*, **5**(1): 95–110.

Gray, S. and Heatherington, L. (2003), 'The importance of social context in the facilitation of emotional expression in men', *Journal of Social and Clinical Psychology*, **22**(3): 294–314.

Harris, L. (2002), 'The emotional labour of barristers: An exploration of emotional labour by status professionals', *Journal of Management Studies*, **39**(4): 553–84.

Hearn, J. (1993), 'Emotive subjects: Organizational men, organizational masculinities and the (de)construction of emotions', in S. Fineman (ed.), *Emotion in Organizations*. London: Sage. pp. 142–66.

Hess, U., Senecal, S., Kirouac, G., Herrera, P., Philppot, P. and Kleck, R. (2000), 'Emotional expressivity in men and women: Stereotypes and self-perceptions', *Cognition and Emotion*, **14**(5): 609–42.

Hochschild, A. (1983), *The Managed Heart: Commercialization of Human Feeling*. Berkeley: University of California Press.

Hutson-Comeaux, S. and Kelly, J. (2002), 'Gender stereotypes of emotional reactions: How we judge an emotion as valid', *Sex Roles*, **47**(1/2): 1–10.

James, N. (1993), 'Divisions of Emotional Labour: Disclosure and Cancer', in S. Fineman (ed.), *Emotion in Organizations*. London: Sage. pp. 94–117.

Kelly, J. and Hutson-Comeaux, S. (1999), 'Gender-emotion stereotypes are context specific', *Sex Roles*, **40**(2): 107–20.

Kramer, M. and Hess, J. (2002), 'Communication rules for the display of emotions in organizational settings', *Management Communication Quarterly*, **16**(1), 66–80.

Levant, R. and Kopecky, G. (1995), *Masculinity Reconstructed*. New York: Dutton.

Lord, R., Klimoski, R. and Kanfer, R. (eds) (2002), *Emotions in the Workplace: Understanding the Structure and Role of Emotions in Organizational Behavior*. San Francisco, CA: Jossey-Bass.

Maccoby, E. (1998), *The Two Sexes: Growing up Apart, Coming Together*. New York: Belknap.

Mann, S. (1999), 'Emotion at work: To what extent are we expressing, suppressing, or faking it?', *European Journal of Work and Organizational Psychology*, **8**(3): 347–69.

Martin, J., Knopoff, K. and Beckman, C. (2000), 'Bounded emotionality at the Body Shop', in S. Fineman (ed.), *Emotion in Organizations*, 2nd edn. London: Sage. pp. 115–39.

Putnam, L. and Mumby, D. (1993), 'Organizations, emotions and the myth of rationality', in S. Fineman (ed.), *Emotion in Organizations*. London: Sage. pp. 36–57.

Rafaeli, A. (1989), 'When clerks meet customers: A test of variables related to emotional expressions on the job', *Journal of Applied Psychology*, **74**(3): 385–93.

Rafaeli, A. and Sutton, R. (1989), 'The expression of emotion in organizational life', in L. Cummings and B. Staw (eds), *Research in Organizational Behavior Vol 11*. Greenwich, CT: JAI Press. pp. 1–42.

Shields, S. (2002), *Speaking From the Heart: Gender and the Social Meaning of Emotion*. Cambridge: Cambridge University Press.

Simpson, P. and Lenoir, D. (2003), 'Win some, lose some: Women's status in the field of human resources in the 1990s', *Women in Management Review*, **18**(4): 191–8.

Steinberg, R. and Figart, D. (1999), 'Emotional demands at work: A job content analysis', *Annals of the American Academy of Political and Social Sciences*, **561**: 177–91.

Sutton, R. (1991), 'Maintaining norms about expressed emotions: The case of bill collectors', *Administrative Science Quarterly*, **36**: 245–68.

Sutton, R. and Rafaeli, A. (1988), 'Untangling the relationship between displayed emotions and organizational sales: The case of convenience stores', *Academy of Management Journal*, **31**: 461–87.

Tannen, D. (1994), *Talking from 9 to 5*. New York: William Morrow.

Tiedens, L. (2000), 'Powerful emotions: The vicious cycle of social status positions and emotions', in N. Ashkanasy, C. Hartel and W. Zerbe (eds), *Emotions in the Workplace: Research, Theory and Practice*. Connecticut: Quorum Books. pp. 71–81.

Van Maanen, J. and Kunda, G. (1989), 'Real feelings: Emotional expression and organizational culture', in L. L. Cummings and B. Staw (eds), *Research in Organizational Behavior Vol. 11*. Greenwich, CT: JAI Press. pp. 43–103.

Wharton, A. (1993), 'The affective consequences of service work', *Work and Occupations*, **20**: 205–32.

Wharton, A. and Erickson, R. (1993), 'Managing emotions on the job and at home: Understanding the consequences of multiple emotional roles', *Academy of Management Review*, **18**: 457–86.

# PART V
# The Future:
# Gender and Computer-mediated Communication at Work

## Chapter 17

# Gender and Electronic Discourse in the Workplace

Rob Thomson

## Introduction

Many workplaces have become highly dependent on computers, not only for keeping records or conducting business, but also for communication between employees. Although this may be an efficient and effective way of communicating, it is important to consider the social implications of computer-mediated communication (CMC). One issue that has received considerable attention in other communication media is gender. Do men and women speak, use and interpret language differently? This chapter addresses these issues in electronic discourse. It appears that although the Internet is inherently gender-neutral, there are gender effects in how people communicate and behave online. If this is the case, then gender must have an effect on CMC in the workplace.

## Overview of Current Research

### Gender and Electronic Discourse

A relatively recent, but increasingly popular means of communication is electronic discourse or CMC. CMC covers a range of means whereby a computer is used to generate text and send it to others via computer networks. This communication medium is interesting because electronic discourse contains elements of both written and face-to-face communication, as well as features unique to CMC (Foertsch, 1993; Lea, 1991; Yates and Orlikowski, 1993). As in face-to-face communication, writers of electronic messages tend to use informal language and paralinguistic features including multiple exclamation marks or capitalization for emphasis (for example, 'he said WHAT!!!, Grrrrrrr'). This suggests that for many people CMC is an extension of informal interpersonal speech. Rintel and Pittam (1997) also report that interaction management strategies such as opening and closing phases in CMC are similar to those in face-to-face communication ('Hi, how are things … chat to you later'). On the other hand, Yates and Orlikowski (1993) give examples where electronic communication is similar to written correspondence. Both show evidence of editing, careful composition, and use of formatting devices such as bullets, headers and lists. This might be more appropriate if the recipient is not a close friend or if the content and context is formal, business or more serious.

In addition to features common to other forms of communication, electronic messages also contain features unique to CMC. These include emoticons or 'smileys' (for example, ;-) :-o ), and may attempt to signify physical actions (for example, jon hugs jane). Another dimension of CMC that mediates social behaviour is synchronicity: whether the conversation takes place in 'real-time', such as a phone conversation, or over a longer period, such as a letter, which could be described as asynchronous. Depending on the specific media (for example, short message service (SMS), discussion board), this can vary and likewise influence the communication and social behaviour.

One major difference between traditional forms of communication and CMC is the anonymity of electronic discourse. On discussion lists and in chat rooms, many people may be identified only by the name they provide, whereas if someone uses a work email, this might not be the case. As such, people may feel freer to experiment with different forms of communication and self-representation than in other media (Reid, 1993). Consequently, some users may be tempted to adopt a different personality, or change their gender or age (Bruckman, 1993; Danet, 1996; Jaffe et al., 1995). This was reported by Bruckman (1993), where many men introduced themselves as women in multi-user-dimension (MUD) environments because women received more attention than men. The language of these users however was much more sexually aggressive than that of women users, and hence their deception was often detected.

Despite the anonymity of CMC, however, there is a growing body of evidence showing that gendered language in CMC is similar to that found in face-to-face and written communication (Herring, 1993, 1994; Jaffe et al., 1995; Rodino, 1997; Savicki et al., 1996; Thomson and Murachver, 2001; Witmer and Katzman, 1997). These studies have shown differences in language features, function and style used by men and women. Moreover, it appears that readers of CMC text are able to predict author gender with a fairly high accuracy (Savicki et al., 1999; Thomson and Murachver, 2001).

However, these gender differences are not so clear-cut. People are very flexible in how they use language, and use different styles depending on recipient, nature of the relationship and the context. For example, most people would speak differently to a friend in a social setting from the way they might to an elderly relative or a senior colleague. Both women and men are capable of using a wide range of language styles, depending on whom they are communicating with. As such, gender-linked language differences have been found to be greater in same-sex groups than when women and men interact together (Bilous and Krauss, 1988; Fitzpatrick et al., 1995; Mulac et al., 1988). This is because both men and women are more likely to use gender-typical speech when they are interacting with others of the same gender. These findings suggest that people are flexible in their use of gendered language and accommodate to the gender-preferential language style used by their partners, which is consistent with communication accommodation theory (see Coupland et al., 1988; Giles et al., 1987).

According to this theory, speakers change their language behaviour in response to that of their conversational partner. If they wish to gain approval, be liked or want to accentuate similarities, they adapt or converge their language to be more like their partner. On the other hand, if they are motivated to accentuate differences, then they may resist this change, or diverge by making their language less like that of their partner. Eisikovits (1987) gives an interesting example of this. She collected transcripts of interviews of male and female adolescents conducted by an older female interviewer. It was found that although the young women decreased their use of slang terms and non-standard speech when talking to the interviewer, the young men used more of these features. Eisikovits argued that the women were motivated to accentuate similarities with the interviewer and converged to the interviewer's speech style. The young men, however, were motivated to make themselves more distinct and hence diverged.

In CMC, a person's own language is influenced by both the gendered style and the gender label of their partner (Thomson et al., 2001). In this study, participants were asked to write email messages to an anonymous 'netpal' over a period of 2 weeks. This netpal was however, a confederate who had either a female or male label (for example, Jane or John) and used either female preferential or male preferential language features. The gendered language styles were created by using templates of features identified as being predictive of gender. The results from this study indicate that the participants' language style was dependent on both their own gender and the style used by their netpal. Although participants did use gender-preferential language, this was modified by their accommodation to the netpal's style. Furthermore, as in the study by Mulac et al. (1990), the style used by the netpal appeared to have the largest effect on participants' own language.

The gender label of the netpal did not have a large effect on the participants' language, but it did affect how much gender-preferential language they used. When the gender of the netpal was different from that of the participant, then the participant used less gender-preferential language than when they were of the same gender. This suggests that the participants not only converged to the language used by their partner, but also to how they believe males and females to speak (Bilous and Krauss, 1988; Coupland et al., 1998; Limbrick, 1991).

In addition to moderating participants' use of gender-preferential language, the netpal label also appeared to influence accommodation. When the gender of the netpal did not match their own, they accommodated less to the male style than when they were of the same gender. Participants were also less likely to accommodate to a male style when a netpal with a female label used it.

The results from this study indicate that when people interact, gender can influence their language in multiple ways. Most people are likely to use a gender-preferential language style. There is, however, considerable flexibility in this. People are influenced by the style used by their partner as well as how they perceive a member of that social group to speak. As gendered language is much more complex than that based on dichotomous gender groups, it is likely that other aspects of gendered behaviour are more flexible than is generally believed.

## CMC and Online Behaviour

Due to the fewer cues to identity in CMC, some theorists have argued that it reduces status differences and barriers to communication (Graddol and Swann, 1989; Kaplan and Farrell, 1994; Keisler et al., 1984; Sproull and Keisler, 1986). The decreased number of social cues in CMC gives users greater freedom from social structures and norms (Keisler et al., 1984). In support of this, one participant in the Kaplan and Farrell (1994) study described how the 'absence of social cues and of immediately perceptible power differentials creates a more comfortable social space'.

Other researchers, however, have argued that CMC is not as equalizing as it was hoped to be (Herring, 1993, 1994; Kramarae and Taylor, 1993; Savicki et al., 1996; Spender, 1995; Truong, 1993). These researchers report that men often dominate open discussion groups, both in amount and control of the topic. This contrasts with the results of Graddol and Swann (1989), however, who found that men and women contributed about the same number of messages. Additionally, Jaffe et al. (1995) found that women were more likely to mask their gender by the use of pseudonyms than men. Although this would distort participation rates, if women feel a need to mask their gender, then perhaps CMC is not as comfortable for women as for men. When users are assumed to be female, they are perceived as more cooperative (Matheson, 1991), in need of technical assistance (Bruckman, 1993), and they are the subject of sexual attention or harassment (Bruckman, 1993; Kramarae and Taylor, 1993; Spender 1994; Truong, 1993).

Decreased social cues, however, can also cause the individual identity of the self and others to become less salient, or deindividuated. As such, this may produce an increase in anti-normative behaviour (Walther et al., 1994). A commonly given example of this is 'flaming' or harsh personal insults. Herring (1994) and Truong (1993) reported that men are much more likely to flame on the Internet than they would face-to-face (but see Witmer and Katzman, 1997, for contrary findings).

Postmes and Spears (1998), however, disputed the idea that deindividuation leads to anti-normative behaviour. Following a meta-analysis of deindividuation research, they concluded that behaviour was not anti-normative per se, but was consistent with the group or situational norms. Violent behaviour in a rioting crowd, for example, may be seen as consistent with situational norms, even though it violates societal norms in other contexts. Flaming may be viewed likewise, as in some situations it may be seen as normative (Lea et al., 1992). Within a group of males, for example, insults and teasing could be common. In electronic discourse within this group, flaming would therefore be seen as normative. Situations of deindividuation appear to increase sensitivity to group or situational norms. This idea, paired with social identity theory (Tajfel and Turner, 1979; Turner, 1987), where individuals have multiple levels of identity from personal to social, leads to the Social Identity and

Deindividuation (SIDE) model (Lea and Spears, 1991; Postmes et al., 1988; Spears and Lea, 1992, 1994; Spears et al., 1990).

The SIDE model predicts that because CMC provides fewer cues to personal identity, a situation of deindividuation is created where personal identity is not particularly salient. Although there is a reduction in cues to personal identity in CMC, there are frequently cues to social identity. This is because it is often possible to predict gender, ethnicity, location and occupation of a user through usernames, server and context of communication. For example, an email address often gives information about workplace and country, and the topic of discussion (for example, depression support group, classical music discussion) gives information about social groups or identity. As such, social identity becomes more salient than it might in other types of communication, thereby increasing awareness and conformity to group norms (Spears and Lea, 1992, 1994). This prediction is supported by a study by Spears et al. (1990), in which the researchers found participants shifted towards group norms when social identity was salient and away from group norms when personal identity was more salient.

Thomson (2002) examined gender-preferential language in discussion lists posted in public forums where gender is more or less salient. Based on the SIDE model, it was assumed that in discussions about female-stereotypical topics and male-stereotypical topics, gender would be more salient than in discussions about non-gender stereotypical topics. Discussions on a range of threads that were female stereotypical, male-stereotypical and gender-neutral were recorded and coded for language features that previous research has shown to be predictive of gender. It was predicted that there would be a higher frequency of female preferential features in discussions about female-stereotypical topics than male or neutral topics. Likewise, it was expected that there would be a higher frequency of male preferential features in discussions about male topics than in discussions about female-stereotypical or gender-neutral topics.

The results from the Thomson (2002) study showed that participants in the selected discussions used gendered language consistent with the topic being discussed. Consistent with predictions, there was a higher frequency of female preferential features in discussions about female-stereotypical topics and a higher frequency of male preferential features in discussions about male topics, than in discussions about other topics. This suggests that participants accommodate to the language style that is expected when discussing gendered topics.

An alternative explanation for these findings is that there are more females taking part in discussions about female-stereotypical topics and are more males taking part in discussions about male-stereotypical topics, hence the greater frequencies of gendered features. Although this may to a certain extent be true, this explanation does not account for the language style used in the discussions about neutral topics. These discussions showed a low frequency of both female and male features rather than a mixture of both. Furthermore, in a few instances, participants have indicated their gender when they have been taking part in a discussion stereotypical of the other gender: 'I am really into fashion, although I don't know much! I hope I will be welcome here in a women's club!'

The findings of these studies bring into question our assumptions about gender and language. If both women and men are able to use either gender-preferential style, then perhaps gender-preferential language is not fixed or inherent to the individual, but is constructed in conversation. This is done through accommodation. When people converse with someone of the other gender, they typically change their own style and converge to the style of their partner. As people converge to the speech styles of each other, their styles converge to a style somewhere between them. Thus, gender differences are constructed and maintained as a feature of the context rather than being inherent to men or women.

This argument does not deny the existence of gender differences, because there is extensive evidence of these differences. Moreover, people are aware of these differences and have beliefs about how women should, and do, speak. In many situations, people may wish, or it is appropriate, to distinguish themselves as a woman or a man. In this context, gender-stereotypical behaviours such as gendered language would be common. Gendered language, however, is not a fixed feature of the individual, because people are capable of using a range of styles depending on the context.

## Implications for Workplace Communication

Although in principle CMC is gender free, it appears that gender is as much a part of communication in online environments as in other media. People are sensitive to gender differences in language use and style, and certainly make judgements based on their perceptions of message senders. For example, Jessmer and Anderson (2001) found that although polite, grammatically correct emails were in general perceived more positively, impolite emails were seen as being authored by high-status males, and polite emails from competent females. As such, patterns and perceptions of electronic discourse may reflect power and status inequalities inherent to many workplace environments.

The influences of gender social perceptions in CMC tasks was highlighted by Matheson (1991), who had participants engage in a negotiation task where the gender of the other participant was known or not given. When gender was not known, there were no differences in perceptions, but when their partner's gender was known, women were perceived as more cooperative and less exploitative than men. This shows that social perceptions and expectations based on gender are present in CMC environments if gender is salient.

CMC may actually, as some theorists have argued ( Biber et al., 2002; Sussman and Tyson, 2000), be more male dominated than other media. Sussman and Tyson (2000) reported that men's discourse was more opinionated and longer than women's discourse, and Biber et al. (2002) found that people perceived misogynist comments and sexual harassment more harassing online than in other environments. Clearly, this should not be tolerated any more than it is in other forms. Unfortunately, many work environments have a hierarchical power structure and discrimination on gender lines is common. It is likely that if this is present in organizations in non-CMC environments, a similar pattern will be found in online communication.

One needs to be careful, however, not to overstate the case for gender differences in online workplace communication. Most research into CMC and online behaviour assumes a degree of anonymity. Often this is not the case in the workplace and an individual's language is more likely to be influenced by knowledge of the recipient and nature of relationship. Gender-linked language differences are clearly context dependent, and in a workplace environment, gender may not be as salient as in more informal social environments. For example Bogoch (1997) found that women lawyers' language style in conversation with clients is role related rather than gender related. Gender differences in communication strategies and style are subtle and can be influenced more by situation, background, status and relationship between the speakers (Burke, 2001; O'Donohue and Crouch, 1996).

**Conclusions and Implications**

Although there is a great deal of flexibility in how we use language, there are gender effects in how we produce, interpret and communicate it. Gender effects are, however, only one factor that influences people's language. The context, relationship between the conversants and the goals of communication are likely to have a larger effect on language than gender. In a work environment, people often know each other and have a history of interactions. Although gender may play a role in the relationship between people, it is most likely that online communication will be a reflection of offline communication. Despite this, however, gender does influence our language, especially with people we do not know. Consequently people need to be aware of how gender influences how we produce and interpret language.

The Internet is inherently gender-neutral, but gender effects are present in CMC as in other forms of communication. This is probably because when the number of cues to personal identity are reduced, cues to social identity become more salient. If gender is salient, it is likely that people will use gender-typical language. However, if gender is not salient, people might use a different social category. This might be based on workplace status, department, location or job. Associated with many of these are beliefs or norms about how one should behave and interact with others from the same or another group. If this is the case, one might expect other language differences in how language is used and interpreted online.

**Recommendations**

The following recommendations arise from the preceding discussion:

- People need to be aware of the limitations of CMC, especially with regard to the lack of paralinguistic features that help us convey and interpret meaning.

For example, an insult given with a grin might not be intended or interpreted as offensive. Although users may try to compensate for this with emoticons, there is a potential for miscommunication.

- Social categories such as gender play a role in how we communicate. These affect the language style and how we construct meaning. As such, it is important to be conscious of how a recipient might interpret a message and make a greater effort to make the meaning clear. Likewise on receiving a message, we need to be open to other possible interpretations of the sender's intentions.

- There is a greater potential for discrimination, harassment and flaming in CMC than other environments if employees' postings are anonymous. Management and employees need to be aware of this, and have clear guidelines on appropriate behaviour and protocols for dealing with problems.

## References

Biber, J. K., Doverspike, D., Baznik, D., Cober, A. and Ritter, B. A. (2002), 'Sexual harassment in online communications: Effects of gender and discourse medium', *CyberPsychology and Behaviour*, **5**: 33–42.

Bilous, F. R. and Krauss, R. M. (1988), 'Dominance and accommodation in the conversational behaviours of same- and mixed-gender dyads', *Language and Communication*, **8**: 183–94.

Bogoch, B. (1997), 'Gendered lawyering: Difference and dominance in lawyer–client interaction, *Law and Society Review*, **31**(4): 677–712.

Bruckman, A. S. (1993), 'Gender swapping on the Internet', paper presented at The Internet Society, San Francisco, CA, August. Retrieved May 21, 2005 from www. mith2.umd.edu/WomensStudies/Computing/Articles+ResearchPapers/gender-swapping.

Burke, R. J. (2001), 'Information sources: Is there a gender issue?', *Corporate Communications*, **6**: 7–12.

Coupland, N., Coupland, J., Giles, H. and Henwood, K. (1988), 'Accommodating the elderly: Invoking and extending a theory', *Language in Society*, **17**: 1–41.

Danet, B. (1996), 'Text as Mask: Gender and Identity on the Internet'. Retrieved May 21, 2005 from pluto.mscc.huji.ac.il/~msdanet/mask.html.

Eisikovits, E. (1987), 'Sex differences in inter-group and intra-group interaction among adolescents', in A. Pauwels (ed.), *Women and Language in Australian and New Zealand Society*. Sydney: Australian Professional Publications.

Fitzpatrick, M., Mulac, A. and Dindia, K. (1995), 'Gender-preferential language use in spouse and stranger interaction', *Journal of Language and Social Psychology*, **14**: 18–39.

Foertsch, J. (1993), 'The impact of electronic networks on scholarly communication: Avenues for research', *Discourse Processes*, **19**: 301–28.

Giles, H., Mulac, A., Bradac, J. J. and Johnstone, P. (1987), 'Speech accommodation theory: The first decade and beyond', in M. McLaughlin (ed.), *Communication Yearbook 10*. Beverly Hills, CA: Sage. pp. 13–48.

Graddol, D. and Swann, J. (1989), *Gender Voices*. Oxford: Basil Blackwell.

Herring, S. (1993), 'Gender and democracy in computer-mediated communication', *Electronic Journal of Communication* (online), **3**(2). Available via e-mail message addressed to Comserv@cios.org. Subject line: Send Herring V3N293.

Herring, S. (1994), 'Gender differences in computer-mediated communication: Bringing familiar baggage to the new frontier', keynote talk at panel entitled 'Making the net*work*: Is there a Z39.50 in gender communication?', American Library Association annual convention, Miami, Florida.

Jaffe, J. M., Lee, Y.-E., Huang, L.-N. and Oshagan, H. (1995), 'Gender, pseudonyms, and CMC: Masking identities and baring souls', paper presented at the annual conference of the International Communication Association, Albuquerque, NM. Retrieved May 21, 2005 from research.haifa.ac.il/~jmjaffe/genderpseudocmc/.

Jessmer, S. L. and Anderson, D. E. (2001), 'The effect of politeness and grammar on user perceptions of electronic mail', *North American Journal of Psychology*, **3**: 331–46.

Kaplan, N. and Farrell, E. (1994), 'Weavers of webs: A portrait of young women on the net', *Arachnet Electronic Journal on Virtual Culture*, **2**(3). Retrieved January 5, 2006 from www.infomotions.com/serials/aejvc/aejvc-v02n3.htm.

Keisler, S., Siegel, J. and McGuire, T. W. (1984), 'Social psychological aspects of computer-mediated communication', *American Psychologist*, **39**: 1123–34.

Kramarae, C. and Taylor, H. J. (1993), 'Women and men on electronic networks: A conversation or a monologue?', in C. Kramarae, H. J. Taylor and M. Ebben (eds), *Women, Information Technology and Scholarship*. Urbana-Champaign, IL: Centre for Advanced Studies, University of Illinois. pp. 52–61.

Lea, M. (1991), 'Rationalist assumptions in cross-media comparisons of computer-mediated communication', *Behaviour and Information Technology*, **10**: 153–72.

Lea, M. and Spears, R. (1991), 'Computer-mediated communication, deindividuation and group decision making', *International Journal of Man Machine Studies*, **34**: 283–301.

Lea, M., O'Shea, T., Fung, P. and Spears, R. (1992), '"Flaming" in computer-mediated communication', in M. Lea (ed.), *Computer-mediated Communication*. London: Harvester Wheatsheaf. pp. 89–109.

Limbrick, P. (1991), 'A study of male and female expletive use in single and mixed sex situations', *Te Reo*, **34**: 71–89.

Matheson, K. (1991). 'Social cues in computer-mediated negotiation: Gender makes a difference'. *Computers in Human Behavior*, **7**(3): 137–45.

Mulac, A., Studley, L. B. and Blau, S. (1990), 'The gender-linked language effect in primary and secondary students' impromptu essays', *Sex Roles*, **23**: 439–69.

Mulac, A., Wiemann, J. M., Widenmann, S. J. and Gibson, T. W. (1988), 'Male/female language differences and effects in same-sex and mixed-sex dyads: the gender-linked language effect', *Communication Monographs*, **55**: 315–35.

O'Donohue, W. and Crouch, J. L. (1996), 'Marital therapy and gender-linked factors in communication', *Journal of Marital and Family Therapy*, **22**(1): 87–101.

Postmes, T. and Spears, R. (1998), 'Deindividuation and anti-normative behaviour: A meta-analysis', *Psychological Bulletin*, **123**: 238–59.

Postmes, T., Spears, R. and Lea, M. (1998), 'Breaching or building social boundaries? SIDE-effects of computer-mediated communication', *Communication Research*, **25**, 689–715.

Reid, E. (1993), 'Electronic chat: Social issues on Internet relay chat', *Media Information Australia*, **67**: 62–70.

Rintel, E. S. and Pittam, J. (1997), 'Strangers in a strange land: Interaction management on Internet relay chat', *Human Computer Research*, **23**(4): 507–34.

Rodino, M. (1997), 'Breaking out of binaries: Reconceptualizing gender and its Relationship to Language', in *Journal of Computer-mediated Communication* (online) **3**(3). Retrieved May 22, 2005 from www.ascusc.org/jcmc/vol3/issue3/rodino.html.

Savicki, V., Kelley, M. and Oesterreich, E. (1999), 'Judgments of gender in computer-mediated communication', *Computers in Human Behavior*, **15**: 185–94.

Savicki, V., Lingenfelter, D. and Kelley, M. (1996), 'Gender language style and group composition in Internet discussion groups', *Journal of Computer-mediated Communication* (online), **2**(3). Retrieved May 21, 2005 from www.ascusc.org/jcmc/vol2/issue3/savicki.html.

Spears, R. and Lea, M. (1992), 'Social influence and the influence of the 'social' in computer-mediated communication', in M. Lea (ed.), *Computer-mediated Communication*. London: Harvester Wheatsheaf. pp. 30–64.

Spears, R. and Lea, M. (1994), 'Panacea or panopticon: The hidden power in computer-mediated communication', *Communication Research*, **21**: 427–59.

Spears, R., Lea, M. and Lee, S. (1990), 'Deindividuation and group polarisation in computer-mediated communication', *British Journal of Social Psychology*, **29**: 121–34.

Spender, D. (1994), 'A history of information media', *Australian Educational Computing*, May: 11–16.

Spender, D. (1995), *Nattering on the Net: Women, Power and Cyberspace*. North Melbourne: Spinifex Press.

Sproull, L. and Keisler, S. (1986), 'Reducing social context cues: Electronic mail in organisational communication', *Management Science*, **32**: 1492–512.

Sussman, N. M. and Tyson, D. H. (2000), 'Sex and power: Gender differences in computer-mediated interactions', *Computers in Human Behaviour*, **16**, 381–94.

Tajfel, H. and Turner, J. C. (1979), An integrative theory of intergroup conflict', in W. C. Austin and S. Wotchel (eds), *The Social Psychology of Intergroup Relations*. Monterey, CA: Brooks/Cole. pp. 33–53.

Thomson, R. (2002), 'Going to the girls' room or the boys' room: Gender in electronic discussion', paper presented at the 8th International Conference on Language and Social Psychology, City University of Hong Kong, July.

Thomson, R. and Murachver, T. (2001), 'Predicting gender from electronic discourse', *British Journal of Social Psychology* **40**: 193–208.

Thomson, R., Murachver, T. and Green, J. (2001), 'Where is the gender in gendered language?', *Psychological Science*, **12**(2): 171–5.

Truong, H. (1993), 'Gender issues in online communications', *Bay Area Women in Telecommunications*. Retrieved January 5, 2006 from www.eff.org/Net_culture/ Gender_issues/gender_issues_in_online_comms.paper.

Turner, J. C. (1987), 'A self-categorisation theory', in J. C. Turner, M. A. Hogg, P. J. Oakes, S. D. Reicher and M. S. Wetherell (eds), *Rediscovering the Social Group: A Self-categorisation Theory*. Oxford: Basil Blackwell. pp. 42–67.

Walther, J. B., Anderson, J. F. and Park, D. W. (1994), 'Interpersonal effects in computer-mediated communication: A meta-analysis of social and antisocial communication', *Communication Research*, **21**(4): 460–87.

Witmer, D. F. and Katzman, S. L. (1997), 'On-Line smiles: Does gender make a difference in the use of graphic accents?', *Journal of Computer-mediated Communication* (online), **2**(4). Retrieved May 21, 2005 from www.ascusc.org/ jcmc/vol2/issue4/witmer1.html.

Yates, J. and Orlikowski, W. J. (1993), 'Knee-jerk anti-LOOPism and other e-mail phenomena: Oral, written, and electronic patterns in computer-mediated communication', paper presented at the 53rd Annual Meeting of the Academy of Management, Atlanta GA, August.

Chapter 18

# The Email Gender Gap

Niki Panteli and Monica Seeley

## Introduction

The study presented in this chapter explores gender differences in email use by focusing on the text-based attributes of email messages. Traditionally, email has been seen to erode social cues in communication processes due to the absence of social context cues, that is, job titles, sex, social importance, hierarchical position, age and appearance (Sproull and Kiesler, 1991a, 1991b). Accordingly, several studies have reported that gender inequalities are significantly reduced in email communication (for example, Dubrovsky et al., 1991; Taha and Caldwell, 1993). Davidson (1995) in particular has suggested that with email as a medium of communication becoming more widespread in organizations, women have more opportunities to raise their voice and get involved in discussions and decision-making processes that concern their workplace.

The main argument of this chapter is that gender cues emerge in text-based email messages and that it is important to take this into account when assessing the level of richness embedded in email communication. The underlying assumption is that there is an organizational context that intertwines with email message texts. Therefore, even though email is often presented as a lean medium, the way text-based messages are constructed and even organized may convey cues that show evidence of gender differences in organizations. Though a key feature of email, there has been little research focusing on the text-based attributes of electronic messages in organizational communication. The present chapter draws upon empirical data to explore the extent to which these attributes differ among male and female employees within the same organizations.

## Overview and Implications of Current Research

Some of the more widely accepted differences between the way men and women manage are summarized in Table 18.1. This is based on a review of the recent literature by Vinkenburg et al. (2000).

**Table 18.1    Gender differences in management styles and behaviour**

| Women – the likelihood | Attribute/characteristic | Men – the likelihood |
| --- | --- | --- |
| Less | Risk taking | More |
| More | Relationship focused | Less |
| More | Communal | Less |
| More | Interpersonal | Less |
| More | Supportive | Less |
| Less | Image conscious | More |
| Less | Autocratic | More |
| More | Participative | Less |
| Less | Directive | More |
| Less | Self-confident | More |
| Less | Career networking | More |
| More | Social networking | Less |
| More | Emotional support networking | Less |
| Less | Political | More |

*Source:* Seeley and Hargreaves (2002) and Vinkenburgh et al. (2000). Reproduced with permission, Elsevier Ltd, from the book: *Managing in the Email Office*, by Monica Seeley and Gerard Hargreaves

Clearly, such differences are often moderated by circumstances such as the organizational culture and context. Whilst this is not the place to argue the true extent of these variations, it does provide a framework from which to review the differences in how men and women use email and the possible explanations. Therefore, even though some research has suggested that women and men do not differ in their use of email (for example Gefen and Straub, 1997), Seeley and Hargreaves (2002), who have observed over 175 executives, have identified some key differences in the way men and women use email and also in their general attitude towards emails. These differences were found in the size of inbox, the speed of responding to emails and the way email is used. For example, it was found that men are more likely than women to send jokes and use email for politics. Further, women are far more inclined to use email to catch up with friends and family and use it to make social arrangements (such as deciding who will do the shopping).

Drawing on these issues, this chapter explores gender differences while challenging the relevance of information richness theory, the most popular media-choice theory in this literature. It argues that the distinctive text-based nature of email messages has been overlooked and that email richness could be uncovered by taking a particular focus on messages sent by males and females.

*Information Richness Theory and Email Use*

Information richness theory proposes that organization participants select communication media depending on their information requirements, that is, ambiguity and uncertainty (Daft and Lengel, 1984). Ambiguity and uncertainty reduction is a function of a medium's capability to achieve information richness; richness is therefore identified as the ability of information to change understanding within a time interval. According to information richness theory, communication media vary in the level of information richness they process depending on their capacity for immediate feedback, the number of cues and channels utilized, personalization, and language variety. In order of decreasing richness, the media classifications are: (1) face-to-face; (2) telephone; (3) personal documents such as letters and memos; (4) impersonal written documents; and (5) numeric documents. Based on these criteria, email as a written and asynchronous form of communication does not meet the requirements for rich communication; it is identified as a lean medium in information richness theory. Trevino et al. (1987) add to this argument by claiming that email is driven mainly by situational determinants (such as distance, expediency, structure, role expectations or time pressures), often by content reasons (that is, for simple and routine messages) and rarely by symbolic factors, implying that email, unlike face-to-face communication, does not have the ability to signal meaning beyond the explicit message that it carries.

This rationalistic view for evaluating the level of richness in email communication medium has been criticized by several researchers. According to Schmitz and Fulk (1991), the theory views richness as a relatively objective feature that is largely inherent in the medium. Their study found that perceived email richness varies across individuals and co-varies with relational social influences and with media experience factors. Despite the arguments in Trevino et al. (1987), Lee (1994) suggests that email messages can be carriers of meanings. Although email itself is not a rich communication medium, it is the meanings given to email messages that contribute to its richness. He stresses that information richness is not just a function of the communication medium, but of the interaction between the communication medium and the organizational context in which it is used. Similarly, Markus (1994) describes the role of organizational context in the choice of communication media. She found that email was used for communication tasks that involved high degrees of ambiguity and was used more intensively by senior managers.

Although it is a written form of communication, email has distinctive text-based characteristics. Generally speaking, unlike spoken discourse where what is said is said and cannot be unsaid, written discourse allows writers to take more time to structure their messages and therefore their text may appear more planned and consequential. Similarly, in email communication, a text can be written, deleted, corrected, rewritten and restructured several times before distribution, without recipients knowing that this has taken place. However, email messages are not necessarily formal, structured and well presented like other written media such as letters and reports. They may have oral characteristics and characteristics that are unique to email instead of, or in addition to, characteristics of written discourse. They can be spontaneously written, brief, with typographical and grammatical errors that resemble conversational speech rather than a well thought out textual language. There are also characteristics seemingly unique to email communication (Spitzer, 1986; Yates and Orlikowski, 1993). Smiley faces and other graphic icons (emoticons) built out of punctuation marks, for example :-), as well as typographical errors are some of the expressive innovations in email communication. Such humoristic patterns do not exist in paper-based messages. The use of asterisks or capital letters for emphasis are also ways for codifying language expressions (Baym, 1995). Clearly, then, the use of email can give an opportunity for the appearance of both verbal and non-verbal attributes in email messages, as well as the evolution of new language and textual patterns among users (Yates and Orlikowski, 1993).

Sarbaugh-Thompson and Feldman (1998) studied differences in the availability, presence and absence and the impact of electronic communications on one's ability to generate trust. In the conventional office setting, people have many opportunities to signal that they are present and trustworthy simply by saying 'hi'. As organizations move towards a more virtual style of operation as in remote working, email is often the primary means of communication. How those communications are constructed and interpreted takes on more importance. Sarbaugh-Thompson and Feldman (1998) suggest that while the use of email has increased, the number of opportunities to communicate socially and hence develop meaningful relationships has decreased. They advocate using email to say 'hi' more often and suggest that for this reason including a greeting in emails is important.

Accordingly, email as a communication medium integrates characteristics found in traditional communication media and enhances possibilities for improved communication across the hierarchy. Email is also a unique medium with characteristics not found in other media (Spitzer, 1986). Its richness may as a result require a different evaluation from that of traditional communication media. This chapter has argued so far that there are characteristics of email communication that were overlooked in information richness theory. It proposes a focus on the text-based nature of email messages. It attempts to refute information richness theory by observing the gender cues evident in email texts.

An email message can be conveyed only through text. It is a written form of communication and unlike paper-based messages, email can be transmitted instantly. Unlike face-to-face or telephone conversations, it can be stored and re-read several times by the original recipient or sent to others using the forwarding function. This chapter looks at differences in how men and women use email through analysis of the content of emails. The text-based and asynchronous nature of emails have been the main reasons advocates of information richness theory describe it as a lean medium. However, unlike other written communication media, email has distinctive text-based attributes that have been neglected from the information richness theory. Email messages have characteristics of written or spoken language, or characteristics unique to email communication, or a combination of all these. Analysis of these different textual patterns reveals gender differences.

*Text-based Gender Cues in Email Messages*

A criticism made earlier about information richness theory is that it fails to take full account of the characteristics of email communication. Earlier studies have shown that email is a richer medium than is reflected in the scale of information richness theory. This chapter adds to this argument by taking primary account of the text-based nature of email messages, which was overlooked in the literature. For example, in a study of emails describing a recent holiday written by men and women for male and female friends, Colley and Todd (2002) found that emails from females contained a higher incidence of features associated with the maintenance of rapport and intimacy than those from male participants and this was more pronounced in the emails from female participants to male friends. Similarly, using a sample of undergraduate students, Jessmer and Anderson (2001) showed that females were perceived to be the authors of polite and grammatically correct email messages, while males were perceived as authoring impolite and ungrammatical messages.

Drawing upon a study by Panteli (2000, 2002), this section highlights that message attributes in electronic communication are socially constructed by the context of the organization in which email is used. In her study on the nature of text-based email messages sent within university departments, Panteli found evidence that messages sent by female staff appear more personal and friendly than those sent by male staff, for these tend to address and/or greet the recipient(s) while avoiding the use of signatures, thus signalling characteristics of spoken communication. For example, none of the female users in the study signed their messages in such a way as to reveal their formal title in the organization. In contrast, about 70 per cent of male users signed their messages. Moreover, none of the messages sent by secretaries and research staff was signed. Clearly, when senders choose to add their signatures to their messages, email reinforces the presence of status differences within a workplace.

The messages sent by females were found to have the most common characteristics of written discourse. Email message 1 (see Figure 18.1), for instance, was sent to a female researcher, Karen, by a female secretary, Helen, after Karen had asked her whether an audio tape had been transcribed. Although Helen replied to Karen shortly afterwards, she added the theme of the message ('RE: INTERVIEW JOHN SMITH, ABC ORGANIZATION') as a way of reminding Karen of the reason for contacting her. She could have instead specified the subject at the top of the email message which, however, she left blank. Email message 1 is structured and formal and shows evidence of careful composition. Moreover, it is informative. Karen (the recipient) is given information not only about whether Helen had finished transcribing a tape, but also how the tape arrived to her (this was known to Karen) and the difficulties that Helen had in transcribing it and how she coped with these difficulties.

By contrast, only about 10 per cent of the messages sent by men were long and structured making use of formative devices such as paragraphs and lists. In the main, male users were more likely than low-ranking staff to send short, unstructured and

.....
Subject:
Priority: normal
Friday 17 May 1996
Dear Karen
RE: INTERVIEW JOHN SMITH, ABC ORGANIZATION
Just a brief note to let you know that I have completed the tape passed to me by yourself, via Liz. I have put a print out of the hard copy in your pigeon hole along with the disk and a back up copy of the disk and the audio tape. Unfortunately, some of the words were very unclear so I have shown them throughout the document like this example ( .. ).
I hope this is okay for your purposes.
Thank you.
Helen Routledge

**Figure 18.1   Email message 1**

I have just found that the next two courses which Computer Services are running on Powerpoint are on 19 and 26 of August – from 2–5pm. [Secretary A] will shortly have some booking forms.
(Mary – I've sent this to all academic staff on my standard mailing list. Can you copy to all admin/sec staff? Thanks)
Professor John Hall
Dept of Beta Studies
Alpha University
Tel:.... (sec. Mary Shaw) fax....

**Figure 18.2   Email message 2**

to the point messages. For instance, email message 2 (see Figure 18.2) was sent by a professor to all members of staff.

Unlike email message 1, email message 2 appears short and conversational, but also directive and instructive. There are two instances where this can be seen. First, the message gives information about the location of the application forms assuming that people in the department are interested in attending. Second, at the bottom of the message, the professor asks his secretary to copy that message to the secretary's distribution list. He could have done this in the form of a conversation without using email to reinforce his status in the department.

It follows that though personalized, friendly and informative, email text, especially by staff at the lower ranks (for example secretaries and support staff), could appear structured and formal as in the case of traditional written discourse. The messages by male staff also have oral characteristics in that their messages appear short, to the point and spontaneous. At the same time, their messages show evidence of formality because they often carry their signatures. The presence of signatures and lack of greetings sustain social and status distances within a relatively small department. These findings reinforce the view of Seeley and Hargreaves (2002) that men tend to be more succinct and very precise, particularly when they are writing to women. Men are less inclined to use greetings or to ask social questions about the family or the weekend in an email. Women tend to be more conversational in style, writing longer, more detailed emails. Women are far more likely to take an extra few minutes to compose the content with the recipient in mind. This is exemplified in the following comment:

> The basis of relationships is connections which means communications. Email can be the bane of our lives but in our frenetic lives it is often the only way. When I send an email, which touches on other people's sensitivities, I spend time composing it. A good manager stays in touch and manages the connections. (Hilary, Marketing Director, international telecommunications company; reported in Seeley and Hargreaves, 2002)

What we see, therefore, is that hierarchical differences may be identified in the way email messages are constructed and structured.

Our analysis reiterates earlier criticisms made about information richness theory (for example, Markus, 1994) that it has failed to fully take account of the characteristics of email communication. Earlier studies have shown that email is a richer medium than is reflected in the scale of information richness theory. In the present study, we add to this argument by taking primary account of the text-based nature of email messages, which was overlooked in the literature. The analysis has highlighted that message attributes in electronic communication are socially constructed by the context of the organization in which email is used. The fact that email has not been established as a formal nor an informal means of communication, means that its users have a degree of flexibility in choosing how to present their messages and what language to use. The degree of flexibility is again influenced by the traditional gender relations within a given setting. Male users speak and write more freely and directly than female users; support for this is given in Pohl and Michaelson (1997). Email therefore as a communication medium signals and refines rather than alleviates gender differences. Beneath the surface of an email as a medium of communication that promotes the equalization phenomenon, there is a continuation of communication barriers between genders.

*Implications for Workplaces*

The need to understand how email is used and interpreted is becoming ever more important as, first, email is increasingly becoming the most frequently used means of business communication and information sharing. Second, organizational challenges are presented, as we live in a global business world and remote working and virtual teams are becoming more evident. Yet, as many organizations are now finding, email misuse accounts for a considerable amount of staff time (Seeley, 2000) and can seriously impact on the organization's ability to deliver its business. Furthermore, the technology of email is changing. In an effort to manage the use of email and improve its usefulness, organizations are now looking at using a wider range of technologies including instant messaging (text-messaging by email) and team-based chat rooms. If email as we know it is seen to be sterile and lacking in any social context, what will be the effect of these other newer, even more barren forms of email? Will they bridge or further widen the gender gap?

For the effective diffusion of email within an organization, and thus for developing more opportunities for idea generation and improved communication across the hierarchy, managers need to be careful that their own email messages do not constrain the potential of the medium. The communication medium itself cannot alleviate gender differential. However, it provides the opportunity for 'relaxing' traditional patterns of interactions by encouraging informal and, most importantly, informative communication across departments and hierarchical layers, among both male and female users.

## Conclusions

The chapter has explored the extent to which email messages differ among male and female senders. We analysed a series of email messages distributed within an academic department over a period of several months and found that email, as a communication medium, signals rather than alleviates gender differences. Therefore, even though email is often presented as a lean medium, the way text-based messages are constructed often conveys the social cues that are traditionally used to determine gender differences in organizations. As a result, the shortcomings in information richness theory become apparent, especially in terms of its relevance for email communication. We need to rethink the concept of richness in email communication and to develop more appropriate tools for measuring information richness. Below we present a series of recommendations for further research, as well as recommendations to practitioners.

## Recommendations

In order to increase generalizability, it would be useful to compare the findings of the studies presented in this chapter with studies of other organizations, private and public, and with a range of organizational characteristics such as, structure (flatter to more hierarchical), size, sector, ratio of female to male employees, and so on.

On a more practical note, some recommendations that can help bridge the gender gap in organizations, regardless of either level or nature of the business, are shown in Table 18.2.

**Table 18.2  Practical recommendations**

| For women | For men |
|---|---|
| • Shorten your emails | • Add some feelings |
| • Focus more on the task and less on the social niceties | • Add some social niceties from time to time |
| • Vary your salutation and sign-off to reflect the sender's and/or the state of the business relationship (for example hi, hello, good morning) | • Vary your salutation and sign-off to reflect the sender's and/or the state of the business relationship (for example hi, hello, good morning) |

## References

Baym, N. K. (1995), 'The Emergence of Community in Computer-mediated Communication', in S. G. Jones (ed.), *CyberSociety: Computer-Mediated Communication and Community*. London: Sage. pp. 138–63.

Colley, A. and Todd, Z. (2002), 'Gender-linked differences in the style and content of e-mails to friends', *Journal of Language and Social Psychology*, **21**(4): 380–92.

Daft, R. L. and Lengel, R. H. (1984), 'Information richness: A new approach to managerial information processing and organization design', in B. Staw and L. Cummings (eds), *Research in Organizational Behavior Vol. 6*. Greenwich, CT: JAI Press. pp. 191–233.

Davidson, K. (1995), 'Liberte, Egalite, Internete', *New Scientist*, May 27: 38–42.

Dubrovsky, V. J., Kiesler, S. and Sethna, B. N. (1991), 'The equalisation phenomenon: status effects of computer-mediated and face-to-face decision making groups', *Human–Computer Interaction*, **6**: 119–46.

Gefen, D. and Straub, D. W. (1997), 'Gender differences in the perception and use of email: An extension to the technology acceptance model', *MIS Quarterly*, **21**(4): 389–400.

Jessmer, S. L. and Anderson, F. (2001), 'The effects of politeness and grammar on user perception of electronic mail', *North American Journal of Psychology*, **3**(2): 331–46.

Lee, A. (1994), 'Electronic mail as a medium for rich communication: An empirical investigation using hermeneutic interpretation', *MIS Quarterly*, **18**(2): 143–57.

Markus, M. L. (1994), 'Electronic mail as the medium of managerial choice', *Organization Science*, **5**(4): 502–27.

Panteli, N. (2000), 'Gender differences in email-based communication: A focus on text-based attributes', paper presented at the IFIP, WG 9.1 Women, Work and Computerization Conference, 'Charting A Course to the Future', Vancouver, Canada, June.

Panteli, N. (2002), 'Richness, power cues and email text', *Information and Management*, **40**(2): 75–86.

Pohl, M. and Michaelson, G. (1997), '"I don't think that's an interesting dialogue" – computer mediated communication and gender', in A. F. Grundy, D. Kohler, V. Oechtering and U. Petersen (eds), *Women, Work and Computerization: Spinning a Web from Past to Future*. Berlin: Springer-Verlag.

Sarbaugh-Thompson, M. and Feldman, M. S. (1998), 'Electronic mail and organizational communication: Does saying "hi" really matter?', *Organization Science*, **9**(6): 685–98.

Schmitz, J. and Fulk, J. (1991), 'Organizational colleagues, media richness and electronic mail', *Communication Research*, **18**(4): 487–523.

Seeley, M. (2000), *Using the PC to Boost Executive Performance*. Aldershot: Gower.

Seeley, M. and Hargreaves, G. (2002), *Managing in the Email Office*. Oxford: Butterworth Heinemann.

Spitzer, M. (1986), 'Writing style in computer conferences', *IEEE Transactions on Professional Communications*, **29**(1): 19–22.

Sproull, L. and Kiesler, S. (1991a), *Connections: New Ways of Working in the Networked Organization*. Cambridge, MA: MIT Press.

Sproull, L. and Kiesler, S. (1991b), 'Computers, network and work', *Scientific American*, **265**(3): 84–91.

Taha, L. H. and Caldwell, B. S. (1993), 'Social isolation and integration in electronic environments', *Behaviour and Information Technology*, **12**(5): 276–83.

Trevino, L. K., Lengel, R. H. and Daft, R. L. (1987), 'Media symbolism, media richness and media choice in organizations: A symbolic interactionist perspective', *Communication Research*, **14**(5): 553–74.

Vinkenburg, C. J., Jansen, P. G. W. and Koopman, P. L. (2000), 'Feminine leadership – a review of gender differences in managerial behaviour and effectiveness', in M. J. Davidson and R. J. Burke (eds), *Women in Management: Current Research Issues Vol. 2*. London: Sage.

Yates, J. and Orlikowski, J. W. (1993), 'Knee-jerk anti-LOOPism and other e-mail phenomena: Oral, written, and electronic patterns in computer-mediated communication', presented at the 53rd Annual Meeting of the Academy of Management, Atlanta, GA, August.

## Chapter 19

# Gender and Diffusion of Email:
# An Organizational Perspective

Mark J. Brosnan

## Introduction

The Internet may well be 'the' technological innovation of the twentieth century (Jackson et al., 2001), penetrating almost every aspect of many organizations. It is less than a decade since the Internet became a mass media technology available to the general public. During this time, the proportion of Internet users who are female has risen from 5 per cent to around 50 per cent (see Jackson et al., 2001). During this same period, there has also been an exponential rise in the number of businesses and homes that are connected to the Internet. Across Europe, the USA and the Far East, surveys report that at the beginning of the twenty-first century, the vast majority of businesses and between half and two-thirds of homes, have access to the Internet (Cole et alet al., 2003). Although the Internet has permeated many aspects of daily life, a large body of research has identified a 'digital divide' that disenfranchises females from the digital revolution (Cooper and Weaver, 2003).

The Internet has two primary functions effectively summarized under the headings 'information' and 'communication'. Information refers to 'surfing' web pages to find information. Communication comprises emailing, online chat rooms, bulletin boards and so on, between people who are physically remote from one another. Of these, emailing, as discussed in the previous two chapters, is by far the most common form of communication via the Internet and has been described as one of the most successful computer applications yet devised (Whittaker and Sidner, 1997). This chapter expands upon the previous chapters to develop an organizational perspective on the use of email to highlight the differential impact upon males and females.

Of course, technology has enabled physically remote individuals to communicate with one another for decades via telecommunications. Email is a qualitatively different medium, as it does not allow for voice. Indeed, the latest developments within telecommunications are to enhance the face-to-face cues through video images of the speakers. Email, however, has remained unchanged since its initial conception. The software surrounding email has enhanced its usability, but essentially the format is a text-based message sender: you type and hit send. You may or may not get a reply at some undetermined point in the future.

The information/communication distinction is interesting, as a gender difference has been reported. Females use the Internet more for communication, whereas males use the Internet more for information (Jackson et al., 2001; Katz and Aspden, 1997; Odell et al., 2000; Weiser, 2000). This has led to findings that males are more experienced, positive and skilled with the Internet – with the exception of email (Schumacher and Morahu, 2001). This is unsurprising, as it reflects a great deal of psychological literature and popular perceptions that females communicate more than males (Eagly and Johnson, 1990; Gilligan, 1982). This chapter discusses the impact that email has upon communication and the detrimental effects this can have for females within organizations.

## Overview of Current Research

*Diffusion of Email*

A recent survey (Cole et al., 2003) of 2000 US homes identified that 62.5 per cent of all Americans use the Internet for communication. On average, people use emails to maintain nine relationships with other people regularly (a regular relationship is defined as weekly contact). Of these nine, one-third are also interacted with face-to-face regularly. This means, on average, that two-thirds of regular relationships are predominantly maintained via email (this excludes exclusively face-to-face relationships, for example with family members with whom you live, but includes more physically distant relatives). The report concludes that email is largely perceived to be a positive technological development by those who use it:

> Substantial majorities of email users say that email is valued, does not require too much time, and is a key method for maintaining connections to people who would not be contacted otherwise. Yet users also remain patient with those who do not use email. (Cole et al., 2003, p. 59)

Of those who have access to the Internet at work, 90 per cent used the Internet to find information for business use and 60 per cent also used this facility at work for personal use. With respect to email, more than 80 per cent reported using email for business and nearly 60 per cent used personal email at work. This is with 45 per cent also believing that their email is being monitored by their employers. The question for employers concerns whether the Internet affects productivity. In a recent study, only 5 per cent of employees felt that access to the Internet made them less productive, while 65 per cent felt the Internet made them more productive; 30 per cent felt that the Internet made them neither more nor less productive (Cole et al., 2003).

*Gender Differences*

It has been argued above that males and females use the Internet a comparable amount, but females email more and men surf the Internet more. Comparable levels of Internet use are a positive development, as a great deal of computer-related research has identified that females are more computer anxious than males (Brosnan, 1998a; Brosnan and Davidson, 1994; see Rosen and Maguire (1990) for a meta-analysis), which has given rise to the term 'the digital divide' to reflect the inequality of opportunity that has prevented some females from fully taking part in, and benefiting from, the technological revolution (Cooper and Weaver, 2003). A large body of research has shown that females of all ages (from 5 years old upwards) have more computer-related anxieties than males, more negative attitudes towards technology than males and use computers less than males. A study by Jackson et al. (2001) replicates this gender difference in computer anxiety, but notes that it is not impacting upon Internet use. Initial investigations into specific Internet anxiety reveal few females are anxious about the Internet (Joiner et al., in press). This may be due to females being able to use the Internet for communication, that is to say an activity that has been traditionally associated with females (Eagly and Johnson, 1990; Gilligan, 1982).

Thus, through email, the Internet represents a critical development in the equalizing of technology uptake between the sexes. Computing can be seen as a male activity and therefore gender inappropriate for females, resulting in heightened levels of computer anxiety in females (Brosnan, 1998a, 1998b, 1998c; Brosnan and Davidson, 1996). Computer anxiety may still be in evidence as the Internet is typically accessed via a computer, suggesting that gender differences in computer-related anxieties are specific to 'pre-Internet computing' activities, such as programming. However, within Internet-related computing, email provides a gender-appropriate application of IT, which may address the digital divide by encouraging active female participation in the digital revolution. Accessing the Internet via media other than a personal computer (for example a Wireless Application Protocol (WAP) phone) may therefore represent a computing forum devoid of any gender differences – but further research is required to substantiate this hypothesis. This is discussed further below. At present, any assessment that the Internet is gender neutral is premature (Sherman et al., 2000).

*An Organizational Perspective*

The gender patterns above are found within organizations (Lind, 2001; Cole et al., 2003). However despite the utopian effects of email described above, there are processes relating to email use occurring within organizations that re-assert traditional gender differences. Email is not always perceived to be the most efficient form of communication. Picard (1997, p. 87) reports that the majority of people 'have lost more than a day's work trying to straighten out some confusion over an email note that was received with the wrong tone'. It is the limitations inherent within email that illuminate gender differences within organizations.

Although used for communication, email is 'affect-limited' (Picard, 1997). By this, Picard means that the expression of emotion, or 'affect', is difficult due to the nature of email. Although the emotional aspects of a face-to-face communication may be subtle, they can have a huge influence upon how the message is perceived. Typically, we do not have the time or skill to select our words with such precision that the tone of a message is totally unambiguous. Rather, as email is text based, messages tend to be shorter than spoken utterances, there may not be an immediate response and contextual information is more difficult to perceive (Riva, 2002). Affect emerges from a two-way communication, that is, communication with a social element. Email allows communication without the 'social'. It is a one-way, asocial communication medium. Even a trail of emails to and fro is a series of one-way communications.

This has led to gender differences in how email is used. Within the office environment, females prefer face-to-face communication to email communication and are more likely to use email to communicate with people who are far away (Boneva et al., 2001). Males, however, are just as happy to email the person in the office next door as speak to them. This can result in two colleagues having differing communication preferences, the female colleague preferring a face-to-face discussion within a socio-emotional context and the male colleague preferring an affect-limited email message. Under this scenario, females attempt to reproduce the socio-emotional aspect of face-to-face communication within email, resulting in gendered patterns of email communication (Savicki and Kelley, 2000). Savicki and Kelley report that females use more self-disclosure and 'I statements', whereas males ignore socio-emotional aspects of the communication (Savicki and Kelley, 2000). Wolf (2000) also reports that females express dimensions such as solidarity, support, positive feelings and thanks in their emails more than males do. Even politeness can identify the sender as female (Jessmer and Anderson, 2001). This is reflected in the findings of Teo and Lim (2000), who report that even when there are no gender differences in the frequency of emailing, females spend longer than males on the task. Thus, in terms of a male perspective on organizational efficiency, females are investing unnecessary time in emailing, epitomized by the title of Herring et al.'s (1995) paper: "'This discussion is going too far!" Male resistance to female participation on the Internet'. For males, email enhances organizational efficiency precisely because it allows for pared-down, to the point, communication.

Additionally, possibly as a result of the lack of socio-emotional context, females have been found to have less message agreement in email communications than face-to-face communications, whereas there are no differences for males. Less social interaction also leads to less message agreement for females only (Guadagno and Cialdini, 2002). Again, research is highlighting that, from a male perspective of organizational efficiency, males use email more efficiently than females. Thus females are likely to spend longer emailing which results in less message agreement, than their male colleagues.

## Implications

Early research into email within organizations identified that email is unable to support the socio-emotional component to communication, that is the social cues that accompany traditional face-to-face communication (Sproull and Keisler, 1986). Sproull and Keisler (1991) concluded that consequently the identities of the emailing individuals tend to fade and vanish. The message becomes dissociated from the context of the identity of the sender. The additional material within emails from females is a reaction to this process, an attempt to contextualize the message with respect to the sender.

Email is perfect for rapidly distributing discrete nuggets of information to any number of recipients, that is, using communication to convey information (one-way communication). 'Email is HEmail'. The removal of social cues allows for shorter, more efficient, communication in affect-limited individuals; typically this characterizes males more than females. The arrival of a long email will therefore not be viewed positively by males. Trying anything more interactive using email is also onerous in terms of time and productivity. Sending an email to a small group of people to a find a convenient time for a meeting often results in a mountain of correspondence about who can make what times. This is an example of attempting to use email for interactive (two-way) communication. 'Email is not SHEmail'.

Communicating asocially can seem like an oxymoron to such an extent that attempts are frequently made to display affect through email. CAPITALS to signify shouting, :-) to signify a smile, ;-) to signify a wink are all attempts to reinsert the oral and visual cues into this affect-limited medium. These icons are termed 'emoticons', and females use them more than males to express positive affect, such as humour, in messages (Riva, 2002). However, the very act of sending an affect-laden email identifies the sender as female. Miller and Durndell (2004) found that gender-related patterns and interaction styles were salient within computer-mediated communication (CMC). A male recipient may simultaneously perceive an affect-laden email as coming from someone who is inefficient and not using technology appropriately, resulting in a resistance to working with the email sender.

Within organizations we therefore have a paradox. While email provides an application within IT where female uptake is higher than that of males, the way in which females use the application may be seen as inefficient by males. The same drive for socio-emotional contact that makes email a gender-appropriate activity for females also drives attempts to counter the affect-limited nature of the medium.

### A Specific Issue: Mobile Phones

The historical perspective on mobile phones is interesting. Currently, most people are emailing having had telephoning as their primary source of remote communication. This leads to telephoning being the basis to which emailing is compared. Emailing is affect-limited compared to telephoning. Telephoning is changing, however, in several ways. Digital mobile telephones have allowed for two major developments (see Plant, 2001 for a report on the social effects of mobile, or cell, phones). The first is videophoning. This is currently expensive, but allows remote communicators to see each other. Again, this technology has been available for a long period; the current developments refer to making this technology available to the general public in a form that can be useful, typically via a mobile phone. This is an obvious development in the sense that it allows for telecommunications to become more comparable to face-to-face communications. Via the internal camera, the speakers can see the faces of those they are speaking to or can focus on an aspect of the environment. In this way, video phoning enhances the social cues in communication over traditional telephoning. If video phoning becomes the normal mode of telecommunication and the basis to which emailing is compared, the differences described above and the responses to them may become accentuated.

The other major development is texting. This too is a text-based mode of communication and typically is much cheaper than telephoning. Possibly as a result of this, the most significant demographic variable determining use of this technology is age, with younger people being far more likely to text each other than older people.

Jeff Gavin and the author have conducted a pilot study to look at the use of texting by 38 students (mostly aged 18–20). Over the period of a month, males made and received more calls than females (means = 436 versus 383 respectively) and more emails (182 and 152 respectively), but females texted more than males (means = 298 versus 196, respectively). While there were no time differences in typing a sentence using a full-size keyboard (both sexes 11 to 12 seconds), females were faster at texting sentences (24 versus 36 seconds with predictive text on and 36 versus 56 seconds with predictive text off). There is some support, then, for the idea that females are more frequent and efficient texters than males. Due to the nature of the medium, it is possible to text a message to a computer and email a message to a mobile phone, thereby blurring the distinction between these two methods of communication. A female entering an organization and moving from texting to emailing may therefore not perceive email to be affect-limited in comparison and consequently not employ the strategies described above to reinsert affect.

Interestingly this mirrors the merging of mobile phones with personal digital assistants (PDAs) that is occurring in hardware. Perhaps the integrated mobile phone PDA technology that allows access to the Internet will allow for an Internet-communication system that does not induce computer-related anxieties (see above). The impact of mobile phones on gender differences in emails is speculative at this stage, requiring further research. Theoretically at least, there is reason to believe that gender differences in emailing within organizations may dissipate if young people continue to text (and do not opt for videophones).

## Conclusions

Although females still report being more computer anxious than males, this does not impact upon Internet use. Specifically, females use the Internet to communicate more than males, while males use the Internet for information-seeking more than females. As alluded to above, this does not mean that all females only communicate and all males only seek information. Rather, there is a gender difference where females and males behave in a way that is significantly different from each other. This is reflected in the way females use email. Females attempt to reinsert the socio-emotional context that is inherently absent from the text-based nature of email. This can result in longer, less-efficient emails that may be viewed negatively by male colleagues.

## Recommendations

What follows are some recommendations for dealing with the problems outlined earlier, aimed particularly at the female email user. Just not using email is not an answer. If you have an email address people will use it and not responding will seem inefficient on your part.

### Strategy 1: Opt Out

On the basis of the research above, refuse to have an email account. Cole et al. (2003) suggest that those who email are not irritated by this. If you need to receive departmental emails or attachments, ask for a departmental email address (for example Department@Organization.com) to be set up for this purpose. Explain that you find email has limitations and that you will use it when you feel it is appropriate to do so. Should you want to send an attachment, then you will use the departmental account to do so. Suggest the organization investigate investing in a videophone method of communication to enhance the social cues and reduce potential miscommunication.

### Strategy 2: If You Can't Beat Them, Join Them

Send short, concise emails to male colleagues, remembering not to be polite. An average of 5 to 13 words is normal (Riva, 2002). This could be complemented by texting on a mobile (cell) phone. This may involve adopting an unnatural style of communication, which is far from ideal. In the long term, it may be that as younger people enter organizations with a great deal of texting experience, email will not be perceived as affect-limited in comparison and the drive to insert affect may diminish.

*Strategy 3: Stick with It*

Female-to-female email communication can remain unaltered in any case. This chapter has highlighted factors that may affect recipients' perceptions of you through your email. Fully informed of this, carry on using email in a way that seems most natural. Educate others in how socio-emotional tone can be conveyed within an affect-limited medium. The benefits that email can have in removing gender differences within the field of IT should not be over-shadowed by resistance from males to affect-laden emails. This may be a little idealistic given the great deal that has been written about the 'glass ceiling'. It would clearly be unfortunate if male resistance to female emailing style provided reinforced glass for this ceiling.

This last point underlines the need for further research within this area, not least because the strategies above challenge females to respond. Much research described above highlights that affect-laden communication is perceived as inefficient and therefore this practice should change. The recommendations above are framed within the context of a drive for 'organizational efficiency' highlighted within the literature as a pertinent consideration for communication and the three strategies represent a response to that context. This mirrors the earlier research of Turkle and Pappert (1990), who identify conforming to the dominant computer culture as a strategy for inclusion within the computer culture. They argue, however, that real advances are made through acceptance of an 'epistemological pluralism', that is, an acceptance of multiple ways of knowing and doing. It is incumbant upon all members of the culture, whether an organizational culture or a computer culture, to respond inclusively to variations within practice, in this instance communicative practice. As technology mediates more and more organizational practices, the issues and strategies idetified by Turkle and Pappert witihin the computer culture become increasingly salient within the organizational culture. Studying the use of CMC within organizations is particularly intersting as it brings together two spheres of knowlege from both oranization-based and technology-based disciplines. Modes of communication are changing rapidly within organizations and the impact of this needs to be evaluated to ensure equality of opportunity within the digital culture of the twenty-first century. Finally, the use of texting and videophone technology may have a significant impact on the way traditional emailing is perceived and highlights the need for research that focuses upon the broad range of technologies used for communication.

### References

Boneva, B., Kraut, R. and Frohlich, D. (2001), 'Using email for personal relationships: The difference gender makes', *American Behavioral Scientist*, **45**(3): 530–49.

Brosnan, M. (1998a), *Technophobia: The Psychological Impact of Information Technology*. London: Routledge.

Brosnan, M. (1998b), 'The impact of psychological gender, gender-related perceptions, significant others and the introducer of technology upon computer anxiety in students', *Journal of Educational Computing Research*, **18**(1): 63–78.

Brosnan, M. (1998c), 'The role of psychological gender in the computer-related attitudes and attainments of primary school children (aged 6–11)', *Computers and Education*, **30**(3/4): 203–08.

Brosnan, M. and Davidson, M. (1994), 'Computerphobia: Is it a particularly female phenomenon?', *The Psychologist*, **7**(2): 73–78.

Brosnan, M. and Davidson, M. (1996), 'Psychological Gender Issues in Computing', *Journal of Gender, Work and Organisation*, **3**(1): 13–25.

Cole, J. and colleagues (2003), *The UCLA Internet Report – 'Surveying the Digital Future'*, UCLA Center for Communication Policy, January. Retrieved March 27, 2005 from ccp.ucla.edu/pdf/UCLA-Internet-Report-Year-Three.pdf.

Cooper, J. and Weaver, K. (2003), *Gender and Computers: Understanding the Digital Divide*. Mahwah, NJ: Lawrence Erlbaum Associates.

Eagly, A. and Johnson, B. (1990), 'Gender and leadership style: A meta-analysis', *Psychological Bulletin*, **108**: 233–56.

Gilligan, C. (1982), *In a Different Voice: Psychological Theory and Women's Development*. Cambridge, MA: Harvard University Press.

Guadagno, R. and Cialdini, R. (2002), 'Online persuasion: An examination of gender differences in computer-mediated interpersonal influence', *Group Dynamics*, **6**(1): 38–51.

Herring, S., Johnson, D. and DiBenedetto, T. (1995) '"This discussion is going too far!" Male resistance to female participation on the Internet', in K. Hall and M. Bucholtz (eds), *Gender Articulated: Language and the Socially Constructed Self*. New York: Routledge. pp. 67–98.

Jackson, L. A., Ervin, K. S., Gardner, P. D. and Schmitt, N. (2001), 'Gender and the Internet: Women communicating and men searching', *Sex Roles*, **44**(5/6): 363–79.

Jessmer, S. and Anderson, D. (2001), 'The effect of politeness and grammar on user perception of email', *North American Journal of Psychology*, **3**(2): 331–46.

Joiner, R., Brosnan, M., Duffield, J., Gavin, J. and Marras, P. (in press), 'Identifying with the net: The relationship between Internet identity, Internet experience and Internet anxiety', *Computers and Human Behavior*.

Katz, J. and Aspden, P. (1997), 'Motivations for the barriers to Internet usage: Results of a national public opinion survey', *Internet Research*, **7**(3): 170–88.

Lind, M. (2001), 'An exploration of communication channel usage by gender', *Work-study: A Journal of Productivity Science*, **50**(6/7): 234–40.

Miller, J. and Durndell, A. (2004), 'Gender, language and computer-mediated communication', in K. Morgan, C. A. Brebbia, J. Sanchez and A. Voiskounsky (eds), *Human Perspectives in the Internet Society: Culture, Psychology and Gender*. Southampton: WIT Press.

Odell, P. M., Korgen, K. O., Schumacher, P. and Delucchi, M. (2000), 'Internet use among female and male college students', *CyberPsychology and Behavior*, **3**: 855–62.

Picard, R. (1997), *Affective Computing*. Cambridge, MA: MIT Press.

Plant, S. (2001), 'On the mobile: The effects of mobile phones on social and individual life', Motorola website. Retrieved March 27, 2005 from www.motorola.com/mot/doc/0/234_MotDoc.pdf.

Riva, G. (2002), 'The sociocognitive psychology of computer-mediated communication: The present and future of technology-based interactions', *CyberPsychology and Behavior*, **5**(6): 581–98.

Rosen, L. D. and Maguire, P. (1990), 'Myths and realities of computerphobia: A meta-analysis', *Anxiety Research*, **3**: 175–91.

Savicki, V. and Kelley, M. (2000), Computer mediated communication: Gender and group composition', *CyberPsychology and Behavior*, **3**(5): 817–26.

Schumacher, P. and Morahu, M. (2001), 'Gender, Internet and computer attitudes and experiences', *Computers in Human Behavior*, **17**(1): 95–110.

Sherman, R., End, C., Kraan, E., Cole, A., Campbell, J., Birchmeier, Z. and Klausner, J. (2000), 'The Internet gender gap among college students: Forgotten but not gone', *CyberPsychology and Behavior*, **3**(5): 885–94.

Sproull, L. and Kiesler, S. (1986), 'Reducing social context cues: Electronic male in organizational communication', *Organizational Behavior and Human Decision Processes*, **37**: 157–87.

Sproull, L. and Kiesler, S. (1991), *Connections: New ways of working in the networked organization*. Cambridge, MA: MIT Press.

Teo, T. and Lim, V. (2000), 'Gender differences in Internet usage and task preference', *Behavior and Information Technology*, **19**(4): 283–95.

Turkle, S. and Pappert, S. (1990) 'Epistemological pluralism: Styles and voices within the computer culture', *Signs: Journal of Women in Culture and Society*, **16**(1): 128–57.

Weiser, E. (2000), 'Gender differences in Internet use patterns and Internet application preferences: A two-sample comparison', *CyberPsychology and Behavior*, **3**(2): 167–78.

Whittaker, S. and Sidner, C. (1997), 'Email overload: Exploring personal information management of Email', in S. Kiesler (ed.), *Culture and the Internet*. Mahwah, NJ: Lawrence Erlbaum Associates.

Wolf, A. (2000), 'Emotional expression online: Gender differences in emoticon use', *CyberPsychology and Behavior*, **3**(5): 827–33.

Chapter 20

# Gender, Group Composition and Task Type in Virtual Groups

Victor Savicki, David A. Foster and Merle Kelley

## Introduction

Two recent trends in the way organizations accomplish work, the use of teams[1] and the use of CMC, allow organizations to leverage the expertise of their employees to accomplish necessary goals, regardless of employees' physical or temporal proximity. These 'virtual teams' allow rapid assembly of teams of experts to solve urgent problems. Utilizing such teams effectively could provide an organization with tremendous advantage in today's hypercompetitive business climate. For example, the use of virtual teams allows work to be accomplished at any time (asynchronous communication) and avoids expensive and complicated travel arrangements for team members. The emergence of these two trends and the concomitant increase of women in the workforce have led researchers to examine exactly how the use of CMC to accomplish organizational goals is impacted by the gender of team members under various work task conditions. The purpose of this chapter is to review current theory and research on CMC communication in accomplishing tasks as it relates to the variable of gender. Specifically, this chapter will examine the relationship among gender, team composition, task type and both group processes and effectiveness for teams using CMC communication.

## Overview of Current Research

*Communication, Group Processes and Group Outcome Linkages*

Conventional wisdom states that effective communication is the key to any successful team. But what is 'effective' communication and how is it linked to successful team performance? According to Bales (1950), effective team communication focuses on what he termed both 'task' and 'maintenance' behaviours. Task behaviours are focused on accomplishing the goal at hand. These include such behaviours as asking for or sharing information, summarizing the statements of others and checking for comprehension. Maintenance behaviours focus on developing and preserving cooperative relationships among group members. Such behaviours include supporting and praising others, encouraging participation and relieving tension. To put the task versus maintenance functions in perspective, only 40 per cent of group meeting time is devoted to task-focused discussions, even in task-oriented, computer-mediated meetings (Olson et al., 1992). Unfortunately, the result of Bales's labelling of these functions as 'task' and 'maintenance' is that, although maintenance functions require work and effort on the part of the group, the maintenance function is sometimes not seen as a part of the 'task' that the group must accomplish. Consequently, teams often do not attend to underlying socio-emotional dynamics of the group that impact the group's performance on the task.

Clearly, attention to the socio-emotional dynamics of a group has consequences for the productivity of the group (Kormanski, 1990). For example, Potter and Balthazard (2002) found that group communication styles were related to group performance on collaborative group decision-making tasks. Specifically, they found that a constructive interaction style, characterized by a balanced concern for both task and maintenance behaviours, cooperation, creativity, free exchange of information, and respect for others' opinions, was related to teams making fewer errors and having increased synergy (teams performing better than their best individual member). Additionally, they found that groups characterized by aggressive (placing personal achievement above group goals) or passive (emphasizing harmony) styles, were likely to make more errors and have lower levels of decision acceptance and member satisfaction. Consequently, it appears that maintaining intergroup relationships enhances the cooperative nature of the group and, in some cases, group performance.

## Gender Differences in Communication

A large body of research has examined differences in normative male and female communication patterns. Research indicates that men and women in the mainstream US culture tend to form separate speech communities (Labov, 1972). Labov defined 'speech community' as a sub-culture whose members share a set of norms regarding communication practices. These speech communities differ in their linguistic styles because it is common for a language to have many alternative ways of saying the same thing. Men's and women's speech communities also differ on assumptions about what the goals of communication are and what strategies are best employed for reaching those goals.

According to Wood (1994), there are six primary features of women's community of talk. Women seem to strive for equality by sharing experiences, verbally showing support for others, using speech that fosters connections and relationships, making efforts to sustain conversation by inviting others to speak, usually responding in some way to what others say and, lastly, using details, personal disclosures, anecdotes and concrete reasoning. Masculine speech communities also demonstrate distinctive characteristics. Men often speak to exhibit knowledge, skill or ability, use speech to accomplish instrumental objectives, make use of conversational dominance, tend to express themselves in fairly absolute, assertive ways, communicate abstractly and tend not to be highly responsive on the relationship level of communication because they give minimal response cues. Accordingly, it appears that women's normative communication patterns naturally facilitate relationship maintenance, thereby increasing the likelihood of cooperation and effective group performance. Consequently, one would expect that women would perform better on group tasks that require a great deal of cooperative effort.

In addition to notable differences between men and women in their verbal communication pattern, a large body of research indicates that women, compared to men, are more sensitive to non-verbal cues, especially when making judgments regarding facial cues (Hall, 1998). Arguably, these facial cues (for example, smiling, gazing and expressions) facilitate relationship maintenance by indicating liking and acceptance or dislike and rejection. Because non-verbal cues primarily facilitate socio-emotional regulation within the group, it is unlikely that these cues would exercise any strong, direct effects on the task aspects of group functioning. It is predicted, however, that impairing a group's ability to accomplish maintenance activities by removing non-verbal communication channels may have a negative impact on group effectiveness; especially when faced with tasks requiring a great deal of cooperative effort. Further support for this argument comes from media richness theory (Daft and Lengel, 1984, 1986), which contends that group performance improves when individuals use 'richer' media (for example, face-to-face interaction that provides the message recipient with access to tone of voice and non-verbal cues in addition to the message content).

This is not to argue, however, that women's performance will not be comparable to men's on various tasks using CMC. Although women tend to utilize non-verbal information more than men to maintain socio-emotional balance in the group, women's normative verbal communication style also more strongly emphasizes maintaining this balance compared to men's communication patterns. Consequently, although women may be more affected by the loss of non-verbal communication channels, they may be able to compensate for this loss through their normative verbal communication. In sum, there are well-documented gender differences in both verbal and non-verbal communication styles. The next section will examine how these differences are manifested in, and affected by, CMC.

*Gender Differences in CMC*

Previous research on gender differences in non-verbal communication suggests that women may be affected by the loss of non-verbal cues (involved in relying on text-based CMC) more than men. Consequently, researchers hypothesized that women would be affected more than men by the relative poverty of cues in CMC and loss of non-verbal information. We are suggesting, however, that women, more than men, will also be able to rely on other communication avenues to accomplish the maintenance tasks of the group.

Dennis et al. (1999) examined the hypothesis that women, more than men, would be affected to a greater extent by the loss of media richness (such as non-verbal information) when using CMC. They manipulated 'media richness' by contrasting problem solving in male, female and mixed gender dyads using face-to-face communication and the 'less rich' CMC. Women dyads' performance was enhanced in the face-to-face condition; none of the other dyads showed any effect of differences in performance based on 'media richness'. They concluded that women are more sensitive than men to non-verbal communication and therefore more affected by its absence in CMC.

In another recent study, Guadagno and Cialdini (2002) found that when women had a prior face-to-face interaction with a female partner, their subsequent CMC experience with that partner was enhanced and they were more likely to agree with their partner. This was true even when the face-to-face experience was manipulated to be competitive in nature. Men, on the other hand seemed only to be affected by a highly competitive face-to-face discussion prior to the CMC experience with that same individual. Under that circumstance, they were less willing to align their attitudes with their partner. These results support the hypothesis that women are more sensitive than men to non-verbal communication and therefore more affected by its presence in face-to-face communication.

Despite the removal of important non-verbal communication channels when using CMC, research has shown that gender differences in communication style using CMC mimic those of face-to-face communication. Early in the investigation of CMC, two interesting predictions were made concerning the effects of using a more anonymous communication medium on group communication. At first, some writers (Graddol and Swann, 1989; Landow, 1992) hypothesized that anonymity, in the form of the absence of clues about the gender and status of the communicator, would lead to more parallel communication by men and women.

Herring (1993, 1994), however, noted anecdotally that there were enough obvious gender differences in email messages that it was often possible to tell whether a given message was written by a man or woman solely from the rhetorical and linguistic strategies. She noted that women's language often contained attenuated assertions, apologies, questions, a personal orientation and supportive statements. Men's language, on the other hand, was more likely to contain strong assertions, self-promotions, rhetorical questions, an authoritative orientation and the use of humour and/or sarcasm. Consequently, it seems that CMC between the genders mimics face-to-face communication regardless of the lack of the more obvious cues about gender.

Most of these early studies, however, focused on the behaviour of the individuals and looked for differences between the genders in individual performance in CMC. What was not known was how gender affected group performance when using CMC. Some scientists hypothesized that anonymity, in the form of lack of personal identification, would contribute to more extreme stereotypical communication styles by men and women. Previous research (Hiltz et al., 1986) indicated that increasing anonymity can lower inhibitions resulting in persons engaging in more extreme normative behaviour. Consequently, in situations where participants cannot be identified, the groups themselves may become 'gendered'; that is, they may rely heavily on masculine or feminine communication norms, depending on the gender composition of the group.

Herring (1994) described CMC in groups on the Internet as 'gendered', depending on the gender composition of the groups. She indicated that individuals are influenced by the overall pattern of communication within the group so that norms evolve to support a style of communication that seems to represent the proportions of men and women. Empirical support for the notion of 'gendered' groups was provided by Savicki et al. (1996c). They found that Internet discussion groups with higher proportions of men were marked by higher calls for action, and groups with higher proportions of women were marked by higher use of self-disclosure and stronger efforts at tension and conflict reduction. Consequently, group composition, along with the use of CMC, is likely to have a strong impact on the extent to which groups engage in both task and maintenance behaviours.

*Gender, Group Composition and Communication Competency in Virtual Teams*

A series of studies by Savicki and Kelley and colleagues (Savicki et al., 1996a, 1996b, 1996c; Savicki et al., 1998; Savicki et al., 2002) supported the assertion that it is not gender alone, but rather the group culture developed by differing proportions of men or women in virtual groups that has an indirect effect through communication styles employed in those groups. These studies examined the influence of this group culture on both group processes and outcomes. The results are summarized below.

Female-only groups tended to behave online differently compared to male only groups. Specifically, women in such groups wrote more words, they showed themselves through self-disclosure and 'I' statements, they interacted directly with other group members and they avoided argumentativeness and flaming (Savicki and Kelley, 2000). They avoided the 'collective monolog' (Hewes, 1986) that seemed to describe much of the interaction in male-only groups.

Interestingly, even when male-only groups, prior to group interaction, were instructed (Savicki et al., 1998), and even specifically trained (Savicki et al., 2002) to use the more effective communication style, the male-only group norms for communication overcame instruction and training to create a more sterile communication pattern. Group norms developed in the 'gendered' pattern suggested by Herring (1994) seemed to exert a powerful influence on communication competencies.

*Task Type, Group Composition and Performance in Virtual Teams*

The treatment of the topic 'task type' in the CMC literature has revolved around the notion of fit between the type of task undertaken by a virtual group and the qualities of the media through which the group interacts. McGrath and his associates (McGrath, 1984; McGrath et al., 1993; McGrath and Hollingshead, 1993; Straus and McGrath, 1994) predicted a relationship between task type, the medium used to perform the task and indicators of group performance and satisfaction. McGrath hypothesized that the higher the task demand for complete idea discussion and decision making, the poorer it will be supported by the relatively cueless, text-based CMC medium. Such theorizing reflects the confluence of the group process research described above and the theory of media richness (Daft and Lengel, 1984, 1986), which argues that there is an optimal fit between situational equivocality and media. That is, CMC, with its absence of non-verbal cues would be more supportive of low-interdependence tasks (idea generation and intellective tasks) than of high-interdependence tasks (preference and cognitive conflict).

In considering task type as it applies to the CMC context, we adopted Huang's (2003, p. 18) definition: 'A task is a set of problems and issues confronting a group that aims to seek a solution acceptable to its members'. Much of the research concerning task type in CMC is based on McGrath's (1984) circumplex theory of task processes in small groups. In this model, categories of task were based on four basic processes: (1) generating ideas; (2) choosing alternatives; (3) negotiating; and (4) executing tasks. In the circumplex model, these processes are related to each other within a two-dimensional space with the horizontal dimension indicating the degree to which the specific task contains cognitive versus behavioural components. The vertical dimension indicated the degree of interdependence required for task completion ranging from collaboration to coordination to conflict resolution. Only the cognitive side of the circumplex was studied in CMC, since behavioural interaction was excluded by virtue of the disconnect in space and often time presumed in most CMC formats.

Thus, four specific task types were specified. First, creativity tasks or idea generation required the least interdependence, since group members could generate ideas independently and, in many cases, too much interdependence could actually reduce the quantity and divergence of ideas developed. Second, intellective tasks required some discussion concerning alternatives, but, since the solving of problems in this task type was evaluated by an external standard of correctness, less negotiating was required. For the third type, decision-making or preference task, which had no verifiably correct answer, negotiation and expressions of judgment, opinion and value were more prominent. Finally, cognitive conflict tasks required the most coordination because they rely most on expressions of emotion and valuing, and presume that a consensus will be arrived at to defuse the conflict. These categories of task have received much attention in CMC research because of their hypothesized relation to qualities of the CMC medium.

In the computer-based, group support system (GSS) literature, support for the task type-media richness relationship has been mixed. While there seems to be relatively consistent support for the benefits to group performance of intellective tasks under the structure that GSS provides, this benefit does not extend to preference tasks, nor to satisfaction with either the decision arrived at or the process of the group generally (Huang, 2003; Huang and Wei, 2000; Tan et al., 1994). As a summary statement, Huang comments that '[g]roup decision outcomes in a GSS environment could be adversely affected when the communication medium was too lean for the preference task but not when the communication medium was too rich for the intellective task'

(p. 18). The GSS structure, by design, eliminates many of the types of interactions necessary for the valuing and affect-laden discussion necessary in preference and cognitive conflict tasks, since these activities were seen as potential distracters from, or even barriers to, optimal group performance (Huang, 2003). Thus, current GSS software does not well support those tasks. In addition, most virtual teams do not have access to GSS facilities, so it may be more useful to extend the context of the media richness-task type beyond the GSS environment.

In non-GSS CMC contexts, several studies have found that other variables are powerful enough to overcome the communication challenges inherent in the CMC medium with its absence of cues to non-verbal communication (George et al., 1990). For example, Savicki et al. (1996b) found gender group composition and the communication patterns generated by all-woman virtual groups overcame the bareness of text-based communication so that these groups were able to discuss and share ideas in ways that produced accurate decisions. The gender composition and communication variables gave those groups an advantage in both an intellective task and a preference task. A communication style that emphasized self-disclosure, self-referent opinion statements and direct conversation with, and reaction to, other group members while virtually eliminating argumentativeness and flaming allowed groups to both perform well, and to experience high levels of satisfaction in comparison to those groups not using this communication style. Social presence (Rice, 1993) could be demonstrated in spite of the medium, which did not support the usual, non-verbal modes of expressing such presence.

Additionally, some models of group decision making specifically identify the necessity for groups to switch back and forth between intellective and preference type activities as they progress toward a high-quality decision that will be effectively implemented (Vroom and Yetton, 1973). Decision making reflects only one of many activities that groups undertake during their lifespans. Others include 'socializing, joking, teaching members skills, and norms, fighting/conflicting, establishing power and status relations, and meeting individual needs for sympathy, acceptance and self-development' (Huang, 2003, p. 17).

The closest approximation to the group norms and communication patterns found in the Savicki and Kelley studies appears in Tan et al.'s (2000) study employing the dialogue technique to enhance communication in electronic teams. The goal of this technique was to facilitate a shared mental model for group members. The dialogue methodology required virtual teams to move through three stages. In the first stage, small talk, members shared personal information. In the second stage, members discussed what they believed to be good communication practices and shared examples of such practices and the values that underlie them. In the third stage, a team mental model was constructed to establish group norms concerning communication. Activities to support these stages of development were required during a same time, different place, warm-up session at the beginning of the virtual team process. Outcomes indicated that groups that developed a shared mental model via this technique not only had higher cohesion, team collaboration, and perceived decision quality in early stages of virtual teaming, but also that this advantage over control groups continued at later stages of virtual team interaction (Tan et al., 2000). Structured interaction to support a group mental model seemed to be effective with the Singaporean sample in this study, where instruction and brief cognitive training was not effective with a US sample. It is unclear how much of this difference was accounted for by the modes of training or the differing cultures, but the dialogue technique provides a reasonable explanation for the effectiveness of female-only groups in the Savicki and Kelley studies.

## Implications for Developing Virtual Teams

In a review of virtual team literature, Horvath and Tobin (2001) developed a list of competencies for virtual teams that included a set of teamwork skills that they found increased virtual team performance: communication, relationship building and management, leadership, and decision making and implementation (pp. 249–52). One communication competency specifically describes the need to use 'verbal, non-verbal and written' modes (2001, p. 249) in order to overcome the absence of usual non-verbal cues, and to avoid miscommunications. While the CMC medium itself overcomes some of the limitations of face-to-face communication (for example, it acts to some degree like a nominal group, facilitating more equal participation), users must compensate for other limitations that CMC creates. There is no reason, however, to believe that CMC has to detract from a virtual team's interaction if appropriate competencies are learned (Horvath and Tobin, 2001; Potter and Balthazard, 2002).

The effective communication style identified in these studies seems to illustrate the communication competency that balances task and maintenance functions called for to produce high functioning virtual teams. In addition, through communication competency, it seems that factors of social presence (Rice, 1993) help to support virtual team attitudinal competencies of collective understanding and swift trust (Horvath and Tobin, 2001), the foundation for cooperative group behaviour.

## Conclusions

Groups utilizing constructive communication styles that emphasize balanced concern for working on the task itself and maintaining positive socio-emotional dynamics within the group are more likely to have higher levels of cohesion, cooperation and, in some cases, performance compared to groups using more aggressive or passive interaction styles. This constructive style appears to be particularly efficacious for groups performing tasks requiring discussion of alternatives, negotiation and expressions of emotion and valuing (for example, intellective and preference tasks). Using CMC to accomplish these intellective or preference tasks may make the process more challenging, but not impossible. Because CMC is a more 'impoverished' communication medium, it may be more difficult for groups to maintain positive socio-emotional dynamics when key vocal (such as tone of voice) and non-verbal (such as facial expressions, eye contact) information is not present. Savicki, Kelley and colleagues in their various studies did find, however, that groups can overcome some of the challenges inherent in using CMC. A series of studies examining the effects of CMC and group composition on task accomplishment showed that, even when using CMC, groups composed of all females tended to adopt a constructive interaction style more quickly than all-male or mixed-gender groups. In these studies, female-only groups compensated for the poorer communication media by engaging in more self-disclosure, interacting directly with other group members, avoiding argumentativeness, and being more open to influence from others compared to all-male or mixed-gender groups, behaviours that mirror normative patterns of female communication. These findings suggest that, when groups develop and maintain positive socio-emotional group dynamics, it is possible for groups to establish norms for using CMC that will facilitate successful accomplishment of both task and maintenance behaviours.

Developing and maintaining positive group relationships is a critical but often overlooked group task. According to Tuckman and Jensen (1977), group development occurs in four stages: forming, storming, norming and performing. In the forming stage, group members focus on getting to know one another, being accepted and learning more about the group (for example, making small talk, telling jokes, sharing stories of past exploits). During the storming stage, group members work to find their 'role' within the group and decide how much a part of the group they wish to be. In the norming phase, group members develop shared expectations regarding acceptable and non-acceptable behaviour (including communication style). The fourth stage, performing, is where the group focuses on completing the task at hand (for example, intellective or preference task). Accordingly, effective groups must accomplish a great deal of work in laying a foundation that facilitates constructive communication prior to the group focusing on its primary task.

## Recommendations

It is within the context of Tuckman and Jensen's model that we present recommendations for enhancing the effectiveness of groups using CMC. In order to enhance a group moving through group development stages quickly so that the group will perform effectively, specific behaviours may be linked to specific stages. Addressing these behaviours should have the effect of helping the group reach its potential in an efficient fashion, even in the cue-reduced CMC context.

### Forming

More efficient resolution of the forming stage will occur when group members share personal information with each other, identify themselves and their affiliations clearly in CMC communications (for example sign all messages), use 'I' statements to indicate ownership when expressing opinions and feelings, and define the problem so that all group members share a common interpretation of what the problem is.

*Storming*

Movement through the storming stage will be facilitated when group members discuss group and individual goals so that members have a clear understanding of what the group is trying to accomplish, refrain from insulting or criticizing others, focus on ideas not people, and maintain a supportive tone even when disagreements emerge. Disagreements and divergent opinions are to be expected, and sometimes even encouraged. It is the manner in which disagreements are dealt with that affects the resolution of this stage.

*Norming*

In the norming stage, group members can make the process more effective by encouraging all group members to emphasize maintaining positive group relationships and devoting time specifically to working on maintenance tasks. There are several specific CMC actions through which group members can express their acceptance of personal responsibility for maintaining positive socio-emotional group climate. These include the following:

- using short, single-subject messages whenever possible;
- responding directly to the person whose idea they are discussing even if the whole group will read the message;
- clearly labelling any emotion expressed in a message;
- avoiding sarcasm, irony and humour, since they often don't work in CMC because the message does not come across as intended;
- communicating in a conversational manner, for example, by not being rigid about grammatical structure or precise spelling or formal modes of address;
- indicating their state of mind when sending a message (such as 'I'm tired today, sigh!') helps convey in CMC what non-verbal cues do in face-to-face meetings;
- avoiding responding to messages while emotional, because misinterpretations are very common in CMC – group members should pause and re-read the message, consider the source, and check their understanding with the author rather than reacting impulsively.

The above specific suggestions should help solidify a functional socio-emotional atmosphere.

*Performing*

Finally, while in the performing stage, a group can accomplish its task more effectively by focusing on accomplishing the task at hand without losing sight of the necessity of maintaining a facilitative socio-emotional climate. Discussion time spent on non-task communication can pay benefits in group productivity.

**Notes**

1. The terms 'team' and 'group' are used synonymously in this chapter. A group or team is defined as two or more individuals who interact with one another and who are dependent upon one another to achieve their goals.

## References

Bales, R. F. (1950), *Interaction Process Analysis: A Method for the Study of Small Groups*. Reading, MA: Addison-Wesley.

Daft, R. L. and Lengel, R. H. (1984), 'Information richness: A new approach to managerial behavior and organizational design', *Research in Organizational Behavior*, **6**: 191–233.

Daft, R. L. and Lengel, R. H. (1986), 'A proposed integration among organizational information requirements, media richness, and structural design', *Management Science*, **32**: 554–71.

Dennis, A. R., Kinney, S. T. and Hung, Y. C. (1999), 'Gender differences in the effects of media richness', *Small Group Research*, **30**: 405–37.

George, J. F., Easton, G. K., Nunamaker, J. F. and Northcraft, G. B. (1990), 'A study of collaborative group work with and without computer based support', *Information Systems Research*, **1**: 394–415.

Graddol, D. and Swann, J. (1989), *Gender Voices*. Oxford: Basil Blackwell.

Guadagno, R. E. and Cialdini, R. B. (2002), 'Online persuasion: An examination of gender differences in computer-mediated interpersonal influence', *Group Dynamics*, **6**(1): 38–51.

Hall, J. A. (1998), 'How big are non-verbal sex differences? The case of smiling and sensitivity to non-verbal cues', in D. J. Canary and K. Dindia (eds), *Sex Differences and Similarities in Communication: Critical Essays and Empirical Investigations of Sex and Gender in Interaction*. Mahwah, NJ: Lawrence Erlbaum Associates. pp. 155–77.

Herring, S. C. (1993), 'Gender and democracy in computer-mediated communication', *Electronic Journal of Communication*, **3**: 1–17.

Herring, S. C. (1994), 'Gender differences in computer-mediated communication: Bringing familiar baggage to the new frontier', paper presented at American Library Association annual convention, Miami, FL, March.

Hewes, D. E. (1986), 'A socioegocentric model of group decision-making', in R. Y. Hirokawa and M. S. Poole (eds), *Communication and Group Decision-making*. Newbury Park, CA: Sage. pp. 262–92.

Hiltz, S. R., Johnson, K. and Turoff, M. (1986), 'Experiments in group decision making: Communication process and outcome in face-to-face versus computerized conferences', *Human Communication Research*, **13**: 225–52.

Horvath, L. and Tobin, T. J. (2001), 'Twenty-first century teamwork: Defining competencies for virtual teams', in M. M. Beyerlein, D. A. Johnson and S. T. Beyerlein (eds), *Virtual Teams*. Oxford: Elsevier Science. pp. 239–58.

Huang, W. W. (2003), 'Impacts of GSS generic structures and task types on group communication process and outcome: Some expected and unexpected research findings', *Behaviour and Information Technology*, **22**: 17–29.

Huang, W. W. and Wei, K. K. (2000), 'An empirical investigation of the effects of group support systems (GSS) and task type on group interactions from an influence perspective', *Journal of Management Information Systems*, **17**: 181–206.

Kormanski, C. (1990), 'Team building patterns of academic groups', *Journal for Specialists in Group Work*, **15**: 206–14.

Labov, W. (1972), *Sociolinguistic Patterns*. Philadelphia, PA: University of Pennsylvania Press.

Landow, G. P. (1992), *Hypertext: The Convergence of Contemporary Critical Theory and Technology*. Baltimore, MD: Johns Hopkins University Press.

McGrath, J. E. (1984), *Groups: Interaction and Performance*. Englewood Cliffs, NJ: Prentice-Hall.

McGrath, J. E., Arrow, H., Gruenfeld, D. H., Hollingshead, A. B. and O'Connor, K. M. (1993), 'Groups, tasks, and technology: The effects of experience and change', *Small Group Research*, **24**: 406–20.

McGrath, J. E. and Hollingshead, A. B. (1993), 'Putting the "group" back in group support systems: Some theoretical issues about dynamic processes in groups with technological enhancements', in L. M. Jessup and J. S. Valacich (eds), *Group support systems: New Perspectives*. New York: Macmillan. pp. 78–96.

Olson, G. M., Olson, J. S., Carter, M. R. and Storrøsten, M. (1992), 'Small group decision meetings: An analysis of collaboration', *Human–Computer Interaction*, **7**: 347–74.

Potter, R. E. and Balthazard, P. A. (2002), 'Virtual team interaction styles: Assessment and effects', *International Journal of Human–Computer Studies*, **56**: 423–43.

Rice, R. E. (1993), 'Media appropriateness: Using social presence theory to compare traditional and new organizational media', *Human Communication Research*, **19**: 451–84.

Savicki, V. and Kelley, M. (2000), 'Computer mediated communication, gender and group composition', *CyberPsychology and Behavior*, **3**: 817–26.

Savicki, V., Kelley, M. and Ammon, B. (2002), 'Effects of training on computer mediated communication in single or mixed gender small task groups', *Computers in Human Behavior*, **18**: 257–69.

Savicki, V., Kelley, M. and Lingenfelter, D. (1996a), 'Gender and small task group activity using computer mediated communication', *Computers in Human Behavior*, **12**: 209–24.

Savicki, V., Kelley, M. and Lingenfelter, D. (1996b), 'Gender, group composition and task type in small task groups using computer mediated communication', *Computers in Human Behavior*, **12**: 549–65.

Savicki, V., Lingenfelter, D. and Kelley, M. (1996c), 'Gender, language style and group composition in Internet discussion groups', *Journal of Computer Mediated Communication* (online), **2**. Retrieved February 2, 2005 from www.ascusc.org/jcmc/vol2/issue3/.

Savicki, V., Kelley, M. and Oesterreich, E. (1998), 'Effects of instructions on computer-mediated communication in single- or mixed-gender small task groups', *Computers in Human Behavior*, **14**: 163–80.

Straus, S. G. and McGrath, J. E. (1994), 'Does the medium matter? The interaction of task type and technology on group performance and member reactions', *Journal of Applied Psychology*, **79**: 87–97.

Tan, B. C. Y., Raman, K. S. and Wei, K. K. (1994), 'An empirical study of the task dimension of group support system', *IEEE Transactions on Systems, Man, and Cybernetics*, **24**: 1054–60.

Tan, B. C. Y., Wei, K. K., Huang, W. W. and Ng, G. N. (2000), 'A dialogue technique to enhance electronic communication in virtual teams', *IEEE Transactions on Professional Communication*, **43**: 153–65.

Tuckman, B. and Jensen, M. (1977), 'Stages of small group development revisited', *Group and Organizational Studies*, **2**: 419–27.

Vroom, V. H. and Yetton, P. W. (1973), *Leadership and Decision Making*. Pittsburgh, PA: University of Pittsburgh Press.

Wood, J. T. (1994), *Gendered Lives: Communication, Gender, and Culture*. Belmont, CA: Wadsworth.

# Index

abruptness 106
active listening 150
advancement, women's 1, 32, 50, 96–7, 100
  *see also* promotion
advisor-client communications 6
  affiliative-instrumental communicative styles 84–6
  call centres 88, 89–90
  client roles 88–9
  cross-cultural 91
  difficulties 87–8
  future directions 91–2
  time constraints 90–1
  variable styles 86–7, 90
  vocabulary 89
  *see also* call centres
aesthetic labour 8, 144, 151
affect-limited communication 263, 264, 267, 276
affiliative communication styles 6, 84–6, 90, 92
Africa 96, 101–2
ageism 203
agentic communication 5, 42, 69, 71–2, 73, 74–6, 76–7
aggressive behaviour 106, 201–2, 240, 271
aggressive linguistic forms 54
all-women groups 276
Amazone 198
ambulance control centre
  *see* medical emergency control room
androgynous behaviour 52, 57, 61
anger 11, 226, 230–1, 233
anonymity 240
anti-normative behaviour 242–3
anxiety 117

computer 12–13, 132–3, 262, 265
archetypes
  cultural 196–8
  dynamic 198–9
  female 196, 199, 206
  male 197
argumentativeness 276
Ashcraft's relationship framing 19–20, 21–3
Asia 96, 120, 121, 136
assertiveness 23, 102, 106, 188
assimilation model (equal opportunities) 1, 2, 3, 13–14, 136, 185
Athena 198
Australia 58, 104, 183, 185, 187
authority 72–3, 76, 203
  *see also* power
Automatic Call Distribution (ACD) 1, 143

Bahrain 101, 102, 103
barriers to women's advancement
  biases 32, 176
  communication and information systems (CIS) 134
  communication styles 50, 96–7
  negotiation 211–12
  *see also* 'glass ceiling'
Baxter, Judith 8–9
Bem Sex Role Inventory (BSRI) 44
binary thought 198, 206–7
board meetings 8–9, 154–64, 158–60
breadwinner role 27, 42, 60
Brosnan, Mark 12–13
bullying 7, 113–16, 119
Burma 121
business culture 52, 56